PERSON

Persons

Human and Divine

Edited by
PETER VAN INWAGEN
and
DEAN ZIMMERMAN

CLARENDON PRESS · OXFORD

OXFORD
UNIVERSITY PRESS

Great Clarendon Street, Oxford OX2 6DP

Oxford University Press is a department of the University of Oxford.
It furthers the University's objective of excellence in research, scholarship,
and education by publishing worldwide in

Oxford New York

Auckland Cape Town Dar es Salaam Hong Kong Karachi
Kuala Lumpur Madrid Melbourne Mexico City Nairobi
New Delhi Shanghai Taipei Toronto
With offices in
Argentina Austria Brazil Chile Czech Republic France Greece
Guatemala Hungary Italy Japan South Korea Poland Portugal
Singapore Switzerland Thailand Turkey Ukraine Vietnam

Oxford is a registered trade mark of Oxford University Press
in the UK and in certain other countries

Published in the United States
by Oxford University Press Inc., New York

ISBN 978-0-19-927751-3

Printed in the United Kingdom by
Lightning Source UK Ltd., Milton Keynes

For Philip L. Quinn

In Memoriam

Acknowledgements

Almost all the essays in this book were presented at a workshop that took place February 8–9, 2004, in Princeton, New Jersey. The meeting was supported by the Pew Christian Scholars Program, which also sponsored two other, larger conferences on the nature of human persons—July 22–24, 2001 in Skaneateles, New York; and September 5–8, 2002, in Princeton, New Jersey. The editors thank the Pew Charitable Trusts and the Christian Scholars Program for their generous support. We thank the authors and the many other participants in these meetings for their diligence and geniality. And we are grateful to Jason Turner and Matthew Benton for their help in preparing the manuscript for publication.

Contents

IV. EMBODIMENT AND THE VALUE OF PERSONS

V. PERSONHOOD IN CHRISTIAN DOCTRINE

List of Contributors

Robert M. Adams is a Fellow in Philosophy, Oxford University.

Peter Forrest is a Professor in the Philosophy Department, University of New England (Australia).

W. D. Hart is a Professor and the Chair of the Philosophy Department in the University of Illinois at Chicago.

John Hawthorne holds the Wayneflete Chair in Metaphysical Philosophy, Oxford University.

Hud Hudson is a Professor and the Chair of the Department of Philosophy, Western Washington University

Brian Leftow is Nolloth Professor of the Philosophy of the Christian Religion, Oxford University.

Trenton Merricks is a Professor in the Corcoran Department of Philosophy, University of Virginia.

Alvin Plantinga is the John A. O'Brien Professor of Philosophy, University of Notre Dame.

Philip Quinn (deceased) was the John A. O'Brien Professor of Philosophy, University of Notre Dame.

Michael C. Rea is a Professor in the Department of Philosophy, University of Notre Dame.

Howard Robinson is a Professor of Philosophy at Central European University and Honorary Research Fellow in the Department of Philosophy at the University of Liverpool.

Lynne Rudder Baker is a Professor in the Department of Philosophy, University of Massachusetts, Amherst.

Richard Swinburne is Emeritus Nolloth Professor of the Philosophy of the Christian Religion, Oxford University.

Peter van Inwagen is the John Cardinal O'Hara Professor of Philosophy, University of Notre Dame.

Hong Yu Wong is a research student at University College London.

Takashi Yagisawa is a Professor in the Department of Philosophy, California State University, Northridge.

Dean Zimmerman is an Associate Professor in the Department of Philosophy, Rutgers, the State University of New Jersey.

Three Introductory Questions:
Is Analytic Philosophical Theology an Oxymoron? Is Substance Dualism Incoherent? What's in this Book, Anyway?

Dean Zimmerman

I

A Tripartite Introduction

The essays within this book—all of which appear here for the first time[1]—are philosophical explorations of the nature of persons. Those comfortable using the word "analytic" to describe the kind of philosophy that now thrives in the philosophy departments of most Anglophone universities will say that we are all analytic philosophers. (Shortly, I shall have more to say about the problematic adjective "analytic".) As a consequence, there is much within this book that is continuous with current philosophical debates about the nature of persons. On the other hand, the authors have theological concerns that do not arise for most contributors to the philosophical literature on persons. Most of the contributors are Christians or strongly identify with the Christian theological tradition. (W. D. Hart and Takashi Yagisawa are the only authors who, so far as I know, have no theological axe to grind—certainly, none is evident in the short, jointly authored paper included here.) The essays explore the philosophical implications of theological and ethical doctrines that have been central to Christianity. And there are options on the table that are not usually taken seriously in mainstream philosophical debates. One might ask whether we think we are doing philosophy or theology. The answer, in most cases, is a bit of both. When Christian

---

[1] Section 1 of Alvin Plantinga's essay partially overlaps his "Against Materialism", *Faith and Philosophy*, 23/1 (2006), pp. 3–32.

analytic philosophers tackle the traditional problems of philosophy of religion, they inevitably produce work that could just as well be called "philosophical theology"—an enterprise that was once popular with philosophers, theologians, and many scholars who were equally at home in both disciplines.

Every chapter concerns the metaphysical nature or ethical value of persons. Even the two essays largely about the divine persons of the trinity contain a good deal of discussion of the contrasting case of ordinary human persons. One of the most frequently discussed questions is, in effect: what should Christians think about the relationship between human persons and human bodies? Of course a compelling case for a single answer to this sort of question should not be expected, given the theological diversity within Christianity—a diversity reflected in this volume, with its mix of Catholics and Protestants from a variety of theological traditions. Still, there is a great deal of common ground; and we have much to learn from one another.

Christianity is often thought to require a dualistic conception of human persons, according to which each of us has (or perhaps simply *is*) an immaterial soul that survives death and awaits reunion with the body at a general resurrection. Unsurprisingly, the book begins with spirited defenses of the sorts of immaterialism and dualism that have traditionally dominated Christian thinking about the nature of persons. For several decades, however, philosophers and theologians have been questioning the inevitability of Christian opposition to materialism. Indeed, at present there seem to be more Christian philosophers defending materialism (as a theory about human persons, not about the deity) than dualism—at least in print. In this volume, at least six of the authors defend the compatibility of Christian faith with a materialist metaphysics of human persons.

My introduction has three parts: The first (Section II) is basically historical. I attempt to explain how it has come to be that philosophical theology, when done in the (so-called) analytic style, is unpopular among theologians—even among theologians who have deep philosophical interests. Philosophy has always been, and arguably continues to be, at least the handmaid (and sometimes the dominatrix) of theology. And, for many decades now, analytic (in the broad sense defined below) has been the preferred philosophical flavor in most of the larger Ph.D.-granting programs in Great Britain and North America. But analytic philosophy is largely regarded as tedious and irrelevant by scholars in seminaries, departments of theology, and departments of religious studies—including even the philosophically-oriented scholars in these settings. Section II is, in part, an appeal to *you*, if you belong to this group: Please don't simply toss the book aside, now that you've discovered the authors are a bunch of analytic philosophers! Give us a chance! My description of recent interactions between philosophy and theology is intended to show that analytic philosophy got a bum rap; perhaps it will convince one or two theologians or Continental philosophers with theological interests that analytic philosophy of religion deserves another look.

After my excursus on the unhappy early history of analytic philosophy's relations with theology, I turn to a more properly philosophical task in Section III: describing the distinction between substance materialism and substance dualism—something that figures prominently in most of the essays. The distinction requires clarification, largely because some materialists are careful to define "substance dualism" in unfriendly ways—for example, in such a way that, to be a substance dualist, one must either believe a contradiction or be hostile toward all things scientific. The third part of the Introduction (Section IV) is a synopsis of the rest of the book.

II

Philosophers among the Theologians

Many of the high points in Christian scholarship have been equal parts philosophy and theology. None of the authors here would pretend to be the next St Augustine, St Anselm, or St Thomas Aquinas; nor even the next Samuel Clarke, Joseph Butler, or Jonathan Edwards. But the essays in this collection resemble their greatest achievements in at least two respects: the authors raise questions that are at once philosophical and theological in nature, and they appeal to both philosophical and theological considerations in their attempts to answer them.

Several of the authors, although based in philosophy departments, have theological training or a lifetime of serious engagement with theology. Others would consider themselves amateur theologians, or relative newcomers with much to learn. Some may be venturing onto theological turf with trepidation. But the philosophical questions that Christians face are as urgent as ever; and, as philosophers and theologians have become ever more specialized, the two disciplines have fewer scholars who can credibly wield all the tools needed to work in the area of overlap. As in other subjects that demand interdisciplinary treatment, the problems of philosophical theology can no longer be reserved entirely for scholars who are equally expert in each of the overlapping disciplines. Given the degree of specialization in both philosophy and theology, there will be few such people, and they will tend to be "synthesizers", dependent upon the philosophers and theologians in the trenches. Surely some Christian philosophers who are theological novices, and some theologians without strong backgrounds in philosophy, will have to be pressed into service for the work to be done in our jointly held territory; and the two groups obviously need to be in conversation with one another.

Unfortunately, there is very little dialogue between Christian philosophers in the analytic tradition and Christian theologians. For there are vast differences between the philosophical canons and methods of Christian analytic philosophers with theological interests, on the one hand, and most Christian theologians with philosophical interests, on the other.[2] When the groups do interact, terminological and methodological differences (and sometimes, sadly, prejudice and mistrust) hinder fruitful exchange.[3]

Given the recent histories of the two disciplines, this lamentable state of affairs should not seem too surprising. During the twentieth century, Western philosophy effectively split into two quite different streams: "analytic philosophy" and "Continental philosophy", though neither label is very appropriate, and neither stream very unified. The parting-of-the-ways was, of course, a long, gradual process, with its roots in nineteenth-century disagreements and divisions. But within the Anglophone academy, it was not until the middle of the twentieth century that a sharp division became noticeable. During that period, the difference between analytic approaches and other ways of doing philosophy came to seem extremely stark to many scholars in Britain and the United States. The Continental–analytic rift began to widen, gradually forcing all those with a stake in philosophy—including, naturally, many theologians—to choose sides. Unfortunately, at that critical juncture, analytic philosophy was extremely hostile to the aims of theology. Those committed to the work of philosophical theology found that they could not breathe in the noxious atmosphere created by logical positivism, the dominant mid-century movement within analytic philosophy. And so most Christian theologians and many Christian philosophers moved their boats decisively and entirely to the Continental stream.

As the distance between the two rivers has grown, portaging between them has become nearly impossible. And so, today, Christian philosophers in the analytic stream find it difficult to understand theologians and philosophers in the Continental stream, and vice versa. Individual commitments to Continental or analytic philosophical traditions were expressed in curricular decisions, hiring practices, and conferrals and denials of tenure. By now, the division is institutionalized; very few departments that contain a sizable number of philosophers are genuinely "pluralistic"; one rarely finds numerous representatives of both streams living

---

[2] A good sense of the current state of affairs can be gleaned from the essays in William J. Wainwright (ed.), *God, Philosophy, and Academic Culture* (Atlanta: Scholars Press, 1996). The contrast explored in Wainwright's collection is between those philosophers of religion whose primary professional home is the American Philosophical Association and those more closely associated with the American Academy of Religion. I take it that the latter group would include most scholars with philosophical interests who work in seminaries, and in theology and religious studies departments.

[3] Conferences that bring together theologians and Christian analytic philosophers can easily devolve into sniping and quarreling. The most noteworthy attempts to bring representatives of the two groups together are probably the UCLA and University of Notre Dame conferences that produced the collections: Thomas F. Tracy (ed.), *The God Who Acts: Philosophical and Theological Explorations* (University Park, Pa.: Pennsylvania State University Press, 1994); and Eleonore Stump and Thomas P. Flint (eds.), *Hermes and Athena: Biblical Exegesis and Philosophical Theology* (Notre Dame, Ind.: University of Notre Dame Press, 1993). I was present at the UCLA conference, and joined the faculty at the University of Notre Dame the year after their conference. Both events were somewhat acrimonious; there were unpleasant public exchanges between philosophers and theologians, and few signs that either group thought they had much to learn from the other.

harmoniously, side by side. Within philosophy, there are several famous cases of strong departments severely weakened or utterly destroyed by protracted battles between analytic and Continental factions. Communication and cooperation between analytic and Continental philosophers is likely to remain sporadic, at best, for the foreseeable future.

Philosophical theology is not, of course, impossible to do while navigating the Continental stream. But it is not your grandparents' philosophical theology. Christian doctrines—including those explored in this book, such as the trinity and incarnation, the immortality of the soul and the resurrection of the body—once prompted theologians to indulge in a good deal of philosophical system-building. Many theologians took their task to include the articulation of Christian doctrines in terms of the philosophical concepts and categories available in their day and age, or at least competitors of or successors to those concepts and categories. When they found existing concepts inadequate to the task, they attempted to modify them, sometimes reviving older philosophical traditions to supplement or challenge philosophical orthodoxy. In any case, theologians once did a good deal of what most authors in this book are doing: affirming doctrine, and developing philosophical systems (including, inevitably, some serious metaphysics) within which those doctrines make sense. Although these doctrines are still the subject of illuminating scholarly work by theologians, much less of it is philosophical theology of this old-fashioned sort. To some extent, the decline of overt philosophical system-building is probably due to a broader, more practical, more historically sensitive conception of theology—one that is, in general, less beholden to philosophy. But that is not the whole story. Even the explicitly philosophical work that comes from a department of theology or religious studies will seldom look like the philosophical theology of earlier generations, or the analytic philosophical theology in this book.

The reason for the difference is simple: Philosophers in the Continental tradition tend to be extremely skeptical of philosophical system-building and metaphysical theorizing, activities that were once central to the task of philosophical theology. Herein lies one of the biggest differences between the two streams: Continental philosophers tend to believe that it is no longer possible to engage in grand philosophical speculation with a clear conscience, at least not once one has absorbed the morals to be drawn from some subset of: Kant, Nietzsche, Freud, Marx, Heidegger, Derrida, etc. Analytic philosophers, on the other hand, do not believe that the arguments of these philosophers—or, in many cases, the *suspicions* raised by them—justify such radical conclusions about philosophical method.

Because of the preference for Continental philosophy in most seminaries and religious studies or theology departments, budding theologians who want to take philosophical theology seriously will usually be expected to utilize the philosophical tools provided by Continental philosophers. Many other important figures would be added to the list of Continental luminaries in the previous paragraph: for example, Dilthey, Merleau-Ponty, Habermas, Gadamer, and Ricoeur. Above all, however, Heidegger is where much Continental philosophical theology begins. Almost invariably, however, analytic philosophers are deeply skeptical about the value of Heidegger's work. And so, much current philosophical theology is bound to seem to them to be not only impenetrable but also fundamentally misguided.

The landscape of philosophical theology retains a few recognizable landmarks. Familiar queries about the nature of God, creation, and the afterlife are still sometimes raised by philosopher-theologians more at home in Continental traditions; and distant echoes of the old answers may be heard in important figures such as Wolfhart Pannenberg or Jean-Luc Marion.[4] But even these echoes will be of little help to those in the analytic stream. The majority of philosophers trained in the universities of Great Britain and North America reject the presuppositions of most postmodern, Continental theorizing. By now, the two rivers have, to use Michael Dummett's metaphor, emptied into very different seas.[5] So, whatever insights might be gleaned from the works of Pannenberg, Marion, and others doing philosophical theology in dialogue with Continental philosophers; they are largely unavailable to Christians in the analytic tradition.

I do not look for a major rapprochement between analytic and Continental philosophers (although, if there is movement on this front, I should hope that some of its impetus would come from increased understanding between Christian philosophers and theologians). My aims here are modest. Analytic philosophy left some very negative impressions upon theologians who abandoned it several generations ago. I merely want to point out that the analytic philosophy they rejected was something of an aberration within the tradition: it was quite unlike both analytic philosophy in its earliest days and the analytic philosophy of the last thirty or forty years. Most of the philosophical work that has been called "analytic" throughout the last hundred years bears little resemblance to the narrow and stultifying doctrines that ruled when theologians set off for what seemed, then, to be friendlier waters. Given the current distance between analytic and Continental philosophy, it would be natural if those trained in the latter failed to realize how analytic philosophy has changed since those days. It is my hope that, if more theologians knew what analytic philosophy was really like, more of them would be willing at least to dip their toes into our stream, or encourage their students to explore it seriously. Some might even come to like it, enlarging the ranks of the theologians willing to help analytic philosophers in the interdisciplinary work of philosophical theology.

---

   [4] Cf. Wolfhart Pannenberg, *Metaphysics and the Idea of God*, trans. Philip Clayton (Edinburgh: T. & T. Clark, 1990); and Jean-Luc Marion, *God Without Being*, trans. Thomas A. Carlson (Chicago: University of Chicago Press, 1991).
   [5] Cf. Michael Dummett, *Origins of Analytic Philosophy* (London: Duckworth, 1993), 26 [cited in Charles Taliaferro, *Evidence and Faith: Philosophy and Religion since the Seventeenth Century* (Cambridge: Cambridge University Press, 2005), 293].

What Analytic Philosophy Is, Was, and Wasn't

Many theologians and Christian philosophers who belong to groups that rejected analytic philosophy early in the last century assume that the analytic river is still patrolled by theologian-eating sharks; that the only kind of philosophical theology capable of surviving here is a meager and reductionistic "analysis of religious language". But the analytic stream was only toxic for theologians (and metaphysicians and ethicists and . . .) for at most a third of its hundred-year history.

One thing that should be pointed out right away is that the word "analytic" in "analytic philosophy" means very little—at least, when used broadly, with "Continental" as the contrasting term. The only definitions of "analytic philosophy" that come close to tracking its actual application are ones that appeal to historical connections and self-identification, not method or positive doctrine. A. P. Martinich's counterfactual criterion is on the right track: analytic philosophers are those who "would have done philosophy the way Moore, Russell, and Wittgenstein did it if they had been doing philosophy when Moore, Russell, and Wittgenstein were".[6] I should put it this way: The distinctive thing about analytic philosophers is that they see themselves as the rightful heirs of Russell and Moore, or of philosophers who saw themselves as the rightful heirs of Russell and Moore, or . . . . "Analytic", so understood, is an adjective grounded very loosely in the way some philosophers measure their debts to philosophers active at the beginning of the twentieth century. To be an analytic philosopher is to have certain philosophical heroes, to admire their impact upon philosophy in a certain time and place—even if one disagrees with most of what these first analytic philosophers actually believed, and even if one largely rejects the details of their philosophical methodology.

Many academics outside analytic philosophy seem to believe that "analytic" just *means* the view that all important philosophical problems can be dissolved by some kind of careful attention to language. But if that were what it meant, "analytic" would be badly misapplied—both by those who wear it proudly and those who apply it pejoratively. It is far better to say that being an analytic philosopher does *not* require belief in linguistic resolutions of all philosophical problems, since only a few of the most famous philosophers of the last forty years who have been called "analytic philosophers" have believed any such thing. Furthermore, the term had no such implication when it was introduced, in the early years of the twentieth century. "Logical analysis", when it became Russell's rallying cry at the beginning of the revolt against idealism, did not mean "linguistic analysis". Initially, at least, it had nothing to do with reducing philosophical problems to puzzles about language. It referred to his belief that *facts*

---

[6] Introduction, in A. P. Martinich and David Sosa (eds.), *A Companion to Analytic Philosophy* (Malden, Mass.: Blackwell, 2001), 5.

could be understood by analyzing their constituents; it stood for his opposition to the idealist's "holism", their contention that analysis of facts is impossible. And the "facts" in question were taken, by Russell and Moore, to be existing chunks of the world, not sentences. Facts, for the earliest analytic philosophers, included real objects and universals as constituents; they were not linguistic entities of any sort.[7]

There is no denying, however, that the schools of analytic philosophy ruling the roost during the middle third of the last century—primarily, logical posit-ivism and the "quietism" of the later Wittgenstein—were intent upon turning philosophical problems into linguistic problems. Logical positivists imposed verificationist constraints upon the meanings of words; and their verificationism made life difficult for those trying to do philosophical theology while remain-ing in conversation with philosophers.[8] According to the most strident logical positivists, theological statements are sheer nonsense—meaningless noises mas-querading as important assertions.[9] In the 1950s, some post-positivists (many influenced by the later work of Wittgenstein) started saying things that seemed, superficially, to be a little friendlier to theology. They were willing to allow that characteristic theological statements and other expressions of religious sentiment are, at least, *meaningful*. Theological discourse constitutes a legitimate, but pecu-liar, "language game". However, when they explained the sort of "game" they had in mind, it became clear that they were not really interested in the way the vast majority of those who "play" this "game" actually use theological statements. Sentences such as "God created the world" or "Jesus rose from the dead" are not used by religious people to make *assertions*, they alleged. There is no question of their being true or false. According to R. M. Hare, for example, they express an attitude of some kind—apparently, something like an expectation that things will come out right in the end, though Hare is none too clear about exactly what attitude constitutes religious "belief". Whatever exactly a theologian means by saying "God created the world", Hare is sure that she is not making a claim with which atheists disagree.[10] R. B. Braithwaite was more explicit: Theological statements are really expressions of a resolve to behave according to some moral

---

[7] For more description of what "analytic" meant to the earliest analytic philosophers, see my "Prologue: Metaphysics After the Twentieth Century", in Dean Zimmerman (ed.), *Oxford Studies in Metaphysics* (Oxford: Oxford University Press, 2004), pp. ix–xxii.

[8] These philosophers also made life difficult for Russell and the rest of the old guard of analytic philosophers, such as C. D. Broad and H. H. Price; so there was always considerable opposition within analytic philosophy itself to each of the movements that so badly mistreated theology—because they badly mistreated metaphysics, ethics, and much else besides. See my "Prologue", pp. xvii–xix.

[9] A. J. Ayer, in his positivist manifesto *Language, Truth and Logic* (New York: Dover, 1952; first published in 1936), argued that "all utterances about the nature of God are nonsensical" (p. 115); and, for a time, a surprisingly large number of analytic philosophers found his arguments plausible.

[10] Cf. R. M. Hare's contribution to "Theology and Falsification", by Antony Flew, Hare, and Basil Mitchell, in Antony Flew and Alasdair MacIntyre (eds.), *New Essays in Philosophical Theology* (London: SCM Press, 1955), 99–103.

code while thinking about (though not necessarily *believing*) Bible stories.[11] Such philosophers often paid lip service to the Wittgensteinian mantra that "the meaning of any statement is given by the way in which it is used".[12] They claimed to be simply attending to the actual use of religious words by ordinary religious believers; but, really, the only usage they could possibly have been describing was their own peculiar habit of continuing to say things like "God created the world" and "Jesus rose from the dead" after having ceased to believe in God or the resurrection. At mid-century, the two most powerful philosophical movements in analytic philosophy offered theologians and religious philosophers two options: When someone says "God created the world" or "Jesus rose from the dead", he is talking pure nonsense; or, at best, he is expressing some positive attitude or resolve that he shares with many atheists.

During the period of positivist rule, an indomitable little group of British philosophers (mostly Anglicans) persevered. Theologians and philosophers such as F. R. Tennant, Austin Farrer, A. C. Ewing, H. H. Price, Ian Ramsey, H. D. Lewis, Basil Mitchell, and a few others carried on with "philosophical theology as usual", while also remaining dogged sparring partners with the dominant figures in analytic philosophy. Meanwhile, many Catholic philosophers and theologians looked for alternative philosophical perspectives that seemed friendlier toward theology. The two front-runners were Whitehead's Process Philosophy and Personalism. For good or ill, both movements have faded almost completely from the philosophical scene. Of course many Catholic philosophers and theologians remained loyal to St Thomas. Frequently, and understandably, they gave up trying to articulate their views in dialogue with the main currents of analytic philosophy—though now many Thomists are deeply engaged with philosophical theology as practiced by analytic philosophers, some even willing to call themselves "analytical Thomists".[13]

But the positivists' dogma that theology (and metaphysics and ethics and . . .) is meaningless was not part of analytic philosophy at its origins; and it was soon rejected, as positivism passed from the scene. Initially, "the philosophy of analysis" meant a fully metaphysically-loaded commitment to *realism* in opposition to the idealisms of Bradley, Bosanquet, and others. Its founders—Russell and Moore—never went along with the extreme positivist dogmas of the 1930s, which led Carnap, Ayer, and others to consign theology to the same dustbin as metaphysics. Nowadays, hardly any analytic philosophers will still try to argue

---

[11] R. B. Braithwaite, "An Empiricist's View of the Nature of Religious Belief" (first published in 1955), reprinted in Basil Mitchell (ed.), *The Philosophy of Religion* (Oxford: Oxford University Press, 1971), 72–91.

[12] ibid. 77.

[13] Examples include Brian Davies, Eleonore Stump, and J. B. Haldane (Haldane describes himself as an "analytical Thomist"). For examples of their work, see Davies, *The Thought of Thomas Aquinas* (Oxford: Clarendon Press, 1993); Eleonore Stump, *Aquinas* (London: Routledge, 2003); and John Haldane, *Faithful Reason* (London: Routledge, 2004).

that theological statements are meaningless, or that the very idea of God is obviously incoherent; and the ones who do are regarded as dinosaurs from a bygone era—the unaccountable age when positivists ruled the earth.[14] Although it took some time for the traditional problems of metaphysics and philosophy of religion to return to center stage, the movements that had pushed them into the wings did not themselves flourish for very long.

Today's analytic philosophers do not think all philosophical problems can be eliminated by some magic bullet of "linguistic analysis". And we engage in all sorts of traditional philosophical enterprises that the positivists declared anathema. Some of us build metaphysical systems of great complexity, defending Platonic universals, Aristotelian essences, and all manner of old-school metaphysical entities.[15] Many of us are moral realists, a few even developing ethics based on natural law or divine commands.[16] Some defend traditional arguments for the existence of God.[17] And one can do these things and remain a respected member of the profession, publishing papers on such topics in the most prominent journals.

A large number of Christians have found a comfortable home in the world of analytic philosophy. The Society of Christian Philosophers has the largest membership of all the special interest groups meeting in conjunction with the American Philosophical Association;[18] and many of its members have been awarded the highest honors our guild can confer.[19] How is it that a space for Christian philosophers has come to open up within the current philosophical

[14] Cf. e.g. Kai Nielsen's treatment at the hands of Anthony Kenny in the *Times Literary Supplement*, 18 January 2002 ("A Genial Solitude").

[15] To see the wide range of traditional metaphysical positions that are alive and well today, one need only glance through the table of contents of any recent metaphysics anthology—e.g. Stephen Laurence and Cynthia Macdonald (eds.), *Contemporary Readings in the Foundations of Metaphysics* (Malden, Mass.: Blackwell, 1998), or Jaegwon Kim and Ernest Sosa, *Metaphysics: An Anthology* (Malden, Mass.: Blackwell, 1999).

[16] John M. Finnis is a distinguished philosophical exponent of natural law within jurisprudence; cf. Finnis, *Natural Law and Natural Rights* (Oxford: Oxford University Press 1980). Divine Command Theory has been defended by two of the most respected analytic philosophers of their generation: Robert Merrihew Adams and Philip Quinn. Cf. Adams, *The Virtue of Faith* (New York: Oxford University Press, 1987), chs. 7 and 9; and Quinn, *Divine Commands and Moral Requirements* (Oxford: Clarendon Press, 1978).

[17] For a survey of recent work on arguments for the existence of God, see William E. Mann (ed.), *The Blackwell Guide to the Philosophy of Religion* (Malden, Mass.: Blackwell, 2005), chs. 4, 5, and 6.

[18] At least, the SCP had the largest membership around 1980, according to Kelly James Clark; cf. Clark (ed.), *Philosophers Who Believe* (Downers Grove, Ill.: InterVarsity, 1993), 9–10.

[19] Many people, both inside and outside philosophy, have taken note of the emergence, within the last thirty-five years, of a surprisingly large number of distinguished and outspoken Christians in analytic departments. The phenomenon has even come to the attention of mainstream news media, such as *Time* magazine (7 April 1980). For detailed accounts of the renaissance of Christian scholarship within mainstream analytic philosophy, see Clark (ed.), *Philosophers Who Believe*; Thomas Morris (ed.), *God and the Philosophers* (New York: Oxford University Press, 1994); and the penultimate chapter of Charles Taliaferro's *Evidence and Faith: Philosophy and Religion since the Seventeenth Century*.

climate? One should not lightly dismiss the answer Alvin Plantinga is said to have given, when asked this question by a bemused, thoroughly secular colleague at a cocktail party: "It's the work of the Holy Spirit." (Plantinga is a master of the jaw-dropping retort.) But more mundane explanatory factors can be cited, as well.

For one thing, despite allegations to the contrary from Continental philosophers, analytic philosophy is, in at least one important respect, thoroughly "postmodern". Overweening confidence in the power of reason to arrive at incontrovertible truth is supposed to have been a hallmark of the modern period. (Was it really? I am not so sure. But never mind; it has, by now, been built into the definition of "modern", and its rejection is supposed to be part of what it means to be "postmodern".) Although analytic philosophers still put a lot of stock in *truth*, they generally admit that there is little in philosophy that we can claim to *know* to be true with much confidence—at least not when it comes to substantive philosophical theories, as opposed to conditional claims about which philosophical theories are consistent with which. There is simply too much disagreement among equally intelligent and well-informed experts within philosophy for us to make extravagant claims to certainty.

Of course almost every philosopher still *believes* various philosophical theories—the ones that seem, after careful reflection, to do the most justice to the sorts of evidence that count in favor of philosophical theories. But what kind of evidence is that? When assessing the adequacy of an ethical or epistemological or metaphysical theory, analytic philosophers consider things like: the theory's ability to retain most, if not all, of their firmest pre-theoretical convictions about the subject matter it purports to describe; the naturalness of the theory's fit with other philosophical views they hold; the theoretical virtues it displays, such as simplicity or the unification of what seemed to be disparate phenomena; and other hard-to-quantify theoretical virtues. No wonder, at the end of the day, we can still disagree! But most of us, after careful consideration of alternative theories, still end up *believing* one of them. We know what can be said on behalf of rival theories, but the evidence seems to us to favor one, even though many of our peers do not see it that way; and so we come to believe the theory—reasonably, but, no doubt, fallibly. If this sort of modesty is "postmodern", then most analytic philosophers are, to that extent, postmodern.

These days, then, the average analytic philosopher recognizes her precarious epistemological situation, and admits that reasonable people have reached radically different conclusions from her own. She knows that there are respectable philosophers who hold views that seem, by her lights, to be "crazy". But these crazy philosophers are people whose criticisms are often important, and might even prove devastating; and their positive views must also be taken seriously, however different they may be from her own. It is my impression that almost every analytic philosopher regards quite a few of her contemporaries in this way; and philosophers who harbor no special anti-religious animus are, as it turns out, generally willing to extend a similar courtesy to Christian philosophers. A few seem even to understand that their own naturalist commitments might seem crazy to us.

I do not want to overstate the strength of Christianity within the Anglophone philosophical world. Although numerous outspoken Christians are highly respected in analytic circles, many of our colleagues still regard the persistence of religious belief among otherwise intelligent philosophers as a strange aberration, a pocket of irrationality. As in many other parts of the academy, expressions of disdain for religion—Christianity in particular—are more socially acceptable among philosophers than in the culture at large. But Christians should be prepared to be regarded as a little bit crazy; if we do not at least *try* to respond to the occasional barbed remark with equanimity, should we claim to be followers of Christ? Thankfully, at present, Christian philosophers can be forthright in the expression of their faith and still be taken seriously as scholars. Some of us will still have plenty of opportunities to learn humility, and we must try to be thankful for those as well.

The Need for Cooperation

Unless philosophy always trumps theology, or vice versa, the only way to tackle the problems of philosophical theology with integrity is to keep both philosophical and theological considerations on the table, after the manner of Augustine or Edwards. As in any subfield that belongs to two highly specialized disciplines, there must be collaboration among experts from both disciplines. Christian analytic philosophers have become intensely interested in the traditional questions of philosophical theology, and have produced a large body of work; but when we look for help in this enterprise from theology, we do not find many theologians attempting to articulate Christian doctrine in ways analytic philosophers can understand. There are a few out there ("some of my best friends are theologians"), mainly from the conservative wing of Anglicanism, and from the many evangelical seminaries and colleges in the United States and Canada. Within Catholic philosophy departments, there are philosophers who are also, in effect, theologians; and some of them find ways to make themselves understood by analytic philosophers. But, the numbers from all three categories seem pretty small, compared to the numbers of Christian analytic philosophers working in philosophy of religion. And those Christian philosophers who do not fit neatly into one of these three subcultures must rely on scholarship from theological traditions that are bound to seem somewhat alien.

Naturally, each party to an interdisciplinary conversation of this sort runs the risk of saying things that will sound shockingly naïve to the other. Most Christian philosophers in the analytic tradition have little, if any, formal training in biblical criticism or the history of doctrine, for instance; so we have plenty to learn. But, given the diminished role philosophy tends to play in theological training, and the dearth of analytic philosophy within seminaries and theology departments, the same is no doubt true of most of the theologians who could engage with us in the project of philosophical theology. So I end this section with an appeal to theologians and Christian philosophers outside the analytic tradition: find out for yourselves whether analytic philosophy is really so arid as you have been told. See if it has anything convincing to say in response to the arguments (or the "hermeneutics of suspicion") used by Continental philosophers to undermine our more traditional approach to philosophy. And then consider whether analytic philosophy might not be, after all, a context in which philosophical theology could flourish. The editors and authors of this book are convinced that it can and, to an impressive degree, does. We hope the contents of this volume help support that conviction.

III

A Dearth of Dualists

To say that dualism is on the defensive in both philosophical and theological circles would be a gross understatement. The idea that we are thinking, immaterial substances interacting with non-thinking, material bodies is widely thought to be incoherent or at least subject to devastating philosophical, scientific, and even theological objections. In this book, several of the authors argue that materialist conceptions of human persons are, for various reasons, inferior to a metaphysics of immaterial selves; but there is at least as much defense of the compatibility of various Christian doctrines with materialist conceptions of human beings. Still, the amount of attention paid to dualism in these pages will seem sadly retrograde to many readers.

By my lights, however, dualism still belongs on the table. I do not deny that there are powerful Ockhamistic reasons to doubt dualism: we know there are plenty of material objects composed ultimately of unthinking physical particles,[20] but why go on to posit an *extra* realm of purely mental things? A very good question, surely, and one not easily answered. I also have to admit that I find many of the traditional arguments for dualism relatively easy to resist.[21] On the other hand, I am not much impressed by the positive arguments against dualism—that is, arguments other than those based upon a reasonable

---

[20] Or do we?—see Adams's essay, Chapter 1 of this volume, for an argument that it is the purely non-mental substances that are problematic, not the immaterial, thinking selves.

[21] For some of my doubts about modal arguments and unity of consciousness arguments, see my "Two Cartesian Arguments for the Simplicity of the Soul", *American Philosophical Quarterly*, 28 (1991), 217–26; and the entry "Dualism in the Philosophy of Mind", *Encyclopedia of Philosophy*, 2nd edn (New York: Macmillan, 2005), 113–22.

Ockhamistic resistance to needlessly positing nonphysical entities.[22] Some anti-dualist arguments are simply very bad (Plantinga pokes fun at some unimpressive arguments in his contribution to this volume). Others take as their target only the more implausible forms of dualism, ignoring more popular varieties that are at least as a priori likely as the extreme kinds.[23] The most interesting anti-dualist arguments target substance dualism by taking aim at one of its implications: a dualism of mental and physical properties. Dualists seem forced to admit that some mental properties are just as fundamental as anything posited by fundamental physics; and, barring some implausible parallelism of mental and physical events, dualists must also posit special causal laws linking the mental (e.g. phenomenal) properties with the fundamental properties already central to physics. There are real puzzles about the form such laws would have to take, a couple of which will be sketched in my discussion of property dualism, below. Although I should not want to downplay their seriousness, they are not problems faced only, or even primarily, by substance dualists. Although highly controversial, property dualism is a real contender in contemporary philosophy of mind; and many of its defenders (notably, David Chalmers[24]) are not substance dualists. Those who, like myself, find property dualism utterly compelling—independently of any reason to accept a dualism of soul and body—will not be overly impressed by objections to substance dualism that take aim at property dualism.

I have attempted, in a small way, to defend some of these outlandish assertions elsewhere.[25] And I have also argued that any *sensible* materialism about human persons—any view according to which I am identical to some familiar kind of physical object, such as a human organism or brain—is a lot harder to maintain

---

[22] For an admirably fair-minded presentation of the case against dualism, one can do no better than to consult Paul M. Churchland, *Matter and Consciousness* (Cambridge, Mass.: MIT Press, 1985), 7–22. I would call his overall strategy "Ockhamistic". However, the "argument from neural dependence" (p. 20) is an important part of his case that might seem more direct—not simply a matter of pointing out that, whatever souls are supposed to do, one can assign their job to some physical object and thereby avoid positing extra entities. The argument from neural dependence relies, however, upon the assumption that, if a dualism concedes that the soul needs a functioning brain in order to think, it is thereby made less plausible. Why should one think this is so? Perhaps because, in the absence of independent activities that it can perform unaided, there is less reason to posit a soul as an additional entity—a serious objection, but one that seems Ockhamistic in spirit. Still, I have to admit that I am papering over a lot of subtle issues by calling all the best arguments against dualism "Ockhamistic".

[23] For example, Ernest Sosa's interesting argument against interaction between souls and bodies depends upon the Cartesian assumption that souls cannot have a more intimate relation to some regions of space than to others; cf. Sosa, "Mind–Body Interaction and Supervenient Causation", *Midwest Studies in Philosophy*, 9 (1984), 271–81. Many dualists have denied this, however; and few, if any, of the traditional motivations for dualism require that souls be altogether "outside of space".

[24] See Chalmers, *The Conscious Mind* (New York: Oxford University Press, 1996).

[25] See my "Should the Christian Be a Mind–Body Dualist?", in Michael Peterson and Ray Van Arragon (eds.), *Contemporary Debates in Philosophy of Religion* (Malden, Mass.: Blackwell, 2004), 315–27; and "Dualism in the Philosophy of Mind".

than most materialists seem to realize.[26] In this volume, however, I leave the arguments for and against dualism to others.

The Varieties of Dualism: Property Dualism

As a sort of prelude to the debates between dualists and materialists that are to come, I now provide a taxonomy of mind–body dualisms—beginning with "property dualism", a thesis compatible with materialism about human persons; and proceeding to "substance dualism", a category subsuming a broad spectrum of doctrines that posit a distinction between soul and body. Some philosophers are skeptical about whether a stable doctrine of interactionist substance dualism can even be formulated; if their skepticism were justified, many of the controversies within these pages would evaporate. I aim to dispel that skepticism here.

Throughout history and as far into prehistory as we can see, the majority view of humankind seems always to have been that there is more to a person than the body; and that an "afterlife" is possible because this "something more"—the soul or spirit—does not pass away with the death of the body. In contemporary philosophy, this doctrine is often called "substance dualism", and contrasted with various forms of "property dualism"—the thesis that the mental properties of persons are significantly independent of or in some other way distinct from the physical properties of persons. Typically, property dualism is identified with the failure of some class of mental properties to "supervene upon the physical" (as in the essay by van Inwagen in this volume).

The denial of the supervenience of the mental upon the physical is tantamount to the denial of a very weak form of a thesis usually called "physicalism". It is generally assumed by those who accept the label "physicalist" that physics has a privileged place among the sciences. In physics, one finds the most precise descriptions of the physical world, and the closest we can come to exceptionless laws. The advance of physics is usually thought to represent progress toward an ideal, true physics—a scientific theory that is "in the style of" present-day physics, explaining all the sorts of events physics now attempts to explain along with whatever new phenomena might turn out to be relevant to the occurrence of these sorts of events. Ideal physics may forever remain beyond our ken, but it is the terms of ideal physics that would provide the means to tell the full, fundamental truth about the nature of matter. "Physicalism" is the conviction that ideal physics would provide the means to—in some sense—"completely describe" our world, without adverting to spookily mental entities or forces.

The physicalist picture I have just sketched really combines two distinct elements. (i) The true description of our universe in the language of ideal physics will not include, as part of its basic ideology, overtly mental terms; so,

---

[26] See my "Material People", in Michael Loux and Dean Zimmerman (eds.), *The Oxford Handbook of Metaphysics* (Oxford: Oxford University Press, 2003), 491–526.

talk about "acts of will", "sharp pains", "reddish after-images", and the like will not be required in stating fundamental laws. (ii) Although we may always need to make use of "higher-level" sciences and laws to explain the behavior of macrophysical objects, including human beings, nevertheless, the true physics of our world would "completely describe" the world in the sense that a full physical description would "settle everything": a world exactly resembling ours in all the details specifiable in the language of ideal physics (and without any extra entities or extra fundamental properties added on) would *have* to be like our world in every respect, including every mental respect. This "settling everything" clause is usually called "global supervenience"—everything about our universe "supervenes upon" or is determined by the way in which fundamental physical properties are exemplified throughout the universe.[27]

Many philosophers reject physicalism because they believe that some kinds of mental property fail to supervene upon the physical. In other words, they believe that the complete specification of the physical structure of a world like ours in purely non-mental terms leaves open various possibilities for the distribution of mental properties over the creatures in that world. According to these opponents of physicalism, the mental "floats free", to some extent, of the physical. For example, if brain states of a certain sort are lawfully correlated with a certain kind of pain, and if experiencing this sort of pain does not supervene upon the physical properties exemplified in and around brains in our world, then it is a matter of contingent law that brain states of this sort generate this kind of pain. They could have been lawfully associated with a different kind of sensation, or perhaps no sensation at all.

"Property dualism" means different things in the mouths of different philosophers. But, more and more frequently, it is used simply to mean the denial of physicalism either because there are brutely mental powers or properties that interact with the physical world (as in the scenario sketched by Hart and Yagisawa in their chapter); or because global supervenience fails—that is, because the complete description of the universe in the terms of fundamental (ideal) physics is compatible with a different distribution of mental properties (as in the epiphenomenal property dualism defended by David Chalmers). In either case, the mental properties exemplified in our world would be to some degree independent of what one might call the *purely* physical properties—that is, all the properties and forces posited by fundamental physics, with the exception of any that might have to simply be identified with mental states or powers.

The fact that one class of properties can vary independently of another does not rule out the possibility that some things may have both kinds of properties.

---

[27] There are vexed questions about how to make physicalism more precise. For a window onto the debate, see Carl Gillett and Barry Loewer (eds.), *Physicalism and its Discontents* (Cambridge: Cambridge University Press, 2001), esp. chs. 1, 2, and 3: David Papineau, "The Rise of Physicalism"; Barry Loewer, "From Physics to Physicalism"; and D. Gene Witmer, "Sufficiency Claims and Physicalism: A Formulation".

If one restricts attention to the observable shapes and colors of medium-sized objects, color properties and shape properties are independent in this way—the distribution of colors over objects does not supervene upon the distribution of shapes. Paint could have been applied, leaving all objects the same shape but with differences in some of their colors. Despite this independence of shape and color, a single object, such as a red ball, can have both color properties and shape properties. The ball does not need to have a part that is red but shapeless and another part that is spherical but colorless.[28] In other words, a dualism of color and shape properties is compatible with a monistic view about the subjects of these properties. Analogously, a dualism of mental and physical properties is compatible with a monism about their subjects. Property dualists who are substance materialists believe that the mental and physical attributes of persons are independent in something like the way color and shape are; nevertheless, they believe that they are attributes of a single thing—in our case, a human person (or perhaps some smaller part of the human body[29]) consisting entirely of ordinary matter.

Although property dualism may not imply a dualism of immaterial, thinking substances and unthinking material bodies; nevertheless, substance dualism is usually thought to imply property dualism. If mental properties belong to entities that are not composed of ordinary matter, it is hard to see why anyone would think that global supervenience holds. So most problems facing property dualism confront substance dualists, too. And there are important objections to property dualism, such as: if any causal relations exist between the mental and the physical, then property dualism will imply inelegant and otherwise implausible causal laws.

Richard Taylor and Keith Campbell offer variations on this last theme.

What we must conceive, then, is a physical change within the brain, this change being wrought not by some other physical change in the brain or elsewhere but by an *idea*. . . . Conceive, then, if possible, how an *idea* can effect such a change as this, how an idea can render more permeable the membranes of certain brain cells, how an idea can

---

[28] This claim is false, if a certain sort of "trope metaphysics" is correct. According to trope theorists, such as D. C. Williams ("On the Elements of Being: I and II", *Review of Metaphysics*, 7 (1953), 3–18 and 171–92), for every fundamental property of a thing, there is a "trope" or instance of that property. Trope theorists generally also hold that objects consist of maximal bundles of "coinherent" tropes; and that a trope that is an instance of a certain property confers that property upon every bundle of tropes with which it is coinherent, including sub-bundles of the largest bundle (I detect this doctrine in Williams; cf. his remarks about the mind, pp. 18 and 171). The largest bundle is the thing we would ordinarily have taken to be the *only* substance with the property; but this sort of trope theorist posits many "thinner" substances that also have it. A trope metaphysics of this sort undermines the distinction between substance and property dualism. The existence of fundamental mental properties that are independent of physical properties implies the existence of sub-bundles which include mental tropes without physical tropes. These sub-bundles, since they are composed of mental property tropes but not physical property tropes, are nonphysical mental substances.

[29] Some substance materialists do not identify themselves with the entire human body, but rather with just the brain or nervous system, or even a single hemisphere.

enter into a chemical reaction whose effect is the diffusion of sodium ions at a certain place, or how an idea can move the particles of the cortical cells or otherwise aid or inhibit chemical reactions occurring therein. Try, I say, to form a conception of this, and then confess that, as soon as the smallest attempt at any description is made, the description becomes unintelligible and the conception an impossible one.[30]

If the dualists are right, events in the brain, of a complexity which defeats the imagination, can cause effects of great simplicity in the spirit. For example, the experience of seeing a red circle on a white ground requires brain activity involving millions of cells. And vice versa, so simple a mental event as deciding to go to bed sets in train, on the Dualist account, cortical events of the most staggeringly complicated sort.

Because no mechanism connects matter with spirit, such causal connections must be primitive, fundamental ones. In no other case are there fundamental connections between the simple and the complex. In no other case is the effect of a complex activity quite different from any composition of the effects of part of the complex. Matter–spirit connections, if they occur at all, are quite unlike any others. And unless panpsychism is true, they occur only in tiny fragments of the universe.[31]

Paul Churchland raises a similar problem. Considering the hypothesis that "mental properties are *fundamental* properties of reality . . . on a par with length, mass, electric charge, and other fundamental properties", Churchland notes that a property dualist might cite, as historical precedent, other cases in which a property was thought to be reducible but turned out to be fundamental—for example, "electromagnetic phenomena (such as electric charge and magnetic attraction)" which were once thought to be "just an unusually subtle manifestation of purely *mechanical* phenomena" but ultimately had to be added to "the existing list of fundamental properties".

Perhaps mental properties enjoy a status like that of electromagnetic properties: irreducible, but not emergent. Such a view may be called *elemental-property dualism*. . . . Unfortunately, the parallel with electromagnetic phenomena has one very obvious failure. Unlike electromagnetic properties, which are displayed at all levels of reality from the subatomic level on up, mental properties are displayed only in large physical systems that have evolved a very complex internal organization. . . . They do not appear to be basic or elemental at all.[32]

The remarks of Taylor, Campbell, and Churchland appear in introductory texts; and so they are, understandably, rather sketchy—gestures in the direction of more rigorous arguments. But no property dualist should deny that these authors have put their fingers on some serious worries. All three lay these burdens (with justice) at the feet of those defending a dualism of immaterial soul and purely physical body. But it is important to note that they are, in the first

[30] Richard Taylor, *Metaphysics*, 4th edn (Englewood Cliffs, NJ: Prentice-Hall, 1992), 22.

[31] Keith Campbell, *Body and Mind*, 2nd edn (Notre Dame, Ind.: University of Notre Dame Press, 1984), 50–1.

[32] Churchland, *Matter and Consciousness*, 12–13.

instance, objections to *property* dualism; and that many philosophers (including many philosophers who are not substance dualists, and probably all of the dualists in this volume) accept these forms of property dualism for reasons that have nothing to do with the stronger forms of dualism. So, however important and impressive these arguments may be, when fully deployed, their force will often have dissipated before they could begin to undermine a philosopher's commitment to substance dualism.

Varieties of Dualism: Substance Dualism

Substance dualism goes further than property dualism, denying monism about the *bearers* of physical and mental properties. Philosophical dualists such as Plato and Descartes—and, more recently, Karl Popper, Richard Swinburne, and William Hasker—disagree about many details.[33] But they have this much in common: (*a*) they believe that, for every person who thinks or has experiences, there is a thing—a soul or spiritual substance—that lacks many of the physical properties the body shares with unthinking material objects; and (*b*) they believe that this extra thing is essential to the person, and in one way or another responsible for the person's mental life. Until recently, "dualism" (as a term for a theory about the relation between mind and body) just meant what is now called "substance dualism". "Property dualism" is a recent coinage. Not long ago, virtually *everyone* was a property dualist, so there was little need to draw a distinction. The definition I propose seems to me to correspond nicely to the way "substance dualism" is now applied, and to the way "dualism" was used before the need arose to distinguish between substance and property dualism.

There are two important ways in which the above definition is vague: how many properties can a soul share with the stuff in unthinking objects before it is just another physical object? And how "responsible" must the soul be for a person's mental life? It seems to me that the points at which philosophers usually begin to wonder whether "dualism" should apply to a philosophical view are explained nicely by the different answers that are given to these two questions. As a theory of mind–body relations attributes more of the same properties to souls and inert matter, or makes the soul less directly responsible for thinking, we become more reluctant to call the view "dualism", without qualification. There is a range of possible answers to these two questions, and the answers can be roughly ordered as more and less dualistic in flavor. On the proposed definition, then, "substance dualism" becomes a label for a range of views spread out along one end of a spectrum—a spectrum of possible

---

[33] Cf. Karl Popper and John C. Eccles, *The Self and its Brain* (Berlin: Springer-Verlag, 1977); Richard Swinburne, *The Evolution of the Soul*, revised edn (Oxford: Clarendon Press, 1997); and William Hasker, *The Emergent Self* (Ithaca, NY: Cornell University Press, 1999).

mind–body theories running from extreme dualisms (like those of Plato and Descartes) to straightforward versions of materialism. The presence of a small area of indeterminacy within the spectrum does not count against the definition, since it is intended to capture the meaning of a familiar but somewhat imprecise term.

How is the Soul "Responsible" for a Person's Mental Life?

I begin exploration of the differences among (substance) dualists by canvassing ways in which clause (*b*) has been understood. In what way is the soul responsible for a person's mental life?

Dualists are deeply divided over the question whether a person is identical with an immaterial substance, or a composite of immaterial soul and physical body. Many dualists agree with Plato: persons are entirely immaterial. Each person just *is* a soul, related to a physical body like pilot to ship. Other dualists identify a person with a whole composed of soul and body. Among these "composite dualists", further differences emerge: some, like Richard Swinburne (and, perhaps, Descartes, who sometimes seems to identify himself with a composite of soul and body), ascribe a person's mental properties to her soul and her physical properties to her body. On this view, there is a thing unlike ordinary physical objects that thinks the person's thoughts, and then there is the person, and they are not identical. The person is identical to a larger thing that includes the thinking soul as a part.

This sort of composite dualist elaborates clause (*b*) by saying that, although I am not identical with my soul, it is nevertheless "responsible for my mental life" in virtue of somehow having or undergoing that mental life *for* me. The explanation raises some obvious and awkward questions. If the composite person *also* thinks, then there are two thinkers who cannot tell themselves apart. If the composite does not, strictly speaking, think; then *persons* do not, strictly speaking, think. A soul does a person's thinking just as the stomach does a person's digesting. Neither alternative is a happy one.[34]

There is at least one view that has some claim to being a version of composite dualism but that gives a very different account of the responsibility for thinking that is mentioned in (*b*). According to St Thomas Aquinas, when soul and body are united, it is wrong to attribute mental states to the soul. Nevertheless, the soul does explain how it is that a person can have the ability to think; and, at death, the soul is responsible for an ongoing mental life in an even more direct way, acquiring the ability to think all by itself, in its disembodied state. So clause (*b*) remains more-or-less true, though the soul's responsibility for the

---

[34] Eric Olson presses these objections to composite dualism in "A Compound of Two Substances", in Kevin Corcoran (ed.), *Soul, Body and Survival* (Ithaca, NY: Cornell University Press, 2001), 73–88.

person's thinking is not so direct as on other forms of dualism—until death, at least.

Aquinas's souls are notoriously hard to understand; but they make some kind of sense within the framework of Aquinas's broadly Aristotelian metaphysics.[35] According to both Aquinas and Aristotle, "accidental forms" explain a thing's accidental properties, while a "substantial form" explains its being or essence. Following Aristotle, Aquinas calls the substantial forms of living things "souls", and the soul of a human being includes his entire complex physical and mental nature. A human being's substantial form gives a hunk of matter the distinctive structure of a living human body, and so it is responsible for the physical abilities of the person composed of that hunk of matter. The very same substantial form is also responsible for the mental abilities of the person. And it is the person as a whole, a physical thing resulting from a combination of matter and form, that exercises both kinds of abilities. If one can wrap one's mind around an Aristotelian metaphysics of form and matter, that much will seem fairly unproblematic. What is harder to see is how something capable of playing the role of a "substantial form" could come to be able to think after death, while not "informing" any matter. Aristotle did not think this was possible. But, according to Aquinas, although the soul that persists after death is not identical to the person whose soul it was, the soul does retain the ability to think. *Who* this thinker is remains something of a mystery.

The Thomistic doctrine of the soul is, by all accounts, a borderline case of mind–body dualism. While body and soul are united, the Thomist's soul has no mental properties—it is not itself a mind or even a part of the person, in the ordinary sense of "part". The way in which it is "responsible for my mental life" is quite indirect; allowing that it is "responsibility enough" to satisfy clause (*b*) in the proposed definition of dualism would extend the meaning of "dualism" to include views that have not usually been thought to qualify. The soul is a formal cause of a human person's ability to think, and also a formal cause of such physical abilities as motility. The soul "conveys" both sorts of powers, but in a funny, "formal" way. The soul does not itself exemplify these powers (while the human person exists, at any rate), and so it does not confer them by simply having the powers and being a part of a human being. And the soul does not confer them upon a physical human being by pushing bits of matter around until they have the right sort of configuration or structure to think or move. Efficient causes do that. Rather, the soul is introduced as the configuration or structure itself—a relatively abstract thing, at least when

---

[35] Eleonore Stump and Brian Leftow elucidate St Thomas's account of the human soul in quite different—but perhaps ultimately complementary—ways. See the chapter "Forms and Bodies: The Soul" in Stump's *Aquinas*; and Leftow's "Souls Dipped in Dust", in Corcoran (ed.), *Soul, Body and Survival*, 120–38.

compared with the full-fledged human being, providing a relatively abstract explanation of how a thing can have these abilities. Platonists posit a different sort of thing to play the role of configuration or structure, one that is even more abstract. But that should not make a Platonist about universals automatically qualify as a substance dualist *about minds and bodies*. By parity of reasoning, Thomists should not be categorized as substance dualists just because the formal explanations they give of mental and physical abilities appeal to immaterial forms.

An example of a Platonist materialist may shed light on the subject. Consider a type–type materialist—someone who identifies mental property types with physical property types; for example, the property *being in pain* with the property *having a functioning brain with C-fibers firing*. If she is also a certain kind of Platonist, she will introduce universals as the metaphysical grounds for attributing *all* structures and configurations—in particular, then, she will suppose that the physical property types she identifies with mental property types are universals. Is she a substance dualist? A type–type materialist would not normally be thought to be a substance dualist; few philosophers would take her views about universals to be relevant to the question whether she is a *mind–body* dualist. If the fact that the Aristotelian's extra entities (e.g. St Thomas's substantial forms) are not like ordinary physical objects makes the view dualistic, then the fact that the Platonist's extra entities (universals) are not like ordinary physical objects should automatically make Platonism dualistic. But "dualism" has not normally been applied in that way (e.g. no one has ever called David Armstrong a dualist simply because he believes in universals, and therefore cites physical universals as the formal causes of mental states; rather, he remains a paradigmatic substance materialist). Unless there is some deep reason to suppose that the real meaning of "dualist" in our mouths does not track our considered application to individual cases, belief in immaterial formal causes should not be sufficient to make one a dualist.

I conclude, then, that St Thomas's view about the way in which the soul is responsible for a human being's ability to think is too indirect to decisively satisfy clause (*b*). Whatever its merits, Thomistic dualism is at best a borderline case of substance dualism. This result is not a surprising departure from ordinary usage. The proponents of Thomistic dualism often recommend the view by pointing out how very close it is to straightforward versions of materialism about human beings; and they spend a good deal of time arguing about whether it should or should not qualify as a version of dualism.

I turn, then, to more full-blooded dualisms, according to which the immaterial part of a person is responsible for the person's ability to think in virtue of being *itself* a thinking thing, here and now. Because of the problems with composite dualism noted above—could something distinct from a person do her thinking for her, or in addition to her?—the paradigm case will be dualisms that identify persons with immaterial substances.

How Many Properties Can the Soul Share with Paradigmatically Physical Objects?

The first of the two elements in my proposed definition of dualism, above, was this: (*a*) for every person who thinks or has experiences, there is a thing—a soul or spiritual substance—that lacks many of the physical properties the body shares with unthinking material objects. This raises the question: "How many properties can a thinking thing have in common with patently inert matter, before it becomes just another physical object?"

Some opponents of dualism allege an incoherence in the very idea of a nonphysical soul influencing a physical body, based on the answers they give to this question. Daniel Dennett points out that, on any version of dualism that says mind affects matter, the soul should eventually come to the attention of the physicist studying the motions of particles in the brain. But would that not make the soul *physical*? "A ghost in the machine is of no help in our theories unless it is a ghost that can move things around . . . but anything that can move a physical thing is itself a physical thing (although perhaps a strange and heretofore unstudied kind of physical thing)."[36] It might have seemed natural to define substance dualism as any view according to which an "enlargement of the ontology of the physical sciences is called for in order to account for the phenomena of consciousness"; one might have thought that a dualist is someone who posits a mental entity that is "something above and beyond the atoms and molecules that compose the brain".[37] But if the extra thing posited is still *physical*, the view would not be dualistic; and if the extra thing is able to interact with the body at all, it *would* be physical. Attempts to define dualism in terms of the nonphysical nature of souls are incompatible with interactionism.

So Dennett proposes a different way to define "dualism"—a definition guaranteed to make dualism unacceptable to anyone who hopes that persons can be studied in a principled way: the dualist is someone who declares that "how the mind works. . . is quite beyond human ken". [38] A philosopher or scientist may posit an extra, mental entity not composed of ordinary matter, and still be a good materialist, so long as the new entity is "scientifically investigatable"; the view only becomes genuinely dualistic when the extra entity is said to be something that cannot be studied scientifically. The hallmark of the dualist is his or her "fundamentally antiscientific stance";[39] to be a dualist is, by definition, to be a mystery-monger, a despiser of science.

Dennett offers us a choice of definitions, then: either "dualism" means something that is incompatible with interactionism; or it means something incompatible with the possibility of a scientific study of the mind. But has Dennett really exhausted the alternatives? On the face of it, the paradigm cases

---

[36] Daniel Dennett, *Consciousness Explained* (Boston: Little, Brown, 1991), 35.
[37] Ibid. 36.   [38] Ibid. 37.   [39] Ibid. 36–7.

of dualists include people like Descartes and Sir John Eccles—philosopher-scientists or scientist-philosophers who suppose that the mind interacts with the brain, and that its powers and mode of operation could, in principle, be studied scientifically. Are there really only two ways to define "dualism", each incompatible with its application to paradigmatic dualists?

Not all critics of dualism define the view in such an unfriendly manner. Paul Churchland and Keith Campbell, for instance, understand substance dualism in terms that are acceptable to its major proponents. They grant that there is a spectrum of coherent conceptions of persons that should all qualify as substance dualisms, some of which make souls more like ordinary inert matter than others. They admit that there are some legitimate motivations for adopting a view from this spectrum, and they realize that these motivations do not require the more extreme forms of dualism. And then they go on to offer substantive, serious criticisms of all forms of substance dualism.[40] But Dennett is not the only philosopher who attempts to defeat dualism largely by means of tendentious definitions.[41] And so the dualist has plenty of motivation for clarifying what he might mean by calling souls "nonphysical" or "immaterial".

Given his importance in the history of philosophy, and the importance of dualism within his metaphysics, it is understandable that Descartes has become the paradigmatic dualist; and that his conception of the differences between body and soul is sometimes taken to be the only version of dualism worth discussing. Cartesian souls are nonphysical in a very strong sense: unlike physical objects, they are not spatially located; unlike the physical world as Descartes conceived of it, souls have no parts, but are instead "simple substances"; and they are in no way dependent upon the physical world for their continued existence or ability to think.

To make these three Cartesian doctrines essential to any view worthy of the label "substance dualism" would, however, be perverse. The adherents of animistic religions, spiritualists and other believers in ghosts all posit a dualism of distinct substances; and so they have naturally been called "dualists". Most prominent philosophers who describe themselves as substance dualists (e.g. Richard Swinburne, William Hasker, and W. D. Hart[42]) depart from one or more Cartesian tenet.

The truth of the matter is that "substance dualism" (and just plain "dualism", back when most philosophers took some kind of property dualism for granted)

---

[40] Churchland, *Matter and Consciousness*, pp. 7–10; Campbell, *Body and Mind*, 41–8.

[41] Jay Rosenberg makes use of a somewhat similar—though in many ways more interesting—defeat-by-definition strategy against dualists. See Rosenberg, *Thinking Clearly about Death* (Englewood Cliffs, NJ: Prentice-Hall, 1983), ch. 2; see esp. 59–63, in which souls are stipulated to have no properties other than "performance capabilities"; by definition, souls cannot have many of the "categorical" properties dualists have traditionally attributed to souls, such as phenomenal states and other modes of experience. Rosenberg's unfriendly definition leaves souls categorically naked, and an easy target for his anti-dualist argument.

[42] W. D. Hart, *The Engines of the Soul* (Cambridge: Cambridge University Press, 1988).

has been used to characterize any of the views on one end of a spectrum. Cartesianism lies at the extreme dualistic end of the spectrum; straightforward versions of materialism are at the other extreme; but there is no neat, perfectly sharp, way to sort all possible theories that belong on the spectrum into two categories, dualisms and materialisms. Views closer to the dualistic end posit entities that lack many of the attributes of ordinary physical objects and their microphysical parts. But every dualist must admit that souls have *some* characteristics in common with uncontroversially non-thinking physical things. What is not perfectly precise is the answer to this question: how many can they have in common and still qualify as "nonphysical substances"?

It is ridiculous to foist upon dualists the view that souls and the matter in non-thinking objects are not alike *in any important respect*. After all, if there were such things as souls, they would resemble physical objects in being "concrete", or "non-abstract", and many important shared properties follow from even this much resemblance. To begin to see the similarities that simply *must* be recognized by any sensible dualism, one need only catalogue the signal attributes typically ascribed to abstract entities. If abstract entities, such as numbers and universals, exist at all, they are probably *necessary* beings. Abstracta are often thought to be outside time, or at least immutable. And intrinsic duplication among abstracta seems impossible; there would be no room for two exactly similar but distinct universals. Has anyone thought that souls were as unlike concrete physical objects as universals are? The souls typically posited by dualists contrast with abstracta in exactly the ways physical objects do. Souls, like bodies, are contingent, temporal, and susceptible to change. And there is nothing obviously wrong with positing two exactly similar physical particles or two exactly similar souls.

So no dualist should be saddled with the thesis that bodies and souls have *no* important attributes in common. But precisely what properties are being withheld from souls, then, when the dualist calls them "nonphysical" or "immaterial"? Assuming a mechanistic physics, with all physical interactions due to contact, Descartes could plausibly identify the physical with the spatially extended; physical properties imply spatial extension, and a multiplicity of parts. But if electrons or gluons turn out to be partless, as some have surmised, should one conclude that they are *nonphysical*? Would it not be better to say that, if electrons are partless, they are physical objects that happen to resemble Cartesian souls in one more respect than Cartesian matter resembles souls?

There is no guarantee that similar problems will not arise again for anyone who, like Descartes, relies on the details of *current* physics to mark the boundaries of the physical. Suppose that today's gluons, leptons, electrons, etc. should go the way of phlogiston, because today's physics turns out to be but a crude approximation of some radically different theory. Or suppose there happen to be sentient creatures much like humans but whose bodies are composed of materials not mentioned in today's physics. Such scenarios should not be taken to verify substance dualism, surely.

Should "nonphysical substance" be taken to mean "a substance lacking any of the properties mentioned in the 'final, true physics' "—since, whatever properties might figure prominently in "final physics", they are unlikely to be highly general, such as *being contingent* or *being mutable*? There are problems in this direction as well. Suppose neuroscientists were to detect unexplained motions of molecules in the brain, ultimately concluding that they must be the immediate effects of thoughts; and suppose that parapsychologists were to find evidence that the thinkers of these thoughts can pass from one brain to another. Physicists would surely be forced to posit basic physical laws involving mental states, and substances whose nature was mental, not physical. In that case, mental substances would end up having properties that appear in the final, true physics; but surely substance dualism would be *vindicated* by these discoveries, not *disproven*.

Despite these initial setbacks in the search for a general definition of "nonphysical substance" acceptable to all who are typically called "substance dualists", there are several characteristic dualistic doctrines that reveal basic points of agreement and that allow for a measure of relative distance from a paradigmatic substance materialism.

One point of agreement between dualists as different as the sophisticated Cartesian and the unsophisticated animist is that there are a great many things in the world that lack mentality of any sort; and that, associated with each human person, there is a thinking thing, a soul, not composed of the same kinds of stuff as these nonmental things. The animist and spiritualist may think of the soul as extended or composite; but they deny, at any rate, that it is made of things that can be found in objects completely devoid of mentality. To be a substance dualist, then, one must at least accept what might be called "compositional dualism":[43] on the one hand, there are things that cannot think and that are made entirely of parts that cannot think; on the other hand, there are things that can think; and, whether or not the latter have parts, they at least do not have parts in common with any of the former things.

There is more to being a substance dualist than affirming compositional dualism, however. Consider a traditional spiritualist metaphysics, according to which there is a special kind of stuff, ectoplasm, found only in spirits, and resembling ordinary matter only in being composite and spatially located. Ideally, such a view ought to fall somewhere on the dualistic side of the spectrum of mind–body views, even though it is not the extreme dualism of Descartes. Compare this view with the (arbitrary and unmotivated) theory that the soul is a point-sized thinking substance that has the same mass as a proton and the same charge as an electron; and that every substance with a similar mass and charge is capable of thought. This rather bizarre theory qualifies as compositional dualism; but it seems to me to be much further away from Cartesianism, and

---

[43] Not to be confused with "composite dualism", discussed above.

more deserving of the label "materialist" than the spiritualist's metaphysics of ectoplasm. It should not matter much where *precisely* the line between materialism and dualism is drawn; some might want to categorize the bizarre proton-mass-cum-electron-charge soul theory as a kind of dualism, while others might insist upon calling ectoplasm a special, intrinsically mental physical substance. From the point of view of defending the coherence of the very idea of substance dualism, all that matters is the fact that there is a spectrum of possible theories about mind–body relations running from the *clearly* dualistic to the *clearly* materialistic; and that the boundary between dualisms and materialisms, though vague, can be drawn in a principled way.

To generalize, then: a version of compositional dualism is further from materialism, and more deserving of the name "substance dualism", the fewer properties are said to characterize both substances capable of thought (and their parts, if any) and substances utterly incapable of thought. Descartes lies far to the dualistic side of the spectrum. Although his souls and bodies are somewhat similar, simply in virtue of being concrete substances, they have very little else in common. Less extreme dualists have posited simple souls with spatial location.[44] Still others, while remaining compositional dualists, suppose that the soul is both spatially located and divisible.[45] W. D. Hart's souls are spatially located and also possessed of a kind of "psychic energy", transformable into kinetic energy.[46] On this view, the same amount of energy can characterize a purely physical system and a soul—a further similarity between the two types of substance. Still, Hart's souls lack charge, mass, spin, and all other interesting intrinsic properties characterizing the particles constituting ordinary matter. And measurable degrees of psychic energy are supposed to be definable in terms of the propensity to sustain beliefs, not in terms of physical effects; so even this quasi-physical quantity seems grounded in the mental nature of Hart's souls, rather than in any intrinsic features they share with ordinary matter.

There may well be no sharp line dividing substance dualism from substance materialism; one can at least imagine versions of compositional dualism according to which souls are just sufficiently like insensate matter to make it unclear whether the view belongs on the dualist side of the spectrum. Nevertheless, the distinction between substance dualism and substance materialism remains an important and natural one, even if slightly vague; and the vagueness becomes largely inconsequential, since the area of indeterminacy is largely unoccupied. Analogously, the distinction between being alive and being dead is still well worth making, despite the possibility of a brief period when a body is not definitely either one; and the slight vagueness in the notion of death has never

---

[44] E.g. Hermann Lotze, in *Outlines of Psychology* (Minneapolis: S. M. Williams, 1885).

[45] E.g. Hasker, *The Emergent Self*, 192; and Hasker, "The Souls of Beasts and Men", *Religious Studies*, 10 (1974), 265–77 (esp. 275–6).

[46] Hart, *Engines of the Soul*; and Hart and Yagisawa, this volume, Ch. 6.

led philosophers to triumphantly deny that organisms can die! "Dualism", as it has traditionally been used in the philosophy of mind, admits of the possibility of borderline cases; but that does not show that dualism could not possibly be true.

IV

Preview of Coming Attractions

The first two parts of the book contain a series of defenses of idealist and dualist theories of human persons. In the third part, two representatives of the "new wave" of Christian materialists have their say (the essays by Baker and Merricks in Parts IV and V also advance the Christian materialist cause). In the fourth part, Quinn and Baker defend the thesis that the bodily nature of human persons is essential to their dignity and value—a point of view that Christians (along with adherents of many other religions) have often been tempted to deny. Finally, various conceptions of personhood are put to work in the exploration of four central Christian doctrines: the incarnation, the resurrection of the dead (including the resurrection of Christ), original sin, and the trinity.

Here is a more detailed synopsis of the chapters:

Idealism

Chapter 1. In "Idealism Vindicated" Robert M. Adams argues that a thing-in-itself or substance must have positive qualitative properties that are not purely formal, and that the only such properties with which we are acquainted are qualities of consciousness. This provides the basis of an argument that we have no adequate reason to posit the existence of soulless substances that would have no properties relevantly similar to qualities of consciousness. A type of idealist hypothesis is proposed that allows our physical science to be tracking a metaphysically real causal order. But, at bottom, the universe consists entirely of thinking, experiencing subjects—finite persons and the infinite God.

Chapter 2. Descartes put human souls "outside of space"; Howard Robinson explores the idea that souls are also in some sense "outside of time"—at least, outside the temporal order that is part of what he calls (following Wilfrid Sellars) the "scientific image". Robinson's metaphysics of persons is offered as part of a larger, idealist package in which God's role is crucial.

Dualism

Chapter 3. John Hawthorne identifies some neglected Cartesian principles about the essential properties of substances. They provide the materials for a more interesting, and perhaps even more defensible, argument for dualism than the ones that are typically attributed to Descartes.

Chapter 4. Alvin Plantinga offered a modal argument for dualism in his famous book *The Nature of Necessity*.[47] In this volume, he advances another modal argument on the basis of the conceivability of my surviving arbitrarily rapid changes in the parts of my body. He notes that some people are suspicious of the sort of intuitions about possibility he relies upon in such arguments; it is easy to confuse not seeing that something is impossible with seeing that it is possible. So Plantinga offers a second argument for dualism that proceeds from an intuition of *impossibility*, namely, the impossibility of a material structure's having *belief content*. He concludes with extensive reflections on specifically Christian reasons for being a dualist.

Chapter 5. Richard Swinburne's arguments for dualism are well known. Here, he offers a new support for dualism based upon the non-supervenience of the mental. He introduces a concept of an *event* according to which there is no more to the history of the world than all the events that have happened. All events can be described canonically as the instantiation of properties in substances (or events) at times. He then introduces a certain conception of the "names" of a property, a substance, and a time; anyone who knew the names of the properties, substances, and times involved in every event (in the sense of "name" he stipulates) would know (or could deduce) everything that happens in the history of the world. He defines the category of the *mental* (whether property, event, or substance) as that to which one subject has privileged access; the category of the physical as that to which there is no privileged access; and the category of the pure mental as that which contains no physical component. Using these categories, he argues that there are mental and pure mental properties, events, and substances; and that these are not identical with, and do not supervene on, physical properties, events, and substances. Human beings are, he concludes, pure mental substances. Consequences are drawn for the Christian doctrines of life after death and the resurrection of the body.

Chapter 6. A responsible dualist should be able at least to sketch how causal interaction between mind and matter is possible. But causation seems inevitably to involve the flow of energy. So a dualist should be able to make sense of the idea that energy might be transferred between mind and matter. That is what W. D. Hart and Takashi Yagisawa attempt to do in "Ghosts Are Chilly".

Chapter 7. Soul–body interaction as imagined in the previous chapter would seem to depend upon the soul's being spatially located. But on many versions of dualism, the soul is not spatially related to anything—and this generates a "pairing problem". Normally, one explains why one arrow hits one target, and

[47] (Oxford: Clarendon Press, 1971); the argument appears on pp. 65–9.

another arrow hits another target, by describing the spatial relations between archers and targets. But if souls are "outside of space" altogether, no such explanation can be given of the fact that one soul interacts with one body, and another soul interacts with another body. Hong Yu Wong examines this explanatory challenge to Cartesian interactionism, raising serious objections to John Foster's response to it. Foster posits laws of nature that apply only to particular soul–body pairs; Wong objects that, given the nature of human bodies, such laws are quite implausible.

Materialism

Chapter 8. Global materialism is the thesis that everything (other than abstract objects if such there be) is material. Local materialisms are theses to the effect that everything within some specified domain, such as the created world or the natural world, is material. A local materialist, like van Inwagen, may accept the existence of God or of angels. In "A Materialist Ontology of the Human Person", he attempts to combine a Platonic ontology of abstract objects with a local materialism according to which human persons are material substances. He then goes on to examine the consequences of his theory for "token–token identity theory"—the view that "tokens" of mental state types, such as types of pain, are identical with "tokens" of physical types, such as types of brain processes—and also for property dualism.

Chapter 9. Although Hud Hudson accepts a thoroughgoing materialism about human persons, he nonetheless reaches the conclusion: "I am not an animal!" Much of the inquiry into whether a human person is identical to a human animal (i.e. a biological organism of the species Homo sapiens) revolves around the debate between those who endorse some version of the "psychological criterion of personal identity" and those who endorse some version of the "bodily criterion of personal identity". Much of this latter debate, in turn, centers on intuitive responses to thought experiments that are notorious for a number of features (none of which is that of generating decisive answers to questions about the persistence conditions of persons). In his chapter, Hudson explores what he takes to be a more promising approach. He defends the thesis that a human person, although a material object, is not a human animal; and he does so while largely sidestepping the "criterion of personal identity" dispute. He appeals, instead, to what he calls a "big-picture, best-candidate, general metaphysics defense" of a theory of personal identity. The most plausible general account of the metaphysics of material objects, together with a few other convictions about ourselves—including, for Christians, belief in the possibility of surviving death—should lead us to the conclusion that we do not have the persistence conditions of human animals.

Embodiment and the Value of Persons

Chapter 10. The late Philip Quinn, in his essay "On the Intrinsic Value of Human Persons", explores his topic by asking what values are violated when persons suffer great evils—abominations, horrors, and atrocities. His starting point is recent work on great evils by philosophers such as Marilyn Adams, Claudia Card, and Susan Neiman. Using as evidence the magnitude of the evils of cannibalism, incest, rape, torture, and mutilation; Quinn argues that an important component of the value of persons resides in the fact that they are embodied creatures of flesh and blood. His aim is to correct what he takes to be the narrowness of our philosophical tradition, in which the value of persons has been located almost exclusively in their possession of such mental capacities as free will and reason. He seeks a more balanced view that takes seriously the simple truth that human persons are not disembodied angels.

Chapter 11. Lynne Rudder Baker is also responding to the fact that, when Christians emphasize the dignity and value of human persons, they often find the source of this dignity in the assumption that persons have immaterial souls or libertarian freedom. In "Persons and the Natural Order", Baker briefly canvasses some reasons to doubt that human persons have either immaterial souls or libertarian freedom, and then presents a view of human persons that locates the dignity and value of persons elsewhere: in the property of *inwardness* made possible by a first-person perspective. She defends a distinctive, broadly materialistic approach to the dignity of human persons; and argues that it is congenial to the most important aspects of Christian teaching about our nature.

Personhood in Christian Doctrine

Chapter 12. In earlier chapters, there are defenses of a wide variety of views about a human person's relation to her animal body. The most straightforward theory, represented by van Inwagen, is identity: a human person just is her body, just is a living, breathing human organism. Hudson and Baker think humans coincide with, but are not identical to, the organisms that are their bodies. Plantinga and Swinburne think humans are substantial souls, related to their bodies by particular causal relations. In "The Word Made Flesh: Dualism, Physicalism, and the Incarnation", Trenton Merricks describes the differences amongst these views; and considers how, on each, a Christian would understand the doctrine of the incarnation. He takes it to be a theological desideratum for a theory of the incarnation that Christ should be related to his human body in the way each of us is related to his or her human body. He explores the different relationships between person and body implied by the competing metaphysics of human persons, and considers the results for a theology of the incarnation. He then argues that the theological preferability of a certain interpretation of the incarnation vindicates one of the theories of person–body relations. According to Merricks, belief in the incarnation supports the view that humans are identical with their bodies; that they are—contra Hudson, Baker, Swinburne, and Plantinga—human animals.

Chapter 13. Peter Forrest brings both theological and scientific considerations to bear upon the nature of persons in his chapter, "The Tree of Life: Agency and Immortality in a Metaphysics Inspired by Quantum Theory". He develops an account of what material objects, including human beings, are; and of what human beings, as agents, do. This account has the advantages of the notorious Many Worlds interpretation of quantum theory, without some of its more counter-intuitive consequences. His "fibrous-universe" metaphysics provides scope for the free agency of human persons; it explains how immortality is possible, making allowance for several mechanisms by means of which the resurrection of Christ and the general resurrection of the dead could be achieved; and it coheres with current scientific theories about the nature of the physical world.

Chapter 14. One important motivation for believing that we are free is that moral responsibility requires freedom and we are clearly morally responsible for at least some of our actions. Michael Rea's "The Metaphysics of Original Sin" explores the question whether the traditional Christian doctrine of original sin undermines this motivation by undermining the claim that moral responsibility requires freedom.

Chapter 15. The doctrine of the trinity has it that there are three Persons in one God. Such odd arithmetic requires explaining. Many explanations begin from the oneness of God, and try to explain just how one God can be three divine Persons. Augustine and Aquinas pursued this project, which Brian Leftow calls "Latin Trinitarianism". In "Modes without Modalism", Leftow describes the difficulty of preventing Latin Trinitarianism from devolving into "Modalism"—a view rejected by most Christian theological traditions. He argues that not every mode-concept one might bring into trinitarian theology begets Modalism. In particular, John Locke made use of a concept of a mode that proves congenial to the formulation of Latin Trinitarianism. We are not ourselves the sort of beings for whom Locke's theory of personal identity is true, argues Leftow. But the three persons of the trinity are.

PART I
IDEALISM

1

Idealism Vindicated

Robert M. Adams

What I want to present in this paper is a case, or rationale, for a sort of idealism. Modern metaphysical idealism enjoyed a distinguished history, and a flourishing and sometimes dominant position, in European philosophy from the early part of the eighteenth century to the early part of the twentieth century. Since then it has fallen on hard times. Not that it has been refuted. Its appeal in modern thought has rested, as I will try to explain, on certain deep problems about supposed soulless substances; and those problems have neither gone away nor been solved in a non-idealist way, so far as I can see. But other intellectual motives have led philosophical interest away in other directions.

I should acknowledge at the outset that *idealism* may not be the happiest name for the position I advocate. It suggests the thesis that bodies or material or physical objects are merely ideas or objects of thought or perception; that their being or *esse*, in Berkeley's famous formulation, is their *percipi*, their being perceived; or that they are merely intentional objects, having, in a more medieval phrase, a merely intentional being. Before finishing I will sketch a view of this sort; but what I am asserting does not go that far. It is that everything that is real in the last analysis is sufficiently spiritual in character to be aptly conceived on the model of our own minds, as experienced from the inside. This thesis, which does not yet tell us anything positive about the metaphysical understanding of physical properties and physical facts, might perhaps more accurately be called *mentalism*, rather than idealism. Some possible developments of it might seem more clearly panpsychist than idealist. It seems to me right, nonetheless, to call my view a form of idealism, in a broad sense, because that is the established name of a historic philosophical tradition in which I certainly stand.

For helpful comments on this essay I am indebted to Marilyn McCord Adams; to Peter van Inwagen, my commentator when I presented it on 29 December 2003 to the Eastern Division of the American Philosophical Association; and to those who commented on it after its presentation at the University of California, Berkeley, on 12 March 2002 (as the Foerster Lecture on Immortality), to a Pew workshop on the metaphysics of the human person on 7 September 2002, and to philosophical gatherings at Macquarie University and the Research School of Social Sciences of the Australian National University and at the universities of Southern California, Notre Dame, Oxford, and York.

My thoughts on this subject are heavily indebted to great philosophers of the seventeenth and eighteenth centuries, especially Leibniz and Berkeley, but also Hume and Kant. This will not be a primarily historical paper, however. I will borrow freely from their views and arguments, and as freely adapt them to my own purpose, which is to offer you in my own voice a sort of vindication of idealism. I have chosen to begin it autobiographically, by recounting how I became an idealist as a teenager.

I came to idealism spontaneously when I was about 15, by thinking about ordinary physical objects with which I dealt on a daily basis. I remember sitting outdoors on a nice sunny day, pulling out blades of grass and asking myself, "What is it, in itself, for this blade of grass to exist?" I could see its green color and smell the fresh grass scent; but Miss Quinn, my ninth grade science teacher, had explained to us, in accordance with the preponderance of modern thought, that such qualities are subjective, aspects of the way objects appear to us rather than of their physical nature. The size and shape of the blade of grass, long and pointed, which I could also see and feel, were allowed to belong to the object, but that didn't satisfy me. It seemed there should be something *filling* the size and shape, and there should be something it was "like" in there—something as robustly qualitative as the green color, but really intrinsically characterizing the physical object.

I wondered whether, if I could penetrate the surface of the object and look inside it, I could discover what sort of thing it was in itself. That's hard to do with something as thin as a blade of grass; but I thought about somewhat thicker things that I had broken open, with the destructive curiosity of the young—pencils, for example, made of wood and graphite, more used then than now. But when I broke the pencil, the inside presented the same issues as the outside. The inside and the outside were indeed different. The pencil was yellow on the outside but mostly pink inside, with dark gray or black in the very center. These are still colors, however—subjective as I'd been taught, a matter of how the object looks to me. My finding them in the middle of the object gets me no nearer to knowing what the object is like in itself.

It was at this point that the idealist hypothesis occurred to me. Perhaps there is nothing that the physical object is like in itself. Perhaps it isn't anything in itself. Maybe all there is to it is the way it looks, feels, smells, and tastes to me.

These thoughts open one to a lot of philosophical questions. I'm not sure how many of them occurred to me when I was 15. One I do remember asking myself is, "How come my friend Mike has perceptions so similar to mine if the perceptions aren't caused by physical objects that are independent of them?" The answer I gave was similar to Berkeley's, though I hadn't yet heard of Berkeley. Mike and I had similar perceptions because God caused us to have similar perceptions so that we could communicate with each other. Whether or not I did then, I could obviously have given Berkeley's kindred answer to the question, "How come my perceptions are ordered as if they were produced by interaction with independently existing physical objects?" God causes them to be so ordered, so that I can live an organized life. Like Berkeley, I did not think as much as I perhaps should have about the question, "How do I know that anyone but me really exists?" Like him I was more puzzled about bodies than about minds. A year or two later, when I first ran across a mention of Berkeley, as a philosopher who held that *esse est percipi*, "to be is to be perceived", I thought, "That's the philosophy for me!"

I have indulged in this bit of intellectual autobiography because I think it encapsulates, in a fairly intuitive form, an approach to these matters that I still find persuasive. In narrating it I have introduced three of the themes that I will now develop in a form that is fuller and (I hope) philosophically more precise. The first is that idealist thoughts about physical objects arise from views characteristically associated with modern science. The second theme is that a central problem about supposed unperceiving objects is what intrinsic qualities they would have. And the third theme is what to make of the causal order that most idealists do indeed suppose produces our perceptions, since they do not suppose that we merely imagine the world.

1. MODERNISM

David Hume declared that

The fundamental principle of [the modern] philosophy is the opinion concerning colour, sounds, tastes, smells, heat and cold; which it asserts to be nothing but impressions in the mind, deriv'd from the operation of external objects, and without any resemblance to the qualities of the objects.[1]

Hume perhaps exaggerates the importance of this principle, but it is at least very characteristic of early modern philosophy and science in its contrast with the Aristotelian scholasticism that it rejected and largely succeeded in replacing. Aristotelians allowed that the forms of "colour, sounds, tastes, smells, heat and cold" present to the mind in sensation do have a "resemblance to the qualities of the objects", and this view is deeply connected with the central role of the concept of *form* in the Aristotelian philosophy.

On scholastic Aristotelian views, things are what they are by virtue of forms that are in them. The most fundamental things are called substances and are what they are by virtue of *substantial* forms; in the case of living substances, such as an oak tree, a fish, or a human being, the substantial form is the *soul* of that thing. But there are also *qualitative* forms; things are hot and red, for instance, by virtue of possessing qualitative forms of heat and redness. It is common to interpret these Aristotelian forms as properties, or perhaps particular occurrences

---

[1] David Hume, *A Treatise of Human Nature*, I. iv. 4: Selby-Bigge edn (Oxford, 1888), 226.

of properties; and that is not wrong. But what is fully as important about them is that they were conceived as *causes*—real, active causes. The substantial form or soul of a plant or animal causes the growth of the organism, for instance, by an inherent teleology. And qualitative forms can cause similar qualitative forms in many instances, as the heat of a hot body propagates heat in bodies that touch it.

This was important for scholastic Aristotelians' theories of sense perception, which they conceived, naturally enough, as a causal interaction. Making a long story very short, we may say that most of them held that, under appropriate conditions, a sense-perceptible qualitative form—say of white color, present on the surface of this paper—propagates a series of forms similar to itself in a medium (illuminated air in this case) and eventually in the eye, with the result that a similar form is ultimately presented to the soul. The important point here for our present purpose is that on prevalent scholastic views the form of color present to the mind in sensation does resemble a form really present in the object perceived.[2]

Aristotelian forms can be seen as linking body and mind. By virtue of the similarity of perceptible forms in the perceiver and the perceived, the mind can see in sense perception something of what bodies are like, qualitatively, in themselves. And by virtue of being, itself, a substantial form, and being conscious of many of its own operations, the mind might have some insight into what it is like for a substantial form to be and act in any substance—though the Aristotelians themselves were less interested in this last point than some early modern philosophers were.

In truth many early modern philosophers, notably including Descartes, thought Aristotelian theories of form projected altogether too much of the mind into the physical world. And the conception of forms as causes in the physical world was precisely the part of Aristotelianism that they wanted most to overthrow, because they believed that better and scientifically more useful explanations could be obtained with a more austere conceptuality. Many of them, notably including Descartes again, adopted a *mechanical* ideal of physical explanation. In the most austere conception of the ideal, all causal interactions in the physical world were to be understood mechanically—that is, in terms of geometrical properties and motions of bodies which interact only by touching and pushing each other. It follows from this conception that in a mechanical interaction only geometrical properties and motions of bodies can be either causes or effects. So if all the properties of bodies are to be explained mechanically, it follows that nothing but geometrical properties and motions can be admitted as a property of bodies.

---

[2] In this paragraph I am relying heavily on the very helpfully less abbreviated version of the long story in Anneliese Maier, "Das Problem der 'species sensibiles in medio' und die neue Naturphilosophie des 14. Jahrhunderts", in her *Ausgehendes Mittelalter: Gesammelte Aufsätze zur Geistesgeschichte des 14. Jahrhunderts*, ii (Rome: Edizioni di Storia e Letteratura, 1967), 419–51.

That excludes "colour, sounds, tastes, smells, heat and cold", on the plausible assumption that, as perceived by the mind, they are something over and above geometrical properties and motions. These qualities, which came to be called "secondary", were thus confined to the mind. Bodies might of course have mechanical properties by which they act on our sense organs in such a way as to cause sensations of color or taste; and some philosophers would be willing to call configurations of such mechanical properties by the names of colors and tastes, if their connection with the relevant types of sensation is reliable enough. According to the austerely mechanistic theory, however, nothing over and above geometrical properties and motions is thereby ascribed to the bodies; and that turns out to be the key point for my argument.

This mechanistic view receives elegant articulation in Descartes's theory of corporeal substance. He identifies the essence of corporeal substance with extension—that is, with the property of being continuously spread out in three spatial dimensions. All the other properties of bodies—that is, all their mechanical properties, their sizes, shapes, and states of motion and rest—he treats as "modes" of extension—that is, as merely *ways* of being extended, and not "forms" added to extension. The Cartesian can argue that the other, "secondary", sensible qualities, such as odors and flavors, are not similarly ways of being extended, and are therefore not qualities of bodies.

2. QUALITIES

Descartes inferred several interesting consequences from his thesis that extension is the essence of corporeal substance. One of these consequences is particularly likely to seem scandalous to us. Descartes concluded that there is no real difference between body and space, and hence that there cannot be any empty space. For space, empty or full, must be extended in three dimensions, as body is; but then, since extension is the whole essence of body, there is nothing in the idea of body, qualitatively speaking, that is not also contained in the idea of space.[3]

Our first objection to Descartes on this point may be that his conclusion is likely to conflict with physical science, since many physicists have found reason to postulate empty space. But a more metaphysical objection may also occur to us. We probably had thought that the idea of body contains much more, qualitatively speaking, than the idea of space. If that is false on Descartes's view, does that mean that he has enriched, perhaps implausibly, the idea of space? It seems not, for all he is saying about space is that it must extend in three dimensions, and we already knew that. So then has he impoverished, perhaps implausibly, the idea of body, making it as hollow as the idea of space? That seems likelier.

---

[3] Descartes, *Principles of Philosophy*, II. 11 and 16.

That is indeed the theme of one of the most interesting of Leibniz's many arguments against Descartes's thesis that extension is the essence of corporeal substance.

For *extension* signifies nothing but a repetition or continuous multiplicity of that which is spread out—*a plurality, continuity, and coexistence of the parts*; and consequently it does not suffice to explain the very nature of the substance that is spread out or repeated, whose notion is prior to that of its repetition. (G iv. 467/W 104)[4]

The basic idea in this argument is that extension is a relation, which cannot constitute a substance without presupposing some positive intrinsic nature of the terms of the relation. The same holds for geometrical properties and motions, the Cartesian modes of extension, which are purely features of spatiotemporal relationship. On a purely mechanistic account, as Kant puts it, "corporeal things are still always only relations, at least of the parts outside one another."[5]

The intuitively compelling point here, I think, is that a system of spatiotemporal relationships constituted by sizes, shapes, positions, and changes thereof is too incomplete, too hollow, as it were, to constitute an ultimately real thing or substance. It is a framework that, by its very nature, needs to be filled in by something less purely formal. It can only be a structure *of* something of some not merely structural sort. Formally rich as such a structure may be, it lacks too much of the reality or material of thinghood. By itself, it participates in the incompleteness of abstractions.[6]

What can fill the otherwise abstract structure of spatiotemporal relations? Think about our visual fields. There shapes, for instance, are shapes of colors—colored lines and areas of color (which may change over time, corresponding to motion). Within the visual field the colors literally fill in the shapes; and it is because shapes need a filling that we can hardly imagine, visually, a shape without some chromatic property. And it is because of the qualitativeness of colors that they bring to the context something that is not merely formal and structural. In a more general way, then, we may conjecture that the reality of a substance must include something intrinsic and *qualitative* over and above any formal or structural features it may possess.

I believe this conjecture is substantially correct. But colors, of course, are "secondary" qualities. On typical modern views those qualities whose peculiar

---

[4] A similar argument is found in G iv. 364–5/L 390 (1692 or earlier), in G ii. 169–70, 183/L 516, 519 (1699), in G iv. 589 (1702), in G vi. 584, and in several other texts. I refer to texts of Leibniz by the following abbreviations. G = *Die philosophischen Schriften von Gottfried Wilhelm Leibniz*, ed. C. I. Gerhardt (Berlin, 1875–90; repr. Hildesheim: Olms, 1965), cited by volume and page. L = Leibniz, *Philosophical Papers and Letters*, trans. and ed. Leroy E. Loemker, 2nd edn (Dordrecht and Boston: Reidel, 1969). W = *Leibniz Selections*, ed. Philip P. Wiener (New York: Scribners, 1951).

[5] Immanuel Kant, *Critique of Pure Reason*, A 283–B 339.

[6] I have discussed Leibniz's and Kant's views on this subject more historically in R. M. Adams, *Leibniz: Determinist, Theist, Idealist* (New York: Oxford University Press, 1994), 326–33, and "Things in Themselves", *Philosophy and Phenomenological Research*, 57 (1997), 810–11.

character we apprehend only visually, and which fill in the shapes in our visual field, are confined to the mind.[7] If there is anything corresponding to them on the surfaces of bodies outside the mind, it is only a structure of primary qualities, and on the Cartesian view will be only a structure of spatiotemporal relations still waiting to be filled in by something more qualitative. Do we know of any qualities that can do the job and that may exist outside the mind? That is a historically situated version of the problem about bodies that puzzled me as a teenager.

In the respect that now concerns us, our conception of our minds seems richer and fuller than our conception of bodies. Early modern thought, having expelled from bodies such clearly qualitative and non-structural sensed qualities as colors and smells, readily found a home for them in the mind, identifying them as qualities of sensory images or sensory states, or (as I will usually say) qualities of consciousness. They have not generally been regarded as properties of the mind or thinking thing itself; the mind itself is not blue or sweet-flavored. The mind or thinking thing does, however, have such properties as having a blue visual image and experiencing a sweet taste; and these properties derive from that subjective sort of blueness and sweetness an irreducibly qualitative character that is much more than merely formal or structural.

Can we conclude that minds or thinking things derive from such qualities of consciousness (though perhaps not from them alone) the kind of positive, non-formal, qualitative content that they need if they are to be substances or complete things in themselves? I believe so, and I believe this opens a way to the conclusion that there are thinking things that, in possessing qualities of such fundamental reality, are indeed things in themselves. In saying so I leave unanswered, for the time being, many metaphysical questions about the thinking substances: whether they endure longer than an instant, for example, and whether they are immaterial or whether, on the contrary, they have physical as well as psychological properties—and even whether my self is such a substance or whether it is rather a structured complex thing some of whose constituents are such substances. My present point is just that, whatever else may be true of them, things that think have in qualities of consciousness a kind of positive content that substances as such require.

In saying even this much I imply that we do have knowledge of qualities of consciousness, in our own experience, as qualities that can belong to a substance or thing in itself and can constitute, at least in part, the reality of such a thing. This is a controversial assumption—controversial in its reliance on self-consciousness as a source of knowledge about the metaphysically real. Those who would reject it might appeal to Kant, who held that not only bodies, but also our own minds,

---

[7] I assume here the correctness of the typically modern thesis of the subjectivity of the "secondary" qualities. Some philosophers still dissent from it, and I would argue for it at length in a much fuller development of my defense of idealism.

are known to us in experience only as appearances. Our inner sense, he says, "presents even ourselves to consciousness only as we appear to ourselves, not as we are in ourselves".[8] Not having time to review here the complex reasons for this position in Kant's critical philosophy, I will simply say that despite those reasons, in some of its implications it has always struck me, as it struck some of his first readers, as one of Kant's least plausible doctrines. As regards qualities of consciousness, at any rate, which are our central concern here, though they were not a main concern of Kant's doctrine, such a relegation of the experienced self to the realm of appearance is very hard to accept. When we see colors and taste tastes we surely know, if we know anything at all, that something is going on that involves those qualities, as features of our consciousness, in a metaphysically primal way.

The thesis that qualities of consciousness are known to us only as appearances does have its contemporary defenders.[9] They are typically motivated by an interest in the alleged possibility of a reduction of mental properties to physical properties. Such a reduction seems to me implausible from the outset for the sort of reason I have just suggested. Here we can add another reason. I believe intrinsic, non-formal qualities have an indispensable role to play in the constitution of substances or things in themselves, and I suspect that such qualities are known to us only as qualities of consciousness or by analogy with qualities of consciousness. If those points are correct (as I think the argument of this paper will tend to confirm), is it not perverse to seek to eliminate unreduced instances of such qualities, not only from bodies, but from the universe altogether?

Now if it is indeed right that things in themselves must have intrinsic, non-formal qualities, and that such qualities must be conceived as qualities of consciousness or analogous to qualities of consciousness, it follows that things in themselves must be conceived as all having qualities of consciousness or qualities analogous to qualities of consciousness. And that is at least very close to the conclusion that things in themselves must be conceived as having a spiritual or mental or at least a quasi-mental character. But is it really true that all intrinsic non-formal qualities must be qualities of consciousness or strongly analogous to qualities of consciousness? Have we even canvassed all the known properties of bodies that might be candidates for this role?

3. CAUSALITY AND QUALITIES

In thinking about possible intrinsic properties to be ascribed to bodies, we should not now restrict our consideration to the "primary" and "secondary" qualities

---

[8] Kant, *Critique of Pure Reason*, B 152–3.

[9] For an elegant example see Derk Pereboom, "Bats, Brain Scientists, and the Limits of Introspection", *Philosophy and Phenomenological Research*, 54 (1994), 315–29.

of early modern mechanistic natural philosophy. Since Newton, no property of matter has been more important for modern thought than *mass*. It is natural to ask whether mass might be the "filling" of positive content that an otherwise empty spatiotemporal structure of geometrical and kinetic properties needs in order to constitute a substance, but such a solution takes us into metaphysical territory of special interest and difficulty. I take it that 'mass' is used in science as an undefined term, but that what physics tells us about mass is its causal role, including its dynamical effects on such factors as inertia and gravitational attraction. For working purposes mass may be treated as a family of causal powers or dispositions known and measured only through the geometrical and kinetic properties of their effects. So perhaps the obvious place to look for qualities of bodies that might solve our problem about them is among their powers and dispositions.

Of course we cannot very well appeal to causal properties to solve our metaphysical problem unless we are metaphysical realists about causality. If there is nothing more to causality than observable regularities of occurrent properties, as many Humeans have held, then we are thrown back again on non-causal properties to find the qualitative content we need. I will not pursue that direction here, however, because I believe that causal properties are so deeply implicated in our ordinary views of things that non-realism about causality undermines any sort of metaphysical realism, and is indeed quite implausible. Certainly I see little point in a metaphysical realism about physical objects that does not include a metaphysical realism about causality.

Powers and dispositions have figured prominently in discussions of the constitution of substances. I don't want to discuss here whether powers and dispositions are *required* for the existence of a substance, as many philosophers have held. What I do want to discuss is whether they *could* assume the role of qualities in constituting a substance. More precisely: could powers and dispositions provide *all* the positive intrinsic content needed for the existence of a substance, without its possessing any *occurrent* or non-dispositional qualities? My answer to this question is negative. From this point on in this paper I shall restrict the signification of 'quality' and 'qualitative' to *occurrent* qualities, qualities that are more than merely dispositional. I believe that without such qualities, powers and dispositions constitute an empty (or metaphysically incomplete) relational structure.

They are constituted by relations between the actual or present state of the substance that has them and other possible states of affairs. Fragility consists in a relation between a present state of something and its possible future breaking. Intelligence, as a power, consists in a relation between a present state or nature of something and its possibly understanding things and acting intelligently. Such causal relations presuppose the terms (in this case states or events) related in them, and are intuitively, I think, an empty framework apart from occurrent qualities of those terms. If we are told that A is a power to cause B, that B is a power to cause C, and C a power to cause D—and in general if we are given a network of causally related terms and are told *nothing* about them except their actual and possible causal relations—we have not been told what the whole system is about. It is as if we were given "money" but there were nothing non-monetary that could ever be bought with it. I emphasize that my objection here is to the supposition of a causal network that is not anchored to actuality by *any* occurrent qualities at all. The effects in a causal network will commonly be causes or potential causes too, and will involve further powers; and I have no objection to that, so long as there are also enough occurrent qualities in the system.

The potentially *resulting* state of affairs is particularly important to defining a power or disposition, which is normally understood as a power or disposition to produce a certain state of affairs (under certain conditions).[10] Powers and dispositions will be defective in positive content if they do not derive enough qualitative content from the possibly resulting states of affairs.[11] The concept of a capacity to feel pain, for example, has positive content derived from the qualitative content of pain, whereas the power to cause motion has, thus far, no complete reality to add to the formal framework of spatiotemporal relations to which motion belongs.

Intuition will support rather strongly, I believe, a further claim about the dependence of substantial reality on occurrent qualities. It is not enough for such qualities to be *potentially* present in the system, as defining the powers and dispositions; substances must have occurrent qualities actually and at present. Of the two states of affairs related by a power or disposition, it is the present, actual, grounding state of the substance that is more important for our understanding of what the substance is or is like, actually and at present. If present powers and dispositions of a substance borrow qualitative content from the qualitative content of states of affairs they may produce, that may tell us what the substance could have been like or may yet be like, but no amount of such information will provide, intuitively, a metaphysically complete answer to the question what the substance is like actually and at present. For that we need some present, actual occurrent qualities. A thing that has, actually and at present, no occurrent qualities over and above its powers and dispositions (and its spatiotemporal relational features) is still too empty to constitute a substance.

If intrinsic qualitative content must be sought in *occurrent* properties, it is still not obvious that it cannot be sought in causal properties. For there are occurrent as well as dispositional causal properties. Things not only have powers; they are

---

[10] This point is an old one. See Plato, *Republic* 477C–D.

[11] Michael Ayers goes farther than I do here, saying, "The idea of power . . . has *no* positive content by itself, since its positive content in any particular case is supplied by the observable effect" [Michael Ayers, "The Ideas of Power and Substance in Locke's Philosophy," rev. version, in I. C. Tipton (ed.), *Locke on Human Understanding: Selected Essays* (Oxford: Oxford University Press, 1977), 80; orig. pub. in *Philosophical Quarterly*, 25 (1975), 1–27; emphasis mine].

apt at any time to be actually acting on things and being acted on by things. Occurrent causal properties of things have historically been conceived as actions and passions (where by 'passion' is meant simply a being acted on). Let us focus on actions.

Because actions are occurrent properties, they may have qualitative content in a way that powers and dispositions do not. The mere fact that they are occurrent properties, however, does not assure that their content will be complete enough metaphysically to solve our problem. That's because a causing must be a causing *of something*, and is thus relational, a node in a structure of causal relations. The metaphysical content of the causing can hardly be complete if the content of the something that is caused is metaphysically deficient. Suppose what is caused is a motion; without qualities that we have yet to find, motion is deficient in qualitative content. Adding to it a *causing* of motion adds only something that needs to get from motion a metaphysical completion that it therefore cannot add to motion. This leaves us with a vicious regress, a failure of metaphysical grounding; the whole framework is still intuitively too empty to constitute a substance.

That an action is an occurrent causing is therefore not enough to solve our problem. If we can find complete enough qualitative content in an action, it is likeliest to be in what I will call *activities*.[12] An activity is an action whose present reality does not consist merely in producing, or tending to produce, effects distinct from the action itself. The content of an activity, accordingly, should not need to be completed by the content of an effect distinct from it.

Are there activities, in this sense, that have intrinsic qualitative content? This question is difficult—too difficult to receive an adequate discussion in the space that can be allocated to it in the proportions of this paper; but I believe there are. For example, deciding to do something, and trying to understand something, seem to me to be activities of the relevant sort; and actually understanding anything arguably is too. My learning to recognize these activities in myself was a learning *what they are like*.

These examples belong to the mental realm. They are activities of which I am conscious in myself.[13] That is no accident. If there are activities with a positive intrinsic qualitative character of which one cannot be conscious in oneself, it is hard to see how I would know that. I do not think, therefore, that we can find in activities, or more broadly in causal properties, a clear case of intrinsic qualitative

---

[12] The choice of this term is obviously inspired by a traditional translation of *energeia* in Aristotle, but I make no claim to be interpreting Aristotle here.

[13] They are also characterized by intentionality. Their intentional objects, on my view, are metaphysically derivative entities, internal features of the activity, and therefore do not compromise the self-containment of its positive content. By the same token, my ascription of self-containment and the relevant metaphysical completeness to the content of activities characterized by intentionality commits me to what is called "narrow content" and to the rejection of the most radical sort of externalism about the mental; on the latter, cf. Tyler Burge, "Individualism and the Mental", *Midwest Studies in Philosophy*, 4 (1979), 73–121, and the extensive literature inspired by it.

character that is not a quality of consciousness. In fact I do not see how to find a clear, known case of the requisite qualitative character that is not a quality of consciousness. So is it true after all that all intrinsic non-formal qualities must be qualities of consciousness or strongly analogous to qualities of consciousness?

I know of no proof that it is true. It does not strictly follow from the claim that the only intrinsic and not purely formal qualities *known to us* are qualities of consciousness. For how could we prove that there are no such intrinsic qualities that are quite unlike any qualities known to us? But why suppose there are such qualities? In order to ascribe them to bodies, is the obvious answer. But why do that? Let me mention four reasons for *not* doing that.

1. The first is that to the extent that we are talking about qualities with which we do not claim to be acquainted, we lack the most obvious reason for being confident that they are not after all of a somewhat psychological character.

2. An equally obvious point is that to the extent that we assign an essential metaphysical role to qualities quite different from any with which we are acquainted, we have a more obscure and less intelligible view of the universe. This is not an argument of peremptory decisiveness; there could after all be qualities that are quite unknown to us. But it seems reasonable to work, so far as we can, in our theorizing, with qualities with which we are acquainted; and it is surely an advantage in a metaphysical theory if the properties that figure most importantly in it are at least akin to properties with which we are acquainted.

3. The view that in addition to intrinsic non-formal qualities of consciousness there is at least one other type of intrinsic non-formal quality radically different from them seems also to be attended with some of the unattractiveness that is widely thought to afflict metaphysical dualisms. Why suppose the types of fundamental qualities in the universe are more alien to each other than we have to suppose them to be? One way of avoiding a dualism of properties, of course, would be to suppose, as some physicalists do, that qualities of consciousness are reducible to properties of an apparently quite different sort; but is it not, as I have argued, bizarre to do that if qualities of consciousness are the only intrinsic non-formal qualities with which we are acquainted? Why not rather decline to postulate intrinsic non-formal qualities radically different from qualities of consciousness? Wouldn't that be a more plausible way of avoiding dualism?

4. There may also be, in the very nature of the concern about qualitative content that grips us here (or that grips me, at any rate), something that pushes us toward qualities of consciousness as a model for what we are after. An essential motivation of this discussion of intrinsic non-formal qualities is the assumption that if there are things in themselves, there must be something that it is like, in itself, for them to exist. We may well suspect that this notion of what it is like, in itself, for something to be the case is borrowed from our knowing by experience what it is like, in itself, to see red, to be in pain, to feel jubilant, and in

general to be in one conscious state or another. Perhaps nothing could have the relevant kind of "inside", or be anything "in itself", without having something like consciousness. To sum up the point in a slogan, perhaps nothing can be anything *in* itself without being something *for* itself.

4. THE CAUSAL ORDER AND THE REALITY OF BODIES

Thus far I have been making a case for the theses, first, that substances must have intrinsic non-formal qualities, and second, that qualities of consciousness, or qualities very like them, are the only intrinsic non-formal qualities of substances. If we accept that pair of theses, what are we to make of the world of bodies studied by physics? That is the question to which the rest of this paper is devoted.

Two main types of answer to it may be distinguished, which for present purposes may be called idealism (in a narrower sense) and panpsychism. The defining difference between them is that according to idealism spatiotemporal relations are reducible to internal features of qualities of consciousness or of quasi-consciousness, while according to panpsychism spatiotemporal relations are not so reducible, but are primitive external, formal properties of substances and their states. Note that I do *not* say that according to idealism *all* external properties and relations are reducible to *internal* mentalistic features. Most serious idealists are not solipsists; and non-solipsistic forms of idealism will generally admit primitive *causal* relations of some sort between substances. It is the reduction specifically of *spatiotemporal* relations that distinguishes idealism from panpsychism. Reasons why disagreements within the broadly mentalist camp might focus on spatiotemporal relations will emerge in the course of discussion.

4.1. Idealism, in a Narrower Sense

I begin with idealism. For reasons that I think are close kin to reasons that I have suggested, Berkeley held that the spatial qualities of bodies cannot be separated from the "secondary" qualities, such as color, and therefore cannot exist except where the latter exist, in the perceptions of perceiving minds. But Berkeley did not conclude that bodies do not really exist. Like most historic forms of metaphysical idealism, his is in large part a theory of what it is for bodies really to exist.

An idealist conception of the reality of bodies can be built up in layers. A first layer can be expressed, to a first approximation, in two theses that draw in diverse ways on suggestions of Leibniz, Berkeley, and Kant.

(I1) A body that appears to us to exist is a *phenomenon*, an internal intentional object of our sense perception and thought, a character, so to speak, in a story told us by those faculties.

(I2) A phenomenon *really exists*, as a body, at a certain place and time, if
and only if it exists, with a certain causal role, at that place and time,
according to (or "in") the story or stories with which our perceptual
experience coheres, and will continue to cohere, the best (that is, in the
cognitively and practically most satisfactory way).

Appearances of bodies in our ordinary experience satisfy the criterion of reality
enunciated in (I2). Appearances of bodies in dreams, fantasies, and hallucinations
do not satisfy it, because they do not participate in a sufficiently comprehensive
coherence. All of us, in practice, judge of the reality of bodies in accordance with
such a coherence condition. The idealist, as Berkeley shrewdly observed,[14] takes
what everyone treats at least as *evidence* of the reality of bodies, and treats it as *constituting* the reality of bodies, as explaining what the reality of bodies consists in.[15]

Does this allow enough reality to bodies? Leibniz said he would call phenomena
"real enough" if they just satisfied a criterion of this sort, because then experience
would never disappoint the expectations we formed about future experience of
bodies "when we used our reason well".[16] But is that enough if we care not only
about our own experience, but also about things that we suppose to go on outside
our own experience? Most of us care at least about other experiencers whom we
take to exist besides ourselves; and we will hardly be satisfied with (I2) if we
cannot interpret it as requiring real phenomena to cohere also with the experience
of other perceivers (other minds, if you will) that appear as characters in relevant
parts of our coherent story and that we think really exist. Let it be so interpreted.

Moreover, most of us will find it hard to believe that a coherent experience
occurs to us merely by accident. Surely there must be some real causal order, not
just constituted by our experience, that produces the coherence exhibited in our
experience. Given our interest in other minds, we will also expect them to have
a place in such a causal order. And if an appearance is to constitute a *really real*
body, we may think, it should be grounded in such a causal order, in such a way

---

[14] George Berkeley, *Three Dialogues between Hylas and Philonous*, in *The Works of George Berkeley
Bishop of Cloyne*, ed. A. A. Luce and T. E. Jessop, ii (London: Thomas Nelson and Sons, 1949), 235.

[15] John Hawthorne has rightly pointed out to me that that bodies that "really" exist according
to (I2) may not be completely determinate. For some bodies *b* that appear to us to exist, and some
properties *p*, our perceptual experience may cohere equally well with stories according to which *b*
has *p* and with stories according to which *b* lacks *p*, leaving nothing to constitute *b*'s having rather
than lacking, or lacking rather than having, *p*. It is not surprising, nor really objectionable, in my
opinion, that an account of bodies as merely intentional, rather than metaphysically fundamental,
objects should have this feature. For many operators or quasi-operators O:, $\ulcorner O: (p$ or $q)\urcorner$ does
not entail $\ulcorner(O: p)$ or $(O: q)\urcorner$, and for such operators $\ulcorner O: (p$ or not-$p)\urcorner$ commonly does not entail
$\ulcorner(O: p)$ or $(O$:not-$p)\urcorner$. Among the operators of which the latter (as well as the former, more general
claim) is true are: 'It is necessary that'; 'I believe that'; and $\ulcorner$In [or according to] $F\urcorner$ where F is a
piece or body of fiction. I think anyone who accepts (I2) should admit that 'In the empirically real
physical world' may be an operator of this sort, creating an intentional context as $\ulcorner$ In the story $F\urcorner$
does. I take it the Antinomy of the *Critique of Pure Reason* makes it explicit that this is a feature of
Kant's "empirical realism".

[16] G vii. 320/L 364.

that the apparent causal order of the corporeal phenomena is derived from the underlying metaphysically real causal order. Borrowing from Leibniz the term, 'well founded phenomenon', we may enrich our idealist account of the reality of bodies with another and more demanding layer, as follows, again to a first approximation:

> (I3) A body that really exists, in the sense indicated by (I2), really exists as a *well founded phenomenon* if and only if there is a real causal order (real independently of our experiencing) by virtue of which the body appears to us as it does, and in relation to which the causal properties, relations, and/or laws of the apparent causal order in which the body has its role are genuine, though derivative, causal properties, relations, and/or laws.

With (I3), unlike (I2), we take our experience to be *evidence* of a reality (specifically a causal order) that consists in much more than the coherence of our experience. Like (I2), (I3) applies only to bodies that are *phenomena* in the sense that there is actual experience or empirical evidence of their existence. I leave open for now the question whether we should want to extend (I3) to allow for the real (and well-founded) existence of bodies of which no empirical evidence actually exists, if there *would* be such evidence in certain relevant conditions, according to the independently real causal order.[17]

It should also be noted that (I3) leaves open the question whether in the underlying, independently real causal order there would be entities (perhaps even substances) with which (or with sets of which) the real and well-founded bodies could be identified, as the well-founded corporeal phenomena can be identified with sets of monads in the Leibnizian system. I don't think that idealist hypotheses need to offer the possibility of such an identification in order to be plausible, though they may offer it, and I will focus on one that does. An idealist who is sufficiently confident of having the resources for such an identification may be tempted to abandon (I1) and (I2) and their identification of really existing bodies with a sort of merely intentional object; but having something like (I1) and (I2) to fall back on is an attraction of idealism, as idealists have noted, as it insulates the existence of objects of ordinary experience from the fortunes and misfortunes of metaphysical theories. All the arguments in the remainder of this paper, however, regarding mere panpsychism as well as idealism in the narrower sense, will be focused on issues about a supposed ultimately real causal order, and responsive to the considerations that motivate (I3).

As we are developing a mentalist view according to which there are no unperceiving substances, the ultimately real causal order of which we speak will be understood as having its seat also in perceiving substances. There is no need in the present context to decide among a number of alternative ways in which this

---

[17] Such an extension might, among other things, provide for complete determinacy of the physical world.

might be conceived, but it will be worth thinking about some of the alternatives and exploring one of them in more detail.

There are alternatives as to the inventory of perceiving beings. Should we with Berkeley limit the inventory to God and more or less familiar subjects of experience—human minds, souls of animals, plus perhaps angels? Or should we with Leibniz add a vast number (an infinity, Leibniz thought) of much less gifted perceiving things, all of whose perceptions would be unconscious? Leibniz's alternative incurs the obvious difficulty of understanding the notion of unconscious perception, but gives him what some may consider the advantage of supposing an ultimately real thing, or more than one, corresponding to every portion of matter in the realm of real, well-founded corporeal phenomena. A third sort of alternative would recognize a multiplicity of perceivers but no God, though this would limit our alternatives in the next round.

For there are also alternatives regarding the structure of causal relationships among the ultimately real perceiving things. Two historically prominent alternatives presuppose that God is included in the inventory. One alternative is a broadly occasionalist structure (such as Berkeley supposed), in which (with the possible exception of a few kinaesthetic sensations caused directly by ourselves) all our perceptions of the world of corporeal phenomena are caused directly by God. The second alternative is Leibniz's famous theory of pre-established harmony, according to which God has pre-programmed all the other substances, deterministically, so that they will always represent to themselves the same world of corporeal phenomena, and will always make choices in accord with that program. A third alternative—perhaps the only one available without God in the inventory, but also available with God in the inventory—is a structure of direct causal interactions among many different perceiving substances.

To some it may seem a glaring objection to all these alternatives that it remains unexplained *how* the causal connections between perceiving substances (including those in which God is the active cause) are supposed to work. A first response to this objection is that at the relevant, deep metaphysical level, causal connections among perceiving substances are no more mysterious than causal connections among material substances would be. What should indeed concern the idealist here, however, is that without solving the deepest metaphysical perplexities about the nature of causality, physical science and common sense have given us much more highly developed and articulated views of the *structure* of causal relationships among bodies than we have for any supposed direct causal relationships among minds. It may be feared, therefore, that the idealist hypothesis will entail an appalling loss of causal understanding unless it can incorporate in its hypothesized real causal order[18] structures of causal relationship sufficiently isomorphic to those explored by physical science.

---

[18] Not necessarily at the deepest level; cf. John Foster, "The Succinct Case for Idealism", in Howard Robinson (ed.), *Objections to Physicalism* (Oxford: Clarendon Press, 1993), 300–2.

There is reason to believe an idealist hypothesis can satisfy this requirement. Here is one way—an occasionalist way, in which it is supposed that God causes corporeal phenomena to appear to us as they do. The basic idea is that the mathematical structure of the causal order that physics explores has its seat or realization in the mind of God. Suppose God thinks a system of all possible ordered quadruples of real numbers, and assigns to each quadruple a value. In a very simple version the value might be just *occupied* or *unoccupied*. The intended interpretation in this example is that, in accordance with something like Cartesian analytic geometry, the quadruples of real numbers correspond to the points of four-dimensional space–time, and exactly those quadruples are "occupied" that correspond to space–time points at which there is matter. I take it that in some such way a system of quadruples of real numbers in God's mind can provide an interpretation of all the scientifically important spatiotemporal structure of a Euclidean four-dimensional physics.[19]

Suppose further that in assigning the value *occupied* to suitably patterned groups of quadruples of real numbers God causes relevant created perceivers to have experience as of the existence, sizes, shapes, and motions of bodies occupying the corresponding space–time points. Suppose finally that God more or less uniformly follows certain principles in assigning the values *occupied* and *unoccupied* to quadruples of real numbers, and that these principles can be indicated relatively simply by formulating the corresponding principles governing the apparent corporeal correlates. Then we can say that those principles are modeled (more and more accurately, we hope) in the laws of physics formulated by science, which in turn will be in this way derivative but genuine laws. This is a way in which the underlying causal order hypothesized by an idealist theory can have a structure comparable in its articulation to that presented in physical science.

This, of course, is just a sketch of an approach. Perhaps correspondence with our most up-to-date mathematical physics would require that God assign to the quadruples values more complicated than just "occupied" or "unoccupied". Perhaps an ordered plurality of values would be needed for each "point", corresponding to different physical properties, and perhaps some of the values would be probabilities. Maybe a rather different approach would have to be used to model a "curved" Riemannian space–time; but surely that too could be done in an omniscient divine mind.

It is worth noting that that the approach I have sketched is one that does allow the bodies of science and common sense to be identified with entities (though not substances) in the underlying, metaphysically real causal order. We may reach this point by a provocatively indirect route. One currently popular materialist strategy for reducing mental properties to physical properties is what

---

[19] Cf. Rudolf Carnap, *The Logical Structure of the World* (*Der logische Aufbau der Welt*), trans. Rolf A. George (Berkeley and Los Angeles: University of California Press, 1969), §§ 107, 125.

is called "functionalism". In it mental properties are defined in terms of their causal roles or functions, and it is argued that the properties that in fact fulfill those causal roles are physical properties, with which the mental properties can then be identified. I do not find it plausible to define qualities of consciousness in terms of causal roles, but perhaps it is plausible to define bodies and their physical properties in terms of causal roles. Suppose they are so defined; and suppose further that the speculation I have just offered about causal structures in God's mind is in fact correct (as of course I have certainly not shown that it is). That would be a way in which it could be true that bodies *are* sets of quadruples of real numbers, understood as ideas in God's mind, to which God assigns the value "occupied". That would be an idealist truth of a rather old—indeed a broadly Pythagorean and Platonic—type.[20]

It would be nice to close on that triumphally idealist note, but it will probably be more illuminating to have a merely panpsychist sketch to set beside it. So . . .

4.2. Mere Panpsychism

More important than the particular mathematical scheme I have suggested for the construction of a physical world in God's mind is the general point that the cogitative and productive powers of an omniscient, omnipotent deity are virtually guaranteed to provide sufficient resources for the construction of an underlying, idealist causal order with a structure that would be mirrored by that presented in the best possible physical science. An omniscient mind can certainly provide structures as rich in information, so to speak, as any postulated in human science. Structures that human physicists can think an omniscient deity can think at least as well. Given the wealth of resources of a broadly occasionalist (and hence also theistic) version of idealism, is there any reason to prefer a different version?

The likeliest reason might be that intuitions regarding the reality of physical causation seem better respected in postulating an interactionist causal structure, in which many perceiving substances, corresponding in some way to physical objects, exercise metaphysically real causal influence on each other. If there are enough such substances to correspond with all the objects of physics, most of them are presumably not exactly intelligent substances, but have as their positive internal qualities something like the unconscious perceptions or "little perceptions" of Leibniz's mere monads. And the obvious reason *not* to prefer such an interactionist version of idealism to the occasionalist version is that it seems doubtful that the rudimentary perceptions of those many substances contain enough information for the construction of a causal order as rich and well articulated as that of physics. Specifically we may wonder whether the feelings of substances that do not have fairly advanced geometrical perception can contain

---

[20] I am indebted to Todd Buras for the observation that this version of idealism can be analogized to materialist functionalism in this way.

enough information for the construction of space and time from intramental resources which is required for an idealist as distinct from a merely panpsychist theory.

Leibniz, though not an interactionist, is one philosopher who holds that the spatiotemporal order of a complete physical universe can be modeled adequately in the subconscious perceptions of a substance so confused as to be totally devoid of consciousness; but he gives us little help in understanding how that could be. Of course, there may be aspects of reality that we don't understand. We don't know what the structures of subconscious perceptions may be, but we have no reason to doubt that anything as real, metaphysically, as a perceptual state (even a subconscious perceptual state) would have some structure. Perhaps we have no clear reason to deny that it could have a rich enough structure to model the spatiotemporal structure of the world of physical phenomena. But the appeal to ignorance may leave us dissatisfied.

If we therefore doubt that the feelings of the interacting substances could contain enough information, and the right sort of information, for the construction of space and time, we may wish to consider a view that renounces the reduction of space and time, supposing there to be physical substances with primitive spatiotemporal relations, while still holding that the positive internal, non-formal qualities of substances are all mental or quasi-mental. In the terminology we are using at this point, we may wish to consider a merely panpsychist view. Is there a worrisome problem about such a view?

Well, philosophers have sometimes supposed that mental qualities have no spatial location, and that might be thought an objection to ascribing spatiotemporal relations to substances whose sole internal, non-relational qualities are mental or quasi-mental. I think this objection should be set aside, however. The shortest way with it is simply to suppose that spatiotemporal relational properties are indirectly tied to qualities of consciousness (or quasi-consciousness) by *belonging to the same substance*; and it's not at all clear to me that that is not an adequate response to the objection. Refusing to treat a substance's or subject's relation to its properties and relations as primitive would very likely be setting foot on a dangerously slippery slope. And the assumption that ascribing spatiotemporal relations to the same subject as mentalistic properties, such as those of subconscious perception, is more problematic, or more in need of explanation or reduction, than ascribing them to the same subject as ostensibly physical but supposedly internal properties, seems to deserve skeptical questioning.

An example of an ostensibly physical but supposedly internal property would be mass, if mass is not identified with its causal role, but is supposed to be something more occurrent, more qualitative, than a family of powers. Perhaps it will be argued that the plausibility of ascribing such qualities to the same subject as spatiotemporal relations is justified by the the rich causal connections between the internal physical properties and changes in spatial relations. But why would the interactionist panpsychist suppose that feelings (conscious or subconscious) of substances are less richly connected, causally, to changes in spatial relations? Why indeed?—given that the interactionist panpsychist may be expected to hold that the supposed internal physical qualities *are* subconscious feelings, causally related to changes in spatial relations as physics requires the physical qualities to be.

Note that the identification of physical qualities such as mass with feelings, in the position I've just been sketching, requires that some aspect of the feelings have precise *quantity*. How plausible or implausible is that? Kant, I take it, proposed to treat *intensity* of sensation or felt quality as a counterpart of quantity of force; and there is surely some plausibility to the idea that intensity of feeling is quantifiable. If any skepticism arises here, it will probably be about the *precision* with which such intensity can be quantified. Suppose the panpsychist says: we are not able to *know* the quantity of intensity with much precision by feeling it, but it *has*, objectively, a precise quantity, which we are sometimes able to measure quite precisely by its effects, on the assumption that the feeling *is* mass or a physical force. Here we must be careful not to hold against the panpsychist a limitation that may be an inescapable part of our cognitive situation, on *any* interpretation of intrinsic physical qualities. Is the usual sort of physicalist in any better position than the panpsychist to assign precise quantities of mass and physical force? Don't we in fact measure such quantities only by their effects, even if it is supposed that they *have*, objectively, a more intrinsic measure?

To forestall a further possible objection, I should also note that on the panpsychist assumption that, in any intrinsic qualitative aspect they have, physical qualities such as mass and physical forces *are* feelings, the ascription of physical effects to such feelings does not violate the dogma of "the causal closure of the physical"—a dogma I do not mean to endorse, but do not need to criticize in this context.

So far as I can see, therefore, either a broadly occasionalist idealism or an interactionist panpsychism can account for the causal structure of physics as well as a typical physicalist view can.

2

The Self and Time

Howard Robinson

1. INTRODUCTION: TIME, DISCONTINUITIES OF CONSCIOUSNESS, AND IDENTITY

I start this paper from the assumption—which I and others have defended elsewhere—that the human subject—the self—is immaterial and simple.[1] I also want to stay as close as possible to Descartes's intuition that the essence of the self is consciousness. Because he thinks that immaterial substances are essentially conscious, he feels obliged to maintain that we are never wholly unconscious, but, even in the deepest sleep, are dreaming. It is setting out from this problem that I wish to investigate the relation between the self and time. The nature of the problem can be expressed as an argument.

(1) The self is essentially conscious.

(2) Selves have periods of unconsciousness in their existence.

(3) If x essentially possesses F, then, if x exists in time, it cannot exist at a time at which it fails to possess F.

Therefore

(4) If selves essentially possess consciousness, then, if selves exist in time, they cannot exist at a time at which they fail to possess consciousness. (3, Universal Instantiation)

Therefore

(5) If selves exist in time, they cannot exist at a time at which they fail to possess consciousness. (1, 4, *modus ponens*)

---

[1] For defences of this view, see Robinson 2003*a* and Madell 1981.

Therefore

> (6) Either selves do not exist in time—that is, they are atemporal—or they do not exist at the times at which they fail to possess consciousness—that is, given (2), their existence is intermittent. (5, Implication)

> (7) Intermittent existence is impossible.

Therefore

> (8) Selves do not exist intermittently. (7, and not possibly p entails not p)

> (9) Anything that undergoes change exists in time.

> (10) Selves undergo change.

Therefore

> (11) Selves exist in time. (9, 10, Universal Instantiation, *modus ponens*)

Therefore

> (12) Selves are neither atemporal nor intermittent. (8,11, Conjunction)

Therefore

> (13) There is no such a thing as the self. (6, 12, Indirect Proof)

Richard Swinburne (1984:33) seeks to avoid this conclusion by allowing intermittent existence. In an earlier article, I characterized the self as essentially *potentially* conscious, which would allow for periods of unconsciousness. I am unhappy with the notion of intermittent existence, and, if what I say in this paper is correct, it can be avoided. I still feel sympathy for the idea that the self is a unique power or capacity for consciousness, but I also think that the relation of the exercise of that capacity to time can be best illuminated by considering the relation of the self to time. I shall, for present purposes, stand by (1). My strategy will be to try to overcome the argument by challenging the way that the concept of time is employed in it. I shall argue that time is not a monolithic unity, and different kinds of change can mean different temporal orders. And participating in a temporal order in a discontinuous way does not entail discontinuous existence, even when the agent is subject to change and, hence, not atemporal, for it may act *from within* a different temporal framework from that *on which* it acts. This modifies and subverts the argument in the following way. (3) becomes

> (3′) If x is essentially F, then, if x exists in time-order T, it cannot exist at a time within T at which it is not F.

Therefore

> (4′) If selves are essentially conscious, then, if a self exists in time-order T, it cannot exist at a time within T at which it is not conscious.

Therefore

(5′) Selves are either intermittent in their existence, atemporal, or exist in a time-order different from that in which they are deemed to have periods of unconsciousness.

This requires us to modify our understanding of the phenomenon characterized in (2) to

(2′) In so far as selves can be said to exist in physical time, they can be said to undergo periods of unconsciousness.

This leaves open the possibility of understanding such unconsciousness as intermittent participation in physical time, and existence in some other temporal order, rather than intermittent existence or pure atemporality. The challenge is to make sense of the third disjunct in (5′). If we can, then the argument goes no further.

This is an ambitious—not to say rash—project. Is it not obvious that the selves that are *our* selves exist in the very physical time in which we undergo periods of unconsciousness? The way I express this worry hints at an inadequacy in the way the argument has been so far expressed. I refer to the selves as 'we'. There may be a slippage here that was already implicit in (2). That premise was meant to state an obvious truth. The obvious truth, in fact, is

(2a) *People* have periods of unconsciousness in their existence.

In order to derive (2) from this plain datum of experience, we need also

(2b) People (persons) and selves are identical.

(2b) could be described as Cartesian in spirit. There are other traditions which would distinguish the human person from its metaphysical core, which is what I have been calling the *self*. Thomism is one of these traditions, for according to St Thomas the person and his soul are not the same thing, and maybe what I am claiming about the self could be better applied to the soul than to the person as a whole. We can reach (2′) from (2a) with the help of

(2c) People (persons) exist in physical time, and selves can be said to do so, in virtue of being the metaphysical core of persons.

Whether we should prefer (2a) or (2c) is not an issue that I wish to press here, except to remark that the idea that there is a metaphysical core to the human person which is not essentially bound to the empirical temporal order may strike some people as less counterintuitive than the claim that persons as such are not so bound. In so far as people are what result when selves, the soul or the otherwise characterized metaphysical core of persons, participate in the temporal order, then they will be essentially temporal in a way that the self need not be.

In the process of defending the view that persons, at least as far as their metaphysical core is concerned, are not essentially part of physical time, I hope to make plausible the following ideas: (i) time is not a monolithic or overarching phenomenon; (ii) as an aspect of the varieties of time, I claim that what I shall call *Manifest Image Time* (MIT) and *Scientific Image Time* (SIT) are separate realms; (iii) that the self belongs to neither of these, but to a dynamic of its own which allows it to influence or participate in the others.

2. THE STATUS OF TIME

The assumption behind most discussion of the problem concerning the continuity of consciousness that I have just aired, is that, for these purposes, the concept of time is not problematic, and the difficulties lie in providing an adequate account of the self. Time in general is, of course, a very difficult notion, and I believe that how one understands it does in fact make a major difference to one's understanding of the subject's relation to it. If one could have a conception of time which allowed that the self is, in some sense, outside physical or empirical time, then temporal gaps in experience might cease to be gaps in the existence of the experiencing self. I want to look at the prospects for at least loosening the self's relation to and dependence on time.

We have strong intuitions about time. We feel that it must be one unitary phenomenon which is a necessary part of the framework in which all concrete things exist. The feeling is that it makes no sense to say that there might be different kinds of time, or beings outside time altogether. The instinct that non-abstract entities cannot exist outside time is very strong. One might say that common sense combines a Newtonian view that time is absolute and unitary, with a Kantian view that it is an a priori presupposition of any concrete existence. It is a feature of common sense to treat time as an all-pervasive medium, such that it would make no sense to think of something as being outside of it. This has even affected the mainstream philosophical approach to God. Brian Davies (2003: 380) complains that 'If there is anything characteristic of modern American philosophy of religion it is the view that God is temporal.' He has in mind the views, amongst others, of Nelson Pike, Alvin Plantinga, and Nicholas Wolterstorff. If he had not been limiting his attention to America, he could have included Richard Swinburne, Peter Geach, and John Lucas. This is part of a programme which tries to make God simply the limiting condition of something we understand perfectly well, namely a mind or a person. In Davies's words,

It is false, we are told, that God is incomprehensible. He is, in fact, something very familiar. He is a person. And he has properties in common with other persons. He changes, learns, and is acted on. He also has beliefs which alter with the changes in the objects of his beliefs. (2003: 377)

If what I say about human persons in this essay is correct, it might become easier to restore a more traditional way of thinking about God. But I suspect that even the more traditional approach to which Davies wants to return is over-respectful of the centrality of time to our conception of the world. It is striking that, when those who regard God as atemporal want to express what His relation is to the temporal order, they say such things as that He is *simultaneous* with the whole of time, and that it is present to Him, in a sense of 'present' which they explicate as being a form of eternal 'now'. This way of talking leads to some well-known problems, but what is striking about it is that it seems to be an attempt to explain atemporality using temporal notions. One reaction to this is to regard it as a silly mistake, but what it suggests to me is how difficult philosophers have found it to escape from the framework of time: it remains a compulsory reference point. Because of this difficulty, philosophers have spoken as if even the notion of atemporality has to be explained within the framework of temporal concepts, so that the challenge becomes how one can, so to speak, stretch the natural topology of time so that it can accommodate the eternal. Atemporality thus gets explained in terms of a certain kind of *now* or of a peculiar kind of *duration*, namely a limitless one without succession. It is as if an atemporal being is the limiting case of a kind of temporality. In my view, this is to defer too much to the idea that time constitutes a framework to which everything must be related. Paul Helm (1988: 35ff.) has argued convincingly that the sense in which God is immediately *present* to things in the world can be adequately expressed in terms of His direct cognition of, and direct volitional control over, them: no temporal notion of simultaneity is required. Nor can any sense be made of the kind of duration mentioned above, and it is not necessary. What we must do is avoid treating time as if it had an almost a priori status, and see it instead as a feature of experience and of processes. I hope to show that, approached in this way, temporal notions can be tools for understanding the world, not the bars of a cage in which we are trapped.

What I need to do is to show that the self is not a standard participant in physical time as we naturally understand it. I shall end this section with two preliminaries. First, I want to draw attention to an analogy, which is intended to help give legitimacy to the idea that difference of process might give rise to difference of temporal system. We are all familiar with the metaphor of the *biological clock*. These are said to be liable to run at different speeds in different individuals, and so not to be in step with each other or with the official clock, which is based on the solar system. They might also speed up and slow down over time, with respect to other systems. Because they are subsystems within the unified structure of one common system—a unified empirical and physical world with one set of common laws and common elementary parts—we treat the idea that these 'clocks' measure different 'times' as metaphorical. But I want to suggest that if the systems were not simply subsystems of such a unified whole, we would not be obliged to acknowledge a unified metric of time. We saw above that it can be maintained that God's relation to the physical world could be cognitive and volitional, without any temporal component. Perhaps there could be a mind—for example, an angelic one—which is not wholly changeless, as God is, but which relates only cognitively and connatively to the world of physical time. Although the events in its mind might be successive, I see no reason why they should possess the same kind of temporality as that possessed by the physical system. What I mean by not possessing 'the same kind of temporality' is that the events in the angelic thought processes need not be simultaneous with any specific physical times. That they *must* be, can only come from the picture of time as an overarching category. We shall return to this thought later.

The second preliminary is to introduce some relevant jargon. There are three distinctions which I will employ and which, on some interpretations, coincide, and on others, do not. First, developing the distinction that Wilfrid Sellars made between the *manifest image* and the *scientific image* of the world, I shall talk about *manifest image time* (MIT) and *scientific image time* (SIT). I make this distinction in order to claim that, as well as possessing different sensible qualities of the normal sort, so that only the manifest image possesses, for example, secondary qualities in their experiential form, the difference extends to being temporal in different senses. The experienced or lived time of the manifest image, I shall claim, possesses certain features not possessed by the time of the scientific image. The second distinction is McTaggart's distinction between the *A-series* and the *B-series* (McTaggart 1927: Gale 1968). The A-series is characterized by the categories of pastness, presentness and futurity: events are first in the future, then become present, and then are past. The B-series categorizes events by their relations of being *earlier than, simultaneous with,* or *later than* each other. The relations between events in B-series terms do not change. The third distinction is between *flowing time* (FT) and *static* or *block time* (BT). These distinctions might seem to coincide. It might seem that the A-series, with its *moving present* or *moving 'now'*, is what defines *flowing time*, and that temporal flow is what distinguishes the temporality of the manifest world. As no one denies that all time is characterized by the *earlier–later* relations, MIT possesses both A- and B-series features. The time of the scientific image, on the other hand, is the time of four-dimensional space–time and of individuals as Minkowski space–time worms. This is the static or block conception of time as being little more than an extra spatial dimension, and satisfying only the B-series. Ways in which the coincidence of these distinctions can be disputed will emerge in the course of the discussion.

3. TIME IN THE MANIFEST IMAGE

In *Problems of Philosophy* (1912/1959: 29 ff.) Russell suggested that physical space could not be thought of as being qualitatively the way it seemed either visually or in touch. Our knowledge of its physical nature is entirely abstract and formal, as captured in the appropriate geometry. If physical space has an intrinsic qualitative nature (and if it is real and concrete it presumably must), we cannot know what it is. The manifest image differs from the scientific image in respect of these fundamental primary qualities, as well as in secondary qualities. This view of space is well known and, though by no means uncontroversial, often accepted. But Russell (1912) indicates, if he does not quite say, similar things about time. He was, however, more explicit a few years later: 'past, present and future arise from time-relations of subject and object, while earlier and later arise from time-relations of object and object' (1915: 212). More recently, Grünbaum has claimed that

what qualifies a physical event at a time *t* as belonging to the present or as now is not some physical attribute of the event or some relation it sustains to other purely physical events; instead what so qualifies the event is that at the time *t* at least one human or other *mind-possessing* organism M is conceptually aware of experiencing the event at that time. (1968: 17)

Grünbaum compares our experience of presentness with our experience of secondary qualities such as colour (1968: 7), but the comparison need not be restricted to presentness alone. The whole experience of what one might call *felt duration* would be a kind of secondary quality. Just as what we think of as spatial extendedness takes its distinctive qualitative feel from the nature of visual (or tactile) experience, so our empirically interpreted idea of time derives from certain kinds of experience. What we might call the *conceptual properties* of the A-series, which could be considered abstractly as simply the changing of predications, are given empirical content by the 'feel' of duration, which, like visual space, could not exist without experience. On such a view, felt duration ('it seemed to take an awfully long time') and the flowing nature of time, as expressed in the moving *now*, are, like the specifically visual and tactile aspects of space, features of the way we experience the world. By contrast, physical time, in so far as we know it, is only an abstract structural feature of the physical system as a whole, which reflects, perhaps, the directionality of causation, or causal explanation.

One might object to comparing the flow of time to a secondary quality on the following grounds. Secondary qualities are marked by their dependence on one sensory modality. It is because visual space and tactile space are phenomenally different that they can, individually, be assimilated to secondary qualities. But the experience of time is not different in the different modalities, but always the same.

Even if this were so, it would not prevent one from treating the flow of time as a subjective phenomenon, for there is no *necessary* connection between subjectivity and being tied to one sense. I am not convinced, however, that time is experienced similarly in all the modalities. The relation between space and time can be brought out by considering Molyneux's Problem.

The thought experiment known as Molyneux's Problem is meant to bring out the qualitative difference between visual and tactile space. According to that problem, it is assumed that a man blind from birth should suddenly recover his sight. Would he immediately recognize what visual phenomena correlated with his tactile experiences of various shapes, or would he need to learn this correlation empirically? The implication is that he would need to learn it, and that this shows that visual and tactile space are qualitatively different, whilst sharing certain formal geometrical features. It is not easy to concoct a parallel thought experiment for time, to which we can relate as easily as to blindness, but it is not obviously impossible.

Assume—perhaps *per impossibile*, but for these purposes I do not think this rules it out—a creature whose conscious life is normally non-temporal. Then imagine that it should have, disconnectedly, three experiences. One is like what we would describe as a round patch of colour moving from the left to the right of the visual field. Another is like a succession of three notes on the piano. The third is like apprehending some propositions and then realizing that a certain conclusion follows from them. Is there any reason why it should strike this subject that there is any qualitative similarity between what we would regard as the temporal structure in each of these experiences? The intrinsic qualitative natures of those experiences are as different from each other as are the visual and the tactile experiences invoked by Molyneux. Only when Molyneux's subject discovers the role of spatial structure in bringing the various experiences together, as experiences of one world, will the formal similarities between their spatial elements become salient. If they remained as disconnected experiences without a potentially common subject matter, simple phenomenology would not reveal it. This is the situation for the subject whose experience is not generally temporally structured.

This last claim might seem strange. Surely the experiences have spatial or temporal features whether or not these are noticed. On the contrary, my claim is that individual experiences possess only what one might call *proto-spatiality* or *proto-temporality* and not fully fledged spatial and temporal properties. These latter belong to experiences only when they are interpreted in the light of the empirical spatial or temporal medium constructed from them; and this construction is possible—that is, we can have a non-abstract conception of space or time—only if the experiences fit together in a certain way.

To see this, imagine the following case. Suppose there is a blind subject who occasionally has random and disorganized visual sensations, which include elements that we would recognize as shapes. Because these experiences do not coordinate with his tactile experiences, and do not form an ordered structure amongst themselves, they do not partake of that spatiality which is common to touch and sight for the normal perceiver. They possess the materials out of which this could be made—they are proto-spatial—but not spatial in the full sense. The subject who has these sensations is not failing to notice the presence of true primary qualities, for the proto-shapes in his experience have not acquired that status; they do not represent an even seemingly objective realm.

A comparison with the experience of dizziness may be helpful here. There seems to be no other way of describing the experience of feeling dizzy except to say that the world seems to go round and round. But, if one attends to the experience, one realizes that there is no completed seeming circular motion. It is as if things move from one side to the other, and repeat this, without any clear experience of their moving back to the starting point, either by continuous motion or in a jump. What we seem to have is an experience which we can only describe in spatial terms, but which makes no spatial sense. One might, therefore, conclude that the experience of dizziness is an incoherent one. What is happening, one might conclude, is that our system for processing spatial information has become disrupted and confused: without a developed conception of space, such an experience could not occur, for it is essentially a garbled version of our spatial conception. But this is not the only way of looking at it. Alternatively, one might prefer to think in the following way. As an experience, or sensation, dizziness is like what it is like: the idea that it is incoherent makes no sense. It is a perfectly clear and recognizable experience and could, in principle, occur in its own right to an otherwise blind subject who had no conception of visual space. The similarities that it possesses to our standard experiences of visual space seem to leave those of us with normal vision no option but to characterize it in spatial terms, and this leads to paradox. The appropriate conclusion from this might be the following. The dizziness experience in itself is of the same status as proto-spatial experience, except that, from the perspective of being usable to build up a conception of visual space, it is inappropriately formed and useless. That is to say, although dizziness experiences are very similar to the individual experiences from which our conception of visual space is built up, they could not themselves be the foundation of such a construction. Whether such experiences, appropriately organized, could be the foundation for an empirical conception of an objective realm, somewhat analogous to space, is difficult to say. The point of introducing the experience of dizziness, however, was this. It can be taken to suggest that individual experiences do not determinately possess features of the objective realm (which is to say, the standard primary qualities), but their construal as possessing these depends on whether they do (and hence also whether they can) participate in some appropriately organized structure. I am suggesting that this is as true of the experiences on which our conception of empirical time is based, as it is for space.

As a consequence, what I said above about the blind subject who hallucinates random visual sensations is also true for the imagined person with the fragmented time experience. He has no use for the kind of temporality we formalize as the objective time of the manifest image, so there is no reason why he should see his experiences as possessing the same primary quality. It is the applicability of abstract geometry to them collectively that holds the various spatial sensory modalities together (which is not, of course to say that conscious knowledge of geometry is involved, only that experience must in fact be susceptible to this construal). If there were no such application—if the various senses never coordinated, as would be the case with disconnected visual and tactile hallucinations—then there would be no common notion of space. Without the common applicability of bare arithmetical succession, there would be no common notion of time as found in the manifest image. Our conception of space and time, and, in general, of primary qualities *qua* primary, is a result of the susceptibility of certain sensations, in virtue of their intrinsic nature *and* organization, to interpretation in a certain intellectual framework.

Furthermore, treating sensations as intrinsically only proto-temporal helps with some of the problems which are traditionally taken to face the doctrine of the specious present. It does so, moreover, in a way that brings out the relation between the subject and manifest image time. The specious present is postulated to explain our experience of time: just as we could not have a concept of space if all our experiences of space were purely punctiform, so we could not form a conception of time, purely on the basis of experiences that present us with an unextended moment. Furthermore, when we see something moving, we see the movement itself. We do not apprehend the object at a certain position and merely *remember* that it was previously at a contiguous one. The idea that we *in one experience* grasp a small temporal array, transmutes naturally into the idea that *in an instant* we grasp this array. This raises the question of the position of the instant at which the grasping is done in relation to the time array grasped. James (1901: 609) thought that it was in the centre of that temporal spread, so that one experiences into the future as well as into the past. C. D. Broad (1923: 349. See also Mabbott 1951), on the other hand, thought that the experiencing was done from the perspective of the end of the time apprehended and that one was always looking into the past. This controversy rests on two assumptions. One is that the 'temporal' feature that characterizes individual experiences is, in its own right, a part of an objective continuous time. The other is that the act of apprehending it must have a place within that time. These assumptions, together, amount to the thought that there is an overarching temporal medium in which the experiences and their contents take place. The picture I have been presenting is meant to be an alternative to this. First, the 'temporal' feature of individual experiences is only proto-temporal. It is simply a kind of experience which, if combined in the right way with other experiences, can constitute an empirical time order. For this reason, second, the subject that apprehends it stands in no other relation to it than that of being the subject that apprehends it. As it itself is not objectively temporal, there is no reason why the subject that apprehends it, simply by apprehending it, should have to stand in a temporal relation to it. As we saw in the case of God's relation to the physical world, it is wrong to take a relation of direct cognition as, of itself, involving any temporal relation: the relation of apprehending or cognizing is primitive in its own right.

Again, there is an analogy to this in the case of vision. If someone experiences a red square, he will naturally tend to think of himself as located somewhere in front of the centre of that square. We think this way, however, because we have constructed a putatively objective world from our experiences—especially our visual ones—and we naturally locate ourselves as subjects at what seem to be the natural places within that world. But someone blind who underwent the occasional visual sensation would not, it seems to me, experience its content as standing in any spatial relation to him. It would simply be something he is aware of and undergoes. *Mutatis mutandis*, the same is true of proto-temporal experiences, taken individually, in abstraction from the temporal interpretation that their ordering makes possible.

I have so far argued that the subject stands in a non-temporal apprehending relation to proto-temporal experiences, and that it is from such experiences, appropriately ordered, that manifest time is built up. There seems to be a problem, however. Part of the requisite ordering is that the proto-temporal experiences must, amongst other things, perhaps, be presented *successively* to the subject. But is not the notion of *succession* here a temporal notion, and so are we not presupposing time, not constructing it? The response to this is as follows. The time we are talking about is MIT. Just as the contents of specious presents are proto-temporal in relation to this time, so is the succession relation. Let us call this relation the *S-relation*. This relation holds between experiences, or, perhaps more accurately, between acts of experiencing. What I am claiming is that the events that are S-related are not related in MIT. S-relatedness is a relation of a generically temporal type, but more primitive than the relation of temporal succession in MIT, because it is one of the components that contribute to the construction of the latter. The subject stands in a non-temporal cognizing or awareness relation to a set of specious present proto-temporal contents, and these awarenesses are in an S-related series. The result is a period of experience of the kind that goes to make up our manifest world.

Once again, our conclusion can be used to clear up a problem that is supposed to bother the theory of the specious present. The way it clears it up also makes plainer my complaint about the consequences of treating time in a unitary manner.

There is supposed to be the following problem for the specious present. Suppose that one such experience presents a series A–B–C. What will be presented in the next specious present? The initial view might be that, after A–B–C, the next specious present will present D–E–F. This view has faced objections, however. If we call the occasion of the presentation of A–B–C, *P1*, and the occasion of the presentation of D–E–F, *P2*, then it has been objected that, experientially, the connection between C and D would not seem to be like that between A and B, B and C, D and E, and E and F. That is, that within one specious present there would be experience of genuine flow or continuity, between different specious presents there could not be the same kind of fluid connection. This belief that there would be a break of continuity has led to this theory's being called the *pulsation* theory, which implies that experience comes in discriminably distinguishable packages. In response, it has been argued that the next presentation after *P1*, A–B–C, would be *P2*, B–C–D, and *P3* would be C–D–E, etc. This, too, however, has its problems, for it seems to suggest that the same content is repeatedly presented: C, for example, is in *P1*, *P2*, and *P3*. But in the even flow of experience, one does not (seem to) experience the same content in a repeated way.

It seems to me that this problem rests on a misconception. The label 'pulsation theory' implies that the successive presentations happen with temporal gaps between them. But that picture embodies the mistake, which I have already criticized, of placing the *experiencings* in the same time series as is constructed from the contents experienced; and this could be justified only if time was one overarching framework. It seems to me that if one experienced A–B–C, and then D–E–F according to the successive relation, in no way would there seem to be any difference between the relations of C and D and the others. It is true that, when one experienced D–E–F, the experience of A–B–C would be only a memory, but it does not follow from this that one's experience would be as of a series of discontinuous throbs or pulses. So long as, at any given moment, one experiences the flow of a specious present, and remembers what went before it, it will never seem that one's experience is discontinuous. C would be present as part of a 'flow', then D would be present as part of a flow, without any *experience* of break or discontinuity. The interfaces between different presentations are not themselves presented experientially. (There is perhaps an analogy here with the blind spot. We can work out that it must be there, but it is not *experienced* as a hole in the visual field.)

Some confusion on this issue might be caused by thinking in a Jamesian manner. One might think that, within a specious present, events are experienced as 'flowing into' each other, but that, by definition, they cannot be so experienced *between* different experiences, so that, therefore, the sense of continuity between 'pulsating' specious presents must be different from that within them. As a consequence, experience must seem 'granulated' and discontinuous. The talk of contents 'flowing into' each other must not be misconstrued, however. It does not mean that contents 'blur' into each other. It should mean no more than that one experiences the transition, as one does within the specious present. And if one experiences the transition A–B–C, and then, without experiencing any break, D–E–F, this will not present itself as involving any discontinuity. It would be experienced as an even flow. The mistaken view that it would not seem continuous, comes from conceiving the experiencings as 'pulses' or 'throbs' located at a temporal distance from each other. In fact a series of S-related apprehensions pick up the contents without break.

We appear to have arrived at the following view. The experience of time involves four elements: (i) a subject which I take to be a simple entity; (ii) proto-temporal experiences; which are (iii) ordered in the successor or S-relation; and (iv) the having of those experiences, and apprehension of their contents, by subjects, where this relation of subject to experience (and its content) is a primitive relation which is not to be explained in a way that seems to presuppose a temporal component in that relation. One should not, for example, think of the content of the experience as temporally present to the subject, or of the subject and experience as being simultaneous with each other. The awareness in question is more primitive than temporal notions because of the essential role of experience in the construction of our idea of manifest time.

How would adopting this view of time help with our original problem? Our problem was to understand how an essentially conscious subject could endure through periods of time when he is not conscious. The answer is that, at least as far as MIT is concerned, the self does not 'endure through' these times, except in a derivative sense. This is because the self is prior to such time, which is itself a construct from the self's experiences. The self is not in MIT, except derivatively. It is to this self that the basic data of experience—those sensations that have, in themselves, proto-temporal and proto-spatial content—are presented. It follows that the subject is not in the time constructed from its experiences. Of course, once the manifest world is constructed, the subject has a location in it. But, as the subject is prior to this world, his place in it is not a basic fact. Perhaps, following a suggestion made in Section 1, one could say that the self, considered as the metaphysical core of the person, is not strictly in MIT, but that the person is: or one might think of the self and person as participating in MIT whilst not being essentially of it.

4. ARE THE TIMES OF THE MANIFEST AND THE SCIENTIFIC IMAGES REALLY DIFFERENT?

On reflection, it might strike the cautious reader that perhaps the grand conclusion presented at the end of Section 3 was arrived at slightly too easily. It might be questioned whether the fact that the manifest image, including its temporal features, is a construct from experience which is characterized by subjective features really entails that its time is, *qua* time, different from that in the scientific image. So we must now look closely at whether the subjectivity of certain aspects of temporal experience, and the role that this plays in time as it is in the manifest image, really entails that this is a different temporal order from that found in the scientific account of the world.

The manifest image is the world as it appears to us, given our particular sensory capabilities. In its specific nature, it can be thought of as an intersubjective construct from our individual subjective experiences. This world is characterized by the time of common sense, which possesses both A and B features. The scientific image, on the other hand, is the world of the 'view from nowhere'; it is physical reality as it is in itself. This world possesses only the time of the B-series. What is the relationship between these two 'worlds'? Are they only prima facie different, or really different, as I seem to imply above?

The most economical or reductive view is that there is ultimately only one reality, and that is the world of the scientific image—augmented, at some places occupied by brains, by mental events.[2] The manifest image is only a kind of perspective on the scientific image, produced by the sensory experiences which exist among the mental events to which I have just referred. One might move on from this thought in either of two ways. One would be to say that when one refers to events from within the manifest image—that is, when one thinks of them as past or future—one is referring to the same events as are present in the corresponding place within the scientific image. So if one refers to the Battle of Hastings in 1066, conceiving of it as past, that event is the same event as one located in the 'static' time 939 years earlier than 2005. Another view is that, seen from within the manifest image, the event of the battle of Hastings is a logical construction from the appearances that constitute flowing time, and so is not real at all. It is only an intentional object of the 'seemings' that are associated with certain brain events. Both these views have it in common that the flow of time adds no real ontology to the B-series, either because the non-present contents of flowing time are identical with events in static time, or because they are constructs from experiential episodes that occur within static time.

Both these positions hold the view that the reality of 'flow time' (FT) consists in no more than the association of mental events with some events in 'block time' (BT). But then the issue is the nature of this association. Is the association such that, within the realm of the mental, time does really flow, though it does not do so within the 'objective' physical world? Or is it such that the appearance of flow, even within experience, is an illusion? This problem can be brought out by considering two pictures used to illustrate the relation between our experience of a restricted presentness in FT and the underlying physical block. Both involve treating experience as a light that falls upon that part of the physical world that appears, at any given moment, as the 'now' of current experience. On one picture, the light *travels along* the time dimension of the block that is the physical world. If one takes this image seriously—as one must if one is to find it explanatory—the light contrasts with the block, because there has to be a sense in which it—the light—moves, whilst the block remains static. But, if this is so, there is genuine FT in the realm of experience, and some experiences will be past, one present, and some to come, depending on what point the light has reached

---

[2] For present purposes, the question of whether mental states can be identified with the brain-states, or whether some minimal dualism is supposed, need not be raised.

in its transition along the line of time. The other picture seeks to eliminate this compromise with FT. According to it, each moment associated with experience has its own light which casts its brightness only so far as its own 'now' or specious present extends. This creates the illusion that other times are out there in the darkness of past and present, whereas they each have their own light and suffer a similar illusion. This latter picture genuinely eliminates FT, but, as it seems to me, at the price of failing to explain even the appearance of flow and passage. From the perspective of the block, all those times associated with experience possess their limited illumination, and nothing explains the sense of transition from one to the next. What we said above about the construction of MIT is relevant here. Simply to have a collection of proto-temporal experiences would not be enough to constitute flowing time: one needed also the S-relation—the fact of succession—to give the temporal dynamic. The 'fixed light' model lacks an appropriate analogue to the S-relation, which the 'moving light' picture allows.

So the 'many fixed lights' picture fails because it cannot explain even the illusion of motion through time. The 'moving light' picture, on the other hand, though it fails to eliminate the A-series, might still save the unity of MIT and SIT. Indeed, it seems to be built into the analogy of the moving light that what is being illuminated to create the moving 'now' that characterizes MIT is the very same thing as constitutes the events in the four dimensional 'block' of the scientific picture.

The matter is not so straightforward, however. Call the event on which the light is currently falling and which, hence, is 'now', 'E'. The event of E's being illuminated will not be the same event as E's existing or occurring, because, on the 'moving light' model, E's being illuminated was future, is present, and will be past, whilst its existence (as opposed to its being illuminated) obtains timelessly. MIT and SIT must be different time-series, because the former is characterized by both A and B features, but the latter by B features alone. Taking T1 and T2 to be time series, the following seems to follow necessarily from Leibniz's Law:

> If T1 has both A and B features and T2 has only B features, then T1 is not identical to T2.

How, then, should we cope with the seeming fact that, according to the 'moving light' model, it is the same thing that is sometimes illuminated and sometimes not? One possible answer is that, though one event cannot be at two places in one time series, it can figure in two different temporal series. The other is that, strictly speaking, corresponding events in MIT and SIT are not actually identical: in this respect, the 'moving light' metaphor only gives the illusion of accommodating everything within the four-dimensional framework. Either way, there are two different kinds of time. But it will repay the effort to look at different ways of conceiving of SIT, as the possessor of only B properties.

5. WHAT IS SIT?

It is a consequence of my assumption that the 'moving "now"' and duration as we experience it are subjective phenomena, that time in the scientific image lacks A-properties. It is only fair to remark that not everyone would accept this view of the scientific picture. Both presentists and 'growing block' theorists would deny it. Nevertheless, it is *ex hypothesi* for my present purposes that the space–time of science is four-dimensional and involves no growth. What this exactly means, however, is unclear, at least in part because it depends so much on metaphor. Talk of being 'static' and a 'block' is, presumably, not simply literal. Even calling time 'the fourth dimension' is not clear: it is not the fourth spatial dimension: it is not what would make possible a Klein bottle, or one of the thirteen or nineteen dimensions of space invoked by string theorists. In this section, I shall look at some of the ways in which the scientific image can be treated.

(i) There are two *non-realist options*. Within a secular phenomenalist or positivist tradition, the scientific image of the world is usually understood purely instrumentally; it is not an account of how the mind-independent world is in itself. For a Berkeleian idealist or theistic phenomenalist, on the other hand, the scientific image can be regarded as a representation of the divine design for the world: so it does answer to a reality, but not the mind-independent one that we normally imagine the physical world to be. It might seem that in neither of these cases does the question of the *real* nature of SIT arise, because these accounts are not realist. The issue is not so simple, however. If one were to accept that there is a clear and absolute divide between the manifest world and the scientific one, then one might regard the former as straightforwardly real and the latter as straightforwardly instrumental or ideal. But if one regarded the scientific image as an essential part of a proper understanding of the manifest world, then one might be committed to conceiving of it *as* real, even if one did not think that it was.[3] It would still be important in this case to understand how time was conceived within this framework. Because the purely instrumental interpretation makes the task of understanding time within that domain irrelevant, and what one might call the 'as if' or quasi-realist interpretation obliges one to pretend to be a realist, it is the realist option that is relevant to my purposes.

(ii) Dainton (2003: 11) states four-dimensionalism (or BT) in the following way: 'all times and events timelessly coexist and are equally real'. The block theorist has to navigate a Scylla and Charybdis. On the one hand, the conventional A-theorist (though not presentists: see Crisp 2003) accepts the timeless existence of all events, provided that 'timeless' is interpreted as equivalent to the tensed 'is, was, or will be'. Accepting this interpretation would entirely undermine BT. On

---

[3] For a brief defence of the idea that a realist construal might be necessary and correct, irrespective of the ultimate ontology, see Robinson 2003*b*.

the other hand, the block theorist usually wants to avoid interpreting 'timelessly' as equivalent to *permanently*, which takes 'timeless coexistence' as meaning that all events exist all the time. The analogy with space is meant to operate so as to make 'x (timelessly) exists, but not *now*' clear and uncontroversial in the way that 'x exists, but not *here*' is clear and uncontroversial. This ignores the difference between 'x came to be at t' and 'x came to be at p', where 't' is a time, and 'p' a place. The former means x *came into existence* at t, the latter that x, presumed already existent, arrived at location p. One could preserve the parallel between the two only by either (*a*) adopting what one might describe as *solipsism of the current location*, so that something comes into existence by being *here*: or (*b*) by treating the event that occurs at t as having an existence independent of the time at which it occurs, in the way that a place in the block exists whether or not the light is passing over it. No one would wish to adopt the former route to preserving the parallel, and the latter seems to be a form of 'permanence', in the sense that it seems to countenance the existence of an event said to take place at t, outside of t. Grünbaum (1968: 24) explains four-dimensionalism by saying:

According to Minkowski's conception, an event qualifies as a *becomingless* occurrence by occurring in a network of relations of earlier and later and thus can be said to occur "at a certain time t". Hence to assert tenselessly that an event exists (occurs) is to claim that there is a time or clock reading with which it coincides. But surely this assertion does not entail the absurdity that the event exists (occurs) at *all* clock times or "permanently".

Grünbaum is here making two points, one of which is question-begging and the other important. The question-begging point is the assumption that the relations of earlier and later, and the notion of 'clock time' can be preserved in their normal sense whilst detached from the idea of time as flowing. Naively or intuitively put, the notion of a clock seems to be essentially connected with movement and becoming: a clock is essentially a *process* to which other events can be compared. But the second point is the more direct one. Grünbaum interprets the accusation of 'permanence' as being equivalent to the absurd accusation that the block theorist is committed to the view that an event that takes place at t, thereby takes place at all times. If this is the content of the accusation of 'permanence', then the accusation is ridiculous. But if that is not the content of the accusation, what is its content? What can 'permanent' mean if not 'at all times'? Because it is obvious that the critic does not mean to say that the block theorist is committed to the view that the Battle of Hastings takes place at every date in history, he is often interpreted as saying something less obviously absurd. The suggestion that is often made is that the critic is judging the four-dimensional block from the perspective of a 'hyper-time', and it is according to this higher order time that all events in the static block are permanent and, hence, simultaneous. The picture is that, because the 'block' is 'static', 'fixed' or 'frozen', everything in it must be permanent and simultaneous. Although, on this interpretation, the accusation of permanence is not so ridiculous, it is still held to be clearly mistaken, because there is no such a thing as the hyper-time, according to which the permanence is supposedly measured and the critic is thought to be in the grip of a picture.

It is not true, however, that the accusation of permanence involves the postulation of a hyper-time. It involves only the application of certain criteria which are held to be the correct criteria for temporality; and the claim that, judging by those standards, the four dimensional block fails to possess an essential feature of genuine temporality. The accusation is that a world without *becoming* simply has not captured what it is that distinguishes time from space, and that its defenders are in the grip of the misleading picture of 'four-dimensionalism', which pretends that time is just an extra dimension, essentially similar to space.

Furthermore, I argued in the previous section that even the appearance of temporal flow could not be explained without allowing that A-properties are real, at least for experience. It is by the standards of this entirely real empirical time that SIT can be deemed to be static, to the point of being atemporal. SIT can then be seen as a structural analogue of time, without being temporal in the sense in which we empirically understand that notion. In that respect, it is analogous to the unknown nature of physical space, which preserves only formal and structural features from our spatial experiences. The accusation expressed by calling all events in the BT 'permanent', is the accusation that BT lacks an essential feature that distinguishes time from space, and that without the feature of temporal 'becoming', the relations dubbed 'earlier' and 'later' cease to have any real temporal content. This accusation could be convincingly rebutted if the appearance of flow found in MIT could be explained from within the 'block' framework, as the various accounts that appeal to moving or static lights attempt to do. But we found that these fail. As temporal flow cannot be explained within the block framework, there is a genuine FT by the criteria of which events in BT are simultaneous with each other.

6. FOUR-DIMENSIONALISM AND THE DIVINE SPECIOUS PRESENT

The upshot (it is rather too tentative to be called a conclusion) of the discussion so far is that time of the manifest image is a different temporal realm from time in the scientific image, and that the latter has a nature which is remote in all but structural respects from what we normally think of as time. There is, however, an intriguing strategy which might save the intuitive temporality of a time that lacks A-properties. It can be approached by enquiring whether the A-predicates apply within a specious present. On the one hand, the presence of flow within the specious present is essential to it. It is precisely to capture directly in experience temporal flow and movement that the specious present is postulated. But it is also essential to it that this temporal spread is captured in one 'present' or 'now', so, it might be argued, the specious present contains no past or future, but only elements arranged as earlier and later than each other. This is because the subject's relation to each specious present is, as was argued above, like God's relation to the whole of created time, cognitive but not temporal. Within a specious present, it seems that the connection is broken between the idea that time flows and the notion of the moving present. Now if BT were like this—and the whole of time has been claimed to be God's specious present—then there would be no question of earlier than–later than relations in BT not being genuinely temporal, or of the 'block' being 'static' in some undesirable sense. But can this feature of the specious present be preserved in abstraction from the status of that present as a mode of experience?

On the one hand, the fact that God's specious present includes the whole of time, including the kind of flow that we apprehend in our specious present, might suggest that this kind of flow is part of time in the scientific image. After all, the scientific image presents time as it is in the objective physical world and it is this world that God is being supposed to grasp in a specious present. It would seem, therefore, that the flow of God's specious present is not essentially dependent on the fact that it is an object of his experience. On the other hand, I claimed earlier on that there was a strong parallel between the way in which the spatial features of visual experience, and those of temporal experience, are both subjective. Space in the manifest image, which for most of us is modelled on visual space, is constructed from features of visual experience that are definitely subjective. Similarly, in the case of MIT, we build it up from experiences whose nature, taken individually, is proto-temporal and subjective. If MIT as we experience it is a construct from subjective features of our experience, then there is no wholly objective and mind-independent flow-time for God to apprehend. His apprehension of such a thing could only be an aspect of His knowledge of our psychological states.

My conclusion, therefore, is that those who think that a universe with only B-properties is 'static', and that its events are 'permanent' in a way inconsistent with our intuitive notion of temporality, are basically correct. It seems also that what was claimed towards the end of Section 3 is correct: MIT and SIT are different temporal orders, and the self is definitely prior to MIT. But if MIT is not identical with SIT, can we be confident that the self is outside SIT? If it is not also outside that order, will it not also suffer from discontinuous existence within the world of the scientific image?

7. THE SELF AND SIT

Assuming that the world of the 'block universe' can be taken realistically at all, it still remains a question whether the self is a part of that world and, hence, whether the self is caught within that world's peculiar kind of temporality. There are at least three reasons for denying that the self is in SIT.

1. Given that (i) there is no overarching temporal system, and so no presumption that any given entity *must* be in that system as a kind of default; (ii) that experiences, of which the self is the subject, are not in SIT; (iii) that the scientific image generally is fundamentally an account of the world in so far as it can be captured by physical science; and (iv) the self is simple and immaterial: then there would seem to be no reason to think that the self is part of the 'block' world of science, and hence it is reasonable to hold that it is not in that temporal order.

2. If one agrees with David Lewis (1983) that the block picture leads to an ontology of temporal parts, then placing the self within block time would mean that any continuous self really breaks down into a succession of more basic brief temporal entities. But it was *ex hypothesi* for this paper that the self is a simple entity, and so not a composite of parts of any kind. So, if Lewis is right, the simplicity of the self is inconsistent with locating it in SIT. If, however, one does not agree with Lewis that the block entails temporal parts—as, for example, Hugh Mellor (1998) does not—then this argument will not apply.

3. As well as the rather passive 'activity' of experiencing, the self is more literally an agent in thinking and willing. The essentially dynamic nature of such activities does not seem to fit in well with locating the self in a realm that is free of 'becoming'. This is so whether one is a determinist or a libertarian about such acts—they still are genuinely dynamic in a way that the block does not seem to allow.

All these considerations seem to me to show that one is not compelled to regard the self, if conceived in an essentially Cartesian way, as part of the block world of the scientific picture.

8. TEMPORAL RELATIONSHIPS BETWEEN THE DIFFERENT KINDS OF TIME

A question that might seem naturally to arise with this account which represents the manifest and scientific images as possessing their own and separate temporal orders, is: what is the *temporal* relationship between the physical, 'block', universe and the manifest and intersubjective universe? But the answer to this has already been implicitly given. Because these are different temporal orders and there is no overarching, unitary time, there is no *temporal* relationship between the two systems. There are, of course, mappings and explanatory relations from one to the other, which enable us to *think of them as* merely different ways of thinking about the same physical, temporal world. But that is not the fundamental ontological perspective.

Once one has rejected the view that there must be one overarching temporal framework, this initially strange answer—that the two realms have no temporal relation—becomes inevitable. The experience of temporal flow is just a kind of sensation which will bear the imposition of the metric of temporal succession. We take this to be physical time, and so construct the temporal order of our 'manifest image' world. Similarly, our visual and tactile sensations will support the imposition of a geometric reading and we take them as being parts of physical space, and so construct 'manifest' space. But, considered in themselves, in both cases, the sensations lack direct relation to the space and time of the four-dimensional universe, for they are temporal and spatial in different senses from that in which it is.

I have talked above as if the world of the manifest image is straightforwardly the public world of common experience, but this is an oversimplification. The manifest image, as contrasted with the scientific image, is the world of experience as seen by the traditional representative realist. It is the world of the 'veil of perception', and the world of science is the mind-independent world that is responsible for causing it, by causing our sense-experiences. This must be so because what distinguishes the manifest and scientific worlds is the fact that secondary qualities—including, for present purposes, visual and tactile space and experiential time—exist only in the manifest world of experience: it is only through the medium of how things seem to the subject that this world exists. The manifest image must, therefore, be a construct from the experiences of individual subjects. As an aspect of this, MIT—the time of the manifest image—cannot be regarded as a primitive. It will be a construct from the temporality of individuals' experiences. It follows that MIT cannot be thought of as a given within which the experiences of individual subjects are located. We understand and take as a given the temporal ordering within particular episodes of unbroken conscious experience. Indeed, most of the discussion above that was presented as being about MIT in fact concerned how the individual's experience of flowing time was constructed. At that point, I simply ignored the difference between temporality as an aspect of individual unbroken chains of experience—what one might call *phenomenal time*—and the flowing time of the manifest world taken as a whole. To bridge this gap and to correct this omission, we must ask two questions. How does one get from individual stretches of subjective experience, and the associated phenomenal time, to the seemingly public manifest world, and its seemingly public MIT? And what are the fundamental temporal relations, direct and indirect, between different continuous streams of consciousness, given that there is no prior, overarching public MIT in which they are all located?

The first issue seems to echo the problem on which phenomenalism foundered, namely that of constructing the public world out of subjective experience. Although it is true that we are not, in the present case, concerned with a reductive analysis of the physical, as phenomenalism was, but only with constructing the manifest image—how we see the world—there is still the question of how one derives the conception of a public world from material that is private and subjective. This issue, however, can be bypassed, because formal construction, reduction or analysis of physical concepts is not what is at issue. It is enough to say that we *take our experience to be of* a public physical world, and we take phenomenal time to be MIT. So, given the structure of our experience, we are simply able and disposed to read the physical interpretation into it. Logical construction is not required. This is not the whole of the account of how we get to the 'public' manifest image. Understanding our own experience as being a public world only gets us half way to a public world. The public or intersubjective manifest world is the mean or common factor of the manifest worlds of individual perceivers.

The second question concerned the temporal relations between separate conscious episodes, and it raises more fundamental problems. Imagine two subjects S and S*, each with periods of conscious experience, separated by periods of unconsciousness. Take as examples of S's periods of consciousness, E1 and E2, and of S*'s, E*1 and E*2. What kinds of temporal relations hold, on the one hand between E1 and E2, or E*1 and E*2, that is, between experiences of the same subject; and, on the other, between E1 or E2 and E*1 or E*2, that is, between experiences of different subjects? As MIT is something that emerges from the phenomenal time to be found in individual subjects' stretches of conscious experience, it would seem that the relations between them cannot be grounded in it.

The surprising fact is that, just as there is not, at the basic level, any temporal relation between the manifest and the scientific worlds, it would seem that neither can there be a prior temporal relation between different strings of conscious experience, such as E1, E2, E*1 and E*2. Considered as the foundations on which the manifest world and its time order are to be built, they stand in no temporal relation. Within the same subject, different non-continuous conscious episodes, such as E1 and E2 are connected by appropriate matching of mental contents, such as show themselves as memory, continuity of character and purposes, and, generally, all the things that the psychological criterion of personal identity invokes. (I say 'show themselves as' because if we consider the likes of E1 and E2 not as already temporally ordered, but as pieces of a jigsaw the correct ordering of which in virtue of their content constitutes the temporal system in question, then a term such as *memory*, which already has temporality built into it, is not strictly appropriate.) This kind of matching of content does not, of course, obtain across subjects, as between E1 and E*1, for example.

What does it mean to say that there are no prior temporal relations between experiential episodes, such as E1, E2, etc.? Consider two cases. In the first, the experiences of the same subject have the usual relations of content that obtain for a subject; and the experiences of both same and different subjects possess those similarities of content that go with living in the same, relatively stable, physical world. From such contents, a manifest image world, with flowing time exhibiting A-properties, will emerge. In the second case, imagine that the various episodes, though coherent in themselves, entirely lack the matchings of content that normally go with either psychological continuity or living in a shared world. In this case, there would be no manifest image world, and no common temporal flow which related them. They would simply be separate events without any direct temporal connection. Assuming that these experiential episodes are correlated with brain events that have a place in a physical world accurately described by a scientific account, then they could be ascribed indirect temporal relations with each other, via this connection with 'block time'. But, as was argued in Section 4, experiential episodes are not in the same temporal order as those in the scientific image. It follows that my current stream of experience and a conscious day in the life of William the Conqueror stand in no pure temporal flow relation at all. In an experiential sense, it makes no sense to claim that it was 'a long time ago'. They are merely related to different parts of a causal and explanatory structure that is the scientific image. Of course, if a subject like ourselves had an unbroken flow of experience covering a great period of time, like that from 1066 to the present, it would seem to him to be a long time. Such might be the case for a very anthropomorphic deity, but not for an orthodox one.

However strange these conclusions seem, I think they are the natural consequence of taking seriously the Russellian or 'secondary quality' account of temporal flow defended in Section 3. Rather as, for a Lockean, questions of the type 'what colour is it in the dark?' have only a reductive answer, involving an appeal to dispositions or conditionals, and to experiential episodes that are not part of physical space; so, once one realizes that temporal flow is subjective, one must recognize that time in reality breaks down into a 'scientific' world lacking all of time's phenomenal features, and the experiences which exist outside the temporal order of science's world but which in some sense depend upon the structure within the scientific order. The parallel with space is exact. The public manifest or visual spatial universe is essentially underpinned by an abstract structure that lacks any knowable qualitative content, and which is therefore, not spatially like, in any but a formal sense, the space of experience. The same is true for time.

9. PROVISIONAL CONCLUSION

How does this solve the problem of the self's identity through periods of unconsciousness?

The self is not an object in the abstract, structural time that, if construed realistically, constitutes the physical world. Nor is it within any of the various phenomenal time episodes that it experiences. So far, therefore, it has no temporal gaps within its conscious life, because it has no intrinsic temporal structure. But this conclusion seems far too strong, almost assimilating the human subject to God. There must be some way of allowing for the processes of action and development in the self. The active nature of the self was one of the reasons given for thinking that the self is not in the block universe of science, so it is important to give some positive account of the kind of temporality natural to the self.

10. THE TEMPORALITY OF THOUGHT AND THE SENSE OF SELF

The relation of the self to these temporal systems seems to bear at least some analogy to the one that, according to traditional theology, God has to the created world—though without attributing to the self the specifically divine properties of omniscience, omnipotence, eternity or self-subsistence. God is eternal—that is, outside time altogether—because (*a*) there is no process of change within Him; (*b*) He stands in no spatial relation to anything that does change. His relations to it are those of intellect and will. Unlike God, we are cognitively and affectively related to only a small part of the world, namely to or through our own bodies. And, even within that narrow range, the quality of our contact is only distantly analogous to God's supposed relation. I referred in Section 2 to the case of angelic intelligence. Angels, like God, are outside the physical temporal system, but they are not unchanging, as is God. If Peter Geach is right, the nature of human thought partakes in some way of this bridge position.

Geach (1969: 34–41) has argued that the 'activity of thinking cannot be assigned a position in the physical time-series' (34). The reason for this is that, though the expression out loud, or rehearsal to oneself, of a thought using a sentence will be spread through ordinary time, one's grasp of the content must come as a whole. If it did not, then by the time one had reached '1066' in the sentence 'the Battle of Hastings took place in 1066' one's consciousness of the other components of the thought would have passed into history. What the sentence expresses as a whole is the thought of which one is conscious. Thoughts have a unity that a stream of consciousness or images does not. One possible response to this is that it merely reflects the relative coarseness of grain of 'thought talk' as opposed to precise physical descriptions. Such a coarseness is a common feature of most of our ways of assessing the various processes in the world. But Geach insists that thought is a *basic action*: that is, counting something as a thought is not just a way of bringing something else that is going on under a particular concept. The force of 'interpretationalist' accounts of thought is that what Geach denies is indeed what is happening. I cannot discuss that approach here, but it is part of the framework within which I am writing that interpretationalist theories are false. Much of what I say in this paper could be grudgingly accepted as an accurate reflection of the 'logic' of talk about the self, whilst denying that it has any bedrock ontological content.[4] Just as the fact

---

[4] For a brief discussion of this suggestion with regard to the simplicity of the self, see Robinson 2003*a*: 96–8.

grasped in the *cogito* cannot be reductively analysed without losing its essential point, neither can what it is to think a thought. What I say can be seen as working out the consequences of accepting the 'coarse grain' of talk about thought, whilst still accepting thought as a basic action. Geach associates this with the same approach to time as I have adopted.

The difficulty felt over saying that a thought need be neither long, nor short, nor instantaneous comes about, I suggest, from a (perhaps unacknowledged) assumption of a Newtonian or Kantian view of time: time is taken to be logically prior to events, events, on the other hand, must occupy divisible stretches or else indivisible instants of time. If we reject this view and think instead in terms of time-relations, then what I am suggesting is that thoughts have not got all the kinds of time-relations that physical events, and I think also sensory processes, have. (36)[5]

The position seems thus to be the following. The expression of a thought in a sentence is spread out in the normal 'flowing' empirical time. But the thinking of the thought which, in some sense, 'lies behind' (but not necessarily temporally before) this, is not temporally structured in the same way. Something which is implicit in the thought is laid out explicitly in the sentence. One experiences a thought *in* a sentence—or sometimes in other, non-verbal, images—but as a unity that a string of sounds or images does not possess. A point that Geach does not make in this context is that without its empirical expression the thought remains, in a sense, hidden even from its thinker. Without the expression in simple sensory consciousness, one does not have an explicit grasp on one's own thought; but conscious understanding of a thought is not just consciousness of its vehicle, plus certain dispositions. The kind of implicitness which characterizes pure thought is present in much of our mental life, including our sense of our own identity.

Imagine two conscious subjects, *A* and *B*, who have exactly the same current explicit states of consciousness. What I mean by this is that their sense fields seem just the same, and their current conscious thoughts and desires and emotions are exactly the same. But *A* and *B* have entirely different histories; it is just a coincidence that their normal conscious states are exactly similar at that moment. The question is: is what it feels like to be *A* at that time just like what it feels like to be *B*? On the one hand, the way I have described the situation might seem to entail that it is. What can 'what it feels like to be *X*' depend on, other than his conscious states; after all, 'feels like' refers to consciousness. On the other hand, it seems to me that one's memories condition what it feels like to be oneself, even when those memories are not part of explicit consciousness. One might be tempted to unpack this latter thought conditionally. If asked about

[5] I reread Geach's article, for the first time in some decades, only when a draft of this paper was well advanced, and after I had included the reference to Kant and Newton in Section 2. Geach's paper encourages me to think that the line I am taking is more respectable for an analytical philosopher than I had feared.

their past or their beliefs, *A* and *B* would give quite different answers. This is true and important, but it seems to me that there is something current and implicit in the subject's sense of himself that underlies at least some of such responses. Adapting Berkeley's jargon, one might say that part of the *notion* that we have of ourselves includes an implicit or tacit grasp on much information not currently being rehearsed, explicitly, in consciousness. It is still in some broader sense part of the phenomenology of our current existence. (Some useful thoughts on this can be found in Slors (2004), and in his development of the idea of *diachronic mental holism*.)

What is needed for an adequate theory of the self is a framework within which one can explain both the implicit and the explicit forms of the self's self-understanding and expression. My suspicion is that the metaphysical psychology of Plotinus and the empirical (if one can call it that) psychology of Jung give one material for developing such an account. That, however, would be another essay, and one not yet developed to the point where it is fit for the eyes and minds of properly rigorous analytical philosophers!

11. CONCLUSION

The argument of this paper has been both counterintuitive and convoluted. It might help, therefore, to summarize the positions presupposed or defended and look briefly at the metaphysical interpretations of them that are available. The positions, and the location of the relevant discussions in the body of the text, are as follows:

(i) There are simple, immaterial selves (initial assumption, § 1).

(ii) These selves stand in an awareness relation to contents that, taken individually, possess proto-temporal properties. The contents are proto-temporal because, taken individually, the nature of the experience is not sufficient either to constitute or to guarantee the existence of any genuine time series. The awareness relation should not be characterized using temporal concepts ('(temporally) *present* to', § 2). These contents will be part of an A- and-B-property-possessing temporal flow iff, both:

(iii) the individual experiences are S(uccession)-related, and

(iv) there is an appropriate kind of continuity in the contents of the experiences in the series (§ 3). (ii) to (iv) give an account of one continuous period of consciousness of the individual self.

(v) Temporality in the life of the self across several such periods is constituted by appropriate memory-type matchings of content (§ 8).

(vi) The full manifest image world, and its associated temporal flow arises if different subjects' experiences harmonize in the appropriate way (§ 8).

(vii) The structural features of the manifest image are elaborated and explained in the scientific image (§ 5).

(viii) The time of the manifest image world is a different time from that of the scientific image (§ 4).

(ix) And the temporality of thought is different from either (§10), though this is not properly explored in this essay.

(x) Because the two images are in different times, it would not be helpful to talk of an event in one of these realms *causing* one in the other, but it is correct to say that events in the manifest image happen *because of* events in the scientific picture. And, if one has a libertarian account of freedom, one will think that events occur in the scientific image because of things brought about in the manifest world (§ 8).

This last point raises the question of how the relationship between these two realms, the manifest and the scientific, is to be understood. As they are temporally distinct realms, it might seem odd to think of the 'because' invoked in the previous paragraph as a causal one: causes, it might be said, either *precede* or are *simultaneous with* their effects, and these are temporal notions, presupposing that both events are in the same time series. The issue is not quite so straightforward, however. The point of the emphasis on precedence or simultaneity of causes is to rule out backward causation: in other words, it concerns events within the same time series, and says nothing about relations between events in different series. So exactly what the nature of the 'because' is, might depend on which of the following theories one adopts.

(A) Realism with mono-temporalism. According to this theory, the scientific image presents the definitive picture of physical reality and, therefore, of physical time. If the manifest world and the experiences on which it is based can be integrated into the scientific image, then materialist monism is true; if it cannot, then there is some sort of dualism. Nevertheless, whether dualistic or monistic about substances, this theory is monistic about time, *and is the picture this paper has been seeking to replace.*

(B) Realism with temporal pluralism. This is the realist version of the theory for which I have been arguing. The manifest world and the scientific one are both real, and they are separate temporal realms. Things happen in one *because of* things in the other; and, because of the temporal disconnection, this may seem mysterious. Perhaps this theory calls for some kind of occasionalism; perhaps there can be causal influence across temporal realms. Unhappiness with these options might lead one to prefer one of the following accounts.

(C) 'Kantian' conceptual pluralism.[6] The intrinsic nature of reality—if that expression means anything—can only be accessed by means of various kinds

---

[6] I am well aware that this is a multiply deviant use of 'Kantian', but, in this context, I am merely using the name to signify the fact that there is a radical divide between the world as it is 'in itself' and as it is when presented within a certain conceptual framework.

of conceptualization. The manifest image that flows from experience is one of these, and the scientific is another. Because neither is to be interpreted in a simple realist way, there is no need to synthesize them into one unitary account. Amongst other things, their notions of time are different; but because they are both attempts at understanding the same reality, it makes sense to say that events picked out in one way occur *because of* events designated in the other.

(D) The Berkeleian interpretation. On this theory, the scientific image represents either the divine blueprint for the world of experience, or our best approximation to it. Its atemporality is to be explained by its status as a blueprint or template, rather than as embodying a different kind of time. Whilst, in a sense, the manifest world is the only real empirical world, it would be incomplete without the scientific image that represents its intellectual underpinning.

The present author prefers some version of (D), but the more secular-minded reader might be tempted by (C).

REFERENCES

Broad, C. D. (1923). *Scientific Thought*. London: Routledge and Kegan Paul.

Crisp, T. M. (2003). 'Presentism', in Loux and Zimmerman, 211–45.

Dainton, B. (2001). *Time and Space*. Chesham: Acumen.

Davies, B. (2003). 'Letter from America', *New Blackfriars*, 84.

Gale, R. M. (ed.) (1968). *The Philosophy of Time: A Collection of Essays*. London: Macmillan.

Geach, P. (1969). 'What do we think with?', in his *God and the Soul.* Cambridge: Cambridge University Press, 30–41.

Grünbaum, A. (1968). 'The Status of Becoming', in his *Modern Science and Zeno's Paradoxes*. London: George Allen and Unwin. Also in Gale (1968: 322–54).

Helm, P. (1988). *Eternal God*. Oxford: Clarendon Press.

James, W. (1901). *Principles of Psychology*, i. London: Macmillan.

Lewis, D. (1983). 'Survival and Identity', in Lewis, *Philosophical Papers*, i. Oxford: Oxford University Press, 55–77.

Loux, M., and D. Zimmerman (eds.) (2003). *The Oxford Handbook of Metaphysics*. Oxford: Oxford University Press.

Mabbott, J. D. (1951). 'Our Direct Experience of Time', *Mind*, 60. Repr. in Gale (1968).

McTaggart, J. M. E. (1927). *The Nature of Existence*, ii, bk V, ch. 33. Cambridge: Cambridge University Press. Repr. in Gale (1968).

Madell, G. (1981). *The Identity of the Self*. Edinburgh: Edinburgh University Press.

Mellor, D. H. (1998). *Real Time II*. London: Routledge.

Robinson, H. (1987). 'A Dualist Perspective on Psychological Development', in J. Russell (ed.), *Philosophical Perspectives on Developmental Psychology*. Oxford: Blackwell, 119–39.

_____ (2003*a*). 'Dualism', in S. Stich and T. Warfield (eds.), *The Blackwell Guide to the Philosophy of Mind*. Oxford: Blackwell, 85–101.

_____ (2003*b*). 'The Ontology of the Mental', in Loux and Zimmerman (2003: 527–55).

Russell, B. (1912/1959). *The Problems of Philosophy*. New York: Oxford University Press.
_____ (1915). 'On the Experience of Time'. *Monist*, 25: 212–33.
Slors, M. (2004). 'Care for One's Own Future Experiences'. *Philosophical Explorations*, 7: 183–95.
Swinburne, R. with Sydney Shoemaker (1984). *Personal Identity*. Oxford: Blackwell.

PART II

DUALISM

3

Cartesian Dualism

John Hawthorne

In this short paper, I shall examine some key structural features of Descartes's metaphysics, as it relates to mind–body dualism. The style of presentation will partly be one of rational reconstruction, designed to present the Cartesian system in a way that will be of maximal interest to contemporary metaphysicians. Section 1 focuses on five key Cartesian theses about principal attributes. Sections 2 and 3 examine how those theses play themselves out in Descartes's discussion of mind–body dualism.

1. FIVE AXIOMS CONCERNING PRINCIPAL ATTRIBUTES

Let me begin by presenting five axioms concerning principal attributes that, as we shall see, play a key role in Descartes's thinking about the relation of mind to body.

A Cartesian principal attribute is a kind of property to which the following five distinctive principles apply:

Axiom 1. COMPLETENESS: Principal attributes are complete.

Axiom 2. ESSENTIALITY: If a substance has properties belonging to some principal attribute, then it is essential to that substance that is has properties belonging to that attribute.

Axiom 3. UNIQUENESS: If a thing x has properties belonging to a principal attribute, then it has a part y which has that principal attribute as its only principal attribute.

Axiom 4. COMPREHENSIVENESS: For each fundamental property of a thing, there is some principal attribute of the thing that it belongs to.

Axiom 5. EXCLUSIVITY: No fundamental property belongs to more than one principal attribute.

I am grateful to Maya Eddon, David Manley, Dean Zimmerman, and especially Tamar Szabo Gendler for comments on an earlier draft of this paper.

In the remainder of this section, I will say more about what these axioms amount to.

Axiom 1. COMPLETENESS

A kind of property is *complete* iff it is possible that there be a thing whose fundamental intrinsic properties all belong to that kind. We can see Completeness at work in Descartes's replies to the first set of objections to the *Meditations*, where Descartes rejects motion as a candidate principal attribute:

> I can very well understand the motion apart from the shape, and vice versa . . . But I cannot have a complete understanding of the motion apart from the thing in which motion occurs . . . and I cannot imagine there to be motion in something which is incapable of possessing shape.[1]

The reason motion could not be a principal attribute is that it is not complete: there could not be an object whose only fundamental intrinsic properties were motion properties.

It is important to note that the completeness constraint applies only to *fundamental* intrinsic properties. Consider the kind *thinking*. It is clearly not possible that there be a being all of whose intrinsic properties belong to that kind: after all, a purely ratiocinative substance would also have the intrinsic property of not being a banana. Does that mean that thinking could not be a principal attribute, since a thinking thing would also be a non-banana thing? The natural response here is to appeal to a distinction between fundamental and derivate intrinsic properties—akin to David Lewis's distinction between perfectly natural and (more or less) gerrymandered intrinsic properties[2]—and to restrict completeness accordingly. This makes it possible to attach good sense to the idea that the profile of some substance might be exhausted by its mental life, so that 'whatever we find in mind is simply one of the various modes of thinking'.[3]

That said, it is worth remarking that in Descartes's hands the notion of a fundamental property is given a particular spin. Descartes distinguishes those properties that exist in things from those properties that exist merely as 'modes of thinking'. This means, roughly, that there are predicates which express concepts but for which there are no corresponding properties in things. For example, he treats existence and duration as properties that exist only as modes of thinking and thus does not reckon existence a challenge to the completeness of mentality,

---

[1] The Philosophical Writings of Descartes, vol. ii, ed. John Cottingham, Robert Stoothoff, and Dugald Murdock (hereafter CSM) (Cambridge: Cambridge University Press, 1984), 86. (vol. i is 1985, vol. iii 1991.)

[2] See e.g. his 'New Work for a Theory of Universals', *Australasian Journal of Philosophy*, 61 (1983), 343–77.

[3] CSM, i. 210.

even though existence and duration are not intuitively mental.[4] For Descartes, then, the properties relevant to completeness are those that exist in the object. (Obviously, someone might accept something like the principle outlined above without endorsing the Cartesian conception of the fundamental properties of an object.)[5]

Axioms 2 and 3. ESSENTIALITY, UNIQUENESS

Regarding 2. Principal attributes constitute the nature of a substance; they could not do this unless essentiality held.

Regarding 3. Descartes distinguishes simple from composite substances. A composite substance may have more than one principal attribute, but a simple substance exemplifies only one principal attribute. And wherever there is a composite substance with some principal attribute, it has as a component some non-composite substance with that principal attribute. (Note that our concern here is with 'parts' not 'proper parts': if y is non-composite, then the part of y relevant to the principle may be y itself.)

Axioms 4 and 5. COMPREHENSIVENESS and EXCLUSIVITY

Regarding 4. All the fundamental properties of a substance are modes of a principal attribute: if a substance *s* exemplifies a fundamental property p, then p exemplifies a principal attribute associated with *s*.

Regarding 4 and 5. Related challenges to Comprehensiveness and/or Exclusivity can be handled with the strategies introduced in the discussion of Completeness. So, for example, existence can't be treated as fundamental, since either one will have to deny that it belongs to the principal attributes—violating Comprehensiveness—or else treat it as belonging to all of them—violating Exclusivity.

General Remarks

Quite obviously, the axioms are interconnected. For example, and notably, the thesis that it is possible that something have some principal attribute A, together with Uniqueness and Comprehensiveness, entail that A is Complete.

---

[4] See Principle LVII of *Principles of Philosophy*, CSM, i. 212.
[5] Philosophers fond of the Cartesian system who are unhappy with Descartes's conceptualist/anti-realist treatment of a large class of properties will have to look for a different fix for the case of existence and persistence: either claim that existing and persisting are not fundamental in the relevant sense, or else formulate these axioms in a way that sets to one side certain very general properties.

I have spoken of principal attributes as kinds of properties and particular fundamental properties as belonging to kinds. It would hardly be true to the Cartesian vision to think of principal attributes as properties of properties and construe 'belonging to' as 'instantiation'. Far better to think of principal attributes and their modes on the familiar model of determinables and determinates. Principal attributes are determinables for which the above five axioms hold. Modes are determinates of those determinables.[6] Predicates which express neither those determinables nor their modes do not express any fundamental property at all—which, on a Cartesian spin, means that these predicates express modes of thinking about a thing that can be true of the thing despite the fact that they do not correspond to any real property in the thing.

2. THE FIVE AXIOMS AND MIND–BODY DUALISM

According to Descartes, thinking and extension are the only two principal attributes exemplified by God's creatures. If we assume that this is true and that the above five axioms govern principal attributes, many of the familiar features of Cartesian dualism follow as a result. Given Completeness, and the fact that thinking and extension are principal attributes, it follows both that it is possible that there be things that are purely thinking (i.e. whose fundamental intrinsic profile is entirely mental) and there be things that are purely geometrical (i.e. whose fundamental intrinsic profile is entirely geometrical). Given Uniqueness, it follows, moreover, that any possible thinking thing has a part that has thinking as its only principal attribute and that any possible extended thing has a part that has extension as its only principal attribute. Given Comprehensiveness, it follows moreover that any possible thinking thing has a part that is purely thinking (i.e. whose fundamental properties all belong to the attribute thinking) and any possible extended being has a part that is purely geometrical (i.e. whose fundamental properties all belong to the attribute extension). Given Exclusivity, it follows that any possible thinking thing has a part that is thinking and not extended and any possible extended thing has a part that is extended and does not think.

Let us see some of these themes at work in the Cartesian texts. I shall begin with Completeness, which Descartes famously deploys in his replies to the fourth set of objections of the *Meditations* (by Antoine Arnauld). Arnauld complains that nothing interesting follows from the fact that we can be certain of our thinking even while imagining that there are no bodies, urging that this is perfectly consistent with the hypothesis that being embodied is essential to us. He points out that our facility with the relevant imaginative exercise may simply

---

[6] Or, on some of Descartes's uses, trope-like instances of determinates.

be due to the fact that we fail to notice that embodiment is essential to us. He draws an analogy, suggesting that someone might know

for certain that the angle in a semi-circle is a right angle. . . . In spite of this, he may doubt, or not yet have grasped for certain, that the square on the hypoteneuse is equal to the squares on the other two sides; indeed he may even deny this if he is misled by some fallacy.[7]

Descartes replies by distinguishing between adequate and complete understanding. For understanding to be adequate, one has to appreciate all the properties of a thing. But for an understanding of a thing to be complete one has merely to understand it to be 'a complete thing'. He goes on:

the mind can be perceived distinctly and completely (that is, sufficiently for it to be considered as a complete thing) without any of the forms or attributes by which we recognize that body is a substance, as I think I showed quite adequately in the Second Meditation. And similarly a body can be understood distinctly and as a complete thing, without any of the attributes which belong to the mind.[8]

The key thought is that while the relevant understanding is not adequate, it is complete; and this is enough to underwrite a real distinction between mind and body. He makes some similar remarks in correspondence with Gibieuf:

[T]he idea of a substance with extension and shape is a complete idea, because I can conceive it entirely on its own, and deny of it everything else of which I have an idea. Now it seems to me that the idea which I have of a thinking substance is complete in this sense.[9]

I do not on that account deny that there can be in the soul or the body many properties of which I have no ideas; I deny only that there are any which are inconsistent with the ideas of them I do have, including the idea that I have of their distinctness.[10]

It is fairly clear what is going on here. Descartes is claiming, *inter alia*, to be able to see that the kind *thinking* satisfies the criterion of completeness. He does not pretend to have an adequate conception of his own mind: there may be mental properties of his that he is unaware of (just as there are geometrical properties of a right-angled triangle that he is unaware of). But he claims to be able to see that a thing could exist 'entirely on its own' with nothing but mental properties in its fundamental intrinsic make-up. He presumes, moreover, that he can see that mental properties do not suffice for bodily properties—after all, it seems clear that a mentalistic groundfloor could not suffice for extension. And thus Descartes may claim to have successfully conceived of a substance that has mentality but no corporeality, even as he admits that he does not have an 'adequate' understanding of such a thing (similarly, *mutatis mutandis*, for corporeal substance). The relevant exercise of thinking of a mental substance

[7] CSM, ii. 141–2. [8] CSM, ii. 157. [9] CSM, iii. 202. [10] CSM, iii. 203.

without thinking of it as corporeal substance is not a mere abstraction: it involves a positive modal insight that there be a thing whose entire intrinsic life is mental.[11]

No wonder Descartes is unmoved by Arnauld. Given that he takes himself to have successfully conceived of a substance whose fundamental intrinsic character is mental, the only residual concern is that extension might arise as an unnoticed but inevitable epiphenomenon of certain mental properties in a way that certain geometrical properties attach unavoidably to certain types of geometrical configurations. But one can consistently and reasonably claim to know that this couldn't happen. One doesn't need to have a comprehensive understanding of an individual's profile (where a profile is the complete set of its intrinsic properties) in order to know that certain kinds of properties are not necessitated by it; knowing that all the fundamental members of the profile are of a certain type will be a sufficient basis for the relevant knowledge.

(Contemporary philosophers could certainly join Arnauld in complaining about Descartes's claim to have recognized completeness for the kind *thinking* (construed as mentality). Such philosophers would probably concede the prima facie possibility of a thing whose basic intrinsic profile is entirely mental, but would question the trustworthiness of the relevant intuitions given what they take to be the best, all things considered, metaphysical perspective on the world. I do not wish to engage with those philosophers here.)

Suppose that thinking is complete. That, by itself, leaves a number of issues untouched. First, it does not settle whether all, some, or no possible thinking things are *essentially* thinking things. Second, it does not settle whether *I* have as a part something that is thinking but not corporeal. Even granting the possibility of a thing whose entire fundamental profile is mental (a consequence of the completeness of mentality) and which lacks corporeality (a consequence of the fact that no mental profile is sufficient for corporeality), it hardly follows immediately that every possible thinking thing has a part that is incorporeal. Certain of Descartes's contemporaries suggested that thought and extension may be metaphysically independent, but compresent in us:

since these attributes are not opposites but merely different, there is no reason why the mind should not be a sort of attribute co-existing with extension in the same subject, though the one attribute is not included in the concept of the other.[12]

The axioms outlined above offer definitive answers to these further questions. Descartes articulates them most clearly in his *Principles of Philosophy*. In Principle LIII he endorses Uniqueness and Essentiality:

---

[11] To De Launay: 'When things are separated only by a mental abstraction, you cannot help noticing their conjunction and union when you consider them together. But in the case of body and soul, you cannot see any such connection. CSM, iii. 188.

[12] CSM, i. 294–5. The author is Regius, quoted by Descartes in *Comments on a Certain Broadsheet*.

each substance has one principal property which constitutes its nature and essence, and on which all the others are referred.[13]

He then gives voice to Comprehensiveness:

Everything else which can be attributed to body presupposes extension, and is merely a mode of an extended thing; and similarly, whatever we find in the mind is simply one of the various modes of thinking.[14]

A commitment to Exclusivity is then immediately apparent a few lines later in his injunction to 'carefully separate all the attributes of thought from those of extension'.[15]

Given an unwavering commitment to these axioms, one would expect Descartes to have no patience whatsoever with the idea that thought and extension can combine in a substance, unless that thesis is one about composite substances.[16] For given his commitments, there is no room for a simple substance that combines those attributes. And that is precisely the attitude we find. Thus in response to Regius, he says:

when the question concerns attributes which constitute the essence of some substances, there can be no greater opposition between them than the fact that they are different. . . .

As for the attributes which constitute the natures of things, it cannot be said that those which are different, and such that the concept of the one is not contained in the concept of the other, are present together in one and the same subject; for that would be equivalent to saying that one and the same subject has two different natures—a statement that implies a contradiction, at least when it is a question of a simple subject (as in the present case) rather than a composite one.[17]

3. THE JUSTIFICATION OF UNIQUENESS

There is nothing surprising about these remarks given Descartes's background commitments—but they don't take us far in understanding why those commitments are there in the first place. We have seen already that a mere commitment to Completeness will not yet support a commitment to the other theses. The

[13] CSM, i. 210. Uniqueness follows from this in combination with the thesis that all entities are composed of substances.

[14] CSM, i. 210.

[15] He explains in LVI that he is using 'mode' as a name of attributes—the point of that use being to highlight the fact that attributes are modifications of substance.

[16] Note that Descartes's use of 'composite' is rather special. He tells us that 'A composite entity is one which is found to have two or more attributes, each one of which can be distinctly understood apart from the other.' CSM, i. 299. This means that having parts is not sufficient for being composite in Descartes's sense: a purely extended thing has parts, but is not composite since it does not have diverse principal attributes. For Descartes, then, composite means having a composite nature/essence. Given Uniqueness, having parts is necessary but not sufficient for being composite.

[17] CSM, i. 298.

status of Uniqueness is particularly pressing in this regard. Why is Descartes so convinced that things with a mixed nature are composed of things with a simple nature? It is to that question I now turn.

To begin, we should note that Uniqueness has a special appeal within a framework that reckons all the fundamental properties to be either mental or geometrical. Descartes thought the patterns of motion of extended substance provided a supervenience base for everything else in the corporeal world; the four-dimensional geometry of the spatio-temporal manifold fixes everything else. Properties such as mass, color, and so on are not fundamental: they reduce to geometrical facts about the manifold. Nor did Descartes believe in *occupants* of space: he identified matter with space itself. In essence the corporeal world is a world of moving regions of space.

Within such a framework, the hypothesis that at the most basic level there are things that are both extended and thinking is tantamount to the hypothesis that some regions of space think, are conscious, and so on. Should we be so scornful of Descartes's confidence that this was impossible? After all, most philosophers will find it obviously impossible that the number 3 thinks, or that a particular moment in time thinks. Such a commitment relies on our having some kind of modal insight as to what sorts of things can think; and there may be no better reason to think that a region of space could think than that a moment of time or a natural number could think. (Granted, Cartesian regions do not just sit there; they move like a fluid. But granting that static container space could not think, it is hard to see how the mere addition of movement will help much.) Assuming the background metaphysics of corporeal substance, the view that body and mind do not mix at the fundamental level is rather compelling.

Let me now elaborate on the justification Descartes actually gives for Uniqueness, articulated in the following famous passage from Meditation Six:

Hence the fact that I can clearly and distinctly understand one thing apart from another is enough to make me certain that the two things are distinct, since they are capable of being separated, at least by God.[18]

The same theme is frequently reiterated. For example:

the only criterion that we have enabling us to know that one substance differs from another is that we understand one apart from the other.[19]

It is not immediately clear how these passages are supposed to engage an opponent who holds that he is a substance which both thinks and is extended and who denies that he has a merely thinking part. Talk of 'one thing' and 'another' seems already to presuppose there are two substances in view. If there is only one thing to begin with, then there is no *other* thing to be understood apart from it. Meanwhile, if Descartes means to apply the thesis not to things but to

---

[18] CSM, ii. 54.   [19] CSM, iii. 214. To Regius.

conceptions of things, the idea is altogether hopeless: for it ought to have been obvious to him that there can be two concepts ('modes of presentation') of the same thing that can with perfect coherence be thought of as applying to different things.

I think it is illuminating to set these passages alongside Descartes's attack on the coherence of extended atoms. Here are some representative passages:

[A]n indivisible thing cannot have any length or breadth or depth. If it had, we could divide it at least in our imagination, which would suffice to guarantee that it was not indivisible: for if we could divide it in imagination, an angel could divide it in reality.[20]

I say that it involves a contradiction that there should be any atoms which are conceived as extended and at the same time indivisible. Though God might make them such that they could not be divided by any creature, we certainly cannot understand that he might deprive himself of the power of dividing them.[21]

Both cases (minds and atoms) rely on dividing things in imagination. In each case, a real distinction is then inferred. Excessive preoccupation with the status of that inference obscures a more basic question. What does it mean to 'divide something in imagination'? Certainly there are situations of ignorance where, in some sense, we divide things in our imagination. Suppose one thought (falsely) that an angel, say the angel Gabriel, is some complex union of body and soul. One might 'divide Gabriel in imagination', but that would show nothing—one's imaginative exercise is grounded on a false conception of the angel. On the other hand, one cannot insist that imaginative exercises 'count' only if they are based on complete knowledge about a thing. For complete knowledge about a thing would carry the information whether or not it was complex: in that case, one wouldn't need to use one's imagination to test for mereological complexity.

Let me suggest one helpful reconstruction of the Cartesian perspective. I shall begin by focusing on the *simple monadic profile* of things. The simple monadic profile of *s* consists of the set of *s*'s simple fundamental monadic properties. Monadic properties built out of relations—like being five feet from the Eiffel Tower, or having multiple parts, do not count as simple; but being extended, thinking, being rectangular, being in pain do count. One further stipulation: we shall say that a simple monadic profile x is possibly divided into subsets y and z iff it is possible that there exists a being whose simple monadic profile is x and which has parts that compose it whose simple monadic profiles are y and z respectively.

Certain paradigmatic Cartesian exercises in modal imagination involve coming to know that some simple monadic profile x possibly divides into subsets y and z. But such exercises will not by themselves permit one to deduce that a thing with x actually has parts that have y and z respectively. That some possible thing with x subdivides in that way does not show that everything with x does.

[20] CSM, iii. 155. To Mersenne.   [21] CSM, iii. 363. To More.

Descartes seems to have endorsed a certain picture concerning how our understanding is configured, namely:

> *Understanding.* If some simple monadic profile x is possibly divided into y and z, then we are disposed to clearly and distinctly think of anything with x as being composed of something with y and something with z.

He combines this with a basic trust in the calibration of understanding to reality:

> *Calibration.* If our understanding clearly and distinctly divides something in imagination, then that thing is divided in reality.

For this package to run smoothly, one of two scenarios must obtain. Either (i) God was kind enough not to actualize any being whose monadic profile is possibly divided in a certain way but which is itself not actually divided in that way, or else (ii) the following thesis holds:

> *Necessitation.* If simple monadic profile x is possibly divided into subsets y and z then x is necessarily divided into subsets y and z.

The latter thesis is the alternative that best captures Descartes's perspective.[22]

Rather than dwell on predictable worries about Calibration, let us focus on Necessitation itself. That thesis delivers a prohibition on extended atoms. Given that we can see that a region of a certain extension and shape could be composed of smaller subregions, if follows from Necessitation that extended atoms are impossible. And it delivers a route to Uniqueness: given that any simple monadic profile of a being that thinks and is extended could attach to a composite of a being that is merely mental and a being that is merely geometrical, it follows from Necessitation that any profile of that kind necessarily attaches to a being composed of a merely mental and a merely geometrical being.

Now some of us will be quite ready to relinquish the Necessitation thesis. But it is at least worth pausing to acknowledge one potential cost of eschewing it. Just as one might ask after principles concerning the conditions under which a plurality compose a thing, one might also think that there are perfectly general and informative principles concerning the conditions under which a thing *decomposes* into a plurality. Now, obviously, a thing's total intrinsic makeup determines whether it decomposes into a plurality, since whether it has proper parts is

---

[22] My discussion has oversimplified matters somewhat. Given that our knowledge is not adequate—in the Cartesian sense—our minds never engage with complete descriptive information about the monadic profile of a thing. What we in fact do, according to Descartes, is to know enough about the simple monadic profile of a thing to know that its profile is possibly divided into profiles of certain types. That said, the basic mechanism is as above: we are so constituted that insofar as we know that a thing's simple monadic profile is possibly divided into certain kinds of profiles, we are disposed to think (with an internal fanfare suitable to clearness and distinctness) that the thing to which the profile belongs is divided in a corresponding way. And given that our minds are calibrated to reality, such thoughts are unerring.

intrinsic to it. But are there any general and informative principles concerning decomposition?

What bears emphasis is that if Necessitation is wrong, then that makes real trouble for the view that there are such principles.[23] After all, a denial of Necessitation means that there are pairs of possible objects that are duplicates with respect to their simple monadic profile but which differ with respect to mereological complexity. Suppose, for example, that we were to allow for the possibility of a five inch diametrical spherical object that was red all over that decomposed into a plurality of smaller parts, and also the possibility of a five inch diametrical spherical object that was red all over that had no proper parts. Once counterexamples to Necessitation like this are admitted, it seems hardly likely that any informative sufficiency condition for simplicity or complexity can hold of either member of the pair. Now some of us have learnt to live with this and have learnt to recognize that there is no deep incoherence in the putative possibility of extended simples (and thus that the kind of rationalist dream behind Necessitation is chimerical). But we are, I think, in the minority. Those who agree with Descartes that extended atoms are impossible may very well find Necessitation appealing. Where else might they complain?

4. CONCLUDING REMARKS

Our rational reconstruction of Descartes has taken something like the following shape

(1) *Necessitation.* If a simple monadic profile x is possibly divided into subsets y and z, then x is necessarily divided into subsets y and z.

(2) *Possible Division.* The simple monadic profile of any human being x is possibly divided into a subset of fundamental properties pertaining to (conscious) mentality and a subset of fundamental properties pertaining to corporeality.

Therefore

(3) Every human being is composed of a part that is purely mental and a part that is purely corporeal.

The argument is clearly valid. So if we assume Necessitation, the only line of resistance will be a denial of (2). One challenge to (2) relates to the issue of Completeness above: can there be a thing whose entire intrinsic life is mental and which has no corporeal properties? Can there be a thing whose entire intrinsic life is corporeal and which has no mental properties? But that is not the only possible reason for complaining about premise (2). Even if we grant that there

---

[23] At least insofar as they take the form of sufficiency conditions.

could be a zombie that corporeally duplicates me but which has no consciousness that coexists with a non-corporeal being whose entire intrinsic life duplicates mine, and even if we grant that such things could interact, is it clear that the union of those beings would be a simple monadic duplicate of me? For example, it might be argued that while I instantiate consciousness, consciousness would not be instantiated by that union (only by its incorporeal part). In this way, there may be a disanalogy between the application of Necessitation to prohibit extended atoms and its use in securing Uniqueness.

I don't suppose that the above discussion will persuade fence-sitters to endorse a Cartesian metaphysics. Nor do I pretend to have made significant advances in Cartesian scholarship. But I hope to have done something to show that serious intellectual engagement with the Cartesian system—as opposed to frivolous dismissal of its pale caricature—may be metaphysically fruitful.

4

Materialism and Christian Belief

Alvin Plantinga

According to *materialism*, human persons are material objects. They are not immaterial things, or objects, or substances; neither do they contain as parts immaterial selves or souls or entelechies. Their parts are material: flesh and bones and blood, molecules, atoms, electrons and quarks (if in fact there are such things). This view, of course, goes contrary to the vast bulk of the Christian tradition. This is not to say, *pace* Plato (or anyway Socrates), that the body is the prison house of the soul, or that our present attachment to the body is to be deplored, as if it were a temporary, makeshift arrangement (due to sin?) to be jettisoned in the next life. Not at all; on the traditional Christian view, God has designed human beings to have bodies; they function properly only if embodied; and of course Christians look forward to the resurrection of the body. My body is crucial to my well-being and I can flourish only if embodied. As W. H. Auden put it, "I wouldn't be caught dead without my body."

Materialism goes contrary to the Christian tradition; even worse (so I'll argue), it is false. As I see it, therefore, Christian philosophers ought to be dualists. Now most naturalists, of course, are materialists; but so are a surprising number of Christian philosophers.[1] I'll argue that this is a mistake. In "Against Materialism"[2] I also argue that materialism is false. This paper covers some of the same ground as that one. It differs in that it omits a couple of sections; it

In addition to the people mentioned in the text, I thank Michael Bergmann, E. J. Coffman, Evan Fales, Richard Fumerton, Trenton Merricks, William Ramsey, and the members of the Notre Dame Center for Philosophy of Religion discussion group, in particular Thomas Flint and Peter van Inwagen, as well as the others I have inadvertently overlooked.

[1] See e.g. Peter van Inwagen, *Material Beings* (Ithaca, NY: Cornell University Press, 1990), and "Dualism and Materialism: Athens and Jerusalem?", *Faith and Philosophy*, 12/4 (Oct. 1995), 475–88; Trenton Merricks, "The Resurrection of the Body and the Life Everlasting", in Michael Murray (ed.), *Reason for the Hope Within* (Grand Rapids, Mich. Eerdmans, 1999); Nancey Murphy "Human Nature: Historical, Scientific, and Religious Issues", in *Whatever Happened to the Soul?* (Minneapolis: Fortress Press, 1998), 1–30; Lynne Rudder Baker, "Need a Christian Be a Mind/Body Dualist?", *Faith and Philosophy*, 12/4 (Oct. 1995), 498–504; and Kevin Corcoran, "Persons and Bodies", *Faith and Philosophy*, 15/3 (July 1998), 324–40.

[2] In *Faith and Philosophy*, 23/1 (January 2006), 3–32.

also adds sections dealing with (1) the alleged arguments for materialism, and (2) the relevance of Christian theism to the question, and (3) an appendix dealing with the way in which materialists try to explain how it could be that a material structure or event could be a belief. With respect to (2), there are, I believe, at least three points to be made. First, there is Scripture; the New Testament in particular contains much that at any rate strongly suggests that materialism is false. Second, Christian theism is crucially relevant to the epistemology of the situation, and that in at least two ways:

(*a*) Given Christian theism, we know that it is at any rate *possible* that there be immaterial thinking things. God Himself is an immaterial thinking thing; hence, by the argument form *ab esse ad posse*, the most powerful argument for possibility, it follows that immaterial thinking things are possible. Furthermore, Christian theism strongly suggests that there are *created* immaterial thinking things: angels, for example, as well as Satan and his minions.

(*b*) Considerations from the Christian faith are powerfully relevant to the alleged objections to dualism and arguments for materialism.[3]

Finally, certain crucial Christian doctrines (for example, Incarnation and the resurrection of the dead) fit better—much better, I'd say—with dualism than with materialism.

I'll restrict myself, for the most part, to the second of these three points. Section 1 of this paper will follow "Against Materialism" in presenting a couple of "strictly philosophical" arguments against materialism; in Section 2 I'll turn to the considerations from Christian theism.

1. TWO ARGUMENTS FOR DUALISM

Christian philosophers, so I say, should be dualists; but of course dualism itself is multiple, if not legion. There is the view—embraced by Plato, Augustine, Calvin, Descartes, and a thousand others—according to which a human person is an immaterial substance: a thing, an object, a substance, a suppositum (for my Thomist colleagues), and a thing that isn't material. Second, there is the view the name 'dualism' suggests: the view according to which a human person is somehow a sort of composite substance S composed of a material substance S* and an immaterial substance S**.[4]

Third, there is also the important but obscure view of Thomas Aquinas and his followers. Is this a form of dualism? The question is vexed. According to Aquinas,

---

[3] Substance dualism and materialism are not uncontroversial contradictories (perhaps, as some suggest, we aren't substances at all, but events, or maybe momentary collections of mental states, or transtemporal collections of person states or stages). For present purposes, however, I'll take it that substance dualism and materialism are the only relevant positions, and speak indifferently of arguments for materialism and arguments against dualism.

[4] See Richard Swinburne, *The Evolution of the Soul* (Oxford: Clarendon Press, 1986), 145.

a human person is a material substance with an immaterial part, the soul. Aquinas says, of this immaterial part, that it is itself a substance. Furthermore the soul, this immaterial part, has the property of possibly thinking (believing, desiring, hoping, deciding, etc.), and after death, *does* think. But Aquinas, also says that the soul is *the form of* the body.[5] A form, however, at least as far as I can see, is or is like a *property*; and a property, presumably, *can't* think. If the soul is a form, therefore, how can it be capable of thinking?[6] This is a tough question, but perhaps we needn't go into it at the moment. A more pressing question is this: I'll be arguing that it is possible that I exist when my body doesn't; is that a possibility, on Thomas's view? True, on his view my *soul* can exist when my body doesn't; but it also seems, on this view, that I am not identical with my soul. Rather, I am a material object that has an immaterial soul as a part. So (on his view) can I exist when my body does not? If the answer is no, then Aquinas's view is not felicitously counted as a version of dualism; at least it is not among the versions of dualism for which I mean to argue. If, on the other hand, the answer is yes, we can welcome Aquinas (perhaps a bit cautiously) into the dualist camp.

Three more initial comments: (*a*) when I speak of possibility and necessity, I mean possibility and necessity in the broadly logical sense—metaphysical possibility and necessity, as it is also called; (*b*) I won't be arguing that it is possible that I (or others) can exist disembodied, with no body at all, although I believe that this is in fact possible;[7] (*c*) I will make no claims about what is or isn't conceivable or imaginable. That is because imaginability isn't strictly relevant to possibility at all; conceivability, on the other hand, is relevant only if 'it's conceivable that p' is to be understood as implying or offering evidence for 'it's possible that p'. (Similarly for 'it's inconceivable that p'.) It is therefore simpler and much less conducive to confusion to speak just of possibility. I take it we human beings have the following epistemic capacity: we can consider or envisage a proposition or state of affairs and, at least sometimes, determine its modal status—whether it is necessary, contingent, or impossible—just by thinking, just by an exercise of thought.[8]

---

[5] *Summa Theologiae*, I, Q. 75.

[6] For an interesting suggestion as to the answer, see Brian Leftow's "Souls Dipped in Dust", in Kevin Corcoran (ed.), *Soul, Body and Survival* (Ithaca, NY: Cornell University Press, 2001), 120 ff.

[7] I can't help concurring with David Armstrong, no friend of dualism: "But disembodied existence seems to be a perfectly intelligible supposition . . . . Consider the case where I am lying in bed at night thinking. Surely it is logically possible that I might be having just the same experiences and yet not have a body at all. No doubt I am having certain somatic, that is to say, bodily sensations. But if I am lying still these will not be very detailed in nature, and I can see nothing self-contradictory in supposing that they do not correspond to anything in physical reality. Yet I need be in no doubt about my identity" (*A Materialist Theory of Mind* (London: Routledge, 1968), 19).

[8] See my *Warrant and Proper Function* (New York: Oxford University Press, 1993), ch. 6. See also George Bealer, "Intuition and the Autonomy of Philosophy" in Michael DePaul and William Ramsey (eds.), *Rethinking Intuition* (Lanham, Md.: Rowman & Littlefield, 1998), 201 ff.

The Replacement Argument: An Argument from Possibility

I begin by assuming that there really is such a thing, substance, or suppositum as I, I myself. Of course I'm not unique in that respect; you too are such that there really is such a thing as you, and the same goes for everybody else. We are substances. Now suppose I were a material substance: which material substance would I be? The answer, I should think, is that I would be my body, or some part of my body, such as my brain or part of my brain. Or perhaps I would be something more exotic: an object distinct from my body that is constituted from the same matter as my body and is colocated with it.[9] What I propose to argue is that I am none of those things: I am not my body, or some part of it such as my brain or a hemisphere or other part of the latter, or an object composed of the same matter as my body (or some part of it) and colocated with it. For simplicity (and nothing I say will depend on this simplification) I shall talk for the most part just about my body, which I'll name 'B'. (I was thinking of naming it 'Hercules' or maybe 'Arnold', but people insisted that would be unduly self-congratulatory.)

The general strategy of this first argument is as follows. It seems possible that I continue to exist when B, my body, does not. I therefore have the property *possibly exists when B does not*; B, however, clearly lacks that property. By Leibniz's Law, therefore (more specifically, the Diversity of Discernibles), I am not identical with B. But why think it possible that I exist when my body does not? Strictly speaking, the replacement argument is an argument for this premise. Again, I conduct the argument in the first person, but naturally enough the same goes for you (although of course you will have to speak for yourself).

So first, at a macroscopic level. A familiar fact of modern medicine is the possibility and actuality of limb and organ transplants and prostheses. You can get a new heart, liver, lungs; you can also get knee, hip, and ankle replacements; you can get prostheses for hands and feet, arms and legs, and so on. Now it seems possible—possible in that broadly logical sense—that medical science should advance to the point where I remain fully dressed and in my right mind (perhaps reading the *South Bend Tribune*) throughout a process during which each of the macroscopic parts of my body is replaced by other such parts, the original parts being vaporized in a nuclear explosion—or better, annihilated by God. But if this process occurs rapidly—during a period of one microsecond, let's say—B will

---

[9] See, e.g. Dean Zimmerman, "Material People", in Michael Loux and Dean Zimmerman (eds.), *The Oxford Handbook of Metaphysics* (Oxford: Oxford University Press, 2003), 504 ff. Zimmerman himself seems attracted to the thought that "the mass of matter" of which one's body is composed is an object distinct from the latter but colocated with it (although of course he is not attracted to the idea that a person just is this mass of matter). He regards the mass of matter as more fundamental (and therefore more ontologically respectable) than the ever-changing body; so he is inclined to regard the latter as a mere "logical construction" or some other sort of entity dependent upon different masses of matter at different times.

no longer exist. I, however, will continue to exist, having been reading the comic page during the entire process.

But what about my brain, you ask—is it possible that my brain be replaced by another, the brain I now have being destroyed, and I continue to exist? It certainly seems so. Think of it like this. It seems possible (in the broadly logical sense) that one hemisphere of my brain be dormant at any given time, the other hemisphere doing all that a brain ordinarily does. At midnight, we can suppose, all the relevant 'data' and 'information' is 'transferred' via the corpus callosum from one hemisphere—call it 'H_1'—to the other hemisphere—H_2—whereupon H_2 takes over operation of the body and H_1 goes dormant. This seems possible; if it were actual, it would also be possible that the dormant half, H_2, be replaced by a different dormant half (in the same computational or functional state, if you like) just before that midnight transfer; then the transfer occurs, control switches to the new H_2, and H_1 goes dormant—at which time it is replaced by another hemisphere in the same computational or functional condition. In a period of time as brief as you like, therefore, both hemispheres will have been replaced by others, the original hemispheres and all of their parts annihilated by God. Throughout the whole process I serenely continue to read the comics.

This suffices, I think, to show that it's possible that I exist when neither my body nor any part of it exists. What about material objects distinct from my body and its parts, but colocated with it (or one of them) and constituted by the same matter as they? I doubt very much that there could be any such things. If objects of this kind *are* possible, however, the above argument also shows or at least suggests that possibly, I exist when none of them does. For example, if there is such a thing as *the matter of which B is composed*—if that phrase denotes a thing or object[10]—it too would be destroyed by God's annihilating all the parts of my body.

Of course very many different sorts of object of this kind—objects constituted by the matter of my body and colocated with it—have been suggested, and I don't have the space here to deal with them all. However, we can offer a version of the replacement argument that will be relevant to most of them. Turn from macroscopic replacement to microscopic replacement. This could go on at several levels: the levels of atoms, molecules, or cells, for example. (It could also go on at the level of elementary particles—electrons and quarks, if indeed there really are such things, and if indeed they are elementary particles.) Let's think about it at the cellular level. It seems entirely possible that the cells of which my body is composed be rapidly—within a microsecond or two—replaced by other cells of the same kind and in the same state, the original cells being instantly destroyed. It also seems entirely possible that this process of replacement take place while I remain conscious, thinking about dualism and marveling at some

---

[10] ibid.

of the appalling arguments against it produced by certain materialists.[11] Then I would exist at a time at which B did not exist.

But is it really true that this process of replacement would result in the destruction of B? After all, according to current science, all the matter in our bodies is replaced over a period of years with other matter, without any obvious compromise of bodily integrity or identity. As a matter of fact, so they say, the matter in our brains is completely replaced in a much shorter time.[12] Why should merely accelerating this process make a difference?[13]

Well, speed kills. When a part (a cell, say) is removed from an organism and replaced by another cell, the new cell doesn't become part of the organism instantaneously; it must be integrated into the organism and assimilated by it.[14] This takes time—maybe not much time, but still a certain period of time. At the instant the new part is inserted into the organism,[15] and until the time of assimilation has elapsed, the new part is not yet a part of the organism, but a foreign body occupying space within the spatial boundaries of the organism. (Clearly not everything, nor even everything organic, within the spatial boundaries of your body is *part* of your body: think of the goldfish you just swallowed, or a tapeworm.) Let's use the phrase 'assimilation time' to denote the time required for the assimilation of the new part. To be rigorous, we should index this to the part (or kind of part) and the organism in question; different parts may require different periods of time for their assimilation by different organisms. For simplicity, though, let's assume all parts and organisms have the same assimilation time; this simplification won't make any difference to the argument.

That a given part and organism are such that the time of assimilation for the former with respect to the latter is dt for some specific period of time dt is, I take it, a contingent fact. One thinks the velocity of light imposes a lower limit here, but the time of assimilation could be much greater. (For example, it could depend on the rate of blood flow, the rate of intracellular transport, and the

---

[11] One such argument, for example, apparently has the following form: (a) Many people who advocate p, do so in the service of a hope that science will never be able to explain p; therefore (b) not-p. See Daniel Dennett, *Darwin's Dangerous Idea* (New York: Simon and Schuster, 1995), 27.

Another seems to have the form (a) If you believe p, prestigious people will laugh at you; therefore (b) not-p. (or perhaps (b*) don't believe p?) See Daniel Dennett, *Explaining Consciousness* (Boston: Little, Brown, 1991), 37.

[12] "But on the kinds of figures that are coming out now, it seems like the whole brain must get recycled about every other month." John McCrone, "How Do You Persist When Your Molecules Don't?" *Science and Consciousness Review* (web-journal, June 2004, No. 1).

[13] Here I am indebted especially to Michael Rea.

[14] See e.g. David Hershenov, "The Metaphysical Problem of Intermittent Existence and the Possibility of Resurrection, *Faith and Philosophy*, 20/1 (Jan. 2003), 33.

[15] Complaint: this new 'part' as you call it, isn't really a part, at first, anyway, because at first it isn't yet integrated into the organism. Reply: think of 'part' here, as like 'part' in 'auto parts store'. Would you complain that the auto parts store is guilty of false advertising, on the grounds that none of those carburetors, spark plugs and piston rings they sell is actually part of an automobile?

rate at which information is transmitted through neuron or nerve.) God could presumably slow down this process or speed it up.

There is also what we might call 'the replacement time': the period of time from the beginning of the replacement of the first part by a new part to the end of the time of the replacement of the last part (the last to be replaced) by a different part. The time of replacement is also, of course contingent; a replacement can occur rapidly or slowly. Presumably there is no non-zero lower limit here; no matter how rapidly the parts are replaced, it is possible in the broadly logical sense that they be replaced still more rapidly.

What's required by the Replacement argument (or at any rate what's sufficient for it) is

> *Replacement* It is possible that: the cells in B are replaced by other cells and then instantly annihilated while I continue to exist; and the replacement time for O and those cells is shorter than the assimilation time.[16]

Can a Material Thing Think? An Argument from Impossibility

The replacement argument is an argument from possibility; as such, it proceeds from an intuition, the intuition that it is possible that my bodily parts, macroscopic or microscopic, be replaced while I remain conscious. But some people distrust modal intuitions. Of course it's impossible to do philosophy (or for that matter physics) without invoking modal intuitions of one sort or another or at any rate making modal declarations of one sort or another.[17] Still, it must be conceded that intuition can sometimes be a bit of a frail reed. True, there is no way to conduct philosophy that isn't a frail reed, but intuition is certainly fallible. Further, some might think modal intuitions particularly fallible—although almost all of the intuitions involved in philosophy have important modal connections. Still further, one might think that intuitions of

---

[16] "Against Materialism", 3. Contains some Objections and Replies to the argument just sketched out.

[17] Realists will say that there can't be similarity without a property had by the similar things, thus resting on an alleged intuition of impossibility; nominalists will deny this claim, thus resting on an alleged intuition of possibility. In his argument for indeterminacy of translation, Quine claims that the native's behavior is consistent with his meaning 'rabbit state' or 'undetached rabbit part' or 'rabbit' by 'gavagai', thus (despite his animadversions) relying on an intuition of possibility. Similarly for his and others' claims about the underdetermination of theory by evidence. Further, anyone who proposes an analysis (e.g. of knowledge) relies on intuition, as does someone who objects to such an analysis (by proposing a Gettier case, for example). In philosophy of mind we have Jackson's Mary example, Burge's arthritis example, twin earth arguments for a posteriori necessities and wide content, refutations of phenomenalism and behaviorism, and much else besides, all of which rely centrally and crucially on intuition. Materialists either take materialism in the basic way, thus relying on intuition, or they accept it on the basis of argument; every argument for materialism I've seen relies on intuition (e.g. the intuition that an immaterial thing can't cause effects in the hard, heavy, massive material world). Indeed, take your favorite philosophical argument or position: it will doubtless rely on intuition.

possibility are especially suspect.[18] That is because it seems easy to confuse *seeing the possibility of p* with *failing to see the impossibility of p*. You can't see why numbers couldn't be sets; it doesn't follow that what you see is that they *could* be sets. Maybe I can't see why water couldn't be composed of something other than H_2O; it doesn't follow that what I see is that water could be something other than H_2O. And perhaps, so the claim might go, one who finds the replacement argument attractive is really confusing seeing the possibility of the replacements in question with failing to see their impossibility. Granted: I can't see that these replacements are impossible; it doesn't follow that what I see is that they are indeed possible.

To be aware of this possible source of error, however, is to be forewarned and thus forearmed. But for those who aren't mollified and continue to distrust possibility intuitions, I have another argument for dualism—one that depends on an intuition, not, this time, of possibility, but of impossibility. One who distrusts possibility intuitions may think more kindly of intuitions of impossibility—perhaps because she thinks that for the latter there isn't any obvious analogue of the possible confusion between failing to see that something is impossible with seeing that it is possible. Or rather, while there *is* an analogue—it would be confusing failure to see the possibility of p with seeing the impossibility of p—falling into that confusion seems less likely. In any event, the argument I'll now propose is for the conclusion that no material objects can think—that is, reason and believe, entertain propositions, draw inferences, and the like. But of course I can think; therefore I am not a material object.

Leibniz's Problem

I (and the same goes for you) am a certain kind of thing: a thing that can think. I believe many things; I also hope, fear, expect, anticipate many things. I desire certain states of affairs (desire that certain states of affairs be actual). I am capable of making decisions. I am capable of acting, and capable of acting on the basis of my beliefs and desires. I am conscious; and conscious of a rich, kaleidoscopic constellation of feeling, mental images, beliefs, and ways of being appeared to, some of which I enjoy and some of which I dislike. Naturally enough, therefore, I am not identical with any object that lacks any or all of these properties. What I propose to argue next is that some of these properties are such that no material object can have them. Again, others have offered similar arguments. In particular, many have seen a real problem for materialism in *consciousness*: it is extremely difficult to see how a material object could be conscious, could enjoy that vivid and varied constellation of feelings, mental images, and ways of being appeared to. Others have argued that a material object can't make a decision (although of course we properly speak, in the loose and popular sense, of the chess-playing

---

[18] See below, p. 113 ff.

computer as deciding which move to make next). These arguments seem to me to be cogent.[19] Here, however, I want to develop another argument of the same sort, another problem for materialism, a problem I believe is equally debilitating, and in fact fatal to materialism. Again, this problem is not a recent invention; you can find it or something like it in Plato. Leibniz, however, offers a famous and particularly forceful statement of it:

It must be confessed, moreover, that *perception*, and that which depends on it, *are inexplicable by mechanical causes*, that is by figures and motions. And supposing there were a machine so constructed as to think, feel and have perception, we could conceive of it as enlarged and yet preserving the same proportions, so that we might enter it as into a mill. And this granted, we should only find on visiting it, pieces which push one against another, but never anything by which to explain a perception. This must be sought for, therefore, in the simple substance and not in the composite or in the machine.[20]

Now Leibniz uses the word 'perception' here; he's really thinking of mental life generally. His point, in this passage, is that mental life—perception, thought, decision—cannot arise by way of the mechanical interaction of parts. Consider a bicycle; like Leibniz's mill, it does what it does by virtue of the mechanical interaction of its parts. Stepping down on the pedals causes the front sprocket to turn, which causes the chain to move, which causes the rear sprocket to turn, which causes the back wheel to rotate. By virtue of these mechanical interactions, the bicycle does what it does, that is, transports someone from one place to another. And of course machines generally—jet aircraft, refrigerators, computers, centrifuges—do their things and accomplish their functions in the same way. So Leibniz's claim, here, is that thinking can't arise in this way. A thing can't think by virtue of the mechanical interaction of its parts.

Leibniz is thinking of *mechanical* interactions—interactions involving pushes and pulls, gears and pulleys, chains and sprockets. But I think he would say the same of other interactions studied in physics, for example those involving gravity, electromagnetism, and the strong and weak nuclear forces. Call these 'physical interactions'. Leibniz's claim is that thinking can't arise by virtue of physical interaction among objects or parts of objects. According to current science, electrons and quarks are simple, without parts.[21] Presumably neither can think—neither can adopt propositional attitudes; neither can believe, doubt, hope, want, or fear. But then a proton composed of quarks won't be able to think either, at least by way of physical relations between its component quarks, and the same will go for an atom composed of protons and electrons, a molecule composed of atoms, a cell composed of molecules, and an organ (e.g. a brain)

---

[19] There is also the complex but powerful argument offered by Dean Zimmerman, "Material People", 517 ff.

[20] *Monadology*, 17. In *Leibniz Selections*, ed. Philip Weiner (New York: Charles Scribner's Sons, 1951), 536.

[21] Although there are speculative suggestions that quarks may in fact be composed of strings.

composed of cells. If electrons and quarks can't think, we won't find anything composed of them that *can* think by way of the physical interaction of its parts.

Leibniz is talking about thinking generally; suppose we narrow our focus to *belief* (although the same considerations apply to other propositional attitudes). What, first of all, would a belief *be*, from a materialist perspective? Suppose you are a materialist, and also think, as we ordinarily do, that there are such things as beliefs. For example, you hold the belief that Marcel Proust is more subtle than Louis L'Amour. What kind of a thing is this belief? Well, from a materialist perspective, it looks as if it would have to be something like a long-standing event or structure in your brain or nervous system. Presumably this event will involve many neurons related to each other in subtle and complex ways. There are plenty of neurons to go around: a normal human brain contains some 100 billion. These neurons, furthermore, are connected with other neurons at synapses; a single neuron can be involved in several thousand synapses, and there are some 10^{15} synaptic connections. The total number of possible brain states, then, is absolutely enormous, vastly greater than the 10^{80} electrons they say the universe contains. And the total number of possible neuronal events, while no doubt vastly smaller, is still enormous. Under certain conditions, groups of neurons involved in such an event fire, producing electrical impulses that can be transmitted (with appropriate modification and input from other structures) down the cables of neurons that constitute effector nerves to muscles or glands, causing, for example, muscular contraction and thus behavior.

From the materialist's point of view, therefore, a belief will be a neuronal event or structure of this sort. But if this is what beliefs are, they will have two very different sorts of properties. On the one hand they will have *electrochemical* or *neurophysiological* properties ('NP properties', for short). Among these would be such properties as that of involving *n* neurons and *n*∗ connections between neurons, properties that specify which neurons are connected with which others, what the rates of fire in the various parts of the event are, how these rates of fire change in response to changes in input, and so on. But if the event in question is really a *belief*, then in addition to those NP properties it will have another property as well: it will have a *content*. It will have to be the belief that *p*, for some proposition *p*. If this event is the belief that Proust is a more subtle writer than Louis L'Amour, then its content is the proposition *Proust is more subtle than Louis L'Amour*. My belief that naturalism is all the rage these days has as content the proposition *Naturalism is all the rage these days*. (That same proposition is the content of the German speaker's belief that naturalism is all the rage these days, even though she expresses this belief by uttering the German sentence 'Der Naturalismus ist dieser Tage ganz gross in Mode'; beliefs, unlike sentences, do not come in different languages.) It is in virtue of having a content, of course, that a belief is true or false: it is true if the proposition which is its content is true, and false otherwise. My belief that all men are mortal is true because the proposition which constitutes its content is true, but Hitler's belief that the

Third Reich would last a thousand years was false, because the proposition that constituted its content was false.[22]

And now the difficulty for materialism is this: how does it happen, how can it be, that an assemblage of neurons, a group of material objects firing away *has a content*? How can that happen? More poignantly, *what is it* for such an event to have a content? What is it for this structured group of neurons, or the event of which they are a part, to be related, for example, to the proposition *Cleveland is a beautiful city* in such a way that the latter is its content? A single neuron (or quark, electron, atom, or whatever) presumably isn't a belief and doesn't have content; but how can belief, content, arise from, be constituted by, physical interaction among such material entities as neurons? As Leibniz suggests, we can examine this neuronal event as carefully as we please; we can measure the number of neurons it contains, their connections, their rates of fire, the strength of the electrical impulses involved, the potential across the synapses—we can measure all this with as much precision as you could possibly desire; we can consider its electrochemical, neurophysiological properties in the most exquisite detail; but nowhere, here, will we find so much as a hint of content. Indeed, none of this seems even vaguely *relevant* to its having content. None of this so much as slyly suggests that this bunch of neurons firing away is the belief that Proust is more subtle than Louis L'Amour, as opposed, for example, to the belief that Louis L'Amour is the most widely published author from Jamestown, North Dakota. Indeed, nothing we find here will so much as slyly suggest that it has a content of *any* sort. Nothing here will so much as slyly suggest that it is *about* something, in the way a belief about horses is about horses.

The fact is, we can't see how it *could* have a content. It's not just that we don't know or can't see how it's done. When light strikes photoreceptor cells in the retina, there is an enormously complex cascade of electrical activity, resulting in an electrical signal to the brain.[23] I have no idea how all that works; but of course I know it happens all the time. But the case under consideration is different. Here it's not merely that I don't know how physical interaction among neurons brings it about that an assemblage of them has content and is a belief. No, in this case, it seems upon reflection that such an event could *not* have content. It's a little like trying to understand what it would be for the number seven, for example, to weigh 5 pounds, or for an elephant (or the unit set of an elephant) to be a proposition. (Pace the late (and great) David Lewis, according

---

[22] A materialist might take a leaf from those who accept 'adverbial' accounts of sensation, according to which there aren't any red sensations or red sense data or red appearances: what there are instead are cases of someone's sensing redly or being appeared to redly. Similarly, the materialist might claim that there isn't any such thing as the belief that all men are mortal (or any other beliefs); what there is instead are cases of people who believe in the all-men-are-mortal way. This may or may not make sense; if it does make sense, however, a person will presumably believe in the all-men-are-mortal way only if she harbors a neuronal structure or event that has as content the proposition all men are mortal.

[23] See Michael Behe, *Darwin's Black Box* (New York: Free Press, 1996), 18 ff.

to whom the unit set of an elephant *could* be a proposition; in fact, on his view, there are uncountably many elephants the unit sets of which *are* propositions.) We can't see how that could happen; more exactly, what we can see is that it *couldn't* happen. A number just isn't the sort of thing that can have weight; there is no way in which the number seven or any other number could weigh anything at all. The unit set of an elephant, let alone the elephant itself, can't be a proposition; it's not the right sort of thing. Similarly, we can see, I think, that physical activity among neurons can't constitute content. These neurons are clicking away, sending electrical impulses hither and yon. But what has this to do with content? How is content or aboutness supposed to arise from this neuronal activity? How can such a thing be a belief? You might as well say that thought arises from the activity of the wind or the waves. But then no neuronal event can as such have a content, can be *about* something, in the way in which my belief that the number seven is prime is about the number seven, or my belief that the oak tree in my backyard is without leaves is about that oak tree.

Here we must be very clear about an important distinction. Clearly there is such a thing as *indication* or *indicator meaning*.[24] Deer tracks in my backyard indicate that deer have run through it; smoke indicates fire; the height of the mercury column indicates the ambient temperature; buds on the trees indicate the coming of spring. We could speak here of 'natural signs': smoke is a natural sign of fire and the height of the mercury column is a natural sign of the temperature. When one event indicates or is a natural sign of another, there is ordinarily some sort of causal or nomic connection, or at least regular association, between them by virtue of which the first is reliably correlated with the second. Smoke is caused by fire, which is why it indicates fire; measles causes red spots on your face, which is why red spots on your face indicate measles; there is a causal connection between the height of the mercury column and the temperature, so that the latter indicates the former.

The nervous systems of organisms contain such indicators. A widely discussed example: when a frog sees a fly zooming by, the frog's brain (so it is thought) displays a certain pattern of neural firing; we could call such patterns 'fly detectors'. Another famous example: some anaerobic marine bacteria have magnetosomes, tiny internal magnets. These function like compass needles, indicating magnetic north. The direction to magnetic north is downward; hence these bacteria, which can't flourish in the oxygen-rich surface water, move towards the more oxygen-free water at the bottom of the ocean.[25] Of course there are also indicators in human bodies. There are structures that respond in a regular way to blood temperature; they are part of a complex feedback system that maintains a more

---

[24] See Fred Dretske's *Explaining Behavior* (Cambridge, Mass: MIT Press, 1988), 54 ff. See also William Ramsey's *Using and Abusing Representation: Reassessing the Cognitive Revolution* (forthcoming). Materialists who try to explain how a material structure like a neuronal event can be a belief ordinarily try to do so by promoting indicators to beliefs; see below, pp. 136–141.

[25] Dretske, *Explaining Behavior*, 63.

or less constant blood temperature by inducing, for example, shivering if the temperature is too low and sweating if it is too high. There are structures that monitor the amount of sugar in the blood and its sodium content. There are structures that respond in a regular way to light of a certain pattern striking the retina, to the amount of food in your stomach, to its progress through your digestive system, and so on. Presumably there are structures in the brain that are correlated with features of the environment; it is widely assumed that when you see a tree, there is a distinctive pattern of neural firing (or some other kind of structure) in your brain that is correlated with and caused by it.

Now we can, if we like, speak of 'content' here; it's a free country. We can say that the mercury column, on a given occasion, has a certain content: the state of affairs correlated with its having the height it has on that occasion. We can say, if we like, that those structures in the body that indicate blood pressure or temperature or saline content have a content on a given occasion: whatever it is that the structure indicates on that occasion. We can say, if we like, that the neural structure that is correlated with my looking at a tree has a content: its content, we could say, is what it indicates on that occasion. We can also, if we like, speak of information in these cases: the structure that registers my blood temperature, we can say, carries the information that my blood temperature is thus and so.

What is crucially important to see, however, is that this sort of content or information has nothing as such to do with *belief,* or belief content. There are those who—no doubt in the pursuit of greater generality—gloss over this distinction. Donald T. Cambell, for example, in arguing for the relevance of natural selection to epistemology, claims that "evolution—even in its biological aspects—is a knowledge process".[26] Commenting on Cambell's claim, Franz Wuketits explains that

> The claim is based on the idea that any living system is a "knowledge-gaining system." This means that organisms accumulate information about certain properties of their environment. Hence life generally may be described as an information process, or, to put it more precisely, an information-increasing process.[27]

At any rate Wuketits has the grace to put 'knowledge' in scare quotes here. Knowledge requires belief; correlation, causal or otherwise, is not belief; information and content of this sort do not require belief. Neither the thermostat nor any of its components believes that the room temperature is thus and so. When the saline content of my blood is too low, neither I nor the structure correlated with that state of affairs (nor my blood) believes the saline content is less than it should be—or, indeed, anything else about the saline content. Indication,

---

[26] "Evolutionary Epistemology", in P. A. Schilpp (ed.), *The Philosophy of Karl Popper* (LaSalle: Open Court, 1974), 413.
[27] "Evolutionary Epistemology", *Biology and Philosophy*, 1/2 (1986), 193.

carrying information, is not belief; indicator content is not belief content, and these structures don't have belief content just by virtue of having indicator content. And now the point here: I am not, of course, claiming that material structures can't have indicator content; obviously they can. What I am claiming is that they can't have belief content: no material structure can be a belief.

Here someone might object as follows. "You say we can't see how a neural event can have content; but in fact we understand this perfectly well, and something similar happens all the time. For there is, after all, the computer analogy. A computer, of course, is a material object, an assemblage of wires, switches, relays, and the like. Now suppose I am typing in a document. Take any particular sentence in the document: say the sentence 'Naturalism is all the rage these days'. That sentence is represented and stored on the computer's hard disk. We don't have to know in exactly what *way* it's stored (by pluses and minuses, or a magnetic configuration, or something else; it doesn't matter). Now the sentence 'Naturalism is all the rage these days' *expresses* the proposition *Naturalism is all the rage these days*. That sentence, therefore, has the proposition *Naturalism is all the rage these days* as its content. But then consider the analogue of that sentence on the computer disk: doesn't it, too, express the same proposition as the sentence it represents? That bit of the computer disk with its pluses and minuses, therefore, has propositional content. But of course that bit of the computer disk is also (part of) a material object (as is any inscription of the sentence in question). Contrary to your claim, therefore, a material object can perfectly well have propositional content; indeed, it happens all the time. But if a computer disk or an inscription of a sentence can have a proposition as content, why can't an assemblage of neurons? Just as a magnetic pattern has as content the proposition *Naturalism is all the rage these days*, so too a pattern of neuronal firing can have that proposition as content. Your claim to the contrary is completely bogus and you should be ashamed of yourself." Thus far the objector.

If the sentence or the computer disk really *did* have content, then I guess the assemblage of neurons could too. But the fact is neither does—or rather, neither has the right kind of content: neither has *original* content; each has, at most, *derived* content. For how does it happen that the sentence has content? It's simply by virtue of the fact that we human beings *treat* that sentence in a certain way, *use* the sentence in a certain way, a way such that if a sentence is used in that way, then it expresses the proposition in question. Upon hearing that sentence, I think of, grasp, apprehend the proposition *Naturalism is all the rage these days*. You can get me to grasp, entertain, and perhaps believe that proposition by uttering that sentence. How exactly all this works is complicated and not at all well understood; but the point is that the sentence has content only because of something *we*, we who are *already* thinkers, do with it. We could put this by saying that the sentence has *secondary* or *derived* content; it has content only because we, we creatures whose thoughts and beliefs already have content, treat it in a certain way. The same goes for the magnetic pattern on the computer disk;

it represents or expresses that proposition because we assign that proposition to that configuration. But of course that isn't how it goes (given materialism) with that pattern of neural firing. That pattern doesn't get its content by way of being used in a certain way by some other creatures whose thoughts and beliefs already have content. If that pattern has content at all, then, according to materialism, it must have *original* or *primary* content. And what it is hard or impossible to see is how it could be that an assemblage of neurons (or a sentence, or a computer disk) could have original or primary content. To repeat: it isn't just that we can't see how it's done, in the way in which we can't see how the sleight of hand artist gets the pea to wind up under the middle shell. It is rather that we can see, to at least some degree, that it can't be done, just as we can see that an elephant can't be a proposition, and that the number seven can't weigh 7 pounds.

Parity?

Peter van Inwagen agrees that it is hard indeed to see how physical interaction among material entities can produce thought: "it seems to me that the notion of a physical thing that thinks is a mysterious notion, and that Leibniz's thought-experiment brings out this mystery very effectively."[28]

Now I am taking this fact as a reason to reject materialism and hence as an argument for dualism. But of course it is a successful argument only if there is no similar difficulty for substance dualism itself. Van Inwagen believes there *is* a similar difficulty for dualism:

For it is thinking itself that is the source of the mystery of a thinking physical thing. The notion of a non-physical thing that thinks is, I would argue, equally mysterious. How any sort of thing could think is a mystery. It is just that it is a bit easier to see that thinking is a mystery when we suppose that the thing that does the thinking is physical, for we can form mental images of the operations of a physical thing and we can see that the physical interactions represented in these images—the only interactions that can be represented in these images—have no connection with thought or sensation, or none we are able to imagine, conceive or articulate. The only reason we do not readily find the notion of a non-physical thing that thinks equally mysterious is that we have no clear procedure for forming mental images of non-physical things. (*Metaphysics, 176*)

So dualism is no better off than materialism; they both have the same problem. But what precisely *is* this problem, according to van Inwagen? "we can form mental images of the operations of a physical thing and we can see that the physical interactions represented in these images—the only interactions that can be represented in these images—have no connection with thought or sensation or none we are able to imagine, conceive or articulate." As I understand van Inwagen here, he is saying that we can imagine physical interactions or changes in a physical thing; but we can see that the physical interactions represented in

---

[28] *Metaphysics* (2nd edn; Boulder, Colo.: Westview, 2002), 176.

those images have no connection with thought. We can imagine neurons in the brain firing; we can imagine electrical impulses or perhaps clouds of electrons moving through parts of neurons, or whole chains of neurons; we can imagine neural structures with rates of fire in certain parts of the structure changing in response to rates of fire elsewhere in or out of that structure: but we can see that these interactions have no connection with thought. Now I'm not quite sure whether or not I can imagine electrons, or their movements, or electrical impulses; but it does seem to me that I can see that electrical impulses and the motions of electrons, if indeed there are any such things, have nothing to do with thought.

Another way to put van Inwagen's point: no change we can imagine in a physical thing could be a mental change, that is, could constitute thought or sensation, or a change in thought or sensation. But then we can't imagine a physical thing's thinking: that is, we can't form a mental image of a physical thing thinking. And this suggests that the problem for materialism is that we can't form a mental image of a material thing thinking. But the same goes, says van Inwagen, for an immaterial thing: we also can't imagine or form a mental image of an immaterial thing thinking. Indeed, we can't form a mental image of any kind of thinking thing: "My point", he says, "is that nothing could possibly count as a mental image of a thinking thing" (p. 177). Materialism and dualism, therefore, are so far on a par; there is nothing here to incline us to the latter rather than the former.

Thus far van Inwagen. The thought of a physical thing's thinking, he concedes, is mysterious; that is because we can't form a mental image of a physical thing's thinking. But the thought of an immaterial thing's thinking is equally mysterious; for we can't form a mental image of that either. This, however, seems to me to mislocate the problem for materialism. What inclines us to reject the idea of a physical thing's thinking is not just the fact that we can't form a mental image of a physical thing's thinking. There are plenty of things of which we can't form a mental image, where we're not in the least inclined to reject them as impossible. As Descartes pointed out, I can't form a mental image of a chiliagon, a 1,000-sided rectilinear plane figure (or at least an image that distinguishes it from a 100-sided rectilinear plane figure); that doesn't even suggest that there can't be any such thing. I can't form a mental image of the number 79's being prime: that doesn't incline me to believe that the number 79 could not be prime; as a matter of fact I know how to prove that it *is* prime. The fact is I can't form a mental image of the number 79 at all—or for that matter of any number; this doesn't incline me to think there aren't any numbers.

Or is all that a mistake? Is it really true that I can't form a mental image of the number seven, for example? Maybe I *can* form an image of the number seven; when I think of the number seven, sometimes there is a mental image present; it's as if one catches a quick glimpse of a sort of partial and fragmented numeral 7; we could say that I'm appeared to numeral-7ly. When I think of the actual world, I am sometimes presented with an image of the Greek letter alpha; when I think of the proposition *All men are mortal* I am sometimes presented with a sort of fleeting, fragmentary, partial image of the corresponding English sentence. Sets are nonphysical, but maybe I can imagine the pair set of Mic and Martha; when I try, it's like I catch a fleeting glimpse of curly brackets, enclosing indistinct images that don't look a whole lot like Mic and Martha. But is that really imagining the number seven, or the actual world, or the pair set of Mic and Martha? Here I'm of two minds. On the one hand, I'm inclined to think that this isn't imagining the number seven at all, but instead imagining something connected with it, namely the numeral 7 (and the same for the actual world and the set of Mic and Martha). On the other hand I'm a bit favorably disposed to the idea that that's just how you imagine something like the number seven; you do it by imagining the numeral 7. (Just as you state a proposition by uttering a sentence or uttering certain sounds.) So I don't really know what to say. Can I or can't I imagine non-physical things like numbers, propositions, possible worlds, angels, God? I'm not sure.

What is clear, here, is this: if imagining the numeral 7 is sufficient for imagining the number seven, then imagining, forming mental images of, has nothing to do with possibility. For in this same way I can easily imagine impossibilities. I can imagine the proposition *all men are mortal* being red: first I just imagine the proposition, for example, by forming a mental image of the sentence 'All men are mortal', and then I imagine this sentence as red. I think I can even imagine that elephant's being a proposition (I imagine the relevant sentence and then imagine it in the shape of an elephant). David Kaplan once claimed he could imagine his refuting Gödel's Incompleteness Theorem: he imagined the *Los Angeles Times* carrying huge headlines: 'UCLA PROF REFUTES GÖDEL; ALL REPUTABLE EXPERTS AGREE'. In this loose sense, most anything can be imagined; but then the loose sense has little to do with what is or isn't possible. So really neither the loose nor the strong sense of 'imagining' (neither the weak nor the strong version of imagination) has much to do with possibility. There are many clearly possible things one can't imagine in the strong sense; in the weak sense, one can imagine many things that are clearly impossible.

What is it, then, that inclines me to think a proposition can't be red, or a horse, or an even number? The answer, I think, is that one can just see upon reflection that these things are impossible. I can't form a mental image of a proposition's having members; but that's not why I think no proposition has members; I also can't form a mental image of a set's having members. It's rather that one sees that a set is the sort of thing that (null set aside) has members, and a proposition is the sort of thing that cannot have members. It is the same with a physical thing's thinking. True, one can't imagine it (in the strong sense). The reason for rejecting the idea, thinking it impossible, however, is not that one can't imagine it. It's rather that on reflection one can see that a physical object just can't do that sort of thing. I grant that this isn't as clear and obvious, perhaps, as that a proposition can't be red; some impossibilities (necessities) are more clearly impossible (necessary) than others. But one can see it to at least a significant degree. Indeed, van Inwagen might be inclined to endorse this thought; elsewhere he says: "Leibniz's thought experiment shows that when we carefully examine the idea of a material thing having sensuous properties, it seems to be an impossible idea."[29] But (and here is the important point) the same clearly doesn't go for an immaterial thing's thinking; we certainly can't see that no immaterial thing can think. (If we could, we'd have a quick and easy argument against the existence of God: no immaterial thing can think; if there were such a person as God, he would be both immaterial and a thinker; therefore . . .).

Van Inwagen has a second suggestion:

> In general, to attempt to explain how an underlying reality generates some phenomenon is to construct a representation of the working of that underlying reality, a representation that in some sense "shows how" the underlying reality generates the phenomenon. Essentially the same considerations as those that show that we are unable to form a mental image that displays the generation of thought and sensation by the workings of some underlying reality (whether the underlying reality involves one thing or many, and whether the things it involves are physical or non-physical) show that we are unable to form any sort of representation that displays the generation of thought and sensation by the workings of an underlying reality. (*Metaphysics*, 177–8)

The suggestion is that we can't form an image or any other representation displaying the generation of thought by way of the workings of an underlying reality; hence we can't see how it can be generated by physical interaction among material objects such as neurons. This much seems right—at any rate we certainly can't see how thought could be generated in that way. Van Inwagen goes on to say, however, that this doesn't favor dualism over materialism, because we also can't see how thought can be generated by the workings of an underlying *non*-physical reality. And perhaps this last is also right. But here there is an important dissimilarity between dualism and materialism. The materialist thinks of thought as generated by the workings of an underlying reality—that is, by the physical interaction of such physical things as neurons; the dualist, however, typically thinks of an immaterial self, a soul, a thing that thinks, as *simple*. An immaterial self doesn't have any parts; hence, of course, thought isn't generated by the interaction of its parts. Say that a property P is *basic* to a thing x if x has P, but x's having P is not generated by the interaction of its parts. Thought is then a basic property of selves, or better, a basic activity of selves. It's not that (for example) there are various underlying immaterial parts of a self whose interaction produces thought. Of course a self stands in causal relation to its body: retinal stimulation

---

[29] "Dualism and Materialism: Athens and Jerusalem?", *Faith and Philosophy*, 12/4 (Oct. 1995), 478. That is (I take it), it seems to be necessary that material things don't have such properties. Van Inwagen's examples are such properties as *being in pain* and *sensing redly*; the same goes, I say, for properties like *being the belief that p* for a proposition p.

causes a certain sort of brain activity which (so we think) in turn somehow causes a certain kind of experience in the self. But there isn't any *way* in which the self produces a thought; it does so immediately. To ask, "How does a self produce thought?" is to ask an improper question. There isn't any how about it.

By way of analogy: consider the lowly electron. According to current science, electrons are simple, not composed of other things. Now an electron has basic properties, such as having a negative charge. But the question, "How does an electron manage to have a charge?" is an improper question. There's no how to it; it doesn't do something else that results in its having such a charge, and it doesn't have parts by virtue of whose interaction it has such a charge. Its having a negative charge is rather a basic and immediate property of the thing (if thing it is). The same is true of a self and thinking: it's not done by underlying activity or workings; it's a basic and immediate activity of the self. But then the important difference, here, between materialism and immaterialism is that if a material thing managed to think, it would have to be by way of the activity of its parts: and it seems upon reflection that this can't happen.[30] Not so for an immaterial self. Its activity of thinking is basic and immediate. And it's not the case that we are inclined upon reflection to think this can't happen—there's nothing at all against it, just as there is nothing against an electron's having a negative charge, not by virtue of the interaction of parts, but in that basic and immediate way. The fact of the matter then is that we can't see how a material object can think—that is, upon reflection it seems that a material object can't think. Again, not so for an immaterial self.

True, as van Inwagen says, thought can sometimes seem mysterious and wonderful, something at which to marvel. (Although from another point of view it is more familiar than hands and feet.) But there is nothing here to suggest that it can't be done. I find myself perceiving my computer; there is nothing at all, here, to suggest impossibility or paradox. Part of the mystery of thought is that it is wholly unlike what material objects can do: but of course that's not to suggest that it can't be done at all. Propositions are also mysterious and have wonderful properties: they manage to be about things; they are true or false; they can be believed; they stand in logical relations to each other. How do they

---

[30] But couldn't a material thing also just directly think, without depending on the interaction of its parts? According to Pierre Cabanis, "The brain secretes thought as the liver secretes bile"; couldn't we think of this as the brain (or, if you like, the whole organism) directly thinking, not by way of the interaction of its parts? Well, if that's how a brain thinks, it isn't like the way a liver secretes bile; the latter certainly involves the liver's having parts, and those parts working together in the appropriate way. Further, the idea of a physical thing's thinking without the involvement of its parts is even more clearly impossible than that of a physical thing's thinking by virtue of the interaction of its parts. Aren't those neurons in the brain supposed to be what enables it to think? You might as well say that a tree or my left foot thinks. Consider any non-elementary physical object—a tree, an automobile, perhaps a horse: such a thing does what it does by virtue of the nature and interaction of its parts. Are we to suppose that some physical object—a brain, let's say—does something like thinking apart from involvement of its parts? Talk about appealing to magic!

manage to do those things? Well, certainly not by way of interaction among material parts. Sets manage, somehow, to have members—how do they do a thing like that? And why is it that a given set has just the members it has? How does the unit set of Neil Armstrong manage to have exactly *him* as a member? What mysterious force, or fence, keeps Leopold out of that set? Well, it's just the nature of sets to be like this. These properties can't be explained by way of physical interactions among material parts, but that's nothing at all against sets. Indeed, these properties can't be explained at all. Of course if you began with the idea that everything has to be a material object, then thought (and propositions and sets) would indeed be mysterious and paradoxical. But why begin with that idea? Thought is seriously mysterious, I think, only when we assume that it would have to be generated in some physical way, by physical interaction among physical objects. That is certainly mysterious; indeed it goes far beyond mystery, all the way to apparent impossibility. But that's not a problem for thought; it's a problem for materialism.

2. THE BEARING OF CHRISTIAN BELIEF

As I said above (p. 100) there are three ways in which Christian belief is relevant to the issue of dualism vs. materialism. First, there is Scripture and perhaps also creedal and conciliar declaration. Second, Christian belief is relevant to the epistemology of the situation, and that in two ways: (*a*) given Christian theism, we know that it is at any rate possible that there be immaterial thinking things, since God Himself is such a thing, and (*b*) these considerations from the Christian faith are powerfully relevant to the objections to dualism and arguments for materialism. Finally, certain crucial Christian doctrines (for example, Incarnation and the resurrection of the dead) fit better—much better, I'd say—with dualism than with materialism. Here I'll confine myself to the second,[31] beginning with just a brief remark on the first.

The Scripture obviously contains a great deal that is relevant to our question; and in my opinion these scriptural declarations heavily favor dualism. I am no Scripture scholar, however, and hence am not well qualified to develop this case. Fortunately enough, then, there is clear and authoritative work by someone who does have credentials in this area: John Cooper's philosophically sensitive examination of the bearing on biblical teaching on our question.[32] I have little to add to Cooper's balanced and nuanced discussion;[33] I would

[31] For a discussion of the bearing of Christian belief on the doctrine of Incarnation, see my "On Heresy, Mind, and Truth", *Faith and Philosophy*, 16/2 (April 1999).

[32] *Body, Soul, and Life Everlasting: Biblical Anthropology and the Monism–Dualism Debate*, 2nd edn. with a new preface (Grand Rapids, Mich.: Eerdmans Publishing Co., 2000).

[33] In the passages with which I am concerned, Cooper is arguing that Paul asserts or presupposes, not merely that a person is not identical with his body, but that in addition there is an 'intermediate

simply like to call your attention to three Pauline passages, together with Cooper's comments on them. These passages (among many others) are, I believe, vastly more smoothly and plausibly understood in terms of dualism than in terms of materialism. People have indeed come up with interpretations in accord with materialism; these interpretations, in my opinion, are strained and implausible.

The first passage is 2 Corinthians 5: 6–9 (Cooper's comments: pp. 141–9):

Therefore we are always confident and know that as long as we are at home in the body, we are away from the Lord. We live by faith, not by sight. We are confident, I say, and would prefer to be away from the body and at home with the Lord. So we make it our goal to please him, whether we are at home in the body or away from it.

Second, a parallel passage: Philippians 1: 21–4 (Cooper's comments pp. 151–6):

For to me, to live is Christ and to die is gain. If I am to go on living in the body, this will mean fruitful labor for me. Yet what shall I choose? I do not know. I am torn between the two: I desire to depart and be with Christ, which is better by far; but it is more necessary for you that I remain in the body.

Third, 2 Corinthians 12: 1–4 (Cooper's comments pp. 88, 28, 149–51):

I must go on boasting. Although there is nothing to be gained, I will go on to visions and revelations from the Lord. I know a man in Christ who fourteen years ago was caught up to the third heaven. Whether it was in the body or out of the body I do not know—God knows. And I know that this man—whether in the body or apart from the body I do not know, but God knows—was caught up to Paradise.[34]

Parity Again

Turning now to the epistemological considerations, return first to the discussion of parity (pp. 113–8 above). Peter van Inwagen concedes that the idea of a thinking material thing seems to be an impossible idea; but he thinks or is inclined to think that the same goes for the idea of an immaterial thing's thinking. Here I believe he is mistaken: as far as I can see, there is no apparent impossibility in the idea of an immaterial thing's thinking. It is not the case that when we consider the state of affairs consisting of an immaterial thing's thinking, that state of affairs

state' between death and resurrection during which a person exists disembodied. I'm not concerned to argue for or against the claim that human persons exist disembodied at some points in their careers; I want only to call attention to the point that in these passages Paul certainly appears to endorse dualism.

[34] Cooper doesn't comment on 2 Peter 1: 13–14, a non-Pauline passage expressing the same sentiment: "I think it is right to refresh your memory as long as I live in the tent of this body, because I know that I will soon put it aside, as our Lord Jesus Christ has made clear to me." Here Peter pretty clearly distinguishes himself from "the tent of this body" and thinks of death as putting aside, separation from, the body.

seems impossible. Nor is the dualist committed to the existence of an underlying immaterial reality whose workings somehow generate thought; that may be an impossible idea, but the dualist isn't committed to it. (Of course I agree that in the strong sense of 'imagine' (above, pp. 113–115) it isn't possible to imagine an immaterial thinking thing.) But suppose van Inwagen were right; suppose the state of affairs of an immaterial thing's thinking seemed, on reflection, quite as clearly impossible as that of a material thing's thinking. What would follow? Would it follow that these two states of affairs are on an epistemic par?

Not at all. For suppose we take Christian theism seriously. Then we are already committed to the existence of a thinking immaterial being: God himself. (We'll probably also be inclined to suppose that there are other immaterial thinkers: angels, perhaps, and Satan and his minions.) The appearance of impossibility in an immaterial object's thinking, if there were such an appearance, would therefore be an illusion, a sort of inexplicable tendency on our part to form a suite of false beliefs, all related to the false intuition that it is not possible that an immaterial thing think. Here, then, is a way in which Christian theism is related to the question of materialism vs. dualism: even if (contrary to fact, as I see it) it did seem on reflection impossible that an immaterial thing think, so that dualism and materialism would be on a par in this regard, Christian theism would lead us to see that there isn't epistemic parity here after all. What it would lead us to think instead is that the apparent impossibility of an immaterial thing's thinking is an illusion.

Objections to Dualism (Arguments for Materialism)

The above arguments for dualism and others like them are, I believe, powerful arguments. Like philosophical arguments generally, however, they are not of that wholly apodictic and irrefragable character Kant liked to claim for his arguments; they are defeasible. It is possible to disregard or downgrade the intuitions of possibility and impossibility to which they appeal, just as it is possible to produce convoluted interpretations of the relevant scriptural evidence. Further, if there were really powerful arguments against dualism or for materialism, then perhaps the appropriate course would be to embrace materialism, or to take refuge in agnosticism. But *are* there any such powerful arguments? You might think so. As Paul Churchland, Jaegwon Kim, and many others say, dualism is the natural, baseline belief of humankind, not an invention of Plato or Descartes; but according to Daniel Dennett, "The prevailing wisdom, variously expressed and argued for, is *materialism*: there is only one sort of stuff, namely *matter*—the physical stuff of physics, chemistry, and physiology—and the mind is somehow nothing but a physical phenomenon. In short, the mind is the brain."[35] Presumably there must be some pretty powerful arguments to move

[35] Dennett, *Explaining Consciousness*, 34.

so many from the baseline position of dualism to materialism. Paul Churchland concurs, "Arguments like these have moved most (but not all) of the professional community to embrace some form of materialism."[36] Where are these powerful arguments? The fact is there aren't any. Most of them seem to have very little force; even the best doesn't survive a closer look. Here there is a clear bearing of Christian theism: the fact is, I think, none of the usual objections to dualism has any purchase at all on someone committed to Christian theism. In particular, the most widely cited and influential argument against dualism—the claim that an immaterial object can't cause changes in the hard, heavy, massive physical and material world—should carry no weight whatever with someone so committed.

Of course many arguments have been proposed for materialism; I'll restrict myself to seven that seem to be among the most important and significant.

Soul Stuff?

The first argument needn't detain us long. According to Michael Levin and others (i.e. Churchland and Dennett), substance dualism fails because the stuff a self is supposed to be made of is mysterious, or obscure, or even inconceivable:

> The trouble, I suggest, is this: we can say what sort of stuff a material thing is an individual piece of, while no one has any idea of the sort of stuff a self is an individual piece of. . . . It is in this sense that it is impossible to form an idea of what the substance dualist's self is. While there are descriptions that can identify a self, we cannot refer to it as a P of S, for we do not know and evidently cannot imagine the *stuff* it is a piece of, or the sort of piece it could be.[37]

But this objection is massively unimpressive. First, note that it would equally be an objection to propositions, properties, states of affairs, sets, numbers, and other abstract objects. Consider, for example, the proposition *All men are mortal*: we don't know and can't imagine the sort of stuff that proposition is made out of or is a piece of. More poignantly, from Levin's perspective, the same would go for many of the entities postulated by contemporary physics: what is the stuff an electron is a piece of? According to the most widely accepted theories, an electron is a perturbation in a field—so is the stuff in question a *field*? But is a field 'stuff'? Or a piece of stuff?

More important, though: the objection rests on a misunderstanding. Selves, according to the dualist, aren't made of any stuff at all, not even very fine, filmy, gossamer, ghostly soul stuff. Levin apparently assumes that everything there is has to be made of stuff of some kind or other: but why think a thing like that? Propositions, properties, sets, possible worlds—these things are not made of

---

[36] P. Churchland, *Matter and Consciousness* (Cambridge, Mass.: MIT Press, 1984), 21.
[37] M. Levin, *Metaphysics and the Mind–Body Problem* (Oxford: Oxford University Press, 1979), 79.

stuff and are not pieces of stuff. So why think selves, if immaterial, would have to be made of stuff? Perhaps Levin and others will reply that it's perfectly fine and good for abstract objects like sets and propositions not to be made of stuff, but concrete objects can't enjoy that luxury; they can only be pieces of stuff. But again, why think a thing like that? And once more there is contemporary physics: electrons and fields do not appear to be pieces of stuff; but are they not concrete? Well, perhaps that is part of the problem posed by the mysterious character of the entities postulated by contemporary physics. These things are mysterious in a variety of ways; perhaps we shouldn't be surprised that they are an enigma in this way as well.

In any event, there is a much more decisive answer from the perspective of Christian (or other) theism: God, clearly enough, is not an abstract object; equally clearly, God is not made of any stuff and is not himself a piece of stuff. From a Christian perspective, therefore, this objection to dualism has no bite at all; the Christian is already committed to the existence of concrete beings that are not pieces of stuff.[38] But even apart from such commitment: would anyone seriously want to hold that we have here a significant new argument for atheism? Could anyone argue with a straight face that God, if he existed, would be a concrete object that wasn't a piece of stuff; but every concrete object must be a piece of stuff; therefore there is no such person as God?

Dualism Unscientific?

Dennett, Churchland, and others complain that dualism should be rejected because it is *unscientific*:

There is the lurking suspicion that the most attractive feature of mind stuff is its promise of being so mysterious that it keeps science at bay forever.
    This fundamentally antiscientific stance of dualism is, to my mind, its most disqualifying feature, and is the reason why in this book I adopt the apparently dogmatic rule that dualism is to be avoided *at all costs*.[39]

But our question here is whether dualism is *true*, not whether it, or more likely its proponents, are properly reverential towards science. What I claim for dualism is only that it is true, not that those who embrace it are of good character, or are appropriately deferential towards science, or in other ways estimable. Perhaps those who promulgate dualism adopt wholly unacceptable stances, even going so far as *lese majesty* towards modern science itself; perhaps they are in still

---

[38] There is also a sort of general and widespread impression that the very idea of an immaterial concrete substance (an immaterial self or thinker) is weird or crazy or implausible. This shows, once more, the importance of fashion and zeitgeist in philosophy; prior to (e.g.) 100 years ago that idea wasn't considered weird; and we haven't learned anything in the last 100 years to show that it really is weird. In any event, however, from a Christian or theistic perspective the idea is anything but weird; the first being of the entire universe is an immaterial thinking substance.

[39] Dennett, *Explaining Consciousness*, 37.

other ways wholly objectionable: what has that to do with the truth or falsehood of dualism? Materialists like Daniel Dennett sometimes adopt an unpleasantly triumphalist tone; Dennett also suggests that Baptists should be confined to zoos, lest they contaminate the rest of us with their noxious views on evolution, etc.:[40] should we conclude that materialism must be rejected?

But the fact is there is no reason at all to think dualists do or must display anything as heinous as an unscientific attitude—at least they need not do so just by virtue of being dualists. We have discovered many fascinating things about the brain and its organization, about the structure and behavior of neurons, about the ways in which damage to various parts of the brain is correlated with mental and physical disorders, about the correlation between certain kinds of mental activity (memory, vision) and increased blood flow and electrical activity displayed in certain areas of the brain, (leading us to say that those activities are 'located' in those areas), and much else. Need a dualist reject these discoveries? Need she decry, downgrade, denigrate, or disapprove of the scientific activity that leads to these discoveries? But is this a serious question? *Of course* she needn't do those things. Indeed, there is no reason at all why dualists can't enthusiastically join the scientific enterprise here. The fact is some dualists have done exactly that, and have been leaders in the field, with no conflict whatever with their dualistic views and no compromise whatever to their intellectual integrity.[41] According to dualism, I am an immaterial object intimately linked to a body; nothing follows with respect to whether and in what way appropriate brain condition is a necessary condition of proper mental function (see below, pp. 133–5). Therefore nothing prevents a dualist from being wholly enthusiastic about brain science. This whole issue is nothing but a red herring.

Explanatory Impotence?

Paul Churchland objects that dualism is *explanatorily impotent*:

Compare now what the neuroscientist can tell us about the brain and what he can do with that knowledge, with what the dualist can tell us about spiritual substance, and what he can do with those assumptions. Can the dualist tell us anything about the internal constitution of mind-stuff? Of the nonmaterial elements that make it up? Of the laws that govern their behavior? Of the mind's structural connections with the body? Of the manner of its operations? Can he explain human capacities and pathologies in terms of its structures and its defects? The fact is, the dualist can know none of these things, because no detailed theory of mind-stuff has even been formulated. Compared to the

---

[40] *Darwin's Dangerous Idea* (New York; Simon and Schuster, 1995), 515–16.

[41] An example would be Wilder Penfield (who made impressive contributions to the 'localization' of memory); see his *The Mystery of the Mind* (Princeton: Princeton University Press, 1975). Another would be Nobel Prize winner John Eccles; see his *Facing Reality: Philosophical Adventures by a Brain Scientist* (New York and Berlin: Springer, 1970) and *The Wonder of Being Human* (New York: Springer, 1984).

rich resources and explanatory successes of current materialism, dualism is less a theory of mind than it is an empty space waiting for a genuine theory of mind to be put in it.[42]

Here we have once more the mistaken idea that the dualist is committed to some kind of soul stuff. But there are two further and fundamental problems with Churchland's objection. First, this might be a good objection to a *scientific hypothesis* to which there was a much more fruitful and explanatorily powerful alternative. But why think dualism is a scientific hypothesis? What Churchland offers is an objection to dualism only if the latter is proposed as hypothesis, something designed to explain the phenomena, something that gets whatever warrant it enjoys by virtue of the excellence of the explanation it provides. But why think of dualism like this? Perhaps the dualist accepts dualism because she believes, first, that there is such a thing as she herself, and secondly, that she couldn't be a material object; she knows she is conscious, for example, and believes that no material object can be conscious. The question how much dualism does or doesn't explain is irrelevant; maybe it doesn't explain much of anything, but why should that be anything against it?[43] I believe that propositions, unlike sets, don't have members; maybe that doesn't explain much, but so what? It's not being proposed as a scientific hypothesis. Similarly an atheologian might complain that many characteristic Christian doctrines—Trinity and Incarnation, for example—aren't good explanations of the phenomena. But that would be an objection only if those doctrines were proposed as hypotheses, explanations of some range of phenomena; and they aren't.[44]

Secondly, the objection seems to suggest that the materialist can or does have an explanation of all these things, but the dualist doesn't or can't. That is of course mistaken; as I argued above, brain science is just as open to the dualist as to the materialist. Well, perhaps the idea is that the materialist can explain these things *as a materialist*, but the dualist can't do so as a dualist. But this looks like an illicit attempt to credit materialist metaphysics with the warrant enjoyed by the relevant science. It isn't as a materialist metaphysician that the materialist has these explanations; it is rather as someone who knows something about the brain and its connections with human behavior and pathologies. And of course there is nothing to prevent the dualist from knowing the very same things. Happily, you don't have to be a materialist to engage in brain science. Indeed, perhaps the shoe is on the other foot. Brain science investigates, among other things, the relation between brain activity and mental activity. Clearly it is arguable (proved by the fact that I've been arguing it) that if materialism were true, there wouldn't be any

---

[42] Churchland, *Matter and Consciousness* (Mass.: MIT Press, 1984), 19.

[43] Of course the term 'explain' is something of a weasel word, and explanations are multifarious. We can imagine a dualist suggestion that, given that material objects can't be conscious, think, believe, make decisions, take actions, and the like, dualism 'explains' the fact that human persons can do those things. That would be a slightly different but analogically connected sense of 'explain'; and in that sense, says the dualist, dualism can explain these things and materialism cannot.

[44] See my "Is Theism Really a Miracle?", *Faith and Philosophy*, 3/2 (1986).

such thing as mental activity; hence, from that perspective, it's the materialist who can't sensibly engage in brain science, at least of the sort that investigates those connections.

Conservation of Energy?

Still another scientific or quasi-scientific objection: according to Daniel Dennett and others, dualism violates the scientifically approved principle of conservation of energy:

> concentrate on the return signals, the directives from mind to brain. These, ex hypothesi, are not physical; they are not light waves or sound waves or cosmic rays or streams of subatomic particles. No physical energy or mass is associated with them. How, then, do they get to make a difference to what happens in the brain cells they must affect, if the mind is to have any influence over the body? A fundamental principle of physics is that any change in the trajectory of any physical entity is an acceleration requiring the expenditure of energy, and where is this energy to come from? It is this principle of the conservation of energy that accounts for the physical impossibility of "perpetual motion machines", and the same principle is apparently violated by dualism. This confrontation between quite standard physics and dualism has been endlessly discussed since Descartes's own day, and is widely regarded as the inescapable and fatal flaw of dualism.[45]

Here Dennett conflates two separate objections to dualism: first, the claim that an immaterial substance can't have causal consequences in the hard, ponderous, massive physical world, so that if dualism were true, human beings would be unable to act in the physical world; and second that the principle of conservation of energy prohibits an immaterial object from acting in the physical world. I'll turn to the first below; here I am concerned with the second. Note first that, again, the theist is already committed to the thought that an immaterial substance—God—can (indeed does) act in the physical world. God has created the world, and also sustains it. Further, according to Christian doctrine, God does much more; for example, he raised Jesus from the dead. And of course many Christians believe God has acted in the world on many occasions, enabling the Israelites to cross the Red Sea, appearing to the apostle Paul, multiplying the loaves and fishes, and much else. Indeed, many Christians believe that God is at present constantly active in the world and constantly active in our lives, strengthening us in time of trouble, offering grace, answering prayers. Clearly this objection, if it has any merit, is as much an objection to Christian belief as to dualism.

Does it have any merit? In a word, No. It is perfectly possible for God to create *ex nihilo* a full-grown horse in the center of the Notre Dame campus without in any way violating the conservation principles. God says: "Let there be a horse in the middle of the North Quad!" The horse suddenly appears in the

---

[45] *Consciousness Explained* (Boston: Little, Brown), 35.

middle of the quad; there need be no violation of conservation of energy. Clearly this needn't violate *global* conservation; for he could deduct an equal amount of energy elsewhere in the universe; the total energy of the system, that is, the universe, would then remain constant. But of course there is local conservation as well as global; and it is harder to see how there could be local conservation of energy if God created that horse *ex nihilo*. That is because it's not easy to find, for each relevant system, an analogue of creating a horse in one part of the universe and deducting the appropriate amount of energy elsewhere. So perhaps creating a horse *ex nihilo* is incompatible with local conservation: if God were to create that horse, energy would fail to be conserved in at least one system.

It doesn't follow, however, that God's creating that horse is precluded by any of the conservation laws of physics or that his doing so violates those laws. That is because the conservation laws are deduced from Newton's Laws; those laws are conditionals whose antecedents include the condition that the system in question is closed; the conservation laws—of momentum, charge, mass, energy, mass/energy, etc.—are therefore said to hold for *closed* or *isolated* systems. Thus Sears and Zemansky,

This is the principle of conservation of linear momentum: When no resultant external force acts on a system, the total momentum of the system remains constant in magnitude and direction.

More generally,

The internal energy of an isolated system remains constant. This is the most general statement of the *principle of conservation of energy.* The internal energy of an *isolated* system cannot be changed by any process (mechanical, electrical, chemical, nuclear, or biological) taking place *within* the system. The energy of a system can be changed only by a flow of heat across its boundary, or by the performance of work. (If either takes place, the system is no longer isolated.)[46]

But of course a system—the physical universe, say—in which God creates *ex nihilo* a full-grown horse is not, obviously, a closed or isolated system. It is clearly not one that is subject to no resultant external force. Therefore the conservation laws do not imply that the quantity in question remains constant in it. More specifically, from the system's being closed it follows that the relevant reference frame is inertial, and hence that the Lagrangian (roughly, a function giving the difference between the kinetic and potential energy of the system) of the system is independent of time (its partial derivative with respect to time is zero). It also follows that the Lagrangian is unaffected by a translation of the entire system in space.[47] But these conditions can't both hold for any system in which this horse

---

[46] *University Physics* (Reading, Mass; Addison-Wesley, 1964), 186 (bold and italics removed from original), and 415 (italics in original).

[47] See Marion and Thornton, *Classical Dynamics*, 4th edn (New York: Harcourt Brace College Publishers, 1995), 217, 219. (I am indebted to Brian Pitts for this reference, and for help throughout this section.)

suddenly appears. For example, if the space of the system is just the space into which the horse is suddenly introduced, the Lagrangian of the system will depend on time; it will assume different values before and after the horse is created.

The same considerations clearly apply to Dennett's claim that dualism (taken as involving the claim that an immaterial self can cause effects in the physical world) is incompatible with the law of the conservation of energy. He neglects the fact that the law in question applies only to closed systems, ones not subject to any outside force. This condition clearly won't hold for any physical system—my body, or brain, or part of my brain—in which an immaterial self causes a change. This objection, therefore, is wholly without force. It's not that it gives one some reason, perhaps only a weak reason, for rejecting dualism; it provides no reason at all.[48]

Can an Immaterial Substance have Causal Consequences in the Material World?

Dennett appears to be confusing conservation of energy with the (alleged) causal closure of the physical—the idea, as he puts it, that "anything that can move a physical thing is a physical thing" (*Consciousness Explained*, 35.) Strictly speaking, this is not an objection to dualism as I defined it: the thought that human beings are not material objects but are immaterial substances. That view, just as it stands, doesn't entail that (human) immaterial substances *can* cause effects in the physical world. Dualism as thus defined is compatible, first, with *occasionalism*, the doctrine embraced by Malebranche and others. According to occasionalism, it is only God who causes changes in the physical world, but, for example, God takes my willing to raise my arm as an occasion to cause my arm to rise. Dualism is compatible, secondly, with Leibniz's *pre-established harmony*, according to which mental events don't cause physical events, but from time immemorial God has instituted a correlation between mental events, such as my willing or trying to raise my arm, and physical events, such as my arm's rising. Dennett's objection is really to *dualistic interactionism*, according to which human beings are immaterial substances that can act, can cause changes, in the physical world. I don't mean to argue against either pre-established harmony or occasionalism, and in fact the latter has its attractions.

So consider the current objection as directed against dualistic interactionism; even so, it still has no force. First, the doctrine or dogma of the causal closure

---

[48] Another definition of closure for a system: a system is closed if and only if there is no flow of energy across its boundaries. As Sears and Zemansky put it above, "The energy of a system can be changed only by a flow of heat across its boundary, or by the performance of work." But this is clearly not a correct definition of closure; if an external agent causes something to occur within a system S (creates a horse within S, say) but without causing a flow of energy across the boundaries of S, S is still clearly not a closed system. This definition would be accurate up to logical equivalence only if it were impossible, in the broadly logical sense, that God create a horse within a system without causing an energy flow across the boundaries of the system.

of the physical is not a deliverance of current science: it is more like an article of faith or perhaps a pious hope on the part of materialists. Science says nothing at all to imply that there aren't any immaterial substances, and nothing at all to imply that if there are some, they can't cause changes in the physical world. Is there then any reason to believe this dogma? Although not strictly relevant to my case, it is of interest to note that causal closure depends heavily on the correct analysis or account of causation. On one of Hume's accounts, causation is fundamentally a matter of constant conjunction (with the 'cause' preceding the effect): "we may define a cause to be *an object followed by another, and where all the objects, similar to the first, are followed by objects similar to the second.*"[49] But of course there is no reason in the world why a mental event (i.e., an event involving only an immaterial substance) shouldn't be related, in this way, to a physical event (one involving only a physical substance). There is no reason in the world, therefore, why my willing to raise my arm shouldn't cause my arm to rise, even if I am an immaterial substance.

Immediately after the above passage from the *Inquiry*, Hume proposes a different account of causation: "Or in other words, *where, if the first object had not been, the second never had existed.*" David Lewis presents a fuller version of this second account. Say that an event *d* depends causally on an event *e* iff the counterfactual *If e had not occurred, d would not have occurred* is true. Then

Let *c, d, e,* be a finite sequence of actual particular events such that *d* depends causally on *c, e* on *d*, and so on throughout. Then this sequence is a *causal chain*. Finally, one event is a *cause* of another iff there exists a causal chain leading from the first to the second.[50]

Again, it is obvious that there can be this kind of counterfactual relation between mental events and physical events. Suppose, for example, that I am an immaterial substance and that something like Leibniz's pre-established harmony is the truth of the matter: from before the foundation of the world, God has decreed and established a correlation between my mental states—my tryings and willings, my efforts and endeavors–and what happens in the physical world. I will to raise my arm; my arm rises; if I had not willed to do so, it would not have risen. On the Lewisian account, therefore, my willing to raise my arm causes it to rise, and this despite Leibniz's explicit aim to propose a theory according to which mental and physical events are correlated but not causally related. The moral is this: given a Humean/Lewisian account of causality, causal closure of the physical isn't plausible—unless, of course, there *aren't* any immaterial substances, in which case it is trivial. Indeed, given a Humean/Lewisian account of causality, the difference between dualistic interactionism and pre-established harmony can hardly be so much as stated. The same goes for another venerable

[49] *An Inquiry Concerning Human Understanding*, (LaSalle: Open Court Publishing Co., 1956), section VII, 83.

[50] "Causation", *Journal of Philosophy*, 70/17 (Oct. 1973), 563. Lewis later added some bells and whistles to fend off certain counterexamples.

contrast: that between dualistic interactionism and occasionalism. For if, as on occasionalism, my willing to raise my arm is the occasion for God's causing my arm to rise, then presumably God would not have caused it to rise if I had not willed to raise it; hence the counterfactual *If I had not willed to raise my arm, my arm would not have risen* is true, so that on the Lewis account my willing to raise my arm causes it to rise. In order to state these distinctions, and this objection to dualism, we must suppose that causation involves more than constant conjunction and more than counterfactual dependence: it must involve something further, something in the neighborhood of *production, making*, a sort of causal oomph or force, a necessary connection of some kind.[51] So to consider this objection, let's assume that causality is more than counterfactual dependence.

Now the objection that an immaterial substance can't have causal effects in the material world is usually stated as a rhetorical question: "How is this utterly insubstantial 'thinking substance' to have any influence on ponderous matter? How can two such different things be in any sort of causal contact?"[52] The answers, of course, are supposed to be "It can't" and "They can't". This objection is perhaps the most widely urged of all the objections against dualism; according to Churchland and Dennett it is widely thought conclusive.[53] But what is there to be said for it? From a Christian or theistic perspective, obviously, nothing at all. The claim is that no immaterial substance can cause effects in the hard, heavy, massy physical world. But this is a claim a theist can't take seriously: for of course *God* is an immaterial substance who causes effects in the hard, heavy, massy physical world. Therefore it can't be a true general principle that immaterial substances can't have causal effects in the physical world. This objection, even if the most widely accepted and respected of them all, should carry no weight with Christian theists.

I suppose someone might say that God is an immaterial substance that can have effects in the physical world, but he is the only immaterial substance that can do a thing like that; no finite immaterial substance can do such a thing. But why believe that? What is the or even a reason to think it true? True: we have little or no insight into how it is that an immaterial substance can cause changes in the physical world; but we have equally little insight into how it is that a *material* substance can cause changes in the physical world. Causation as a non-Humean relation among finite substances is something of a mystery; but it is no more mysterious where one of the relata is material and the other immaterial than where both are material or both immaterial.

---

[51] It is the difficulty of making clear this kind of connection that is part of the charm of occasionalism; in the case of divine causation, the connection isn't obscure at all; it's just broadly logical necessity. Every world in which God says 'Let there be light!' is a world in which there is light.

[52] Churchland, *Matter and Consciousness*, 11.

[53] See also Anthony Kenny, *Descartes* (New York: Random House, 1968), 222–3.

The Pairing Problem

Objection 5 is usually formulated (if that is not too strong a word) by way of rhetorical questions; thus, for example, Churchland: "How is this utterly insubstantial 'thinking substance' to have any influence on ponderous matter? How can two such different things be in any sort of causal contact" (above, p. 129)? Jaegwon Kim provides a notable exception; he actually develops a serious and responsible statement of the alleged problem. (In his case 'formulate' is certainly not too strong a word.) Kim's efforts here go so far beyond the usual that they deserve to be treated as a separate objection to dualism.

Kim begins by pointing out that the usual rhetorical-question formulations of the objection have nothing to be said for them. By way of a more serious effort, he asks us to suppose that "Smith and Jones are 'psychophysically synchronized': each time Smith's mind wills to raise his hand, so does Jone's, and vice versa, and every time they will to raise their hands, their hands rise."[54] What is it that makes it the case that it is *Smith's* willing, not Jones's, that causes Smith's hand to rise? After all, both willings are spatiotemporally related to the event of Smith's hand rising in the same way: they occur at the same time, and neither is spatially related to that event. So in virtue of *what* is it that Smith's willing, rather than Jones's willing, causes Smith's hand to rise? We can't answer by pointing out that Smith wills that *Smith's* hand rise, while Jones wills that *Jones's* hand rise for, says Kim, what makes a given body B the body of a given person S is that S is able to cause changes in B *directly*. (I can raise my arm directly; I can raise yours only by taking hold of it with my hand and then raising it.) But then bodily ownership, for the dualist, is explained by way of psychophysical causation; therefore we can't use bodily ownership to explain psychophysical causation.

Kim presumably won't be satisfied with the answer, "Well, we don't so far have a problem except in cases of people who are psychophysically synchronized, and people are very seldom psychophysically synchronized." His idea would be that the dualistic interactionist (hereafter dualist) is committed to the *possibility* that there be cases of psychophysically synchronized people where nonetheless it is Smith's willing, not Jones's, that causes Smith's arm to rise. And if there were such cases, there would have to be something, some further factor X, that determined, grounded, made it the case, that Smith's willing, not Jones's, causes Smith's arm to rise. In the case of causation on the part of material beings, that further factor would involve spatio-temporal relations; but those aren't available to the dualist.

Still, there may be an easy answer: there is an asymmetry about these willings. What Smith wills is that *this* (pointing to the hand) hand rise. Of course this hand is Smith's; but willing that Smith's hand rise is not the same thing as willing that *this* hand rise, even if this hand is Smith's. So Smith but not Jones wills that

---

[54] "Lonely Souls: Causality and Substance Dualism", in *Soul, Body, and Survival* (Ithaca, NY: Cornell University Press, 2001), 30–43 (33).

this hand rise, and Jones but not Smith wills that *that* hand rise. And the further factor X that makes it the case that Smith's willing causes Smith's hand to go up is that Smith wills that this hand go up; similarly, of course, for Jones and *that* hand. But Kim can easily amend his example so as to sidestep this reply: suppose that both Smith and Jones will that Smith's hand rise and do so at the same time: by virtue of what is it that *Smith's* willing, as opposed to Jones's, causes Smith's hand to rise? As Kim puts it,

There are two souls, A and B, and they perform a certain mental action, as a result of which a change occurs in material substance M. We may suppose that mental actions of the kind involved generally cause physical changes of the sort that happened in M, and, moreover, that in the present case it is soul A's action, not soul B's, that caused the change in M. Surely such a possibility must exist. But ask: What relation might perform the job of pairing soul A's action with the change in M, a relation that is absent in the case of soul B's action and the change in M? Evidently, no spatial relations can be involved to answer this question, for souls are not in space and are not able to bear spatial relations to material things ('Lonely Souls', 36).

Kim's thought, then, is that in any case where an event A causes an event B, there must be some factor, some X, in virtue of which it is A that causes B, in virtue of which A is paired with B. In the case of material events, this factor X, he suggests, will be a matter of spatio-temporal relations, although he doesn't say what, in general, these spatio-temporal relations would be. Spatio-temporal relations aren't available to do the job for the dualist, however, because temporal relations by themselves obviously can't do the job, and the soul isn't in space. But there don't seem to be any other candidates for the pairing relation; so there is a deep difficulty for the dualist here, one in virtue of which dualism should be rejected.

What can the dualist say for herself? First, is it really clear that in any case of causation, there must be this factor X that pairs up event A with event B, that makes it the case that A is the cause of B? I have two worries here. First, it isn't clear that spatio-temporal relations suffice for the pairing job; at any rate if we take quantum mechanics seriously. On some interpretations of quantum mechanics objects don't have a determinate position, or indeed any position at all, between collapses of the wave function; presumably the same goes, therefore, for events involving those objects. Of course there are other interpretations of quantum mechanics that lack this feature; so perhaps this isn't a serious worry for Kim.

Second and more important: why must we suppose that *there is* such a factor X? The question is: when event A causes event B, what is it that pairs A with B, rather than with C or D? What is it that makes it the case that A causes B? But maybe this is a confused question, or at any rate a question that conceals a contentious philosophical position. Consider the similar and oft-asked question about identity over time. What is it that makes it the case that object A at time t is identical with object B at some earlier time t*? Similarity? Causal connections of certain kinds? Many answers have been proposed, but none seems to work. And perhaps the right answer to the question is: there isn't anything (anything *else*, so to speak) that makes it the case that A is identical with B. Identity doesn't have to supervene on other properties. Of course there are necessary conditions of A's being identical with B. For example, both A and B must exist, and (perhaps) must have existed at each time between t and t*; and if A and B are physical objects, then (perhaps) there must be a continuously occupied spatio-temporal path between the location of A at t and that of B at t*); but there isn't anything that makes it the case that A at t is identical with B at t*. Couldn't it be the same in the case of causation? Why does there have to be something, a state of affairs or something else, that makes it the case that event A causes event B? This is not an easy question. It is intimately connected with this question: which is prior: causal laws, or individual examples, cases, of causation? That is also a difficult question, and it may have different answers for divine causation on the one hand and creaturely causation on the other.

But we don't have to have answers to these difficult questions in order to see that the pairing problem, if there really is a pairing problem, is not a problem for dualists who are also theists. Medieval and Renaissance theists held, of course, that God creates the universe and sustains it and its parts in existence. But they also held that God *concurs* with every causal transaction that takes place; this concurrence is both necessary and sufficient for a given event (or substance) A to cause a given event B. Now one might suspect that this concurrence doctrine is metaphysical overkill—little more, really, than an attempt to pay God unnecessary (and unwanted) metaphysical compliments. If there really is a pairing problem, however, divine concurrence offers an easy solution: the relevant factor distinguishing Smith's willing from Jones's willing is that God concurs with the state of affairs *Smith's willing causing Smith's arm to rise*, but does not concur with *Jones's willing causing Smith's arm to raise*. That's the further factor X that makes it the case that it is Smith's willing that does the causing.

Perhaps Kim would want to reply as follows: divine concurrence is a solution to the pairing problem only if theism is viable, and theism is viable only if it is possible that God cause events in the world. Now Kim apparently thinks this pairing problem would hold for *any* alleged cases of causation on the part of an immaterial substance: "the difficulty we have seen with Loeb's interpretation of Descartes as a Humean in matters of causation, I believe, points to a more fundamental difficulty in the idea that mental substances, outside physical space, can enter into causal relations with objects in physical space" (p. 35). He might therefore suppose that the pairing problem affects alleged divine causation just as much as creaturely causation. For according to theism, God is not in space (and, some say, not in time either). Therefore the factor X that answers to the pairing problem in the case of material objects, that is, some relation to space and time (or space–time) isn't present in cases of divine causation. No doubt the theist is committed to the possibility that both God and someone else, an angel, perhaps, will that something happen; what is it that makes it the case that it is *God's* willing that causes the event, rather than the angel's? Not spatio-temporal relations, clearly; but then what? What is that factor X in the case of alleged divine causation?

But here there appears to be an easy answer. According to classical theism, it's a necessary truth that whatever God wills, takes place. It's a necessary truth that if God says, "Let there be light," then there is light. Necessarily, if God says, "Let Adam come into existence," Adam comes into existence. So what is it that makes it the case that God's intentions cause what they cause? To ask that question is like asking, "What is it that makes an equiangular triangle equilateral?" The answer is (broadly) logical necessity; it's necessary that whatever God wills comes to be, just as it's necessary that every equiangular triangle be equilateral.[55] Accordingly there isn't a problem about that factor X in the divine case; but then divine concurrence solves the pairing problem, if there really is such a problem, for the case of immaterial created substances.[56] Here is another objection to dualism, or argument for materialism, that ought to have no purchase at all upon a Christian (or other) theist.

Localization and Dependence

According to Nancey Murphy:

In particular, nearly all of the human capacities or faculties once attributed to the *soul* are now seen to be functions of the brain. Localization studies—that is, finding regional structure or distributed system in the brain responsible for such things as language, emotion and decision making—provide especially strong motivation for saying that it is the brain that is responsible for these capacities, not some immaterial entity associated with the body. In Owen Flanagan's terms, it is the brain that is the *res cogitans*—the thinking thing.[57]

Localization studies show that when a given sort of mental activity occurs, certain parts of the brain display increased blood flow and increased electrical activity. Paul Churchland adds that mental activity is also in a certain important way *dependent* on brain activity and brain condition:

[55] This is part of the attraction of occasionalism. It is hard to see what causality amounts to in the case of secondary or created causes, just as it is hard to see what necessity amounts to in the case of "natural" necessity, the sort of necessity that natural laws are supposed by, for example, D. M. Armstrong in *What is a Law of Nature?* (Cambridge: Cambridge University Press, 1983) to have. (Armstrong has since revised the views.) But it is easy to see what causality amounts to in the case of God's causing something: it's just a matter of logical necessity.

[56] Kim, obviously, is certainly among the most thoughtful materialists; and he finds both reductive and non-reductive materialism deeply problematic. This should incline him towards dualism; but of course he also thinks there is this pairing problem for dualism. If he thinks the pairing problem is the only serious problem for dualism, and if he agrees that divine concurrence offers an easy (theistic) solution to that problem, then wouldn't he have here a powerful theistic argument?

[57] Warren Brown, Nancey Murphy, and H. Newton Malony (eds.), *Whatever Happened to the Soul?* (Minneapolis: Fortress Press, 1998), 1.

Alcohol, narcotics, or senile degeneration of nerve tissue will impair, cripple, or even destroy one's capacity for rational thought. Psychiatry knows of hundreds of emotion-controlling chemicals (lithium, chlorpromazine, amphetamine, cocaine, and so on) that do their work when vectored into the brain. And the vulnerability of consciousness to the anesthetics, to caffeine, and to something as simple as a sharp blow to the head, shows its very close dependence on neural activity in the brain. All of this makes perfect sense if reason, emotion and consciousness are activities of the brain itself. But it makes very little sense if they are activities of something else. We may call this the argument from the *neural dependence* of all known mental phenomena.[58]

It isn't true at all that it makes very little sense to say that activities of the immaterial self or soul are dependent in this way on the proper function of the brain. Still, this argument from localization and neural dependence is perhaps the strongest of the arguments against dualism. That may not be much of a distinction, given the other arguments are substantially without any force, at least for someone committed to Christian theism. But this argument does seem to carry a certain minimal force; at any rate dependence and localization phenomena do suggest the possibility that the brain is all there is here. Taken as a serious argument, however, and looked at in the cold light of morning, it has little to be said for it. What we know is that for at least many mental functions or actions M, there are parts of the brain P such that (1) when M occurs, there is increased blood flow and electrical activity in P, and (2) when B is damaged or destroyed, M is inhibited or altogether absent. Consider, therefore, the mental activity of adding a column of figures, and let's assume that there is a particular area of the brain related to this activity in the way suggested by (1) and (2). Does this show or tend to show that this mental activity is really an activity of the brain, rather than of something distinct from the brain?

Not obviously. There are many activities that stand in that same relation to the brain. There is walking, or running, or speaking, or waving my arms and moving

---

[58] *Matter and Consciousness*, 20. See also Thomas Nagel's "Concealment and Exposure and Other Essays" (New York: Oxford University Press, 2002); in the course of a long, detailed, and subtle discussion, Nagel argues that there is a logically necessary connection between mental states and physical states of the following sort: for any mental state M there is a physical state P such that there is some underlying reality R, neither mental nor physical but capable of having both mental and physical states, which has essentially the property of being such that necessarily, it is in P just if it is in M. (And perhaps it would be sensible to go on from that claim to the conclusion that it is not possible that I exist when my body B does not.) Nagel concedes that it seems impossible that there be such a reality; his argument that nonetheless there really is or must be such a thing is, essentially, just an appeal to localization/dependency phenomena: "the evident massive and detailed dependence of what happens in the mind on what happens in the brain provides, in my view, strong evidence that the relation is not contingent but necessary" (p. 202), and "The causal facts are strong evidence that mental events have physical properties, if only we could make sense of the idea" (p. 204). The particular route of his argument here is via an argument to the best explanation: he suggests that the only really satisfactory explanation of those localization/dependency phenomena is the existence of such an underlying reality. (Of course if that is what it takes for a really satisfying explanation, we may wonder whether there *is* a really satisfying explanation here; are we guaranteed that all phenomena have what we take to be really satisfying explanations?)

my fingers: for each of these activities there is a part of my brain related to it in such a way that when I engage in that activity, there is increased blood flow in that part, and when that part is damaged or destroyed, paralysis results so that I can no longer engage in the activity. Who would conclude that these activities are really activities of the brain rather than of legs and trunk, or mouth and vocal cords, or arms? Who would conclude that my fingers' moving is really an activity of my brain and not of my fingers? Ric's rock climbing is dependent on appropriate brain activity; it hardly follows that rock climbing just *is* an activity of his brain. Digestion will occur only if my brain is in the right condition; how does it follow that digestion is really an activity of the brain, and not an activity of the digestive system? My brain's functioning properly depends on blood flow and on the proper performance of my lungs; shall we conclude that brain function is really circulatory or pulmonary activity? All of my activities depend upon my ingesting enough and the right kind of food; shall we see here vindication of the old saw 'you are what you eat'?

The point, obviously, is that dependence is one thing, identity quite another. Appropriate brain activity is a necessary condition for mental activity; it simply doesn't follow that the latter just is the former; nor, as far as I can see, is it even rendered probable. We know of all sorts of cases of activities A that depend upon activities B but are not identical with them. Why should we think differently in this case?[59]

Well, perhaps someone will say that in the cases I've been citing, we know on independent grounds that there are two kinds of activities; we know that digestion is an activity of stomach, intestines and the like, and not just of the brain, even if brain activity is a necessary condition of digestion. But (so the objector continues) just that knowledge is what is lacking in the case of mental activity; we don't know of something distinct from the brain that is involved in mental activity. Suppose that were so: we would still have at best a massively weak argument for materialism, for (obviously) the fact that we don't know of such a thing hardly shows that there isn't any such thing. Should we pay much attention to an atheologian who argued that since we don't know of an all-powerful, wholly good, all-knowing being who has created the world and sustains it in existence, there isn't any such being? But in any event it isn't true that we don't know of something distinct from the brain that is involved in mental activity. The above arguments for dualism, I claim, gives us, at the very least, good reason to hold that thinking is not, or not merely, an activity of the brain. But then it is not the case that thinking is an activity of the brain and nothing else.

In conclusion, then: there are powerful arguments against materialism. When we consider the bearing of Christian belief upon materialism, we find still more

---

[59] A related argument for materialism has it that the great theoretical benefits of *identifying*, for example, pain with C-fiber firing, warrant accepting materialism. For discussion of this claim, see the last section of "Against Materialism".

reasons to reject it in favor of dualism. Were it not for my respect for my materialist colleagues, I would certainly say "Never has so implausible a doctrine been so widely accepted!"[60]

APPENDIX: INDICATION AND CONTENT

I argued above that a material structure or event isn't the right sort of thing to have belief content; this problem has not been lost on materialists, canny lot that they are. In trying to deal with it, they typically ignore Leibniz's problem and instead offer suggestions as to how it might be that a neural object or event could have (original) content after all. Most attempts to do so begin with *indicators*, or *indication*, or *indicator meaning* as outlined above.

The first step is to call these structures, the ones correlated with external or internal conditions of one kind or another, 'representations'. Indeed, the idea that such structures are representations has become so common that it is part of the current background assumptions in cognitive neuroscience.[61] Those patterns of neural firing in the frog's brain are said to be representations of flies, or bugs, or small flying objects, or small black objects (there is usually considerable latitude of choice as to what gets represented); those magnetosomes in anaerobic bacteria are said to represent north, or the direction towards oxygen-free water, or the lines of the earth's magnetic field; the structures in your body that respond to the temperature of your blood are said to represent that temperature.

Now the terms 'represent', 'representation', and 'representative' are multiply ambiguous. Webster's *Third International* gives a whole host of analogically connected meanings: you can send your representative to a meeting; your state or national representative represents your interests (we hope); an artist can produce a representation of a battle; a musical passage can represent a storm; x's and o's can represent football players, and a dotted line can represent where the tight end is supposed to go, a scale model of Mt Rainier can represent Mt Rainier. This term is therefore something of a weasel word, a property that often gets exploited in philosophy of mind or cognitive science contexts. Since the term is ordinarily used without explicit definition, it is often hard to know just what is meant by calling those indicators 'representations'; shall we say that wherever you have causal or nomological correlation, you have representation? Shall we say that smoke represents fire (and fire represents smoke), that the rate at which the wheels of my car turn represent the speedometer reading, and that trees budding represent spring or warmer weather (and vice versa)? I guess we can say these things if we like; it's a free country, and the term 'representation' is flexible enough to allow it.

But here is the crucial next step: efforts to understand belief materialistically typically try, somehow, to promote these representations to *beliefs*. In so doing, they ordinarily simply ignore Leibniz's problem—the fact that it looks as if a material thing can't think, or be, a belief. But this procedure is also unpromising in its own right: representation of this sort is nowhere near sufficient for belief. The gas gauge on my car may represent

---

[60] Well, *almost* never. Verificationism, which was as widely accepted in the 1940s and 1950s as materialism is now, is at least equally implausible.

[61] See Ramsey, *Using and Abusing Representation: Reassessing the Cognitive Revolution.*

the amount of gasoline in the tank, and the weight on the bolts holding the tank to the frame, and the volume of air in the tank, and other things as well; nothing in the relevant neighborhood has beliefs on these scores. Those magnetosomes perhaps represent the direction to oxygen-free water; neither they nor the bacteria that contain them believe that's the way to oxygen-free water. Those internal structures that indicate and thus represent your blood pressure do not believe that your blood pressure is thus and so, and neither (most of the time) do you. The thing to see is that no amount of this indication and representation, no matter how gussied up, is sufficient for *belief.* Clearly a material object *can* be a representation in *some* sense: Michelangelo's *David* for example, is a representation of David, and a few weird lines in a cartoon can represent George Bush. But it doesn't follow that a material structure can be a belief, or that it can have propositional content.

There are many ways in which materialist thinkers try to promote indication or representation to belief. I can't of course comment on them all; I'll content myself with brief comments on a couple of the most prominent.

First, there is Jerry Fodor's suggestion. It is plausible to suppose that there is a certain neuronal structure or event that is involved in the perception of cows, and that is caused by cows, and that indicates cows. These structures, says Fodor, have the content cow. But note further that these structures can also, under certain conditions, be caused by other things—a moose in the twilight, or under certain conditions maybe a large cat, or a perhaps a scale model of a moose. What confers content on such a structure—the content cow—is that there being structures of that sort that are *not* caused by cows, is asymmetrically dependent upon there being structures of that sort that *are* caused by cows: "But 'cow' means *cow* and not *cat* or *cow or cat* because *there being cat-caused 'cow' tokens depends on there being cow-caused 'cow' token, but not the other way around.*"[62] This also seems monumentally unpromising, at least if taken as presenting a necessary and sufficient condition.[63] Perhaps we can rewrite Fodor's suggestion more explicitly as follows:

> (F) A token cow indicator C* of type T has the content cow just if there being non-cow-caused tokens of T depends on there being cow-caused tokens of T, but not conversely.

Thus there is, we may suppose, a certain neural structure ordinarily caused, in human beings, by the perception of a cow; in certain circumstances, however (twilight, for example, or great distance) that token will be caused, not by a cow, but by a moose or horse, or cat, or cow picture, or too much whiskey, or whatever. Tokens of this type T have the content cow, however, because if there weren't any cow-caused tokens of T, there wouldn't be any non-cow-caused tokens of T; but there could perfectly well be cow-caused tokens of T even if there weren't any non-cow-caused tokens of T.

Taken as a specification of a necessary and sufficient condition, (F) has two problems: the proposed condition is not necessary, and it is not sufficient. First, there are objects about which we have beliefs, of which we have concepts, and denoted by our terms, such that there probably aren't any indicators of them at all. These would comprise the

---

[62] *A Theory of Content and Other Essays* (Cambridge, Mass.: MIT Press, 1990), 91.
[63] And if it isn't intended as a sufficient condition, it won't really be relevant to our current concerns, i.e. it won't suffice to show how representations can be promoted to beliefs.

whole realm of abstracta: properties, propositions, numbers, sets, and the like. These things do not enter into relevant causal relations with us; hence there aren't indicators of them in our brains—or, if there are, they aren't caused by these abstract objects. Hence the condition (F) proposes isn't necessary: we have beliefs about, concepts of, and terms denoting objects that don't cause the relevant indicators. But secondly, (F) is also insufficient: it is much too generous with content. Consider cow pies, for example; they apparently fill the bill specified by (F). Cow pies are cow indicators; furthermore, there wouldn't be non-cow-caused cow pies if there weren't cow-caused cow pies, although there could certainly be cow-caused cow pies even if there weren't non-cow-caused cow pies. But then cow pies, according to (F), have the content cow—which, not to put too fine a point on it, is no more than a load of organic lawn food.

Second, there is Fred Dretske's work, perhaps the most sophisticated and accomplished attempt to explain belief from a materialist perspective.[64] Like the other two, Dretske ignores Leibniz's problem; like them he simply assumes that it is possible for a material thing to think and for a material assemblage of neurons to be a belief. And like nearly everyone else, Dretske begins with the notion of indication, correlation (perhaps nomic, perhaps causal) between events of one kind and events of another. His attempt to explain belief in terms of indication involves two additional ideas. First, the notion of *function*. All beliefs are representations, and representations essentially involve functions: "The fundamental idea [of representation] is that a system, S, represents a property F, if and only if S has the function of indicating (providing information about) the F of a certain domain of objects."[65] So not all cases of indication are cases of representation: the fuel gauge in my automobile indicates the amount of gasoline in the tank, the weight on the bolts holding the tank to the frame, the amount of air in the tank, the air pressure, the altitude, the temperature, the potential across a certain circuit, and many other things; its *function*, however, is to indicate the amount of gasoline in the tank. Hence it represents the amount of fuel in the tank and does not represent those other properties and quantities, fascinating as they may be. This appeal to function enables Dretske to see representational contexts as like belief contexts in being intensional: it may be that it is the function of something or other to indicate a property p, while it isn't its function to indicate a nomically or logically equivalent property q.

But just as not every case of indication involves representation, so, according to Dretske, not every case of representation is a case of belief (or proto-belief, as he tends to put it). He cites the case of the noctuid moth, which, upon detecting the bursts of high frequency sound emitted by the bat's sonar, executes evasive maneuvers. Here we have representation; it is the function of those neural structures registering that sound to indicate the presence of bats, to carry the information that bats are present. But these structures, says Dretske, are not beliefs and do not have belief content. Where C is a structure representing something or other (and now we come to the second additional idea), belief content is present *only if C causes some motor output or movement M, and the explanation of C's causing M is C's carrying the information that it does.* That is not so in the case of those structures in the noctuid moth:

---

[64] See esp. *Explaining Behavior* and *Naturalizing the Mind* (Cambridge, Mass.: MIT Press, 1995).
[65] *Naturalizing the Mind*, 2.

the explanation of why *this* C is causing *this* M, why the moth is now executing evasive maneuvers—has nothing to do with what *this* C indicates about this moth's surroundings. The explanation lies in the moth's genes. (*Explaining Behavior*, 92)

Take a given moth and the neural circuit C whose firing causes those maneuvers M: the explanation of C's causing M is not that C indicates the presence of bats, but the way the neural circuitry of this moth is deployed. The fact that in these moths C represents the presence of bats may explain or help explain why moths of this type have survived and flourished; but the fact that in a given moth C represents bats does not explain why C causes M.

If we don't get belief here, where do we get it? Where there is *learning*, says Dretske (here learning, on pain of circularity, does not entail or presuppose belief). Consider a bird that learns to peck at a red spot because it is rewarded when it does. At first the bird pecks aimlessly, now at the red spot, now at the black spot, now at a shadow on the walls of its cage. But then we reward it when it pecks at the red spot. Soon it will peck only or mainly at the red spot; it has learned something. What has happened here? Well, the bird had a red spot detector to start with; by virtue of learning, that structure came to cause the bird to peck at the red spot. And the structure in question causes the motor output in question *because* that structure indicates a red spot, carries the information that the figure in front of the bird is a red spot. Here, therefore, we do have a case of belief content, says Dretske, and the bird can be said to believe (or proto-believe) that there is a red spot in front of it.

As far as I can see, Dretske's complete account of belief can be put as follows:

(D) x is a belief if and only if (1) x is a state of an indicating element E in a representational system (e.g. the event consisting in the system's being 'on'), (2) x's function is to indicate something F, (3) x is in the mode or state it is in when it indicates something F, (4) x causes some movement M, and (5) the explanation of x's causing M is that it indicates F.

A comment on (3): it's not necessary that, on the occasion in question, x is actually indicating something F; perhaps on this occasion x is misrepresenting. We fix red-colored spectacles on the bird: now its red spot indicator causes it to peck at any spot, red or not. But the red spot indicator is still on, as we might say, even when in fact the spot in front of the bird is black.

This is a complex and sophisticated account. Still, sophisticated as it is, Dretske's account, I think, won't anywhere nearly do the job. First, a couple of semi-technical objections. I believe that $7 + 5 = 12$; nothing, however, carries the information that $7 + 5 = 12$, and indeed $7 + 5's$ *being equal to 12* isn't information. That is because, according to Dretske's (Shannon) conception of information, information is always a matter of reduction of possibilities; but $7 + 5's$ *equaling 12* doesn't reduce the possibilities with respect to anything. The account is therefore too strong; it rules out beliefs that are logically necessary in either the broad or the narrow sense. And just what kind of possibilities are we thinking of here? If causal or nomic possibility is relevant (if carrying information requires the reduction of causal or nomic possibilities), then the account also fails to work for nomologically necessary beliefs, such as that (as current physics has it, anyway) nothing travels faster than light (more exactly, nothing accelerates from a velocity less than that of light to a velocity greater than that of light). This doesn't reduce the nomic possibilities. And what about beliefs about the past? Given that past propositions are 'accidentally necessary', does anything *now* carry the information that Brutus stabbed Caesar?

Further, I believe that Proust is more subtle than L'Amour; is it even remotely plausible to suppose that I must therefore have a Proust-is-more-subtle-than-L'Amour-indicator, a neural structure correlated with *Proust's being more subtle than L'Amour* whose function it is to indicate that Proust is more subtle than L'Amour? Or a structure that fires when in the (virtual?) presence of a pair of writers, one of whom is more subtle than the other? And even if there were such structures, would they have to cause *motion* of one sort or another, for me to believe that Proust is more subtle than L'Amour? Maybe I've always believed this, but never said so, or in any other way displayed this belief in my behavior.

Still further, return to that noctuid moth. Perhaps it was designed by God; and perhaps God designed it in such a way that C, the structure causing that evasive motion, causes that motion because C indicates the presence of bats. Then it would be true that C causes M because of what it indicates (God chooses C to cause M, because C indicates the presence of bats) and, on Dretske's account, the moth would on the appropriate occasions believe that there are bats present. So if the moth came to be by undirected evolution it doesn't have beliefs (or at least doesn't have the belief that bats are present when its bat indicator is activated); if God has designed it, however, then it does have that belief on those occasions. Can that be right? In the same way there are all those internal indicators I mentioned a bit ago: structures whose function it is to indicate blood pressure, temperature, sodium level, sugar level, and the like. These indicators are in fact so constituted that they cause certain kinds of movements. If human beings have been designed by God, then presumably they cause those movements because of what they indicate; that's why God designed the system in such a way that they *do* cause those movements. So on Dretske's account, these structures, or we who contain them, would hold the associated beliefs about our blood temperature, pressure, sodium level, sugar level, and the like. But we don't; if Dretske's account were right, therefore, this would constitute an argument against the existence of God. Clearly it doesn't.

Insofar as they can't accommodate necessary beliefs and beliefs about the past, Dretske's conditions are too strong: they aren't necessary for belief. But they are also too weak: they aren't sufficient either. If his account were correct, then if we have been designed by God, we hold all those beliefs about blood pressure, temperature, sodium content, and the like; but we don't. You may or may not think we have in fact been designed by God; but even if we haven't it is certainly *possible* that we have; hence it's possible that Dretske's conditions hold when no beliefs are present. And really, why should the fulfillment of Dretske's conditions have anything at all to do with belief? So there is this structure that has the function of indicating something and causes what it does because of what it indicates; does that really so much as slyly suggest that something in the neighborhood of this structure holds the appropriate belief, or any belief at all? Consider the thermostat. The bimetallic strip indicates the temperature, and has the function of indicating it. Further, when it bends enough to close the circuit, thereby causing furnace ignition, it causes what it causes because of what it indicates. We designed the thermostat in such a way that when that strip indicates 67 °F, it causes the furnace to ignite; so the explanation of its causing that movement is that it is indicating that the temperature is

67 °F. But neither the bimetallic strip nor the thermostat, nor the furnace nor anything else need believe that the temperature is 67 °F. Even if we set aside Leibniz's problem, we must conclude, I think, that Dretske's account, subtle and powerful though it is, won't anywhere nearly serve as an explanation of how there could be beliefs if materialism about human beings is true.

5

From Mental/Physical Identity to Substance Dualism

Richard Swinburne

I

"Mental properties are the same as physical properties", "mental events are the same as physical events", "mental substances are the same as physical substances" —says many a physicalist. "Mental properties and events supervene on physical properties and events", and "mental substances supervene on physical substances"—says many another physicalist. Whether these claims are true depends first on what is meant by "substances", "properties", and "events", "mental" and "physical", and by "supervene"; and then on what are the criteria for one property, event, or substance being the same as another.

The first issues can be dealt with quickly and to some extent stipulatively. I understand by a property a monadic or relational universal,[1] and by an event the instantiation of a property in a substance or substances (or in properties or events) at times. Any definition of a substance tends to beg philosophical questions, but I'll operate with a definition which does not, I think, beg the questions at issue in this paper. A substance is a thing (other than an event) which can (it is logically possible) exist independently of all other things of that kind

This paper profited much from discussion at three workshops funded by a grant from the Pew Charitable Trusts. I am especially grateful to Howard Robinson for showing me what was wrong with a previous version of the final section of the paper. The opinions expressed in this paper are those of the author and do not necessarily reflect the views of the Pew Charitable Trusts.

[1] I shall count as 'properties' only hard properties, that is properties the truth conditions for whose instantiation in a substance at a time are a matter of how things are with that substance at that time. I limit the class of properties in this way because we do not need to suppose that there are any other properties in order fully to describe the world. Times are periods of time. Causal relations or relations of spatio-temporal continuity relate substances at a period of time.

(viz. all other substances) other than its parts.[2] Thus tables, planets, atoms, and humans are substances. Being square, weighing 10 kilos, or being-taller-than are properties (the former two being monadic properties, the latter being a relational property which relates two substances). Events include my table being square now, or John being taller than James on 30 March 2001 at 10.00 a.m.

There are different ways of making the mental/physical distinction, but I propose to make it in terms of the privilegedly accessible/public.[3] I believe that my way of making the distinction highlights the traditional worries about how the mental can be connected with the physical; but some other ways of making the distinction may do so as well, and similar results to mine are likely to follow from these other ways. So a mental property is one to whose instantiation the substance in whom it is instantiated necessarily has privileged access on all occasions of its instantiation, and a physical property is one to whose instantiation the substance necessarily has no privileged access on any occasion of its instantiation. Someone has privileged access to whether a property P is instantiated in him in the sense that whatever ways others have of finding this out, it is logically possible that he can use, but he has a further way (of experiencing it) which it is not logically possible that others can use. A pure mental property may then be defined as one whose instantiation does not entail the instantiation of a physical property. So "trying to raise one's arm" is a pure mental property, whereas "intentionally raising one's arm" is not; for the instantiation of the latter entails that my arm rises.[4] My definitions have the consequence that there are some properties which are neither mental nor physical—let us call them

---

[2] "The notion of a substance is just this—that it can exist by itself without the aid of any other substance", R. Descartes, *Replies to the Fourth Set of Objections*, in J. Cottingham, R. Stoothof and D. Murdoch (trans.), *The Philosophical Writings of Descartes*, ii, (Cambridge: Cambridge University Press, 1984), 159.

[3] There are in the literature other ways of understanding the mental/physical contrast, the most common of which are the intentional/non-intentional and the non-physical science/physical science contrasts. I expound this solely in terms of events. On the former account a mental event is one which involves an attitude towards something under a description—it is fearing, thinking, believing so-and-so; when the subject does not necessarily fear, think, believe something identical to so-and-so; a physical event is any event other than a mental event. On the latter account the physical is what can be explained by an extended physics, and the mental is what cannot be so explained. The former account has the unfortunate consequence that pains and colour qualia are not mental events; yet these are the paradigmatic troublemakers for "mind–brain" identity, and must count as mental if we are to deal in any way with the traditional mind/body problem. The latter account is hopelessly vague, for it is totally unclear what would constitute a science incorporating present-day physics as still being a physics. Hence my preference for my way of defining "mental" and "physical" properties, events, and—analogously—substances.

[4] Mental properties will include both conscious properties and continuing mental properties. Conscious properties are ones of whose instantiation in a subject, that subject is necessarily aware while they are instantiated—e.g. having the thought that today is Tuesday. Continuing properties are ones for which the exercise of the subject's privileged access depends on her choice to introspect, but which continue to characterize her while she chooses not to ask herself about them—e.g. the beliefs we have while asleep or thinking about other things, and the desires we have which are not currently influencing our behaviour.

"neutral properties". They include formal properties (e.g. "being a substance") and disjunctive properties ("being in pain or weighing ten stone"). A mental event is one to which the substance involved has privileged access; normally this will consist in the instantiation of a mental property, but sometimes it may involve the instantiation of a neutral property (as, for example, does the event of me being-in-pain-or-weighing-ten-stone). A pure mental event is one which does not entail the occurrence of a physical event. A physical event is one to which the substance involved does not have privileged access. A mental substance is one to whose existence that substance necessarily has privileged access, and a physical substance is a substance to whose existence that substance necessarily has no privileged access, that is, a public substance. Since having privileged access to anything is itself a mental property, and someone who has any other mental property has that one, mental substances are just those for which some mental properties are essential. And we may define a pure mental substance as one for which only pure mental properties are essential (together with any properties entailed by the possession of pure mental properties).

I understand the supervenience of one (kind of) property on another in a sense derived from Kim's sense of "global supervenience".[5] A-properties supervene on B-properties iff there are no two possible worlds in each of which every substance has the same B-properties as some substance in the other, but not every substance has the same A-properties as some substance in the other which has the same B-properties as it (and no substance has A-properties without having B-properties). This leads to a natural definition of event supervenience as follows: A-events supervene on B-events iff there are no two possible worlds identical in their B-events but differing in their A-events. The difference between property and event supervenience lies in the fact that events are individuated in part by the substances in which the properties are individuated. If there can be two different substances (in different worlds) with the same B-properties (including relational properties), there could be event supervenience without there being property supervenience. For it could be that each substance S_n which had certain B-properties B_o had to have determinate A-properties, but different ones for different substances—S_1 had to have A_1, while S_2 had to have A_2. Then there would be event supervenience. But there would still be two worlds in which two substances (S_1 in one and S_2 in the other) having all the same B-properties did not have all the same A-properties.

The natural extension of Kim's account of supervenience to substances is as follows: A-substances supervene on B-substances iff there are no two possible worlds identical in their B-substances but differing in their A-substances.[6]

---

[5] See Jaegwon Kim, " 'Strong' and 'Global' Supervenience Revisited", in his *Supervenience and Mind* (Cambridge: Cambridge University Press, 1993), 80–2.

[6] The corresponding definitions in terms of Kim's other sense of modal "supervenience", "strong supervenience" are as follows. A-properties strongly supervene on B-properties iff in all worlds any substance with the same B-properties has the same A-properties (and no substance has an A-property

So (pure) mental properties supervene on physical properties iff there are no two possible worlds in which every substance has the same physical properties as some substance in the other but not the same (pure) mental properties as some substance in the other which has the same physical properties as it (and no substance has mental properties without having physical properties). (Pure) mental events supervene on physical events iff there are no two possible worlds identical in their physical events but differing in their (pure) mental events (and no substance has mental properties without having physical properties.) (Pure) mental substances supervene on physical substances iff there are no two possible worlds identical in their physical substances but differing in their (pure) mental substances.

A possible world is one which is metaphysically possible. I understand by a logically possible world, one whose full description entails no contradiction;[7] whether a world is a logically possible world is therefore something discoverable a priori. Thirty years ago Kripke and Putnam drew our attention to the fact that there were many propositions which seemed not to entail any contradiction but were necessarily true or necessarily false with a necessity as hard as that of logical necessity, and whose truth or falsity were discoverable only a posteriori. These propositions were said to be metaphysically but not logically necessary or impossible. Hence the notion of a metaphysically possible world as one which was different from a merely logically possible world; it had to be both logically possible and one whose full description (in terms of logically contingent propositions) involves no metaphysically necessarily false propositions. Thus "Hesperus is not Phosphorus" or "water is XYZ" (where XYZ is different from H_2O) might seem to entail no contradiction, and yet they hold in no metaphysically possible world. However I share Chalmers's view that the distinction between the logically and metaphysically possible "is not a distinction at the level of worlds, but at most a distinction at the level of statements . . . The relevant space of worlds is the same in both cases".[8] That is, any logically possible world is a metaphysically possible world, and conversely.

without having a B-property). A-events strongly supervene on B-events iff for any substance in all worlds in which it has the same B-properties it has the same A-properties (and no substance has an A-property without having a B-property.) The natural definition for strong substance supervenience turns out to be the same as the definition for global substance supervenience. For both properties and events, strong supervenience entails global supervenience but not vice versa. If there is no global supervenience of properties, events or substances, it follows that neither will there be strong supervenience.

[7] My definition of a "logically possible world" as one whose full description entails no contradiction is more satisfactory than a definition which defines a "logically possible world" as a world describable by propositions not provable to be inconsistent by "logic". For clearly no world can be logically possible if it harbours any contradiction at all. Yet there are innumerable entailments which we can recognize without the entailment being captured by any system of logic so far devised. "This is red" obviously entails "This is coloured", but no system of logic so far invented will show that it does. Our very understanding of a proposition involves some ability to recognize what it entails (quite apart from any system of logic), what one who asserts it is committed to. The notion of entailment is more basic than the notion of a "logic".

[8] David Chalmers, *The Conscious Mind* (Oxford: Oxford University Press, 1996), 68.

The Kripke/Putnam type of metaphysically (but not logically) necessary propositions are all ones in which some substance (property or event or time) is referred to by a rigid designator of a kind which is rather uninformative about the nature of what is referred to. A rigid designator of a substance, property, event, or time is a word which picks out that substance, property, event, or time in every possible world. Rigidifying any uniquely identifying description will yield a rigid designator, but it may tell you very little about what is designated. If "water" is used to refer to whatever has the same chemical essence as the actual stuff in our rivers (and so used with what Chalmers calls its "secondary intension"), we can use the term to say something about that stuff without knowing what the stuff is and so without being able to identify instances of it except the ones in our rivers. However, we can describe logically possible worlds more informatively by using rigid designators of a special kind which I shall call "informative designators". For a rigid designator of a thing to be an informative designator it must be the case that someone who knows what the word means (that is, has the linguistic knowledge of how to use it) knows a certain set of conditions necessary and sufficient (in any possible world) for a thing to be that thing (whether or not he can state those conditions in words, or can in practice ever discover that those conditions are satisfied). Two informative designators are logically equivalent if and only if they are associated with logically equivalent sets of necessary and sufficient conditions. To know these conditions for the application of a designator is to be able (when favourably positioned, with faculties in working order, and not subject to illusion) to recognize where it applies and where it doesn't and to be able to make simple inferences to and from its application. Thus "red" is an informative designator of a property, of which "the actual colour of my first book" is a mere uninformative rigid designator. I can know what "red" means in the sense of being able to identify things as red, and make simple inferences using the word without knowing which things in our world are red. The ability to identify things as red can exist without the knowledge of which things are actually red. But knowing how to use the expression "having the actual colour of my first book" does not give me the ability to recognize things other than my first book as having the colour of my first book.

I am inclined to think that while being "water" (as used in the eighteenth century) is an uninformative designator of a property, being "H_2O" is an informative designator of a property. It is the property of being composed of molecules consisting of two atoms of hydrogen and one atom of water. To be an atom of hydrogen is to be an atom consisting of one proton and one electron. Or rather we may allow that negatively charged hydrogen—hydrogen with an extra electron—is still hydrogen; and so are isotopes of hydrogen, in which there are one or more additional neutrons in the nucleus. A proton is a proton in virtue of its mass, charge, etc.; and an electron is an electron in virtue of its mass, charge, etc. And I can know what it is to have certain mass or charge without discovering which things have what mass or charge, merely by knowing what people would observe (in this case using instruments) if things did have such and such mass or charge. A similar account should be given of what it is to be an atom of oxygen. But maybe physicists in the future would only count something as an electron if it was made of the same stuff as the electrons in the atoms of such-and-such a particular volume of H_2O, while it would be possible for something to have the same mass, charge, etc. as an electron and not to be so composed. In that case knowing what "H_2O" means would as such no longer allow me to recognize new instances of it. To do this, I would need also empirical knowledge of the composition of some actual volume of H_2O. But I believe that the current rules for the use of "H_2O" count anything as an electron which has the same mass, charge, etc. Whether a word is or is not an informative designator a matter of the rules for its use in the language.

A full description of a world will include descriptions of its events in terms of informative designators. If all the events so described are logically compatible, no metaphysically false propositions will be true of that world, for if one was, so would be the logically false proposition obtained by replacing any uninformative designator which it contains by an informative designator of the property or whatever so designated. If "Water is XYZ" were true of it, so would be "H_2O is XYZ"—yet that entails a self-contradiction. Hence all logically possible worlds are metaphysically possible.

This claim of course holds only for worlds where metaphysical necessity is analysable as above. Anyone who makes a claim about what is metaphysically possible or impossible where this is not analysable in the above way owes the reader an explanation of what "metaphysically possible" means. It may well be, as Gendler and Hawthorne say, that "the notion of metaphysical possibility . . . is standardly taken to be primitive", adding in a footnote "in contemporary discussions at any rate".[9] For myself, I simply do not understand what is meant by this notion, unless it is analysable as above, or given some other technical definition. It is simply uninformative to say that it is the most basic conception of "how things might have been".[10] For since this "most basic conception" is supposed to be narrower than logical possibility, it is unclear how it is to be narrowed unless in the way I have analysed.[11]

Given my understanding of a "possible world", whether the physicalist's claims of identity or supervenience are true now depends on the criteria for one property, event, or substance being the same as another. There are some identity

---

[9] T. Gendler and J. Hawthorne (eds.), *Conceivability and Possibility* (Oxford: Clarendon Press, 2002), Introduction, p. 4.

[10] Ibid. 4–5.

[11] I myself have used "metaphysically necessary" to mean (roughly) whatever is the ultimate cause of things or is entailed by the existence of that ultimate cause; and so the "metaphysically possible" is whatever is compatible with the existence of the actual ultimate cause. I give a more precise definition, in *The Christian God* (Oxford: Clarendon Press, 1994), 118–19. But this is certainly not the sense which most writers who use the term have in mind.

criteria which will give him his result and some that won't. Ordinary usage provides no clear criteria, and different aspects of usage can be systematized to provide different criteria. We need a metacriterion for choosing which criteria to use.

Now the history of the world is the history of one thing and then another thing happening, in a sense of "thing happening" which includes both things remaining the same and things changing. I suggest that the things that happen and the only things that happen are events in my sense. It is this substance existing (which can be analysed as it having its essential properties) for a period of time, coming to have this property or relation to another substance at this or that time, continuing to have it and then ceasing to have it. I have adopted the construal of properties as universals (instantiable in more than one different substance) rather than as tropes (particular properties), for the reason that—as far as I can see—there is not anything more or less to the difference between this (e.g.) redness and that one (of exactly the same shade and shape) except in terms of the substances (and times) in which they are instantiated. And, I suggest, there are no other things that happen except events in my sense. Some have cited flashes and bangs as examples of things which happen but are not events in my sense. But they can easily be analysed as the instantiation of properties in regions of space, or (if you do not think that regions of space are substances in my sense), as themselves substances which exist for a very short time.

So I suggest as a metacriterion that we individuate properties, substances, and times in such a way that if someone knows which properties were instantiated in which substances when, they know everything that has happened. A canonical description of an event will say which properties, substances, and times it involves, by picking them out by informative designators—and conjointly the properties, times, and substances involved will form an informative designator of that event. Then it will be the case that someone who knows all the events that have happened under their canonical descriptions knows everything that has happened (and someone who knows all the events that have happened under their canonical descriptions in some spatio-temporal region knows all that has happened in that region). If you do not individuate properties, substances, and times in accord with a criterion derived from this metacriterion, then in order to give a full description of everything that has happened you would need additional metaphysical categories. It would need to be the case, for example, that as well as saying which properties were instantiated when, you would need to say which aspects or features those properties had. It is better not to multiply metaphysical categories beyond necessity. I predict that exactly the same kinds of issue would arise with a fuller system of categories as with the ones which I shall set out below using my system of categories, and that they would require exactly the same kinds of solution. So I stick with my system of categories.

To give some person the knowledge of everything that has happened, it will suffice (given that that person has sufficient logical competence) to list any of many different subsets of all the events. For the occurrence of some events entails the occurrence of other events. There is one event of my walking from A to B from 9.30 to 9.45 a.m., another event of my walking slowly from 9.30 to 9.45, and a third event of my walking slowly from A to B from 9.30 to 9.45. But the third event is "nothing over and above" the first two events. To generalize—there is no more to the history of the world (or the world in a region) than any subset of events whose canonical descriptions entail those of all the events; and no less than any least subset which will do this. There are different ways of cutting up the history of the world into events, and there are many different sets of events, such that there is no more or less to the history of the world than the occurrence of all the events of that set. All this suggests that we should count as the same event not merely two events which involve the instantiation of the same properties in the same substances at the same time, but also two events whose canonical descriptions (their informative designators) entail each other. For if you know that the one has occurred, that puts you in a position (if you have sufficient logical competence) to know that the other has occurred, and conversely. The occurrence of one event is then nothing in the history of the world 'over and above' the occurrence of the other event. Two events could involve the same substances, properties, and times and so be the same event, while having two different canonical descriptions which do not entail each other if, for example, there could be two informative designators of a substance which are not logically equivalent (and that can happen if there can be contingent identity between substances—a possibility which I shall discuss later in the paper). Conversely, the canonical descriptions of two events may entail each other without the properties, substances, and events involved all being the same. One case of this is where a substance having some property entails and is entailed by some part of that substance having that property. For example, a table is flat if and only if that table's top is flat; but the former is not an occurrence in the history of the world additional to the latter, nor is the latter an occurrence additional to the former.

On a Humean picture of the world we need no relations other than spatio-temporal relations between substances to state the history of the world. The history of the world is just this substance (with its properties) coming into existence, acquiring now this monadic property, now losing that one, changing its spatial relations to other substances, and finally ceasing to exist; and a similar history for all the other substances. Causation for Hume is analysable in terms of regularities in the temporal patterns of acquisition of monadic properties and spatial relations. But on an account of causation in which causation is unanalysable and so not reducible to events of the former kind, the history of the world will involve not merely succession but causation. A substance or event causing an event is itself an event (of the instantiation of the relation of causation between the substance or event and the other event), and the history of the world will need then to include such events—though it need no longer mention, as separate events, any events related by the relation of causation; their occurrence is entailed by the event of the one causing the other.

It is not, however, relevant to the present discussion whether a Humean or a non-Humean account of causation is correct. So—to return to the central theme—in order to satisfy my metacriterion how must we individuate properties and substances, so that someone who knew the canonical description of every event of some subset of events which entails the canonical descriptions of all the events would be in a position to know everything that had happened? (Our interest being only in the identity conditions for properties and substances which allow us to say whether there are mental as well as physical properties and substances, I shall not consider the interesting issue of what are the identity conditions for times—e.g. whether (if it is 3 October 2003 today) P being instantiated in S today is the same event as P being instantiated in S on 3 October 2003.)

II

To begin with properties—to satisfy my metacriterion each different feature of the world named by informative designators which are not logically equivalent has to count as a different property; though, since some entail others, we shall not need to mention them all in order to give a full account of the world. It is important to distinguish a description of a property P in terms of some property which it possesses, from an (informative or uninformative) rigid designator of P. "Green" is an informative designator of the property of being green; it applies to it in all possible worlds, and someone who knows what "green" means knows what an object has to be like to be green. "Amanda's favourite colour" or "the colour of spring grass" may function as descriptions of the property green in terms of its properties, possibly (in our world) uniquely identifying descriptions. These words may be used to describe the property of being green by informatively designating a different property—the property of being Amanda's favourite colour or the property of being of the same colour as spring grass—which properties the property of being green possesses. "Green is Amanda's favourite colour" is then a subject–predicate sentence where "Amanda's favourite colour" informatively designates the property of being Amanda's favourite colour and thereby (in our world) describes the property green. It says that the property "green" has itself the property of being Amanda's favourite colour. If it were (unusually) being asserted as a statement of identity between two informatively designated properties, it would be false. But any property name can be turned into an uninformative rigid designator of another property which has the first property. "Amanda's favourite colour" can be used to rigidly designate that colour which in the actual world is Amanda's favourite colour. In that case "Green is Amanda's favourite colour" will be a (true) identity statement. The device of rigidification allows us to turn any uniquely identifying description of something, including a property, into a rigid designator of that thing. But it does not make it into an informative designator of that thing. For someone who knows what the rigidified predicate "the colour of spring grass" means need have no ability to identity any colour property (other than that of spring grass) as being that colour property—for they may never have seen spring grass.

It follows from all this that it is a purely a priori matter (a matter of logical entailment) whether one informatively designated property supervenes on other informatively designated properties. It follows straightforwardly that no mental properties (in the sense of properties which are such that necessarily their subject has privileged access on all occasions of their instantiation to whether they are instantiated in him) are the same properties as physical properties (in the sense of publicly accessible properties, such that no one substance ever has privileged access to whether or not they are instantiated in it)—for the simple reason that their informative designators are never logically equivalent. The property informatively designated by "being in pain" is just such a mental property. Others can find out whether I am in pain by studying my behaviour and my brain states. But I too can study my behaviour (on a film) or my brain states (via mirrors); yet I have a further way of knowing whether I am in pain or not which the others do not have—I can actually feel it. The same goes for all the "qualia" properties, and in my view also for the intentional properties of having such and such beliefs, desires and purposes. On the other hand the properties informatively designated by "being square" or "weighing-10-kilos", or the brain properties of patterns of electrochemical transmission are physical properties in this sense. It follows for similar reasons that mental properties do not supervene on physical properties—since for any world in which some combination of physical and mental properties is instantiated, there is always a world in which the physical properties are instantiated but the mental ones are not. This follows because the canonical descriptions of the events of a world in which any combination of physical properties is instantiated never entail that mental properties are also instantiated, since what anyone can access equally can never entail what only one person can access in a privileged way. And since mental events are ones to which the substance involved has privileged access, and physical events are ones to which the substance does not have privileged access, no mental event can be the same as any physical event,[12] nor can it supervene on one. Clearly too, both

---

[12] It may be useful to compare my argument with Kripke's somewhat similar argument for the falsity of "my pain is my being in such-and-such a brain state". I analyse the version in Kripke's paper "Identity and Necessity" in M. K. Munitz (ed.), *Identity and Individuation* (New York: New York University Press, 1971). Kripke claims, first, that "my pain" (which I shall understand as "me being in pain") and "my being in such and such a brain state" (which I shall understand as "me being in such and such a brain state") are "both rigid designators" (p. 162). Kripke and I are entitled to use these expressions in this way, and that is surely their normal use. But a conclusion will only follow about whether or not they rigidly designate the same event given an understanding of what

mental events (including pure mental events) and physical events occur, and so the former cannot be omitted from a full description of the world.

III

I turn now to substances.[13] For a substance at one time t_2 to be the same substance as a substance at an earlier time t_1, two kinds of criteria have to be satisfied. First the two substances have to have the essential properties of the same species of substance which they are. Fairly clearly there are different ways of cutting up the world into species of substance, any of which would enable us to give a true and full description of the world. Suppose I have a car which I turn into a boat. I can think of cars as essentially cars. In that case one substance (a car) has ceased to exist and has become instead another substance (a boat). Or I can think of the car as essentially a motor vehicle, in which case it has continued to exist but with different (non-essential) properties. All three substances exist—the car which is essentially a car, the boat which is essentially a boat, and the motor vehicle which is essentially a motor vehicle. Yet I can tell the whole story of the world either by telling the story of the motor vehicle, or by telling the story of the car and the boat.

it is for some event to be the event it is. In this case, Kripke claims, we pick out the events "by essential properties". That is, being a pain is essential to the first event and not the second event; and being a brain state is essential to the second event and not the first event. On my view (for which I have given reasons) an event is the event it is in virtue of the substances (or events), properties, and times involved in it. Since the substances and (I assume) times are the same in the events in question, the issue turns on whether the properties designated are the same. The conclusion that the two events are not the same will follow only if "being in pain" and "being in such and such a brain state" are being used not merely as rigid designators of properties, but as informative designators of the properties of being in pain and being in such and such a brain state—that is, do not designate some underlying property by means of its properties of being in pain or being in such and such a brain state. I am using the words in this way, and I would claim it to be the most natural understanding of them; and I am clearly entitled to use the words in this way. Kripke is equally entitled to think of the properties involved in the events as essential—but only given my view that we are entitled by definition to say which properties are essential to an event. Kripke's argument seems to be relying on an intuition that the properties stated are essential to the event; but there is no need for him to do that. He can make it a matter of definition. The conclusion of the non-identity of the pain and the brain state does, however, need a further argument. It will only follow, given my criterion (or some similar criterion) for property identity—that to be identical two properties have to have logically equivalent informative designators, that is, logically equivalent sets of necessary and sufficient conditions for their application (and I have given reasons for using that criterion). From that it will follow that the properties involved in the two events are not the same, and so the events are not the same. Without this an opponent of Kripke might say that the property of being in pain just is the property of being in such and such a brain state. I think that Kripke would be sympathetic to this final move, but he does not actually make it.

[13] I shall assume for the sake of simplicity of exposition that substances "endure" rather than "perdure" through time; that is, in the case of the material objects of our world, that they are three-dimensional (spatial) objects rather than four- (three spatial and one temporal) dimensional objects. But I believe that this assumption can be dropped without any damage to the main argument.

The second requirement for a substance at one time to be the same as a substance at another time is that the two substances should consist of largely the same parts, the extent to which this has to hold varying with the genus of substance. At least five kinds of thing have been called "substances"—simples, organisms, artefacts, mereological compounds, and gerrymandered objects (such as the right top drawer of my desk together with the planet Venus). Despite the view of some that only some of these are really substances,[14] my metacriterion gives no justification for such an arbitrary restriction. For each of these genera of substance there is its own kind of identity criterion, varying with the extent of replacement or rearrangement of parts which is compatible with the continued existence of the substance (e.g. for a mereological compound, no replacement is possible; for artefacts such as a car, boat, or motor vehicle a small amount of replacement is possible). A full history of the world will need to mention only certain genera of substances—for example if it tells us the history of all the fundamental particles (considered as mereological compounds) that might suffice (if we forget for a few paragraphs about obvious problems arising from substances having mental properties). There is no more to any substance than its parts, and the history of the substance is the history of its parts. It might sometimes be explanatorily more simple if one took larger substances, such as organisms, rather than their parts as the substances in terms of which to trace the history of the world; but the causal properties of large substances including organisms are just the causal properties of their parts, even if the latter have causal properties such that, when combined with other parts, they behave in ways different from the ways in which they behave separately. Alternatively, instead of telling merely the history of fundamental particles, we could include in our history of the world organisms and artefacts, saying when they gained or lost parts, or their internal parts were rearranged. We might then need to describe the history of the fundamental particles only in so far as they did not form unchanging parts of the organisms or artefacts. And certainly we could do without describing the behaviour of gerrymandered objects.

Being the same part may itself be a matter of having all the same subparts, and so on forever; or some replacement of subparts may be allowable, but in the end—if we are to operate with a sharp criterion of identity—we must define a level at which no replacement is possible if the subpart is to be the same subpart, a level of what I shall call ultimate parts. Being the same ultimate part will involve, as with any substance, having the essential properties characteristic of the kind—being this hydrogen atom will involve having a certain atomic mass, number, etc. It

[14] See Peter van Inwagen, *Material Beings* (Ithaca, NY: Cornell University Press, 1990), section 13; and Trenton Merricks *Objects and Persons* (Oxford: Clarendon Press, 2001). Van Inwagen considers that mereological compounds, artefacts, and gerrymandered objects do not exist, and so of course they cannot be substances.

will involve also something else, for it to be the same token of that kind—a principle of individuation.

What that principle is depends crucially on what sorts of thing substances are. One view is that substances are simply bundles of co-instantiated properties. The alternative view is that some substances have thisness.[15] A substance has thisness iff there could exist instead of it (or as well as it) a different substance which has all the same properties as it, including past and future related properties such as spatio-temporal continuity with a substance having such and such monadic properties.

If no substances have thisness, then the history of the world will consist of bundles of co-instantiated properties having further properties, including spatio-temporal relations to earlier bundles, coming into existence and ceasing to exist, and causing the subsequent existence and properties of other bundles. There are many different ways (equally well justified by our initial metacriterion for a system of metaphysical categories) to cut up the world into substances at a time, according to the size of the bundle and which members of the bundle are regarded as essential to the substance which they form. And, according to which members of the bundle are regarded as essential, so there will be different ways of tracing substance continuity over time. Ultimate parts will also be individuated by properties. The obvious such property for individuating parts which occupy space is spatio-temporal continuity with a substance having the same essential properties of the species, conjoined perhaps with causal continuity (that is, the earlier substance causing the existence of the later substance); for non-spatial substances, temporal plus causal continuity would seem to be the obvious requirement. And we need some uniqueness requirement, to ensure that at most one substance later than a given substance which satisfies both of these requirements is the original substance. But there are again alternative ways in which these requirements could be spelled out, any of which would allow us to tell the whole story of the world. If we make spatio-temporal continuity necessary for the identity of substances over time, then we shall have to say that if an electron disappears from one orbit and causes an electron to appear in another orbit without there being spatio-temporal continuity between them, they are different electrons. Yet if we insist only on causal continuity, then they will be

---

[15] For a more detailed account of thisness and of what would be evidence that material objects do or do not have thisness, see my "Thisness", *Australasian Journal of Philosophy*, 73 (1995), 389–400. This article has been subject to some detailed criticisms by John O'Leary-Hawthorne and J. A. Cover in "Framing the Thisness Issue", *Australasian Journal of Philosophy*, 75 (1997), 102–8. One quite unjustified criticism which they make is that (p. 104) my "principle concerns intra-world duplication *solo numero*" and that "it is surprising that Swinburne does not explicitly address inter-world versions of his principle". However, I did make it explicitly clear (p. 390) that all the principles which I discussed (including, therefore, that principle in terms of which I defined thisness), "concern not merely the identity of individuals in a given world, but across possible worlds".

the same electron. But we can tell the whole story of the world either way, and both stories will be true; electrons of both sorts will exist.

If, however, some substances have thisness, a full history of the world will have to describe the continuities not merely of bundles of co-instantiated properties, but of the thisness which underlies certain bundles (that is, of what it is which makes the difference between two bundles of the same properties with qualitatively the same history). So it must be a necessary condition of ultimate parts of substances being the same that they have the same thisness.[16] For those physical substances which are material objects, thisness is being made of the same matter. We have then the hylemorphic theory that sameness of a material object requires sameness of essential properties of the species and sameness of underlying matter. We could, contrary to the Aristotelian model, insist that as well as sameness of matter, for an ultimate individual part to be the same individual some essential properties (in addition to those of the species) have to be the same. But it is more natural to insist only on preservation of the essential properties of the species; and in this way we can still tell the whole history of the world. In that case if (and only if) the electron in the new orbit is made of the same matter as the old electron, it is the old electron. Spatio-temporal continuity is now no longer an independent requirement for a substance continuing to exist, but probably (fallible) evidence that the same matter has continued to exist; and so (given that the other arbitrarily chosen essential properties of the species are preserved) that the same material object exists. Spatio-temporal continuity is evidence of sameness of matter in so far as the best (i.e. most probable) physical theory of how matter behaves has the consequence that it moves along spatially continuous paths. I shall in future assume that this theory is probably true.

We do not know whether the inanimate material objects of our world have thisness, and in this respect we do not know what would constitute a full description of our world.[17] If they do, then not any account of the world which describes the patterns of property distribution in the world will be a correct one. We need one which individuates the ultimate parts of inanimate material objects (picked out as such in some clear way) being the same substances only if they have the same matter. Then mereological compounds will have to have the same matter throughout their existence, while organisms may gradually replace matter.

Now, to give the full history of the world, I have claimed, involves listing all the events of some subset which entails all the events that have happened

---

[16] If ultimate parts have the same thisness, then the substance composed of these will have a thisness constituted by these and conversely. I thus reject a view which Gallois calls "strong haecceitism", the view that two objects (O in world w, and O* in world w*) could yet be different, even if they have all the same properties and are composed of identical constituents. See A. Gallois, *Occasions of Identity*, (Oxford: Clarendon Press, 1998), 250–1.

[17] See my article "Thisness" on how physics may provide evidence on whether material objects do have thisness.

under their canonical descriptions. We saw in the case of properties that that involves picking out the properties involved by informative designators. And surely we need to informatively designate the substances too—merely giving a description of them, even a rigidified description, won't tell us what was green or square or in pain. Informatively designating a property involves knowing a certain set of necessary and sufficient conditions for something to be that property. Similar considerations seem to apply to substances. But here we have to note that, while we do know informative designators for many properties, we do not know informative designators for many substances. We often do not know the conditions necessary and sufficient for a substance to be that substance; for often we do not know what would make a later substance or a substance in another world that substance. The first reason for our inability to informatively designate substances is that we do not know with respect to some kinds of substances and in particular inanimate material objects, whether or not they have thisness (and so, for example, are to be individuated partly by their underlying matter) or whether they are to be individuated solely by properties, including (spatio-temporal and/or other) properties of continuity.

So in practice we often pick out material objects by uninformative rigid designators of a kind which we may call quasi-informative designators. They are words associated with a disjunction of two sets of necessary and sufficient conditions for a thing to be that thing (one disjunct applying if the substance has thisness, the other if it does not); but which in practice lead us to identify the same things in the actual world as the thing in question. Thus Hesperus is the actual planet which often appears in the evening sky. If material objects do not have thisness, then being Hesperus consists in being a planet which is a bundle of co-instantiated properties spatio-temporally continuous with those which constitute the planet which appears in the evening sky. If material objects do have thisness, then being Hesperus consists in being a planet made of a particular chunk of matter (i.e. with thisness). Since we do not know whether material objects have thisness, "Hesperus" does not function as an informative designator. But although the nature of Hesperus differs in the two cases, we are likely (when positioned as favourably as we can be) to pick out the same planet as Hesperus on other occasions in both cases. For in the latter case we will use the criterion of spatio-temporal continuity with the matter of the actual planet as evidence of a chunk of matter being the same matter; but satisfying the criterion will be fallible evidence of the sameness of two planets, whereas in the former case it will be what constitutes sameness.

If material objects do not have thisness, then an informative designator of a substance will be a conjunction of informative designators of co-instantiated properties. If we learn that material objects do not have thisness, then we will be able to designate them informatively. 'Hesperus' can function as an informative designator of a planet spatio-temporally continuous with the planet (if any) which actually appears in the evening sky. 'Hesperus' is then an informative designator because I know what is involved in calling something Hesperus, and I can have the ability to identify things as Hesperus without having any empirical knowledge—I don't need to know that there are any planets in order to know what the informative designator means. But if material objects do have thisness and we learn this, in practice humans would still be unable to pick them out by names. This is because we would be unable to identify a planet (e.g. one in the morning sky) as Hesperus without knowing of what chunk of matter the planet which appears in the evening sky is made; we might have fallible knowledge that the same chunk was or was not present in Phosphorus, but we still wouldn't know what that chunk was, except in terms of its properties, which wouldn't enable us to distinguish it from another chunk (in another world) with the same properties. Maybe God can tell the difference between two such chunks, but we humans can only distinguish chunks by properties. There will still be a true description of the world using informative designators of substances, but it will not be accessible to us.

Note that if material objects do have thisness, there will be informative designators of the planets currently picked out by the quasi-informative designators 'Hesperus' and 'Phosphorus', call them 'H' and 'P' such that 'H is P' will be a logically necessary truth, because in each case what constitutes being that planet will be the same—being a planet made of such and such a chunk of matter. But if material objects do not have thisness and 'Hesperus' and 'Phosphorus' are used in the way described in the previous paragraph, then 'Hesperus is Phosphorus' will be a contingent truth; the identity it reports will be a contingent identity. This is because being Hesperus is being spatio-temporally continuous with such and such a planet; and being Phosphorus is being spatio-temporally continuous with such and such a planet; and it would be a contingent matter whether each was spatio-temporally continuous with the other. There would be worlds in which each existed but they were not spatio-temporally continuous.[18] If we use 'Hesperus' and 'Phosphorus' only as quasi-informative designators, we will not know whether the identity is necessary or contingent.

---

[18] It is only identity over time (trans-temporal identity) which can be contingent. Rejecting the necessity of identity for substances of certain kinds though preserving it for others, requires understanding Leibniz's law in a more restricted way for the former. It remains the case that necessarily if $a = b$, Φa if and only if Φb, only so long as Φ is a non-modal property. On how this is to be spelled out, see Gallois, *Occasions*, ch. 6. In espousing contingent identity, I do not commit myself to the stronger thesis of occasional identity—that two objects can be the same at one time but different at another. Gallois brings out that this can only be maintained if trans-temporal identity (identity between an object and an object at another time) is not identity (that is, if the relation is not transitive and symmetrical.) See Gallois, *Occasions*, 113–17. The possibility of contingent identity arises because of the possibility that some substances are mere bundles of instantiated properties, and so the identity of a substance at another time will consist in the spatio-temporal continuity with it of some similar bundle. Contingent identity then allows the possibility that the same substance may be picked out by names that are not logically equivalent(because it is not a matter of logical necessity which bundles are continuous with which other bundles). Given that only hard properties count as properties (see n.1 above), the same possibility does not arise for properties.

However, having only an ability to pick out inanimate material objects by means of quasi-informative designators, we can still know quite a lot about which ones are or are not identical with or supervene on others. Merely knowing to which kind a substance belongs often enables us to say that two substances rigidly designated in different ways are not the same—since they do not satisfy some of the necessary conditions for sameness; even though we cannot nearly so often say that two substances are the same. This table may or may not be the same as the one that was here last week, but it is certainly not the planet Hesperus—for Hesperus is essentially a heavenly body and the table is not. And sometimes quasi-informatively designating may enable us to say that this kind of substance supervenes on that kind. Suppose that there can be just three kinds of motor vehicles—ones which can travel on land (cars), ones which can travel on water (boats), and ones which can travel in the air (airplanes)—and that we have some criterion for determining to which of these kinds a dual or triple-use vehicle belongs. Then motor vehicles supervene on boats, cars, and airplanes—there are no two possible worlds with the same cars, boats, and airplanes, but different motor vehicles. But cars, boats, and airplanes do not supervene on motor vehicles—there can be two possible worlds with the same motor vehicles, but different cars, boats, or airplanes (if, for example, what was a car in one world has been turned into a boat in the other world).

IV

Now suppose that no substances have thisness, and so the bundle view of all substances is correct. Mental substances are those substances which have mental properties essentially. Then whether there are mental substances depends on how one bundles together bundles of properties into substances. Mental properties with physical parts (such as the property of intentionally raising one's arm) are naturally thought of as belonging to the substance to which the physical part belongs. But one may put pure mental properties (such as the property of trying to raise one's arm) either in the same bundle as the physical property to which it is most closely related causally—the one which causes it to be instantiated or whose instantiation is caused by it,[19] or (following Hume[20]) one can put the pure mental properties into a bundle with other pure mental properties to whose instantiation it is related causally (and perhaps also related by relations

[19] As proposed e.g. by Jerome Shaffer, "Could Mental Processes be Brain Processes", *Journal of Philosophy*, 58 (1961).

[20] "The true idea of the mind, is to consider it as a system of different perceptions or different existences, which are linked together by the relation of cause and effect, and mutually produce, destroy, influence, and modify each other", David Hume, *A Treatise of Human Nature*, 1.4.6.

of similarity and apparent memory). On the Humean model clearly there will be mental substances, for some bundles of properties would be individuated by their mental properties. It might seem, however, that on the non-Humean model one could individuate substances solely by their physical properties and regard mental properties as merely contingent members of bundles, and then the only substances would be physical substances. Alternatively one could individuate substances at least partly in terms of mental properties, and then there could be mental substances. Either way of describing the world would yield a full description.

It is, however, not possible to have a full description of the world in which all substances are individuated only by physical properties. For it is an evident datum of experience that conscious mental events of different kinds (visual sensations, auditory sensations, etc.) are co-experienced, that is, belong to the same substance. Any description of the world which had the consequence that co-experienced events did not belong to the same substance would be a false one. Hence, if the substance to which these events occur has physical properties and so a spatial volume, that spatial volume must include within it the total physical cause of those mental events. My having mental properties forces us to recognize as a substance something which (if it has physical properties) has spatial boundaries at a time and over time no narrower than those of the physical correlates of what I co-experience. The identity of the substance is thus constituted by a mental property, that its boundaries are no narrower than the boundaries of the physical correlates of what I co-experience. We cannot cut up the world in an arbitrary way and individuate substances solely by physical properties, and suppose that the mental properties are merely contingent properties of these substances. For even if (as seems not to be the case empirically) the brain basis of, for example, my visual sensations and my auditory sensations were the same, that would not still entail the datum of experience that they were both had by the same person. We can only include that datum in a full description of the world if we suppose that the identity of substances which have conscious mental properties is determined by whether the mental properties which they have at the same time are co-experienced.

It is also an evident datum of experience that certain mental events are had consecutively by the same person. Experiences take time—if only a second or two; and every experience which I have I experience as consisting of two smaller parts. I am the common subject of the experience of hearing the first half of your sentence and the experience of hearing the second half of your sentence. And yet the mere fact that these experiences are caused by events in the same part of the physical substance which is my brain does not entail that. It follows for both of these reasons that we cannot describe the world fully except in terms of mental substances which—if they have physical properties—are the substances they are both at a time and over time, whose boundaries are no narrower than those of the physical correlates of what a subject co-experiences.

It will be evident that it will make no difference to the fact that there are mental substances if the bundle theory of all physical substances is false, and inanimate material objects including brain-molecules have thisness (and so being the same substance is not solely a function of properties, but of the matter in which those properties are instantiated). For still nothing would follow from that for which mental properties were co-experienced. We can describe the facts of co-experience only if we allow the existence of mental substances.

This conclusion is reinforced when we consider some well-known neuro-physiological data and thought experiments. The crucial issue when a patient's corpus callosum is severed is whether (on the assumption that experiences are produced by both half-brains) the experiences produced by his left brain are co-experienced with the experiences produced by his right brain. It is not merely that some ways of dividing up the brain, or defining when it began or ceased to exist, would provide simpler explanations of how the brain or body behaves than do others, but that some ways would entail the non-occurrence of a datum of experience, whose occurrence would be evident to its subject or subjects—that a subject had both sets of experiences, or that he had only one set. Whether there is one person or two is not entailed by which experiences are connected with which half-brains, or anything else physical. To describe what is going on we need to individuate persons in part by the experiences they have, and not by the extent of the unity of a brain. Merely to describe, not to explain, experience, we need mental substances individuated at least in part in this way.

This conclusion is further reinforced when we consider the thought experiment of half-brain transplants. S's brain is taken out of his skull, divided into two halves, these halves are put into two different skulls from which brains have been removed, a few additional bits are added from a clone of S, the bits are connected to the nervous system, and we then have two functioning persons with mental lives. But if we know only the history of all the physical bits, described in terms of their properties (and, if required, their underlying matter) and which mental properties are instantiated in all the persons involved, there seems to be something crucial of which we are ignorant—which (if either) of the subsequent persons is S. Whether S has survived such a traumatic operation seems an evidently factual issue, and yet one underdetermined by the physical and mental properties associated with physical substances. Only if S is a mental substance (to whom the co-experienced experiences occur), can there be a unknown truth about whether or not S has survived this operation—which surely sometimes there will be.

It follows that mental substances are not identical with and do not supervene on physical substances, since there can be worlds in which the physical substances (brains and the extent of their continuity) are the same but there are different mental substances (two in one world, only one in another).

V

My final claim is that human beings, you and I, are pure mental substances (which do not supervene on physical substances). Many thought experiments in the spirit of Descartes seem to describe conceivable situations and so to be strong evidence of the logical possibility of me existing without a body, or continuing to exist when my body is destroyed. Let us take Descartes's original thought experiment.

I saw that while I could conceive that I had no body . . . I could not conceive that I was not. On the other hand, if I had only ceased from thinking . . . I should have no reason for thinking that I had existed. From this I knew that I was a substance the whole nature or essence of which is to think and that for its existence there is no need of any place, nor does it depend on any material thing.[21]

We can make sense of this and many similar suppositions (disembodied life after death, etc.); they do not appear to contain any contradiction—and that is strong evidence that what we appear to conceive is logically possible. But, says the objector, 'maybe they are not "metaphysically possible" '. However that possibility only arises if "I" (or "Richard Swinburne" as used by me) is not an informative designator, but only an uninformative designator (such as a quasi-informative designator) of some substance whose identity is constituted by some underlying factors whose nature is unknown. But clearly it is an informative designator. For I do know the conditions necessary and sufficient for a substance to be that substance. I can recognize (with faculties in working order, favourably positioned, and not subject to illusion) when it applies and when it doesn't and make simple inferences from its application. For I can always pick out myself as the subject of experience and action—infallibly. In this I am in Shoemaker's phrase, "immune to error through misidentification".[22] I cannot recognize that a present conscious experience is taking place and yet misidentify it as yours when it is really mine, or conversely. I can misidentify myself if I pick out myself by means of a body—for example, believing falsely that the person seen in the mirror is me—but that will be a case of illusion.[23]

Of course I can still misremember what I did in the past, and indeed misremember how I used the word "I" in the past. But this kind of problem

[21] R. Descartes *Discourse on the Method*, trans E. S. Haldane and G. R. T. Ross in, *Collected Works of Descartes*, i, (Cambridge: Cambridge University Press, 1972), 101.

[22] Sydney Shoemaker, "Introspection and the Self" in Q. Cassam, (ed.), *Self-Knowledge*, (Oxford: Oxford University Press, 1994), 82.

[23] The need for some sort of qualification on Shoemaker's phrase is the subject of recent discussion. See Analisa Coliva, "The First Person: Error through Misidentification, the Split between Speaker's and Semantic Reference, and the Real Guarantee", *Journal of Philosophy*, 100 (2003), 416–31.

arises with every claim whatsoever about the past. "Green"is an informative designator of a property, but I may still misremember which things were green and what I meant by "green" in the past. The difference between informative and uninformative designators is that (when my faculties are in working order, I am favourably positioned, and not subject to illusion) I can recognize which objects are correctly picked out at a present time by informative designators, but not generally when they are picked out by uninformative designators (in the absence of further information). And I know what a claim about the past or future amounts to when it is made by informative designators, but not when it is made by uninformative designators. I know what would constitute a future or past experience being mine, what it is for some future or past person to be me. Not so with Hesperus or water. I don't know (in the sense defined) what would constitute past or a future substance being water or Hesperus if I am merely in the position of the "water" user in the eighteenth century, or the "Hesperus" user in the early ancient world; or even today—for reasons given above.

I conclude that, in the absence of some hidden logical (and I mean "logical") contradiction in Descartes's description of his thought experiment—to suppose which would be immensely implausible—the experiment shows what it purports to show: Descartes is a pure mental substance. He could exist without anything physical existing, and so pure mental substances do not supervene on physical substances. Each of us can do the same experiment about ourselves and so show that we are pure mental substances.

There are, however, two kinds of pure mental substances—those which do not have a body as a contingent part, and those which do. Ghosts do not have bodies, for example, whereas human beings living on Earth do have bodies. But since the body which is currently mine could continue to exist as a living body without having any causal connection with any mental substance, or could become instead the body of a different mental substance; and since I could under such circumstances go on existing and have a mental life without a body, I now consist of two disjoint parts—my body (the contingent part of me), and the rest of me which we can call my soul (the essential part of me). Since what is required for a mental life is the part of me other than my body, I have a mental life in virtue of my soul having a mental life. But that does not have the consequence that there are two events of thinking going on when I am thinking—my soul thinking and me thinking; since the two canonical descriptions of the event mutually entail each other the events are the same. Human beings are thus a composite of substances of two genera—a soul which is, I suggest, a simple; and a body which is an organism.[24] We could therefore tell the whole story of

---

[24] In "A Compound of Two Substances" (in K. Corcoran (ed.), *Soul, Body and Survival* (Ithaca, NY: Cornell University Press, 2001), Erik.T. Olson argues that there are two serious difficulties for 'compound dualism' (the view that the person who I am has two parts—body and soul) which

the whole by telling the story of souls and bodies, and not mention human beings at all. But if you do include the story of human beings and their souls and bodies part company, we shall then need to include their separate histories. [25]

For me to exist, I need only to have some pure mental property (for example, having privileged access to my beliefs). I do not need to have any particular mental properties. I pick myself out as the subject of certain currently experienced mental properties. But I would pick out the same substance if I used less or more of the properties of which I am currently aware as co-instantiated. Thus suppose I pick out myself as the subject of two separate sensations (say, visual and tactual sensations). But if at the same time I also had two other sensations (say, auditory and gustatory), I could have picked out the same myself by means of those latter sensations. And if I had done so, the fact that I had the former (visual and tactual sensations) would have been irrelevant to who was picked out. But then the same person would have been picked out had I not had those (visual and tactual) sensations at all, the only ones I did have. So I would have been the same person if I had had quite other sensations instead. And since I could have had different mental properties, clearly I could have had different physical properties too (which gave rise to the different mental properties). Or—to take

are not difficulties for simple dualism (the view that I am my soul). The first is that mentioned in the text—that if we (embodied on earth) are not souls, although souls think, then there are two thinking things—me and my soul. In the text I argue that this is unparadoxical, since there is only one act of thinking going on—I think in virtue of my soul thinking. Olson admits (p. 76) that "there are some properties we have in a derivative sense. We are tattooed insofar as our skin is tattooed", but seems to think this unimportant. But innumerably similar examples can be adduced (I give the example of the table and its top on p. 149) and it is all-important. Why these examples don't have paradoxical consequences is because the events are the same: me being tattooed just is my skin being tattooed. We have seen earlier that there are many different ways of describing the world, but some of them don't describe anything "over and above" others of them.

The other difficulty which Olson finds in compound dualism is that (p. 81) it has the "absurd consequence that one could come to be identical with something that was previously only a part of one". Suppose I am embodied on Monday, but my body is then destroyed and I continue to exist in a disembodied state on Tuesday, then Olson claims that (1) I on Monday am the same as I on Tuesday, (2) I on Tuesday am the same as my soul on Tuesday, (3) my soul on Tuesday is the same as my soul on Monday, from which there follows a conclusion incompatible with compound dualism, (4) I on Monday am the same as my soul on Monday. But the false premise is (2). I on Tuesday have one and only one part on Tuesday, my soul. But I on Tuesday am not the same as my soul on Tuesday. This would be occasional identity, which runs into the problem mentioned in n. 18 above. Clearly a substance (of many genera) gains or lose parts while remaining the same substance: and there is no good reason to deny that a substance might come to have only one part. The "absurd consequence" does not follow.

[25] Our normal understanding of ourselves which I analyse in the text is that the parts of our bodies—arms, legs, and so on—are parts of ourselves; and so, given the arguments of this paper, we must think of whole bodies also as parts of ourselves. But, given that bodies are only contingent parts of human beings, we can think instead of ourselves merely as souls causally connected to bodies. Descartes himself seems to oscillate between these two ways of talking. For examples and commentary, see pp. 63–6 of Brian Smart, "How can Persons be Ascribed M-Predicates", *Mind*, 86 (1977), 49–66.

a temporally extended example—suppose I say to myself, "It is 5.00 and time to stop work". I pick out myself as the substance who said all these words to itself. Now it would be the same substance if I had uttered only the first six words; and also the same substance if these had been followed by two different words—"It is 5.00 and time to work harder"; yet a quite different thought would have been had. The words uttered later cannot make a difference to who it was who uttered the earlier words. And it would have been the same substance if I had uttered only the last two words, and also the same substance if these had been preceded by six different words- "I am getting tired and must stop work". Words uttered earlier cannot make a difference to who it was who uttered the later words. Hence, very different sensations or thoughts can be had by the same person from the ones he actually has. And yet a substance might only exist long enough to have these particular sensations or thoughts. The examples therefore suggest that for a substance who exists for a longer period of time, there can be no principled argument for claiming that there are any limits at all to the kind and length of mental life which can be had by that substance. For there could be a sequence of overlapping experiences, each consisting of two parts, the later of which formed the earlier part of the next experience, from which it must follow that the same substance has all the experiences which form the chain, and the later members could be very different in character from the earlier members. So, since what makes me is not the particular mental or physical properties which I have and not the matter of which my body is made, I must have a further thisness which is independent of any thisness possessed by physical matter.

This point is brought out by the apparent conceivability of a world W_2 in which for each substance in W_1 there is a substance which has the same properties as it and conversely (and any physical matter underlying the properties is the same in both worlds), but where a person S who exists in W_1 does not exist in W_2. The person who lives in W_2 the life (physical and mental) which S lives in W_1 is not S. And surely this world could be different solely in the respect that the person who lived my life was not me. For it is not entailed by the full description of the world in its physical aspects and in respect of which bundles of mental properties are instantiated in the same substance that I, picked out as the actual subject of certain mental properties, have the particular physical or mental properties which I do and am connected with the body with which I am connected. Human beings have a thisness which is quite other than any thisness possessed by the matter of which their bodies are made. In consequence of this and earlier thought experiments the Humean view of personal identity as constituted by the causal (and other relational) connections between our actual instantiated mental properties must be rejected.

Since I am a pure mental substance, I may hope to continue to exist after the destruction of my body, and perhaps then to be given a new body. My acquiring a new body will consist in the new body being brought into causal interaction with the pure mental substance which is myself. The "resurrection of the body" of all humans at the "last day" (the "General Resurrection") is a central Christian doctrine. Catholics, Orthodox, and many Protestants also believe that the person continues to exist without a body in the period between death and the General Resurrection. Both these doctrines are fully compatible with the account of human nature which I have defended in this paper.

6

Ghosts Are Chilly

W. D. Hart and *Takashi Yagisawa*

What you can imagine is possible, and you can imagine being disembodied, so you could be disembodied. Thus you do not depend for your existence on that of your body, so the distinctive thesis of Cartesian (and Platonic) dualism is true of you.[1]

Much of the information about the nature of the mind revealed by this central argument for dualism shows up in working out its second premise, that you can imagine being disembodied. A responsible dualist should be able at least to sketch how causal interaction between mind and matter is possible. But causation is the flow of energy.[2] So a dualist should sketch how energy might flow between mind and matter. For example, Paul Grice showed that vision requires that veridical visual experience be caused by that in virtue of which it is veridical.[3] To transpose Grice's result into the disembodied mode, imagine that light rays reaching the region of convergence of a disembodied person's lines of sight from that in virtue of which his visual experience is veridical lose some electromagnetic energy and, at a fixed rate of conversion, he acquires or is sustained in his degree of conviction as to how what he in fact sees is.[4] It is a corollary of this way of imagining

---

We are grateful to Paul Lövland for helpful comments on an earlier version of this paper.

[1] W. D. Hart, *The Engines of the Soul* (Cambridge: Cambridge University Press, 1988).

[2] Ibid., ch. 5.

[3] Paul Grice, "The Causal Theory of Perception," repr. in Robert J. Swartz (ed.), *Perceiving, Sensing and Knowing* (New York: Doubleday, 1965), 438–72. See also Hart, *Engines*, ch. 4. Grice showed that sight requires veridical visual experience caused by what makes it veridical. Visual experience is perspectival, i.e., along lines of sight that converge not so much in a point as in a small region. When visual experience is veridical, these lines of sight coincide with lines in space, and the region of the convergence begins to locate the visual experience, and thus part of the disembodied person. More of him can be placed via other senses, especially touch, and thinking through the requisite causation firms up his location. So disembodied people can be located in space, and yet still disembodied. Indeed, the sphere of radius one yard centered at the midpoint of the segment joining the present centers of mass of the Milky Way and the Crab Nebula fills out a region of space that perfectly well could be, and probably often is, void. It is simply not true that only material objects are located in space. Descartes made a blunder when he said that the essence of matter is extension.

[4] Hart, *Engines*, ch. 10. Of course one wants not just belief but also visual experience to be caused by that in virtue of which it is veridical (where the experience causes or sustains that subsequent belief). On this see ibid., 136–7 and n. 1 attached there.

how the disembodied could satisfy Grice's causal constraint on vision that there would be optical effects of vision in the disembodied. Perhaps their presence would show up as, say, a dimness of the light in the region of convergence of their lines of sight, and that upshot might perhaps in turn remind one of the filminess attributed to ghosts in folklore.[5] Dualism is venerable common sense.[6]

We have imagined (some of) how the disembodied could see. Could they feel hot or cold, could they have experiences like those embodied people have when they touch hot or cold objects? They need not: disembodiment might be like an anesthetic that numbs. But that maneuver seems a retreat of last resort. Let us at least try to be less fainthearted. An embodied person's body loses heat to objects he touches that are colder than his body, but gains heat from hotter such objects. Presumably such losses or gains in body heat cause an embodied person to feel cold or hot. Transposing in the disembodied mode is mostly a matter of dropping out the material middleman, the body. To do so here requires imagining how a disembodied person could be hotter than some cold objects and colder than some hot objects. This in turn will require him to have a temperature, a certain quantity of heat. But, it will be modish to think, heat is mean kinetic energy.[7] Kinetic energy is half the product of velocity squared with mass. So disembodied people could not have temperatures unless they have mass and thus are not disembodied after all. So disembodiment must numb.

This thinking is too hasty, for it is false that heat is mean kinetic energy. Heat moves in three forms: conduction, convection, and radiation. Conduction and convection may be at bottom matters of kinetic energy of massive corpuscles. But radiation crosses empty space innocent of massive corpuscles. Arno Penzias and Robert Wilson discovered that all regions of empty space have at least a temperature of about 3 degrees Kelvin.[8]

There was already reason to suppose disembodied people sources of radiant heat in order to imagine how they could be immaterial without being *eo ipso* immortal.[9] Imagining them as sources of radiant heat (from, say, imperfect efficiency in their mental processes) also shows a way to imagine them having temperatures while still thoroughly disembodied. Then we can imagine them losing some of their heat by radiation to colder nearby material objects, or gaining some heat by radiation from hotter nearby material objects. Now imagine as well that where such changes in temperature occur in them swiftly, they also lose an extra bit of heat (proportional in size to the prior change of temperature), and, at a fixed rate of conversion, acquire or are sustained in their conviction as to

---

[5] Ibid., 143.   [6] Ibid., ix–x and 178.
[7] Saul Kripke, *Naming and Necessity* (Oxford: Blackwell, 1980), 98.
[8] Steven Weinberg, *The First Three Minutes* (London: André Deutsch, 1977), ch. 3.
[9] Hart, *Engines*, 6–7 and 174.

how hot or cold what they are in fact feeling is.[10] It is, as noted, part of this way of imagining how the disembodied could feel hot or cold that they would have temperatures and thus thermal effects. Deferring to folklore, it is fun to put this as a corollary that ghosts are chilly.

[10] See, *mutatis mutandis*, n. 4. The second law of thermodynamics makes it natural to expect this conversion of heat into a sensation of heat to be only imperfectly efficient: were the sensation afterward to degrade into radiant heat, it would yield less than gave rise to it, because some of the heat giving rise to it remained heat (was wasted) in the process.

7

Cartesian Psychophysics

Hong Yu Wong

I

In this paper, I shall examine a certain style of argument against the possibility of a Cartesian psychophysics, and a response to it. Both are due to John Foster.[1]

The argument targets classical interactionism. Allow me to begin by giving a minimal construal of the doctrine:

> (MC) Some sentient creatures are psychophysical unions of material and immaterial substances that have mutual causal influence on each other.

This itself divides into various claims; two are of direct relevance:

> (D1) Material and immaterial substances are distinct.

> (D2) Material and immaterial substances within psychophysical unions have causal influence on each other.

A third claim, which is standardly understood to be part of classical interactionism but is not entailed by (MC) is:

Hommage à John Foster. Thanks to Quassim Cassam, Tim Crane, John Foster, Barry Loewer, Howard Robinson, and especially Michael Martin, Krisztina Orbán, Paul Snowdon, and Dean Zimmerman for discussion and comments. I am very grateful to Michael Martin and Dean Zimmerman for detailed last-minute comments.

[1] Foster has discussed these ideas in a number of places, beginning with the paper he wrote for his first B. Phil. supervision with A. J. Ayer, later published as "Psychophysical Causal Relations", *American Philosophical Quarterly*, 5 (1968) 64–70. More developed versions are to be found in his paper for Ayer's *festschrift*, "In *Self*-Defense", in G. F. Macdonald (ed.), *Perception and Identity* (London: Macmillan, 1979), and in part III, sections 7 and 8 of his monograph *A. J. Ayer* (London: Routledge, 1985). The core argument and response have remained constant, though Foster has changed his mind on the nature of causation and aspects of the dialectic. The most recent account of these matters is in his *The Immaterial Self* (London: Routledge, 1991). The section of direct relevance is "The Problem of Causal Pairings" in ch. 6.

(D3) Immaterial substances are non-spatial; that is, they have no spatial properties.[2]

I will now pause to make two qualifications. First, I do not wish to decide whether classical interactionism is committed to the claim that we are psychophysical unions or that we are immaterial substances with material appendages. The more general formulation is that some sentient creatures *involve* psychophysical unions of mutually interacting substances; but this is rather clumsy so I shall stick with the simpler (MC). In any case, the problems of this essay arise for any interactionist who assents to (D1), (D2), and (D3). Secondly, it is not my intention to spell out a positive conception of immaterial substance in this essay; I am primarily concerned to evaluate the status of an argument that is in play as long as (D1) through (D3) are accepted. For present purposes, it should suffice to say that immaterial substances are non-spatial and essentially mental.

I take it that (D1), (D2), and (D3) are jointly insufficient but necessary for classical interactionism.

The paper is divided into three parts. In the first (Sections II and III), I describe a certain kind of problem for classical interactionism. I begin by considering traditional scepticism about classical interactionism, and use this as a springboard for developing a precise worry about interactionism that also stems from doubts about the possibility of psychophysical interaction given the non-spatiality of immaterial substance—Foster's 'causal pairing problem'. In the second part (Section IV), I set up Foster's response to the causal pairing problem in terms of individualised psychophysical laws. Foster's solution is ingenious, but is, I argue, inconsistent with our conceptual commitment to the *generality* of causation—that the causal relation holds between two entities in virtue of the *kinds* they fall under as opposed to *which particular things* they are. This leads to the third and final part (Section V), where I tease out certain unpalatable consequences of a metaphysics of individualized laws or dispositions. I argue that in order to accommodate the empirical fact of metabolic turnover, the theorist has to be committed to certain radical claims about the nature of human bodies and matter in general. I conclude by briefly considering whether classical interactionism should abandon the claim that immaterial substances are non-spatial.

II

Much of the traditional scepticism about classical interactionism stems from (D3), the non-spatiality of the soul. Anthony Kenny expresses this line of thought, which goes back to Princess Elisabeth of Bohemia, when he writes:

---

[2] I also mean to sidestep the issue of whether immaterial substances are non-spatial or merely unextended. I take it that theories claiming the latter are non-classical.

On Descartes' principles it is difficult to see how an unextended thinking substance can cause motion in an extended unthinking substance and how an extended unthinking substance can cause sensations in the unextended thinking substance. The properties of the two kinds of substance seem to place them in such diverse categories that it is impossible for them to interact.[3]

Kenny's remark highlights a dubious feature of classical interactionism: on Descartes's principles, it is not at all clear how substances with such diverse properties can interact. (This is somewhat exacerbated by Descartes's 'primary attribute' conception of substance—which effectively means that distinct substances can share *no* properties.[4]) But Kenny has little more to say against classical interactionism, resting his case on this brief description of a problem. Here Kenny is not alone. This style of objection is often read as definitive against classical interactionism in contemporary philosophy.

The dialectical force of this traditional objection is, I think, greatly overrated. At best, it issues an *explanatory challenge* to the interactionist: that he may not, as Swinburne does in *The Evolution of the Soul*, take mind–body interaction as a brute inexplicable connection (perhaps only comprehensible by higher beings, like God) while asserting (D1), (D2), and (D3).[5] (I shall call this the 'primitivist' position.) If classical interactionism is to blunt the dialectical force of the explanatory challenge, interactionists must at least *attempt* to make the possibility of mind–body interactionism intelligible. As Jaegwon Kim puts it,[6] the explanatory question is not *how* a being like God links the soul and the body, but rather *what* God is doing when he links the soul and the body; that is, if this is done via some relation *R*, what relation *R* is God using to do the job? I mention God here because the primitivist position often includes the claim that it is not obliged to answer this question because (1) God provides the mind–body link and (2) we couldn't possibly understand *how* he does it. Such a primitivist refuses to meet the challenge to explain *what* God is doing when he links the soul and the body.

There are, however, a number of ways the traditional worry might be developed. One suggestion is that it is the very *diversity* of kinds of substances that leads to the impossibility of classical interactionism. This is justified by a principle to the effect that substances can only interact causally with substances

[3] Anthony Kenny, *Descartes* (New York: Random House, 1968), 222–3.

[4] The disjointedness of families of properties associated with distinct substances does not follow on a 'profligate' conception of properties, on which every predicate corresponds to a property, since distinct substances will at least share the property of being substances. It is clear, however, that Descartes is working with a 'sparse' conception of properties on which they, so to speak, 'carve nature at its joints'. (See esp. his metaphysics of substance as presented in the *Second Meditation* and the *Principles of Philosophy*.)

[5] See the "Prolegomenon to the Revised Edition" of Swinburne's *Evolution of the Soul*, rev. edn. (Oxford: Clarendon Press, 1997) where he expresses sympathy for the 'primitivist' position.

[6] Jaegwon Kim, "Lonely Souls: Causality and Substance Dualism", in K. Corcoran (ed.), *Soul, Body, and Survival* (Ithaca, NY: Cornell University Press, 2001).

of the same kind. Assuming that causation relates *events*, the principle behind the objection can be formulated as follows:

Homogeneity

An event *c* involving a substance *A* can enter into causal relations with another event *e* involving a substance *B* only if *A* and *B* are substances of the same kind.[7]

However, Homogeneity seems to be an excessively strong constraint to place on causation. Consider the case where we have a kind of substance that is like material substance in all respects except that it essentially lacks a property that material substances essentially have, say mass. Call this kind of substance M*. Now we can pose the question of whether events involving M* substances can causally interact with events involving material substances. Absent any obvious reason to the contrary, there does not seem to be any *general* reason why events involving M* cannot causally interact with events involving material substances—unless it can be shown that causal interactions between events involving the two substances *must* be mediated by mass.

But might we not weaken the homogeneity principle to one that only requires the substances to be sufficiently similar? It is, however, crucially unclear what 'sufficiently similar' amounts to in this context. If immaterial substances have spatial addresses at extensionless points, does that mean that they are now sufficiently similar to material substances, and so interaction is possible? The principle doesn't seem to give us any answers here. Whilst the causal principles we have been concerned with only specify necessary conditions on causation, the crucial unclarity of 'sufficient similarity' in this context seems merely to raise the explanatory challenge: that mind–body interactionism needs to be made *intelligible*. This takes us back to the original suspicion about the non-spatiality of immaterial substances.[8]

III

There is, however, another way of developing the traditional scepticism about classical interactionism into a full-scale objection. This, too, springs from

---

[7] An allied principle used is that causal relations are restricted to things of the same ontological category. Again, this is shorthand for the proper formulation in terms of events involving the things in question. (Ducasse objects to this principle; see p. 88 of his "In Defense of Dualism", in S. Hook (ed.), *Dimensions of Mind* (New York: New York University Press, 1960), 85–90.) This is stronger than the principle pertaining to substances. It is prima facie implausible because of apparent counterexamples like the perception of facts, which requires that a fact cause a mental event.

[8] Perhaps one might respond that we don't really know what making Cartesian mental agency intelligible means. But we still need to react to the questions that can be raised. It would be cavalier to simply brush them aside.

doubts about whether (D2) is sustainable given the interactionists' acceptance of non-spatiality, that is, (D3). This style of objection proceeds from general constraints on the nature of causation—in particular, the absence of a contingent dimensional structuring framework for immaterial substances—to the conclusion that material substances cannot interact with immaterial ones because there are no appropriate criteria for pairing causes with effects. The argument is due to John Foster. He calls it the 'causal pairing problem'.

Consider a scene from the Middle Ages: a disputation about mental ontology amongst schoolmen has almost degenerated into fisticuffs. Three philosophers are shooting paper pellets at each other with slings. What makes it the case that the dualist's pellet hits the materialist but not the idealist? The force vector of the dualist's sling was in the materialist's direction, the materialist didn't move in the meantime because he was busy aiming at the idealist, etc. In short, the materialist was appropriately located relative to the dualist. And in general it seems that spatial relations function as contingent structuring relations, insuring that the particular causal relata in any case are logically unique in that situation; that is, we have determinate cause–effect pairs in each situation.[9]

As a working assumption, let us assume what Foster calls the 'nomological assumption':

(NA) The causal relation between two events is completely determined by the non-causal properties and relations of the two events and the obtaining of certain relevant covering laws.

The problem for the interactionist is that, given the possibility of simultaneous exact qualitative mental duplicates and given that he only has a temporal relation to work with as an external pairing relation (since classical interactionism is committed to the non-spatiality of immaterial substances), it is not at all clear that he can find an external pairing relation to facilitate mind–body interaction—a relation to insure that mental causes can be uniquely paired with their material effects and vice versa. To be precise, the interactionist is facing at least two questions here, a general one and a specific one about embodiment:

(A) *The general problem.* Given the lack of an external pairing relation, how can immaterial substances which are non-spatial interact with material substances?

Even if the interactionist can answer (A), he still faces a second challenge to secure the specificity of embodiment:[10]

---

[9] This requirement is perhaps too strong and we will give it up in due course: that there is no criterion for pairing doesn't entail that there cannot be causal relations (cf. the Foster–Tooley indeterminacy-of-pairing case discussed in Section V).

[10] This problem may be exacerbated by intuitions of independence that the interactionist may have regarding disembodiment; but, for the most part, I shall not consider modal theses to which

(B) *The specificity of embodiment.* How can the interactionist's psychophysical laws account for the specificity of embodiment—that is, the fact that *my* mind interacts just with *my* body *and no other*, and vice versa—for the range of sentient creatures that classical interactionism is committed to in its minimal specification (MC)?

Answering (A) does not automatically present an answer to (B); and though questions (A) and (B) are distinct, one fails to answer the question of how interactionism is possible *for beings like us* if one gives an answer to (A) that does not also answer (B).

The natural interactionist strategy at this stage is to hunt down an external pairing relation to supplement the temporal relation and to secure unique causal pairing. An obvious candidate is the relation of embodiment ('*x* is embodied in *y*'). Thus supplemented, the laws yield unique causal pairing—but the account is, unfortunately, circular. Such laws assume the notion of embodiment, which on the dualist account is something like direct causal interaction between a particular mind and its body; *but how then is the dualist to explain this causal attachment?* If we return to a solely temporal pairing relation we have no unique pairing (or unique pairing by luck, as it were). But on pain of circularity, we cannot use a pairing relation such as embodiment.

Most of the time the dialectic stops at this stage. The antagonist cannot think of any suitable external relation and infers that classical interactionism is untenable.[11] For example, Jaegwon Kim concludes from a similar argument that classical interactionism is *unintelligible*. Indeed, he claims that even soul–soul causation is impossible in the absence of a structuring framework, since souls are essentially non-spatial but space is the only dimensional framework Kim can think of.[12]

A charge like that can be met in various ways. One is to hypothesize quasi-spatial ordering relations between non-spatial immaterial entities that would function as a contingent structuring dimensional fabric.[13] (These need not be isomorphic to spatial relations, but need to structure immaterial entities in a way that will at least respect 'quasi-spatial exclusion principles' analogous to spatial exclusion principles.) There is no obvious inconsistency in relating immaterial substances to material substances by these hypothesized relations, and

classical interactionism is standardly thought to be committed. (But see the discussion in Section V for an interesting modal wrinkle.)

[11] See e.g. Ernest Sosa's two articles: "Mind–Body Interaction and Supervenient Causation", *Midwest Studies in Philosophy*, 9 (1984), 271–81; and "Subjects Among Other Things", reprinted in M. Rea (ed.), *Material Constitution* (Oxford: Rowman and Littlefield, 1997).

[12] Kim, "Lonely Souls".

[13] See e.g. p. 146 of Sydney Shoemaker's "Immortality and Dualism", repr. in his *Identity, Cause, and Mind* (Cambridge: Cambridge University Press, 1984) and section 2 of Timothy O'Connor's "Causality, Mind, and Free Will", repr. in K. Corcoran (ed.), *Soul, Body, and Survival* (Ithaca, NY: Cornell University Press, 2001).

by some such relations we seem to have a glimmer of what it might mean to think that immaterial substances can interact with material substances. *Modulo* the difficulties of finding a viable quasi-spatial framework that might provide contingent structuring relations of the appropriate sort, the suggestion seems to make some sense of classical interactionism, and it does not seem to me that any difficulties with finding an appropriate relation can translate into conceptual incoherence for classical interactionism. (It is, however, important to realize that the sense of intelligibility here is thin. As Shoemaker says: "It is not that we have a determinate conception of some kind of immaterial substances, and can conceive of there being things that satisfy this conception. It is rather that we can conceive of having (or acquiring) such a determinate notion, and of believing, intelligibly and consistently, that there are things that satisfy it."[14])

Another way of meeting the unintelligibility charge is suggested by Daniel Garber's response to the charge on Descartes's behalf.[15] Garber writes:

Mind–body interaction seems to be, for Descartes, a paradigm for both mechanist and Scholastic causal explanation. Since there were two main competitors at the time, we can say that, for Descartes, mind–body interaction is the paradigm for *all* causal explanation, it is that in terms of which *all* other causal interaction must be understood. . . . Mind–body interaction must be basic and intelligible on its own terms since if it were not, then no other kind of causal explanation would be intelligible at all; to challenge the intelligibility of mind–body interaction is to challenge the entire enterprise of causal explanation. Furthermore, we *cannot give* a simpler or more easily understood account of causal interaction than mind–body interaction because *there are no more basic or more inherently intelligible ways of explaining the behaviour of anything open to us.* We cannot appeal to analogies with impact to clarify mind–body interaction, as Elisabeth does, not because of any confusion of primitive notions, but because we must work the other way: body–body interaction must ultimately be understood through the notion we have of the way in which the mind acts on the body.[16]

---

[14] Shoemaker, "Immortality and Dualism", 147 n. 8.

[15] See "Understanding Interaction: What Descartes should have Told Elisabeth", in Garber's collection of essays, *Descartes Embodied* (Cambridge: Cambridge University Press, 2001).

[16] Ibid. 188. The textual evidence for Garber's claim that mind–body interaction is the paradigm notion of causation for Descartes comes from two sources. For scholastic explanation, it derives from Descartes's discussion of how understanding the idea of heaviness is derivative from understanding the mind and mind–body union. The relevant passages are in the *Sixth Replies*, in C. Adam and P. Tannery (eds.), *Œuvres de Descartes*, rev. edn. (Paris: Vrin/CNRS, 1964–76) (henceforth, 'AT'), vii. 442. The chain of ideas tracing the intelligibility of mechanistic explanation back to the intelligibility of mind-body interaction is more circuitous. The relevant passages are in Descartes's letters to More in 1649 discussing the nature of motion, AT v. First, all motion is due to God: "motion transferred, motion begun, and motion ended in impact must derive from God himself, shuffling bodies about as part of the process of 'conserving the same amount of translation in matter as He put in it the first moment of creation' (Descartes to More, August 1649, AT v. 403–4)" (Garber, "Understanding Interaction", 184). The burden of proof is now on how we understand divine causation of motion, a problem similar to that for classical interactionism, since God too is incorporeal, and thus unextended. Here Descartes writes that "the only ideal I can find in my mind to represent the way [*modus*] in which God or an angel can move matter is the one which shows

The import of this suggestion is that mental agency is *conceptually primitive*. Garber's idea is that it is open to a classical interactionist to say that we can only understand causation because our experience of agency presents us with instances of mental causation of bodily effects; and that our understanding of causation in other instances is derived from this basic phenomenon.[17] I am sympathetic to the suggestion that our experience of agency constitutes the basic source of causal understanding. But the plausibility of this phenomenological observation concerning conceptual genealogy, while underlining the indispensability of agency and mental causation in our conceptual scheme, fails to buttress classical interactionism. Nothing about the conceptual primitiveness and entrenchment of mental causation in our conceptual scheme helps to make sense of how immaterial substances lacking in spatial properties can enter into causal relations with material substances. It would be a mistake to read the dialectical force of Garber's observation as establishing the possibility of mental causation, given a certain ontology of the mental, after that ontology has been independently established. Nothing has been shown about *how mental causation is possible* within that ontological framework!

That mental agency is conceptually basic for us doesn't mean that *any ontology of the mind–body relation gets mental causation of bodily effects for free*. That gets the dialectic backwards. Rather, given the conceptual primitiveness of mental agency with bodily effects, giving an intelligible account of mental agency specifies a strong constraint on any theory of the mind–body relation. Any credible theory had better be able to give an intelligible account of mental events causing bodily events (or if not, it had better be able to provide a powerful error theory). As such, Garber's point, while conceptually astute, is, so to speak, 'ontology-neutral' and fails to buttress a classical interactionism committed to (D1) through (D3).

In this first part of the paper, we saw how Foster crystallized the vague worries associated with traditional scepticism about interactionism into a specific problem: how is it possible for there to be causal interaction between non-spatial immaterial substances and material substances, in the absence of external pairing relations such as those provided by space? The upshot of our discussion is that, in light of (NA), the interactionist has to answer a question about how we tie down mental events to a specific body. In the next part of the paper, we shall explore Foster's solution to this difficulty.

---

me the way in which I am conscious I can move my own body by my own thought" (Descartes to More, 15 April 1649, AT v. 347). Thus even the way in which we can conceive of God acting upon the world is derived from the conception of how I act on my body.

To enter some disclaimers for Garber: he does not say that this suggestion circumvents all or even any of the problems that have been raised for classical interactionism; but he does think that Descartes had the materials to respond in this way to Elisabeth's inquiries, and that this suggestion is philosophically superior to Descartes's actual responses to Elisabeth.

[17] Endorsing the conceptual necessity of mind–body interaction for understanding causation at large significantly bolsters the case of the primitivist. I am not aware of any primitivist who has taken up Garber's suggestion.

IV

The causal pairing problem appears to be insoluble for the classical interactionist given (NA) and the lack of a *spatio*-temporal framework. Having set up this obstacle to interactionism, Foster then sets out to surmount it. His solution is subtle: he simultaneously undermines (NA) yet manages to secure the specificity of embodiment.

Foster attacks the nomological assumption directly. Using a classic argument for singular causation, he shows that even in physical causation, you get perfectly symmetrical situations where you cannot pair the causes.

The Foster-Tooley counterexample against the nomological assumption runs as follows:[18] Consider two particles x and y, both of type Δ. It is a law that particles of type Δ emit a single flash of light within a 1 metre radius around the particles every 10 seconds. Consider a situation in which x and y are placed adjacent to each other so that there is an area where the radii within which they emit light flashes overlap. At time t, two flashes of light, f_1 and f_2, simultaneously appear in the overlapping 'emitting zone'.

(NA) claims that the causal relation between any two events is fixed entirely by the non-causal properties and relations of the two events and the obtaining of certain relevant covering laws. But this is not true for the case at hand. Fixing the non-causal properties and relations of the flashes f_1 and f_2 and the particles x and y, and the relevant covering laws, fails to determine whether flash f_1 was emitted by x and f_2 by y or the other way around. So (NA) is false.

(In fact, the case constitutes a counterexample to a weaker formulation in terms of supervenience:

> (NA′) There can be no difference in the causal relation between two events without a difference in either the non-causal properties and relations of the events or the covering laws.

If the case described above is a possibility, then we have a situation in which there can be differences in the causal relations between flash and emission events, without differences in either the non-causal properties and relations of the events or the relevant covering laws. Thus, fixing the laws and non-causal factors fails to fix the causal relations. Given this, we can reject (NA) and any other thesis which entails (NA′).)

Here is where Foster's pincer strategy comes into play. Even given singular causation, the interactionist is obliged to explain why *this* brain only directly interacts with *this* mind and *that* brain only with *that* mind; the *specificity* of embodiment needs to be explained. It is important to note, however, that there is

---

[18] See e.g. D. M. Armstrong's presentation of the argument in the chapter on singular causation in his *A World of States of Affairs* (Cambridge: Cambridge University Press, 1997).

an *asymmetry* between cases of symmetrical physical causation and interactionist scenarios. In the case of symmetric physical causation canvassed above, there is *no pressure* to explain why the flash appears here rather than there; but in the case of classical interactionism, we have to explain—even given singular causation and the failure of (NA′)—why *this* mind only interacts with *this* brain (and no other), and *that* mind only with *that* brain (and no other). This is explained by recourse to individualized psychophysical laws.

Rather than hunting for some relation to supplement the temporal one, Foster restricts the scope of psychophysical laws to particular persons.[19] For example,

L(Mary): It is a law that whenever a Φ-event occurs in (Mary's) brain B_M at a time when B_M is of structural type Σ, Ψ-experience occurs a tenth of a second later in (Mary's) mind M_M.

L(Harpo): It is a law that whenever a Φ-event occurs in (Harpo's) brain B_H at a time when B_H is of structural type Σ, Ψ-experience occurs a tenth of a second later in (Harpo's) mind M_H.[20]

(And similarly for other people with the appropriate substitutions.) Foster's solution here is to secure the specific psychophysical arrangement characteristic of embodiment by recourse to an appropriate system of scope-restricted laws—laws which by their scope restriction "limit the fields of influence and sensitivity of each in the requisite way". This is *not* to reinstate the nomological assumption, for the point of postulating the scope-restricted laws is only to explain why psychophysical causal relations are regular and not to reduce them to nomological facts.

But we might worry that scope-restricted laws lack nomological generality. We don't expect that the *identity* of particular objects is a nomologically relevant factor. Rather, we think that causation takes place in virtue of the *kinds* of individuals that enter into the causal relation (and certain other locality conditions); *which particular things* is irrelevant.[21]

---

[19] Peter Unger in his *All the Power in the World* (Oxford: Oxford University Press, 2006) uses individualized dispositions to solve the same problem. Presumably individualized laws will supervene on individualized dispositions or the other way round depending on whether laws or dispositions are more basic in the ontology.

[20] *The Immaterial Self*, 167.

[21] Another worry is that the fact that the interactionist can stipulate such laws doesn't imply that they exist. The interactionist may meet such a worry by showing that the laws do work beyond that which they were designed to do, and this increases their independent plausibility. Worries like this highlight issues of evidential force of various claims in the dialectic. I intend to sidestep these issues; in this paper I concentrate on finding internal problems with Foster's solution. I am interested in what costs we would incur by postulating that Foster's solution describes how things actually are.

In the face of the stipulation objection, in *All the Power in the World*, Unger argues that individualized dispositions are not as weird and rare as we think. He describes a class of 'self-directed' dispositions and argues that these are conceptually independent of space. The objector, he argues, confuses the pairing problem with an individuation problem. Unger is also willing to

Foster responds that scope-restricted laws are not "nomologically capricious", for the "nomological constraints do not vary inexplicably from person to person". Psychophysics is general in a certain sense: whenever there is a psychophysical law for a certain individual, there are exactly similar scope-restricted laws for everyone. We might think of the scope-restricted laws for each individual as instances of a general law:

L $< \Sigma, \Phi, \Psi >$: It is a law that there is some 1–1 correlation between human brains and human minds such that any Φ-event in a brain x of structural type Σ is a tenth of a second earlier than some Ψ-experience in that mind which is correlated with x.[22]

The nomological factor is invariant, discounting the reference to the particular brain and mind in question. It is not that the individualized laws can be *deduced* from L $< \Sigma, \Phi, \Psi >$, since it does not specify which brain is related to which mind—so this does not reinstate the reductionist (NA). L $< \Sigma, \Phi, \Psi >$ specifies that there is a correlation and the individualized laws then go on to secure the causal links.

There is, however, an important proviso: the dualist mustn't go on to account for the unity of a mind in even partially causal terms, otherwise a circularity lurks. For the account of unity presupposes psychophysical causation, while the psychophysical causation account presupposes a prior account of what constitutes a single mind.

But one wonders why there is a need for ineliminable reference to *particular* minds and brains if everyone gets exactly similar laws. Are the individualistic laws Foster posits more than a redescription of the problem? Why is it that we don't need these individualistic laws for causation across the sciences, but we

speculate on the possibility of a space-like framework that minds might reside in, but he uses that to solve the individuation problem.

It is difficult to assess the dialectical force of the individuation problem, but whatever force something like the individuation problem has, there is a certain style of argument against immaterial substances from the lack of a principle of individuation that is flawed. Ernest Sosa in the appendix to his "Subjects Among Other Things" sets out two principles for the metaphysics of individuals, Diversity Cannot Stand Alone (DCSA) and Entities Require Dimensional Framework (ERDF).

DCSA: "No entities x and y can possibly be related only by diversity in such a way that the following three conditions are satisfied: first, x is numerically distinct from y; second, x is otherwise the same as y in every qualitative respect; and, third, x is related to y by no relation that is irreflexive, except only for the relation of diversity (and its deductive progeny)."

ERDF: "If entities x and y belong to the same category, they must fall within a dimensional framework, which requires the presence of some ordering relation that relates the two."

Sosa argues for the former principle (and thus implicitly for the latter) by means of what I call the 'my foot, not my feet argument': the lesson, Sosa argues, is simply that no entities x and y can simply be related by diversity, for otherwise you might have not just one right foot but indefinitely many of them, all related only by diversity. The proper response is that we have no reason to posit so many feet, whereas we seem to have theoretical reasons to posit immaterial substances.

[22] *The Immaterial Self*, 168.

need them for psychophysics? Is the notion of individualistic laws ultimately consistent with our conception of causation?

Notice that even if one rejects (NA)—that is, even if one rejects the unique pairing requirement—that doesn't entail that causation doesn't still happen in virtue of the *kind* of things (and certain other locality constraints) as opposed to *which particular things*. My point is that there is more than one route to a causal pairing problem for the classical interactionist. The route that we've developed (following Foster) concerns the availability of a dimensional background that functions as a contingent structuring framework for causation. Another route is from the notion of causal generality, the idea that causal relations between events happen in virtue of non-haceitistic properties. (A haceitistic property is the property of being identical with a certain particular individual; e.g. *your* being identical with *you*, *my* being identical with *me*, etc. Note that this is *not* the property of being identical with some individual or other, which we all share.) The intuitive plausibility of a thesis of causal generality can be illustrated by a simple thought experiment.

Consider the case of three elementary physical particles, *a*, *b*, and *c*, of kind π. As it happens, *a* repels only *b* and *b* repels only *a*. These two particles fail to interact with *c* no matter how close they are to *c*. In fact, the thought experiment can be set up in two ways: (i) *a* interacts only with *b* regardless of the distance between them, even when *c* is adjacent; or (ii) within a certain distance, *a* interacts only with *b*, but when *b* is not in the appropriate vicinity for interaction and *c* is, *a* still fails to interact with *c*. We do not think that these are plausible scenarios, because we implicitly subscribe to a principle of causal generality.

Though the causal pairing problem can be developed from two directions, there is no doubt that the two assumptions can interact: causal generality entails the impossibility of haceitistic causation (i.e. causation where an entity's identity—as opposed to just the kind it falls under—is relevant, e.g. the sort of scope-restricted laws that Foster posits), whilst the lack of a structuring framework implies the lack of an external pairing relation which pairs cause and effect, given causal generality.

Note that the Foster–Tooley counterexample is not a counterexample to generality but to the supervenience thesis (NA′) and any thesis that entails it. In their scenario, though we do not have determinate causal pairing relations, we can in all of the putative pairings make sense of a causal link in terms of spatial arrangement and the covering law. The scenario is consistent with the thesis of causal generality—that causation takes place in virtue of the *kind* of things that enter into the relation rather than the *particular identity* of the things involved. Thus, the classical interactionist has not yet come to terms with the strong intuition we have of causal generality, since the Foster–Tooley case sketched above against (NA′) is *perfectly consistent* with causal generality, and, as the simple thought experiment illustrates, there is reason to think that our understanding of causation includes a tacit commitment to generality.

I am unable to pursue further the line of argument from causal generality in this paper, since it would take us too far afield. Rather I will hint at how one might pursue the dialectic on whether we are committed to causal generality, since it has largely been left at an intuitive level. The first thing to note is that the pairing problem is not merely a problem about criteria for pairing causes, since there are physical scenarios where the symmetry of the causal situation does not allow us to uniquely pair causes to their effects. Rather, the absence of a criterion for pairing causes is *symptomatic* of an underlying commitment to causal generality and the absence of a dimensional framework that individuates Cartesian minds. One can see this distinction when one considers that if the pairing problem merely consisted in the absence of a *criterion* for pairing, then Descartes would have no problem with it since he posits *singular* representation relations between minds and their bodies. But we do not think that this then shows us how Cartesian psychophysics is possible—we still want to know just how non-spatial minds can interact with bodies. Thus I suggest the real question here is one concerning causal generality.

How, then, might we push the dialectic further? The dualist here is positing a kind of *sui generis* singular causal relation, whose singularity does not consist in spatio-temporal factors obtaining. Can we really make sense of such a singular relation given our commitment to causal generality? It may seem that there is no prima facie inconsistency between these individualistic powers and our conception of causation. But perhaps our understanding of causation involves some commitment to, for example, mechanism (or something similar)—a commitment that requires us to be able to make sense of the causal scenario via spatio-temporally localizable interactions. Or it may be that our concept of causation is interventionist, where, crudely, for x to be a cause of y is for intervening on x to be a way of intervening on y. Interventionist theories of causation do not appeal to the idea of providing a mechanism, but it may be that we are ultimately unable to understand the notion of an intervention in anything but spatio-temporal terms.[23]

Rather than conducting the dialectic at the level of general constraints on causation, I propose to steer the debate toward a specific consequence of a metaphysics of individualized laws. This, I shall argue, illustrates the incongruence of a metaphysics of individualized laws with certain other general metaphysical commitments that we may have. The original problem of psychophysical interaction turns up as a bump elsewhere in the carpet.

---

[23] See e.g. John Campbell's "An Interventionist Approach to Causation in Psychology", in A. Gopnik and L. Schulz (eds.), *Causal Learning: Psychology, Philosophy and Computation* (Oxford: Oxford University Press, forthcoming) and the references there on interventionism. Here I am indebted to discussion with Michael Martin.

V

We now turn to the third and final part of this paper.[24] My argument here consists in teasing out certain unpalatable consequences of a metaphysics of individualized laws or dispositions. I see this as a specific development of the dialectic arising from the inconsistency of individualized laws or dispositions with general conceptual commitments we have about the nature of causation.

The difficulty I shall consider stems from the need of the interactionist to accommodate the empirical fact of metabolic turnover. I shall argue that if the interactionist is to accommodate this within an individualistic metaphysics of causation, he is forced to embrace certain radical claims about the nature of human bodies and matter in general.

Every day, our bodies change large numbers of particles; in particular, my body may assimilate material particles formerly in bodies of other sentient creatures or it may assimilate particles which have never been incorporated into a body. This has the consequence of radicalizing the notion of matter to which the interactionist of Foster's stripe is committed. To establish this, we have to consider the consequences for all the available metaphysical stories about bodies: that they are just swarms of particles, or just a series of mereological sums, or wholes that are not *mere* sums but can undergo change of parts. Let us call these pictures a *nihilist* metaphysics of bodies, a *mereological essentialist* metaphysics of bodies, and a *commonsensical* metaphysics of bodies respectively. Note that even though the discussion will be couched in terms of the relation between minds and bodies, the most relevant entities for psychophysics are *brains*, since we may lose quite a large number of other body parts and still function, but cannot lose our brains. In the following discussion, let 'body' stand for whatever medium-sized organic thing (organ or organism) is connected by laws to the mind.

(A) Nihilist metaphysics

On this metaphysics there is only a swarm of particles shaped 'body-wise'—*but no body*. (There are no swarms either. A 'particle swarm' merely picks out a group of particles in close proximity.[25]) Given metabolic turnover by the 'body', the particles that constitute our 'bodies' will be continually changing. It seems that excepting incorporation into the 'bodies' of mental subjects, material particles do not possess individualistic dispositionality. Even classical interactionists who accept some solution like Foster's are apt to think that causal generality holds except in the case of the psychophysics of sentient individuals. But how then is it possible that material entities can individualistically

---

[24] This section has greatly benefited from extensive comments from Dean Zimmerman.

[25] See e.g. Cian Dorr's "The Simplicity of Everything" (Ph.D. dissertation, Princeton University, 2002) and his more recent "What We Disagree about When We Disagree about Ontology", in M. Kalderon (ed.), *Fictionalist Approaches to Metaphysics* (Oxford: Oxford University Press, 2005).

interact with mental substances?—Do material particles acquire individualistic dispositions when caught up in the life of a mental subject?[26]

The situation gets more problematic once one considers that, at some later time, your 'body' may incorporate some material particles that I shed. Do these material particles then lose their disposition to interact only with *my* mind and then acquire a disposition to interact only with *yours*?

My argument requires two premises and certain simplifying assumptions. The premises are: (1) it seems possible that any material particle that could be incorporated by the 'body' of one mental subject could be incorporated into the 'body' of any other mental subject. This is uncontroversial. And (2) it is implausible to think that material particles acquire individualistic dispositions once incorporated into a 'body'.[27] This is because even though the classical interactionists think that minds can causally influence certain parcels of matter, they do not think that minds can change the *nature* of these parcels of matter. The assumptions: By 'behaviour' I mean to refer to what the term was used for traditionally; that is, externally accessible actions—as manifested in bodily movements. For simplicity, let us assume that we can individuate types of behaviour by the distinct kinds of bodily movement that they involve. Let us also assume that the ability to perform each kind of behaviour is associated with a single 'behavioural disposition' and that the dispositions of individual particles have to coordinate with dispositions of other particles in the body-shaped particle swarm to sustain the large-scale behavioural dispositions.

---

[26] I am conducting the argument with dispositions rather than laws because it is slightly more intuitive. But the argument can be run in terms of laws.

[27] Unger sees no problems with the acquisition of individualistic dispositions on the part of objects, but his approach seems to me to be excessively cavalier. (See *All the Power in the World*, ch. 7, esp. pp. 456–60 on 'bodily flexibility'.) The original problem for classical interactionism is posed by how (D2) is possible given (D3), but with the background assumption that, as Foster puts it, the mental and physical realms are both fundamental and ontologically separate. Foster defines dualism as the conjunction of five claims: (1) There is a mental realm. (2) The mental realm is fundamental. (3) There is a physical realm. (4) The physical realm is fundamental. (5) The two realms are ontologically separate (*The Immaterial Self*, 1). Insofar as the original problem is as I describe it, Unger is changing the game, since he is explicitly denying Foster's fifth assumption. The denial, moreover, is a strong one, since he appears to think that minds can 'infect' particles with individualistic dispositions towards them when they are absorbed into bodies (if they are the bodies of minds). Whilst there is no conceptual incoherence in this, I am sceptical of this way of thinking about matter. After all, the classical interactionist was originally motivated to allow for causal influence of minds on bodies (and vice versa). Affecting the trajectories of particles, say, is not a matter of changing their natures, but rather being (yet another) cause acting on them. Also, Unger appears to think that if a particle joins a mob of particles that are already individualistically directed toward a mind, then that particle can acquire individualistic dispositions toward that mind (p. 460). I discuss and reject this as implausible in the main text. With regard to that passage, it is also unclear whether he is really thinking of hypothetical, general dispositions of the sort that I discuss in the main text (and has slipped into a non-nihilist metaphysics of bodies) or is thinking of bona fide individualistic dispositions.

This paper was written before Unger's monograph was published, though I had access to an early draft. I intend to consider the details of Unger's metaphysics in a later paper.

The upshot of this is that for every single behavioural disposition—individualized, naturally, since it is the ability of *this* mind to act with *this* particle swarm—that an individual sentient being has, every material particle will have to have an individualized disposition for every sentient being that might ever exist in the universe. This is because it has to be able to interact individualistically with any sentient creature whose 'body' incorporates the particle. (I take it that, even though dispositions of individual particles have to coordinate with those of other particles to sustain large-scale behavioural dispositions, these too will have to be directed at the mental individual in question.) But it is an understatement to say that it seems unlikely that each material particle has dispositional sensitivities to all minds that can potentially be embodied in the history of the universe. This, if anything, is a veritable 'combinatorial explosion' of distinct dispositions. Before, where we had a single disposition for each kind of behaviour, now we need a very large family of these—one for each possible sentient creature.

One might respond that this is already the case with familiar physical particles, such as electrons, given the subtlety and highly varied repertory of their reactions to different situations. But it is important to notice that the complexity involved in the case of individualized dispositions is of a radically higher order. In the case of the familiar physical particles, their behaviour can be characterized by a set of relatively straightforward equations and the range of different numerical values solutions to these equations can take. In contrast, the physical particles with individualistic dispositional sensitivities not only have the dispositions that characterize the familiar physical particles, but also must have dispositional sensitivities to all possible mental subjects that can potentially be embodied, which is at least a very large number. Where before one only needed to invoke a single disposition (reacting to different dispositional response partners, in C. B. Martin's lingo) to describe certain behaviour, now one needs a distinct disposition for each sentient individual that might exhibit such behaviour (and a distinct family of dispositions for the behavioural repertory of each individual). In the latter case, there is a veritable 'combinatorial explosion'. Whilst there is no incoherence in this position even when this consequence has been highlighted, I maintain that such a consequence is highly implausible.

Furthermore, since we think that the universe could have existed without any sentient creatures, and since we do not think that the *nature* of material particles is radically altered by the presence of sentient creatures, it is implausible to think that material particles have dispositional sensitivities to mental subjects which they would not have if we or other sentient creatures did not exist—especially since we think that the probability of sentient creatures evolving in a material universe is rather low.[28]

---

[28] Recognition of this point seems to require the classical interactionist to give up the fifth commitment of dualism as Foster defines it. This is a far weaker denial of the commitment to

There are several responses available to a classical interactionist. One is to identify a single particle lodged deep in the brain that is never lost as the locus of psychophysical interaction.[29] It will then serve a function not unlike that of the pineal gland for Descartes, directing further causal traffic in the body. Only this particle needs to have individualized dispositions directed at the mental subject it is psychophysically linked with; and because it is never lost during the life of the sentient creature, the particle need not have dispositional sensitivities to any other individuals.

This solution is unappealing for various reasons. That the particle is not lost does not mean that it does not have to have all the dispositional sensitivities that each material particle must have in order to cope with a situation involving individualized dispositions and metabolic turnover. Though the description of the response did not mention the initial stages of establishing the psychophysical link, a working psychophysics must make sense of the development of sentient creatures. It seems that if a material particle is recruited into a psychophysical system to play the role of this permanent material link, it must *already* be dispositionally sensitive to any mental subject with which it might be psychophysically linked—for otherwise it cannot interact with the mind that it later interacts with individualistically, since it has no resources for causal interaction with particular minds. In the early neonatal stages of brain development, how does the mind manage to 'capture' a particle in the brain to interact individualistically with it? A story according to which particles already have the requisite individualistic dispositions seems more plausible then one on which mental subjects can 'capture' a material particle and 'infect' it with individualistic dispositions directed toward it and no other mental subject. Whatever powers classical interactionists think mental subjects have, surely these do not include powers to induce individualistic dispositions in material particles.

But might not the interactionist who wishes to plump for this solution say that the possibility for individualistic interactions is written into the laws of material particles? These laws are rather like blank cheques (which can be used only once), where the material particle is individualistically directed at the mental subject with which it first comes into contact. On this story, only one particle will come into direct contact with the mental subject: whichever particle is the first to interact with the mental subject and is not already individualistically directed at another individual, that is, any particle 'in the vicinity' that still has a 'blank

ontological separateness, since it is a general consequence of there being sentient psychophysical beings in the world.

[29] Chisholm is said to have held a position like this at one time. But Chisholm's was a materialist position which identified the mental subject with a single particle lodged deep in the brain that is never lost because of considerations about personal identity (as opposed to a view which used a similar strategy for interactionism). His thought there is not unlike that of the rabbis regarding the luz bone. See his "Which Physical Thing Am I?" in P. van Inwagen and D. Zimmerman (eds.), *Metaphysics: The Big Questions* (Oxford: Blackwell, 1998).

cheque'. But how is a non-spatial immaterial subject to interact with a particle that is not yet individualistically directed at it, since there are no obvious pairing relations to secure the causal link between them?

We may summarize the problems for the 'blank cheque' account as follows. Firstly, on this picture the mind is non-spatial, so the notion of 'coming into contact' here is tenuous. Secondly, insofar as the mind is non-spatial, either the particle is already individualistically disposed to interact with it or it is not; if it is, we have the 'combinatorial explosion' of dispositions again; if not, we have no answer to the question how material particles can interact with a non-spatial immaterial mind.

A more interesting response is that there is no combinatorial explosion of dispositions because the dispositions I have ascribed to material particles are *general* dispositions, rather than individualistic ones. The objector reasons as follows: insofar as the dispositions of individual particles have to coordinate with those of other particles to sustain large-scale behavioural dispositions, they will have to be hypothetical powers of the form—'disposed to interact with mind x, if caught up into the ongoing organic life associated with x; disposed to interact with mind y, if . . . y; (etc.)'. But in that case, these dispositions are not individualistic, but general. This is because, rather than having a disposition for each particular mind in the universe, each particle only needs a disposition to interact with whichever mind is associated with the swarm into which it is drawn. This does not require particles to be *selectively sensitive* to particular minds, as is the case with individualized dispositions.

Now, if the dispositions have the alleged hypothetical form, then they are general and there is no combinatorial explosion of dispositions. But defusing the combinatorial explosion in this way also means that the dualist is left with *no* solution to the causal pairing problem, since the only powers in play on this understanding are powers to enable a particle to get caught up in a swarm that can *already* selectively interact with a mind—how selective interaction between swarms and minds is possible in the first instance has yet to be explained. (Remember that by a 'particle swarm' we are merely speaking of a group of particles in close proximity.)

I can think of three ways the dualist can secure this selective interaction:

(1) The dualist may reject the suggestion that the dispositions of material particles are of the general, hypothetical sort, but are truly individualistic. The idea is that each particle can selectively interact with the mind it is attached to, and that the large-scale behavioural dispositions of a swarm to selectively interact with a mind *just consists in* the individualistic dispositions that each particle in that swarm has towards the mind in question. This is committed to a reductive conception of the large-scale behavioural dispositions. Fixing the individualistic dispositions of the particles fixes the large-scale behavioural dispositions of the swarm—even though strictly speaking there's no composite object which possesses this large-scale disposition but only a group of particles

in close proximity. These dispositions will be individualistic as well, since they just consist in the dispositions of individual particles associated with the swarm in question that are directed at a particular mind. The possibility of selective interaction is thus allowed for at the ground level in terms of the individualistic dispositions of particles. But because particles have to be able to interact individualistically with any mind whose 'body' incorporates it, each particle has to have individualistic dispositional sensitivities to all minds that can potentially be embodied in the history of the universe. This way of securing selective interaction is thus saddled with the combinatorial explosion of dispositions.

(2) The dualist may embrace the suggestion that material particles have dispositions of the general, hypothetical kind. This avoids the prospect of combinatorial explosion of dispositions at the level of the dispositions of individual particles, but places the pressure of selective interaction on particle swarms (for all a body is on the nihilist picture is a group of particles in close proximity). The ability of particle swarms to interact selectively with particular minds is then explained by their possession of individualistic dispositions to interact with particular minds. Unlike in the previous scenario, the individualistic dispositions of swarms cannot be understood to consist in the dispositions of individual particles, since these have a general character. (Rather, particles interact with minds in virtue of their joining a swarm that can interact selectively with a particular mind.) The swarm has individualistic dispositions that are over and above any dispositions that the particles in that swarm possess—even though, strictly speaking, there are no such things as swarms, since we are assuming a nihilist metaphysics of bodies. Though I submit that there is some tension in this position, it is not obviously incoherent—at least, not without supplementary metaphysical premises. Assuming that there is no need to reify swarms in order to understand how groups of particles in close proximity can possess individualistic dispositions when individual particles do not, swarms (nihilistically understood) will have to possess individualistic dispositional sensitivities to all minds that can potentially be embodied in the history of the universe—in which case we have a combinatorial explosion of dispositions at the level of these swarms.

(Insofar as the tension I alluded to pushes us toward an anti-nihilist under-standing of swarms, the picture collapses into one of the anti-nihilist metaphysics of bodies considered later. This highlights a difficulty in understanding psycho-physics on a nihilist metaphysics of bodies. Nihilist metaphysics either needs to think in terms of particles interacting individualistically with minds or in terms of swarms. The former departs from our standard conception of psychophysical laws being links between minds and certain medium-sized entities. On the most natural understanding of how the latter is possible, there is pressure to abandon a nihilistic metaphysics.)

(3) The dualist may claim that if groups of particles have special powers to generate minds, then a group of particles can have a singular relation to the mind

it generates.[30] Naturally, this singular relation cannot be explained by recourse to spatio-temporal factors, since minds are non-spatial. Rather it is a kind of *sui generis* singular relation that holds between an individual and the system that generates it, which then provides the basis for selective interaction. The idea is that groups of particles have special powers of this sort: if this group is the first stage of a swarm that is good enough (e.g. sufficiently well-organized) to generate a mind, then it will generate and selectively interact with the particular mind x; if this other group (in some cases, overlapping in membership with the first) is the first stage of a swarm well-organized to produce a mind, then it will generate and selectively interact with mind y; and so on. (Swarms must, of course, be understood nihilistically.)

This appears to both solve the causal pairing problem and drastically reduce the number of individualistic powers the dualist needs to attribute to particles and swarms of them. The plausibility of this proposal also gains by providing the dualist with a skeletal developmental story of how minds and bodies initially hook up. To see that this goes a long way toward reducing the number of dispositions we need to ascribe to particles or swarms of them, consider the kinds of dispositions in play: excepting these special dispositions to generate particular minds when working together with other particles in the first stage of a (mental) life, individual particles would only need to have a general disposition to interact with whichever mind is already interacting with a swarm into which they merge. Thus, on this picture, on top of whatever dispositions we need to ascribe to particles and swarms to explain physical phenomena, we would only need (i) individualistic dispositions of swarms specifying which particular mind that group of particles would generate if they were working together at the beginning of a life, and (ii) just a general disposition on the part of each particle to interact with whichever mind is associated with a swarm into which it is drawn.

If this proposal works, then it provides a pleasing resolution of the difficulties I have unearthed for the dualist. But, as we shall see, it is not without its costs. Given metabolic turnover, the particles that play their part in the group of particles that is one's body will be constantly changing. On this picture, the original group of particles generates and has a singular relation with a particular mind, but because of metabolic turnover, the members of this group are soon scattered around the world and no longer play their original roles in the generating swarm. It is implausible to say that the scattered original group of particles continues to function as that mind's body, as we would then be committed to some minds having scattered bodies; thus groups of particles (each overlapping in members with its predecessor) take their turn to function as one's body. But how is it possible for there to be selective interaction between these later swarms and the mind, once the generating swarm starts to become scattered? After all, the

---

[30] Barry Loewer and Dean Zimmerman independently suggested this response to me.

singular relation holds between the generating swarm and the mind. Since we are working within a nihilist metaphysics, the best answer that the dualist can give is that certain historical facts about the swarm and the mind—that this mind was connected up with a swarm of which this swarm is a descendant—account for the current connection. The dualist will further bolster his response by pointing to there being a local explanation and a continuous path of causal connections back to the initial hook up.

It is, however, unclear that this allows for the possibility of selective interaction between the descendants of the generating swarm and the particular mind in question. Whilst it is true that the current swarm is a descendant of the generating swarm and there is a continuous path of causal connections between earlier and later swarms, the dualist has yet to show that later swarms can selectively interact with the particular mind generated by its first ancestor. Consider the dispositions that we have ascribed: the generating swarm has individualistic dispositions toward the mind it generates and individual particles have general dispositions. Here we only have materials to explain how the generating swarm can individualistically interact with a mind, and then only when those particles remain in close proximity and are appropriately organized. (We can also explain how other particles can interact with that mind by joining that swarm.) If we add historical facts about the current swarm and a continuous path of causal connections to this, we can at best explain how the current swarm is a descendant of a swarm which once generated a particular mind and could individualistically interact with it. I cannot see how the dualist can claim to have allowed for selective interaction for descendant swarms unless he has unwittingly slipped into a non-nihilist metaphysics or has begged the question of how individualistic interaction is possible on a nihilist metaphysics. It is hard to see how a series of swarms can individualistically interact with a particular mind—where the only basis of this is the ability of the generating swarm that they are descendants of to interact selectively with that mind—unless the dualist is implicitly thinking of an entity that can survive changes of parts that selectively interacts with the particular mind in question. I discuss the consequences of individualistic dispositions for non-nihilist metaphysics of bodies in what follows.

Furthermore, even if the dualist solution here can be squared with a nihilist metaphysics, it cannot be squared with another dualist commitment: the possibility of a soul's switching bodies. Assuming the dualist solution works, the generating swarm and its descendants are directed at one particular mind, and that mind can only interact with the generating swarm and its descendants. Thus, the dualist has undercut the need for every swarm to be dispositionally sensitive to every possible mind by positing a singular relation that restricts interaction to a generating swarm plus its descendants and the generated mind. This leaves dualists with a dilemma: they have to either give up the possibility of body change or abandon individualistic dispositions—on pain of losing their solution to the pairing problem. Once again, there is a tension in understanding the individualistic interaction of a swarm-series and a mind in purely nihilistic terms. The possibility of body change for dualists who buy into individualistic dispositions is explored in more depth when we turn to consider a commonsensical metaphysics of bodies, on which bodies can survive changes of parts.

(B) Mereological essentialist metaphysics

On this metaphysics, the body is a mereological sum of particles that are close together and fill a body-shaped region. A theorist who acknowledged metabolic turnover and also held such a metaphysics of bodies would have to accept that we are constantly switching bodies—since, first of all, a body is identical with a mereological sum of particles; secondly, given metabolic turnover, the particles that constitute a body are constantly changing; and, thirdly, a difference in the particles means that we have different mereological sums. Thus on this account we are constantly changing bodies.[31] (The rate of body change is roughly the same as the rate of metabolic turnover.) The consequence of this is that minds have to be able to interact selectively with a whole range of different bodies, and bodies have to be able to interact selectively with all possible mental subjects that can potentially be embodied. Another way to arrive at this consequence is to note that on this account it appears to be possible that you have the body that I have now at some later time (*possible*, I say, however vanishingly low a probability such an event has). Given this possibility, one and the same body has to be able to interact selectively with both your mind and also mine. Once again, we are faced with a scenario on which we have a 'combinatorial explosion' of dispositions.

One might respond that the dualist should rather be committed to the *persistence* of a person's body over time (*as the person's body*, rather than as a scattered object) so that each person's soul interacts with only one body throughout the person's lifetime. But, as we have seen, this is impossible to square with a mereological essentialist metaphysics of the body—given metabolic turnover. A theorist with such a commitment would have to opt for a metaphysics of bodies on which they are not *mere* sums but can survive change of parts. This brings us to the next case.

(C) Commonsensical metaphysics

Finally, on this metaphysics, the body is *coincident with yet distinct from* the body-shaped particle swarms that constitute it; and it can undergo change of parts. One might think that the root of the problem is due to nihilist or mereological essentialist metaphysics of bodies, rather than the individualistic dispositions; but let us see if the undesirable consequences disappear if we move to a commonsensical metaphysics of bodies. On this picture, the mind interacts selectively with a body that is distinct from yet coincident with the material particles that constitute it, but which is such that it can survive change of parts.

---

[31] See Chisholm's *Person and Object* (La Salle, Ill.: Open Court, 1976). He is fully aware of this consequence of his mereological essentialism.

There are a number of questions we might have about bodies on such a metaphysics. Are they material entities? This might strike one as a rather odd question, since the status of bodies as material seems to be as good as that of any other kind of medium-sized ordinary object, like tables. But if it is a general feature of material entities that mereological supervenience holds of them (i.e. the properties of the whole are fixed by the properties and relations characterizing its proper parts), then bodies are not material entities, for mereological supervenience appears to fail for bodies. It seems that there can be a difference in the properties of a body without a difference in the properties of material particles which constitute it. This is a consequence of their possessing individualistic dispositions: there appears to be no reason why the same group of material particles with the same properties, including the same organizational structure (spatial arrangement, etc.) might not come to constitute a body qualitatively identical in every way to another body but with individualistic dispositions directed at a distinct individual. In other words, fixing the material particles and their properties doesn't fix the properties of the body.

But placing the burden of individualistic interaction on bodies is only to move the bump in the carpet somewhere else. We no longer have the material *particles* as dispositionally sensitive to all possible mental subjects, but place their dispositional burden on *bodies*, while not disturbing the common conception of properties that material particles possess. Regardless of whether we think mereological supervenience holds for all material entities, having such a metaphysics of bodies does little to alleviate the more serious difficulty that is an analogue of the developmental problem discussed earlier. In this case, the developmental problem is how the mind manages to recruit a brain (in a body) to interact individualistically with it. Here, as before, we are faced with a dilemma. The interactionist can accept a 'combinatorial explosion' of dispositions (at the level of bodies)—for even if a body is recruited by a mind to play the role of permanent material link, *it* must *already* be dispositionally sensitive to any mental subject with which it might be psychophysically linked, on pain of not being able to interact with particular minds at all, since it has no other resources for interaction. On the other hand, one can reject the combinatorial explosion of dispositions, and be left without a solution to the pairing problem.

The interactionist may respond by asking why there has to be any 'recruiting' at all? In particular, why can't he suppose that—as a matter of brute fact—there is for each actual or merely possible body exactly one actual or merely possible mind, the only one with which this body could possibly have causal commerce?

This brings us to a wrinkle that underscores certain distinctive modal features of individualistic dispositions (laws).[32] If it is a law that *this* very body here (call it *Bob*) is the thing that causes changes in my mind (call it *Mob*) then it seems that even God couldn't have given me a different body, since they are connected

---

[32] Paul Snowdon brought this modal wrinkle to my attention.

by various individualistic laws. Surely, we do not want a view of this world on which it *had* to be this body, Bob, that was causally linked to me.

The interactionist might respond that since God made it a law that Bob individualistically interacts with Mob, surely God could have made a different law linking me to a different body. It is not clear what this means, but even if we permit that God could have written the Book of Laws in such a way that I was linked to a different body, given the *actual* individualistic laws, it is not at all clear that Cartesian minds are permitted to change their bodies—which is an intuition of distinctness from one's body that Cartesians tend to find fairly robust (that is, the intuition that *this* mental life may persist despite changes of body)—even though Cartesian minds may (on standard accounts) be disembodied.[33] Now, the interactionist may allow for body change if he posits individualistic laws with greater complexity. In particular, couldn't God institute nested individualistic laws, such as ones saying that mind x interacts with body y until y is destroyed (or some other event happens), and then x interacts with body z (etc.)? This strategy for allowing body change, however, undermines the earlier interactionist response (that—as a matter of brute fact—there is, for each actual or merely possible body, exactly one actual or merely possible mind with which it could possibly have causal commerce) which was meant to undercut the need for a body to be dispositionally sensitive to all mental subjects to which it can potentially be linked.

Thus either no body change is possible—contrary to Cartesian intuition—or body change is possible. If body change is possible and assuming, as before, that psychophysical interaction cannot alter the nature of bodily entities, we are back with the dilemma of either accepting a 'combinatorial explosion' of dispositions for bodies or lacking a solution to the pairing problem. For a body recruited by a mind to play the role of a permanent material link must *already* be dispositionally sensitive to any mental subject with which it might be psychophysically linked, on pain of not being able to interact with particular minds at all—since it has no other resources for interaction.

I conclude that insofar as the interactionist uses individualized dispositions to solve the pairing problem, he has to be committed to the existence of *some* material entities—whether they be all the fundamental particles that feature in the bodies of sentient creatures or medium-sized material objects—that are

---

[33] Note that my point only requires the Cartesian intuition of distinctness—*this* mental life being able to persist beyond *this* very body—and not the stronger intuition of disembodiment, which plays no role in this argument. It is important to note that *distinctness* of mind and body is a (far) weaker thesis than their *independence*. To see this, consider the Kripkean thesis that because of the persistence of mental phenomena despite possibly radical changes in the realizing physical phenomena, the mental phenomena of the creatures in question are not necessarily identical with, and thus not actually identical with the realizing physical phenomena (given the necessity of identity). Here, whilst mental phenomena are distinct from their physical realizers, they are surely not *independent* of them, for otherwise mental phenomena wouldn't be realized by physical phenomena.

dispositionally sensitive to each and every sentient creature with which they might possibly interact (or having to surrender the Cartesian intuition of distinctness). This is a radical departure from both our ordinary and scientific conceptions of matter and material things. I submit that this is a heavy cost that must be paid by the interactionist of Foster's stripe.[34]

VI

At this stage of the dialectic, it might seem that it would ease the problems of the classical interactionist if he gave up the thesis of non-spatiality of immaterial substances. Whilst I think that the traditional arguments for the non-spatiality of immaterial substances are inadequate,[35] it is not obvious that placing immaterial substances into space does not create other problems (it was not for no reason that

---

[34] That Cartesian psychophysics is committed to radicalizing at least certain parcels of matter is a point that Descartes clearly saw but was lost on the tradition. The issue arises in a slightly different way within Descartes's framework but also relates to embodiment. In the *Sixth Meditation* and elsewhere, Descartes discusses substantial unions and phenomena associated with them such as imagination and bodily sensations. These phenomena, however, can neither be understood as modes of thought nor as modes of extension. Thus substantial unions bring some new metaphysical and phenomenological facts in their train—which are over and above those that characterize material and mental substances considered separately.

The commitment on Descartes's picture to radicalizing certain parcels of matter can be illustrated as follows. On his 'primary attribute' conception of substance, extension is the attribute through which all other attributes of material substances must be understood. A natural development of this is to see the material world as a single extended continuum. (This comes out clearly in Spinoza's development of Descartes's metaphysics of substance.) However, substantial unions impose a constraint on the individuation of bodies. This is because they bring some new metaphysical facts in their train. This in turn has the consequence that certain parcels of matter—those that enter into substantial union—acquire a special status, since they can no longer be *solely* understood in terms of extension. Thus, bodies of minds are the only perturbations on the material fabric that cannot be ignored. Here I am indebted to discussion with Michael Martin. (See John Cottingham's "Cartesian Trialism", *Mind*, 94 (1985), 218–30 for discussion of these issues. Although there is a question as to how Descartes can accommodate the distinctive characteristics of substantial union on his official metaphysics and epistemology of substance, there are no good textual grounds to support a 'trialist' interpretation of Descartes.)

[35] Besides Descartes's arguments to this conclusion, which are generally discredited, I know of two arguments to this conclusion by John Foster (*The Immaterial Self*, 206–12), both of which are, I think, ineffective. (At the start of the chapter entitled "On the Mental Self", he claims to have already shown that mental things are devoid of any physical properties, including location in physical space. I do not think this is true, unless he means that he has refuted all extant versions of materialism, including some weak variety of token identity. And even so, that all versions of materialism are false doesn't imply that mental things are devoid of all physical properties—unless he is illicitly assuming Descartes's 'primary attribute' conception of how to understand substances.)

The first of Foster's two arguments is trivial. He defines a basic mental subject as something which figures as a mental subject in the conceptually fundamental account of the metaphysically fundamental reality. A mental subject is anything which has mental states or takes part in mental activities. Given that he has refuted all extant versions of materialism, the obvious hope for an account on which a corporeal thing might be a basic mental subject will be a causal account; so something like direct causal interaction must take place between corporeal thing and mental states.

immaterial substances were exiled from space). It would seem that if immaterial substances were spatial, they would be subject to spatial exclusion principles (this seems to be an essential part of our conception of denizens of space and the spatial)—principles analogous to those applicable to material objects, such as: no two material objects of the same kind can occupy the same place at the same time. Admittedly, placing immaterial substances in space does not then place them in direct spatial competition with material objects; they are *not* material objects (and *a fortiori* not the same kind of material object as any other material object), and hence there is no bar to them being at the same place at the same time as a material object. But, as Colin McGinn points out,[36] questions concerning whether an analogous spatial exclusion principle applies to mental objects seem to be misconceived: Can two thoughts be spatio-temporally coincident? Can two mental subjects be in the same place at the same time? Though nothing about the mental seems to rule out spatial exclusion principles applying to them, the fact that questions about spatial exclusion which seem constitutive of our concept of the spatial (and spatial occupancy) strike us as awkward when applied to the mental suggests that the application of spatial concepts in the mental realm is at best tenuous (the best case to be made for spatial properties is perhaps that of bodily sensations, because they seem to be directed at a part of the body). Perhaps the motivations of the interactionist who retreats to placing immaterial substances in space would be better served not by placing them in space as such but rather by placing them in the kind of quasi-spatial fabric that we earlier suggested as a scenario on which interactionism might be intelligible. This solution, however, is only a beginning, for an interactionist who attributes quasi-spatial properties to immaterial substances has at best an answer to the first query raised for interactionists, and still needs to tell us how the specificity of embodiment is to be secured?[37]

But then, the argument goes, *ex hypothesi*, this will not be a basic mental subject; because it doesn't figure as a mental subject in the philosophically fundamental account.

The second argument is that, given the falsity of token identity—i.e. given that mental events are non-physical—there is no objective fact of the matter which thing is in pain. He thinks you could in principle assign pain to any corporeal thing and not make any objective error. That's absurd; so corporeal things couldn't be mental subjects. But I see no reason why mental ascriptions cannot be made on the basis of weaker assumptions than token identity, such as appropriately weak supervenience principles, where certain physical systems (possibly larger than individual bodies) are identified as the supervenience base of a mental system and, as such, are ascribed the mental state or event.

[36] See McGinn's "Consciousness and Space", repr. in his *Consciousness and its Objects* (Oxford: Oxford University Press, 2004).

[37] This might involve 'coordinating' the quasi-spatial and spatial dimensions such that the psychophysical units can stay intact (as functioning, single causal units), depending on how the quasi-spatial framework is understood.

VII

My purpose in this essay has not been to urge dualists to give up the ghost, but rather to evaluate the costs of a working classical interactionist psychophysics. We began with certain vague worries associated with traditional scepticism about psychophysical interactionism and saw how Foster crystallized this into a problem about how causal interaction between non-spatial immaterial substances and material substances is possible in the absence of an external pairing relation such as space. In formulating the problem for interactionism in this way, Foster isolates the substantial issue that is behind traditional scepticism. We developed a doubt about the non-spatiality of immaterial substances into a general problem concerning constraints on causation. There we examined Foster's solution to the stark question that he posed for classical interactionism. The ingenuity of the solution—in terms of individualized laws—rests on its simultaneously undermining the nomological assumption whilst still securing the specificity of embodiment. Alas, this appears to conflict with our conceptual commitment to the *generality* of causation—that the causal relation holds between two entities in virtue of the *kinds* they fall under as opposed to *which particular things* they are. I then brought out the costs of embracing a metaphysics of individualized laws: if the theorist of individualistic laws is to accommodate the empirical fact of metabolic turnover, he has to be committed to certain radical claims about the nature of human bodies and matter in general.

Foster has posed in the deepest way how we should understand the problem of classical interactionism, and hence puts us in a position to see why his solution does not work. He still faces—in Merleau-Ponty's ironic turn of phrase—"the problem of how to give the soul a chance of feeling its body".

PART III

MATERIALISM

8

A Materialist Ontology of the Human Person

Peter van Inwagen

I will begin by setting out a metaphysical position that is so abstract that it hardly deserves the name 'position'. (Perhaps it would be better called a 'metaphysical framework'.) This very abstract position constitutes the metaphysical perspective from which I view all philosophical problems, including those problems that pertain to the human person. If you think this perspective is skewed, you will not find much to agree with in what I am going to say about the ontology of the human person.

The most general metaphysical category is the category "thing". I use 'thing' as the most general count-noun. Everything is a thing. A thing is anything that can be referred to by a third-person-singular pronoun—as when I say, "The following is true of everything, that it is identical with itself." The category "thing" comprises everything there is, everything that exists (for I take a stern anti-Meinongian line about non-existents: non-existents simply don't exist: the number of them is 0).

Things divide into two sub-categories, the concrete and the abstract. If there are such things as the following, they are concrete: cabbages, kings, bits of sealing wax, electrons, tables and chairs, angels, ghosts, and God. I myself believe in only some of the things in this list: cabbages, kings, electrons, angels, and God. But I am quite certain that if there were bits of sealing wax, tables and chairs, and ghosts, they would be concrete things. Here is a list of abstract things: propositions, possibilities, sentence-types, sets, properties or attributes, numbers, novels (as opposed to tangible copies of novels), theories, and such miscellaneous items as the key of F-sharp minor, democracy, and the literary form *the epic poem*. I am not sure which of the things in this list I believe really exist (I certainly think some of them do), but I am quite certain that if there is such a thing as, for example, the key of F-sharp minor, it is an abstract thing.

How can we understand this distinction? (That is to say, how can we provide an *explicit statement* of the distinction marked by the words 'abstract' and 'concrete', for, in my view, it is a real distinction and one we can grasp simply by attending to lists of examples. Some philosophers, of course, doubt whether there *are* any clear ideas associated with the words 'abstract' and 'concrete'.) Can we provide a useful definition of either 'abstract' or 'concrete'? (If we could define either, we could define the other as its complement.) Well, I'm inclined to think that if someone says, "A thing is concrete if and only if it has causal powers", that person says something true. But I'm not satisfied that this counts as a definition. One reason, of course, is that the concept "causal powers" needs a good deal of philosophical work. But I see, or think I see, a deeper difficulty: it seems to me that although concrete objects, one and all, have causal powers, and abstract objects, one and all, lack causal powers, this is a fact that an adequate definition of 'concrete' and 'abstract' ought to *explain*. To define a concrete object as an object that has causal powers seems to me, at least in some moods, to be like defining a "word" as a thing that can be spelled correctly or incorrectly. This definition of 'word' does, I suppose, give 'word' the right extension, but one feels that it touches on a rather peripheral feature of words: a definition of 'word' should be such as to explain why words and words alone are things that have spellings. I am therefore not going to offer 'has causal powers' as a definition of 'concrete' object, for I feel somehow that the no-doubt-true statement 'A thing is concrete if and only if it has causal powers' doesn't get at the essence of what it is to be a concrete object; I think we are able to grasp this essence by considering any reasonably comprehensive list of types of concrete object and proceeding to perform some sort of act of abstraction that enables us to see what the common feature of things in the list is. But I doubt whether we are able to articulate the essence we grasp in this act of abstraction. And here is a perhaps related problem that faces us if we understand 'abstract object' as 'object that has no causal powers'. This definition is purely negative: it represents the concept "abstract object" as the concept of a kind of thing that does *not* have a certain property and tells us absolutely nothing about what properties these things do have—beyond, of course, the property *not having causal powers* and its logical consequences. Suppose it had never occurred to anyone that phrases like those in my list of examples of abstract objects were denoting phrases. If some philosopher were to introduce the concept "thing lacking causal powers" into some metaphysical discussion, that would probably suggest to his audience that he had in mind some ghostly sort of thing that could drift about in space and pass through material objects without affecting them or being affected by them. No one, surely, would react by saying anything like, "If there were objects that had no causal powers, that could only be because words and phrases like 'wisdom' or 'the proposition that snow is white' had referents; objects without causal powers would be the referents of phrases like that." It seems, therefore, that one could have the purely negative concept "having no causal powers" without having the concept "abstract object".

Now the metaphysical position or framework I promised you. First, there is only one kind of concrete object: that which has traditionally been called "substance" or "individual thing". And there is only one type of abstract object. I will call this one type "relation". I will first expand on this second statement. Among relations there are 0-term relations, or propositions, 1-term relations (also called properties, attributes, qualities, features, characteristics . . .), and 2-or-more-term relations, which I will call 'proper relations' (on the model of proper fractions and proper subsets). I will not discuss proper relations. I will, however, say something about propositions and properties. Propositions are things that have truth-values. They are things that can be *said*—that is, *asserted*. They are things that can be assented to or denied. (For most propositions, these descriptions are true only in principle, at least as regards human beings. Most propositions are too complicated to be assented to or denied by any human being. The same "true only in principle" qualification will be needed at various points in the sequel. I'll leave it you to supply it.) Properties, by contrast, are things that can be *said of* or *about* something (whether truly or falsely); that it is white, for example. That it is white is one of the things you can say truly of the White House, and you can say it truly of the Taj Mahal, too. But you can't say it truly of the Eiffel Tower or the key of F-sharp minor; you can, in fact, say it only falsely of these objects, for each is non-white. A few properties have traditional names that are, as the linguists say, perfect nominals: 'whiteness', for example, or 'wisdom'. In my view, 'wisdom' is a name for what we say *of* or *about* Solomon and the Cumaean Sibyl when, speaking with reference to them, we say, as appropriate, 'He is wise' or 'She is wise'. But most properties have no such names: one of the things we can say of something is that it is one of the daughters of the forty-third President (we could say this truly of exactly two things; if we said it of Chelsea Clinton or the Eiffel Tower or the number of planets, we'd be saying it falsely of those things). And this property, a perfectly good example of a property in my view, has no one-word name. Typical properties (and, more generally, typical relations) are, as 'whiteness' and 'wisdom' and our more complicated example testify, universals, for, typically, a property can be said truly of—or, to use some more usual idioms, can belong to, be had by, be instantiated by, be exemplified by—two or more things. Not all properties have this feature, however, for there are plenty of things that can be said truly of only one thing (that it is a daughter of the forty-second president; that it is an even prime), and plenty that cannot be said truly of even one thing (that it is a woman who served as President of the U.S. in the twentieth century; that it is both round and square). I thus come down on the side of platonism, as opposed both to nominalism and Aristotelianism. And a very capacious platonism it is. I'd *like* to say that to every meaningful open sentence there corresponds a property, but you probably know why I can't say that. I have to admit that Russell's paradox forces me to confront a mystery: it seems that one of the things you can say about something is that it is a thing of the sort that can be said of things and can't be said truly of *itself*. But it can't *be* that there is any such thing to say about things, despite the fact that one can say truly of wisdom that you can't say it truly of itself, and can say truly of whiteness that you can't say it truly of itself. And *that* certainly looks for all the world like a case in which one and the same thing can be said truly both of wisdom and of whiteness. Well, I'm a metaphysician and am inured to mystery.

It should be evident that properties, as I use the term, are as abstract as anything could be. They can in no way be "constituents" (whatever that might mean) of concrete objects. If there are such things as "tropes" or "immanent universals", they are not properties or any other sort of relation. And, since, in my view, there are only substances and relations, there are no tropes or immanent universals. I don't mind this consequence, for, as far as I can see, the term 'trope' (as used by philosophers), and the term 'immanent universal' are perfectly meaningless. Another perfectly meaningless term—this one over on the "concrete" side of things—would be 'bare particular'. A bare particular would either be what you get when you subtract the tropes from an ordinary concrete object (and thus the term would be meaningless) or else a thing of which nothing is true; and of course, the idea of a thing of which nothing is true makes no sense at all.

One final point about propositions and properties and other abstract objects. They are not among the *invisibilia* that are mentioned in the Nicene Creed. With the possible exception of those abstract objects that in some way "involve" concrete objects (such as "impure" sets and, perhaps, propositions that predicate properties of particular individuals), they are eternal and necessary and hence uncreated. The *invisibilia* that we Christians must not believe to be uncreated are those "unseen" things that have causal powers. (As far as we know, all these things are persons, and, more specifically, angels of some sort. If there are impersonal *invisibilia*, we have not been told about them.) Those who want to say that the doctrine of God's sovereignty implies that he must somehow be the creator of such things as the proposition that snow is white are, to borrow words Whitehead used for another purpose, paying God an ill-judged metaphysical compliment.

I should like to be able to say something useful about substances or individual things. But I can't, not really. Of course it follows from what I have said that substances have causal powers and that anything that has causal powers is a substance. But this statement will not be of much help to anyone who wants to know what a substance is. You might of course want to dispute even this unhelpful statement. You may think that there are things that have causal powers but shouldn't be called substances. If you do, I'll have to ask you what they might be. Tropes? There are no such things. Surfaces? There are no such things. States? *Either* there are no such things or they are some sort of property and thus lack causal powers. Social entities like baseball teams and corporations? I don't know what to say about them, other than to remind you that hard cases make bad law. (I don't mean that I can't think of any way to fit social entities into my ontological framework; I mean I can think of lots of ways to fit them in, and am not sure which is the best.) Stuffs? Well, stuffs are worthy of discussion, but such discussion wouldn't be germane to what I'm going to talk about. Let's just say that if some metaphysician convinced me that I had to add stuffs to my ontology, the addition wouldn't affect anything I'm going to say. Events? Ah, that's a very good question.

Events constitute one of the main challenges to the adequacy of my ontological framework. Our discourse obviously contains many sentences that on some understanding or analysis must express truths and which apparently refer to and quantify over events. I must somehow take account of this fact, and, it would seem, in one of four ways. (1) I might try to show that all true statements that apparently imply the existence of events can be paraphrased as statements solely about the changing properties of and changing relations among substances; (2) I might try to show that events can be understood as substances (of some special sort); (3) I might try to show that events can be understood as properties (of some special sort; (4) I might concede that my ontological framework needs to be expanded and say that there are two sorts of concrete object, substances and events; (5) I might concede that my ontological framework needs to be expanded and say that there are two sorts of abstract object, properties and events. I am not at present clear which of these options I should choose, or even which of them is the most promising. I hope that I shall one day be able to "paraphrase events away" (option 1), but I admit that I have not yet given any serious thought to this project. And I am certain that option 2 is a non-starter (I have included it in the list of options only for the sake of logical completeness). Beyond this, I am forced to admit that I do not know what to say about events. I wish I did, because, while I was writing this essay, I discovered that an important question in the philosophy of mind turns on the question whether there are events. Not an absolutely fundamental question, but one of some significance. In this paper, I'll have to content myself with saying what this important question in the philosophy of mind that turns on the question whether there are events is. This I will do when I discuss the identity theory.

An incidental remark: the fact that I am not sure what to make of events has another consequence, a purely metaphysical one. Because of my uncertainty about the existence and nature of events, I cannot follow Aristotle and define a substance as a thing that has properties but is not itself a property—for events, if such there be, may have properties and yet not themselves be properties. (The same point, of course, could be made in relation to stuffs.)

Here ends my description of the metaphysical framework that underlies my discussion of the philosophy of mind. Let's now turn to you and me, to us human persons. How do we fit into this framework? Well, obviously, we're not relations. True, some philosophers seem to think we're something like a computer program, and a computer program, in my metaphysic, is probably some sort of relation. But I have a hard time believing this is really what these philosophers mean to say, and if they do mean to say this we can ignore them. Whatever I am, I'm a lot more like a poached egg or a waterfall or a hydraulic jack than I am like a computer program; one should therefore take the thesis that I'm a computer program less seriously than one would take the thesis that I'm a poached egg, and that's not very seriously.

If we exist at all, we're substances. Now some philosophers think we don't exist at all. Perhaps it suffices to point out that if they're right, then it's false that some philosophers think we don't exist at all. Their thesis is thus either false or such that no one holds it. And I'm not going to waste my time and yours discussing a thesis that's either false or held by no one.

Perhaps this is as good a point as any at which to mention the "self". (There isn't any *very* good point.) Some philosophers say things like this: that modern neurobiology has exploded the old myth of the self or that the self is a social construct or that Descartes was mistaken in thinking that a sharp boundary could be drawn between self and world. When I hear philosophers say things like this, the first thing I always ask them is whether, when I use the word 'I' I refer, or at least am attempting to refer, to one of the these "selves" (my own, of course). After all, if there are selves and if, when I use the word 'I' I refer to something, it would seem that it must be my Self I refer to. Or if there is such a thing as my Self, and I do *not* refer to it when I use the word 'I', how could it be correct to call this thing my Self? It is not I, it is rather something numerically distinct from me, and how can something that is not I be properly called my Self? Or, if the philosophers I am talking to are of the party that holds that selves are myths, I ask them whether their position is that they do not exist—for if they exist, then, of course, each time one of them uses the word 'I', that use refers to something, and what could that referent be but the self of the speaker? These questions may seem to some to be trivial quibbles on my part, but they are no such thing. They confront the philosophers who talk of selves with a dilemma I have never seen satisfactorily resolved. If they say, "Yes, that's just what your Self is (or that's just what it would be if there were such a thing): what you refer to when you say 'I'," then their theses almost invariably turn out to be nonsense or obviously false or so obviously true that it is hard to think why anyone would bother stating them. (Modern neurobiology has obviously not shown that there are no such things as you and I.) Or, if they say, "No, that's not what your Self is—your Self is not you but something numerically distinct from you; it is [or 'is supposed to be'] something you *have*; it's not what you *are*," then they are never able to give any real explanation of what they mean by 'self': their attempts at explanation turn out to be so much semantical arm-waving. Let this suffice for a discussion of the "self".

We are, I contend, substances. What sort of substances? Well, either material or immaterial substances. (Grave difficulties confront the philosopher who proposes to define 'material' and immaterial'. In this essay, I will ignore these problems.) Or so it would seem. But there is a sort of alternative.

St Thomas Aquinas, as every schoolman knows, teaches that we are some sort of union or amalgam or compound, of a material and an immaterial substance; and such a union could not be classified as either material or immaterial. But the form the position takes in his work scarcely seems coherent. Thomas thinks that I am a union of my soul and my body, the former being an immaterial substance and the latter a material substance. So far, this is fairly plain sailing. But Thomas also thinks that the soul is the *form of the body*. I do not see, and no one has ever been able to explain to me, how something that is the form of a substance can also be a substance. It seems evident to me that the phrase 'the form of my body' must either strictly speaking denote nothing (that is, although this phrase can appear in meaningful and true sentences, it will, "disappear on analysis": for example, the true sentence, 'The form of my body remains constant as long as I remain alive' expresses something that could be more perspicuously expressed by some such words as 'The formal features of my body do not change as long as I am alive') or else must denote some abstract object, some very complex property I have throughout my existence, or some very complex variably polyadic relation that at every moment of my existence then holds among the particles of matter that at that moment compose my body. In the former case, there is, strictly speaking, no such thing as the form of my body. In the latter, the form of my body is an abstract object, and there is no such thing as an amalgam of my body and it—just as there is no such thing as the amalgam of Michelangelo's *David* and the property (a property of thousands of other statues and billions of human beings) *being shaped like a human being*. How could there be an amalgam of two things, one of which was a statue and the other of which was something that you could say about a statue? (Here's another difficulty I see in Aquinas's position: wouldn't the union of my body and the form of my body, whatever the form of my body may be, be simply my body? And isn't my body, without qualification, a material substance? Or is this the same difficulty, viewed from another angle?)

Could something like Aquinas's view, but minus his account of the nature of the soul, be correct? Suppose my soul is a true immaterial substance à la Descartes and my body is a material substance à la, once more, Descartes. Could it be that, *pace* Descartes, I am not identical with *one* of these things (the immaterial one), but am rather a union or amalgam or whole that somehow comprises both of them—and am thus neither a material nor an immaterial substance?

There would seem to be modal problems with this position (call it Cartesian unionism) that do not face orthodox Cartesianism. If Cartesian unionism is true, I am not the immaterial thing that Descartes calls my *mens* or *anima*. Suppose my body were annihilated and no new body replaced it. What would happen to me according to Cartesian unionism? Only one answer is possible: I should cease to exist, for, now that my body has been destroyed, there is no candidate for the office "I" but my *mens*, or the *mens* that was formerly mine. And my *mens* can't be I, since it used *not* to be I—and, as we all know nowadays (I hope we all know this), if x is not identical with y, x is necessarily not identical with y. But what then is the *point* of Cartesian unionism? It seems to be a way of combining the disadvantages of orthodox Cartesian dualism (interaction problems, for example) with the disadvantages of materialism (the implication of materialism that I cannot survive the corruption of my body). In short, if you are a Cartesian unionist, why not become an orthodox Cartesian? And, anyway, isn't it just evident that if at present my thoughts consist in a sequence of alterations (in the abstract metaphysical sense: changes in the properties of) in a Cartesian immaterial substance, and if that sequence of alterations goes on in the same sort of way following the annihilation of my body, I shall continue to exist? More might be said about Cartesian unionism, but I won't say it. I have mentioned Cartesian unionism only for the sake of logical completeness. As far as I know, no one *is* a Cartesian unionist, and I don't propose to discuss at length a position no one holds.

Our exploration of the thesis that I might be something other than either a material or an immaterial substance (namely, the union of a material and an immaterial substance) seems to show that this is not a viable alternative to Cartesianism and materialism. There are, therefore, only two possible metaphysical accounts of the human person (that is, two accounts of what we refer to when we say 'I'): a human person, a human "someone", is either a material substance or an immaterial substance.

I myself believe that we are material substances. I am therefore in one sense of the word a materialist. I am, as one might say, a local materialist. I oppose local to global materialism. A global materialist believes that everything (or every concrete thing) is material. I am not a global materialist, since I believe that God exists and that God is neither material nor abstract (and no doubt angels, in which I also believe, are concrete things that are not material). A local materialist is a philosopher who is not a global materialist but who believes that all objects of some particular sort are material—where that "sort" is a fundamental philosophical category and is such that the objects it comprises have been widely held to be immaterial. In my case, the sort or fundamental metaphysical category is "human person". I believe that human persons are material objects (living human organisms), and that they have no part or aspect that is in any way immaterial.

In my book *Metaphysics*, I presented some arguments for the thesis that we human persons are material substances. These arguments convinced no one. Imagine my astonishment. It is not my intention on this occasion to re-hash the arguments for materialism I have already presented or to present new arguments for this conclusion. (But I'll remind you of one of my *theses*: it may be difficult to see how it's possible for a material thing to think and feel, but it's equally difficult to see how it's possible for an immaterial thing to think and feel.) I want, rather, to discuss various logical and metaphysical confusions into which a great many of my fellow materialists have fallen. For I have to admit that I haven't seen much logical and metaphysical confusion, much sheer *confusion* (as opposed to error; since I disagree with them I am of course committed to thinking they are in error), in the writings of dualists, and certainly not confusions that infect their central positions. There is one major exception to this generalization: John Locke, to whose views I shall turn in a moment, is a very confused dualist indeed. But logical and metaphysical confusion among the materialists amounts to a pandemic. As I lay out the metaphysical confusions into which, I believe, many materialists have fallen, the features of an "unconfused" (by my lights) materialist ontology of the human person will emerge.

One confusion that is very common among materialists, and which I have discussed in print, is inherent in the view that it is possible to be a materialist and to accept a psychological-continuity theory of personal identity. But this confusion does not really have any essential relation to materialism. It is a special case of a more general confusion, the confusion that attends the thesis that it is possible consistently to believe that we are *substances* (material or immaterial) and to accept a psychological-continuity theory of personal identity across time. This was precisely the confusion of John Locke to which I alluded a moment ago. Locke believed that we were immaterial substances *and* accepted a psychological-continuity criterion of personal identity (more specifically, a memory criterion). Accepting both these theses led him to the absurd view that it is possible for one to switch souls. (I model this phrase on the more common phrase "switch bodies".) More exactly, it led him to the impossible view that one and the same person could be identical with one immaterial substance today and with another tomorrow, an evident violation of the principle of the transitivity of identity—and hence a violation of the principle of the indiscernibility of identicals, of which the transitivity of identity is an immediate logical consequence. As far as I know, no other dualists (and, for that matter no idealists) have got themselves into any such logical incoherency as this. Plenty of materialists have, though: just those materialists who think that we human persons really exist (who are not willing to dismiss us as some sort of grammatical fiction) and who accept any sort of psychological-continuity criterion of personal identity. One simple argument for this conclusion is this: any materialist who accepts a psychological-continuity criterion of personal identity must concede that it is possible for a person to *switch bodies*—and in a way not involving the transfer of anything material to the new body from the old body: simply in virtue of the transfer of information present in the brain of one body to the brain of the other body. But such a case of "body switching" or "bodily transfer" would be a case of someone's being identical with one material substance at one time and with another material substance at another time. And the principle of the indiscernibility of identicals tells us that can't happen: for the reality of any body switch, together with the principle of the indiscernibility of identicals, must entail a contradiction. (For example, that a certain person both has and lacks the property of once having been bald, or that someone was once in Room 101 and has never been in Room 101.)

Now having said that materialists who accept a psychological-continuity theory of personal identity must fall into a contradiction, I must qualify my statement. (There's the bit where you say it and there's the bit where you take it back.) Perdurantists can avoid the contradiction. Adherents of relative identity can avoid the contradiction (although I have not heard of any of them who wants to accept a psychological-continuity theory of personal identity). Can anyone else? Is it possible to avoid it without committing oneself to a very strong metaphysical thesis like perdurantism or to a very unorthodox logical thesis like the relativity of identity? (Of course there's nothing *per se* wrong with accepting strong metaphysical theses or unorthodox logical theses, but I don't think it's worth becoming a perdurantist or a believer in relative identity *simply* to be able consistently to subscribe to a psychological-continuity criterion of personal identity; if perdurant-ism doesn't recommend itself to one on grounds independent of the philosophy of mind, one should say that the price isn't worth it—and, of course, the same point applies to the relativity of identity.) Sydney Shoemaker has tried to avoid the contradiction by embracing the thesis that we persons are neither substances nor grammatical fictions but some intermediate sort of thing. Baseball teams and corporations are his supposedly philosophy-of-mind-neutral examples of things having this intermediate ontological status. (Or rather, of things having this *lesser* ontological status, for grammatical fictions are not really *there* to have any sort of ontological status.) According to Shoemaker, baseball teams and persons really exist and are really material objects and really have causal powers, but they are not substances; they therefore are importantly different from tables and chairs and cats and human bodies, which *are* substances. I have examined Shoemaker's views in detail elsewhere. Here I will say only that the possibility of there being something that really exists and really has causal powers but is not a substance seems to me to be a flight of metaphysical fancy. The only way for a thing to avoid being an abstract object is for it to be a substance. As I said a while ago, I am not sure what line to take about the referents of phrases like 'the New York Yankees' but the right thing to say about their referents must be this: either such phrases have (in the strict and philosophical sense, as they say) *no* referent; or their referents are substances; or their referents are abstract objects. There is no other way for an ostensible denoting phrase to be related to the world—and there's an end on't.

A second confusion or family of confusions endemic to the writings of materialists is evident when one considers their attempts to answer the question, What is the relation between the mental and the physical? I will not discuss those materialists who deny the existence of the mental—eliminativists or old-line behaviorists. As Jerry Fodor has said, it's one thing to throw the baby out with the bath-water; it's another to throw out the baby, the bathtub, the washbasin, the toilet, and the bathroom walls and ceiling and floor with the bath-water.

Almost all materialists who accept the reality of the mental accept some form of the so-called token–token identity theory. I want to examine this thesis. What is it that, according to advocates of the token–token identity theory, is identical with what? In my view, attempts to answer this question have engendered widespread confusion. According to most statements of the identity thesis, various items picked out using mental language are said to be identical with "brain processes" or "brain states". But what items, exactly? All sorts of phrases, some of them drawn from everyday language and some of them philosophical inventions, figure in proposed answers to this question. Some of these phrases are meant to be very general and to cover all cases or large classes of cases, and some of them are meant only to serve as examples of special sorts of thing that are identical with brain processes or brain states. Mental states and mental processes, qualia, sentences in the languages of thought, experiences, pains, afterimages, . . . In the case of the more general terms, and this is especially true of the terms 'quale' and 'mental state', it is very rare for materialists to take much trouble over the question what these terms are supposed to mean or what ontological categories their referents are supposed to fall into. I will remark that the terms that figure in the other side of the equation are not much better explained. I think that, in particular, the term 'brain state' could do with a lot of explanation.

Again I ask: what it that, according to the identity theory, is identical with what? I can see only one answer to this question that has any hope of making logical and metaphysical sense: *mental changes* in a material substance, in a physical thing, are, one and all, identical with *physical changes* in that substance—that is, the class of mental changes in a substance are a subclass of the class of physical changes in that substance. But what are mental and physical changes? To answer this question, we need some ancillary definitions.

By a material substance or physical substance, I mean a substance that is composed entirely of elementary particles. (That is to say, a substance each of whose parts overlaps an elementary particle.) Physical changes in a material substance are rearrangements of and interactions among the elementary particles that are its ultimate parts. (I say "its ultimate parts" because I take elementary particles to have no proper parts. But nothing I want to say turns on whether this is indeed so.) By a mental change in a material substance, I mean a change in that substance's mental properties. By a mental property, I mean a property such that, of necessity, if a thing has it at a time, that thing is then either thinking or feeling something. Consider, for example, *that he, she, or it is considering buying a new car*, a thing that can be said truly of lots of people; or consider *that he, she, or it is in pain*, a thing that can (unfortunately) be said truly of lots of sentient creatures. These two properties are mental properties, properties whose more usual names would be something like "considering buying a car" or "being in pain". The materialist who is not an eliminativist or behaviorist will agree, I think, that the material substances who are ourselves have mental properties (at least when they are not in a coma or a deep dreamless sleep), and that at least some mental properties are intrinsic properties. (If Putnam and Kripke are right, some mental properties are relational properties. But it seems evident that there could be no relational mental properties if there were no intrinsic mental properties.) A material substance or physical thing changes mentally when its intrinsic mental properties change. The identity thesis, finally, is that each human person is at any time composed entirely of elementary particles, that the material substances that are human persons have intrinsic mental properties, and that every *change* in the intrinsic mental properties of a material substance is identical with a rearrangement of or an interaction among the elementary particles that compose it.

The identity thesis, so stated, requires its adherents to believe not only in material substances and properties—material substances and abstract, eternal, necessarily existent universals but in changes—that is to say, in events. Advocates of the identity thesis must believe in events each of which is both a change in the intrinsic mental properties of a material substance *and* a rearrangement of or interaction among its constituent elementary particles. If, as I'd prefer to think, there are no events, if there are only substances and relations, then there is no thesis that can properly be called the identity theory. A thesis properly called the identity theory must, obviously enough, assert that something that is in some sense physical is identical with something that is in some sense mental, and if there are no events, I maintain, nothing that pertains to human persons is in any sense mental. Now you may want to suggest to me that if there are, as I maintain, properties, then there is obviously something that is in some sense mental, for there are mental properties. I will make two points in reply. First, mental properties are after all properties: they are abstract, eternal, necessarily existent Platonic objects. We call them "mental" properties because a thing that has them thinks and feels, but they would exist even if nothing thought or felt: they would exist in worlds from which thought and consciousness were entirely absent. Therefore, although I call them mental properties, they are no more mental things than physical properties (such as *that it weighs 60 kilos*) are physical things. This is a point to which I shall return when I discuss "property dualism". My second point is this. If one says that mental properties are identical with physical properties, one is no doubt expressing some form of what is called the type–type identity theory. The point I am trying to make, however, is really a point about the so-called token–token identity theory: my thesis is if there are no events, then there is nothing mental for the token–token identity theorist to identify with something physical.

If there are no events, I contend, there is nothing mental. And yet I am not saying that if there are no events the eliminativists or the behaviorists are right. If there are no events, I contend, the mental is nevertheless real. For, even if there are no events, it is nevertheless true that some things think and have feelings. They really do have those properties. That they have those properties is as real and objective a feature of the world as anything is. If there are events, I contend, there are mental events. But, I say, there are certainly none of those *other* things that, according to most advocates of the identity thesis are identical with some physical item. Even if there are mental events, I say, there are no pains, no qualia, no orange after-images, none of the things that have been said by so many philosophers of mind to be the referents or extensions of the terms and predicates of mental language. (There may be such events as the onset of an after-image or someone's coming to be in pain, but there are no after-images or pains.) I want to try to make it clear what I am saying when I say this, for I find that I am liable to be misunderstood. Let me take you through a particular case, a particular mental episode, in detail. (An unusual one, I concede, for it will involve the evil genius. But he's a very useful piece of conceptual apparatus, and I make no apology for his presence in the illustrative story I'm going to tell.)

Suppose Sally, whose perceptual apparatus is normal in every respect, is examining (under conditions favorable for color-perception) a piece of turquoise—the color of which is, of course, called 'turquoise'. The words 'It is turquoise' could be used to say either of two things about this object (both of them true): that it is made of a certain mineral, *or* that it is of a certain color. The evil genius suddenly removes from the world all physical things that are turquoise in color, including, of course, the piece of turquoise Sally is examining; but, plying his time-honored philosophical trade, he causes her sensations to be just what they would have been if he had not done this. Is there then anything that is turquoise (in color)? I would say no, but some would say yes: there is, they would say, a quale immediately present to Sally's conscious awareness that has the property *being turquoise in color*. Now some of these philosophers will hasten to add that the quale is not turquoise *in the same sense as* the piece of turquoise that was there a minute ago. The color-properties of qualia, they will tell us, are different properties from the color-properties of material things, although in ordinary speech we pair them and use the same name for each member of the pair—a feature of our usage that is responsible for the fallacy or mistake or confusion called *naive realism*. But they will insist, there is a property "being turquoise in color" that belongs to qualia, even if there is a distinct property that goes by the same name and belongs only to physical objects. (Berkeley, will of course, tell us that if, *per impossibile*, there were both these properties, only the property of qualia could properly be called a color.) These properties of qualia were called phenomenal properties when I was in graduate school. I don't know whether they're called that still, but, whatever you call them, I can't make out what they're supposed to be because I don't understand what these qualia are that they're supposed to be properties of. When the evil genius annihilates everything turquoise and causes Sally's state of perceptual awareness to continue unchanged from the way it was a moment ago when she was examining a piece of turquoise, his manipulations and deceptions have left nothing there but Sally. At any rate, there is nothing *concrete* there but Sally. We can if we like say that there are certain properties there, although saying of a place that a certain property is at that place is to say something of dubious significance. No doubt someone who talks that way means only that something at that place has that property. When I say that Sally's state of perceptual awareness is just the way it was a moment ago (or that her sensations are as they were a moment ago) when she was examining a piece of turquoise, I am saying that she has many of the same mental properties as she did then. I am saying that many of the things that were true of her then are true of her still. What else could I be saying? And in saying this I imply the existence of nothing but a substance (in my view a material substance) and some properties, properties she, the material substance, has. These properties are, to be sure, mental properties, but that means only that if they are true of or belong to something at a moment, that thing is thinking or feeling at that moment. A parallel definition of 'physical property' would be: a property is physical if its being true of something implies that that thing is a physical substance. A physical property, therefore, is not a property that has the property *being physical*, which is a property no property could have. To call a property physical is to speak not of *its* nature but of the natures of the things it could possibly be true of. We call a property physical not because it *has* the property *being physical* but because it *entails* that property. And all these points apply, the appropriate changes being made, to mental properties. To call a substance a mental substance is to say something about its nature; to call a property a mental property is to say something about the natures of *other* things, the things it is possible for it to belong to. Both mental and physical properties are abstract, Platonic sorts of things; just as the terms "novel" and "history" do not represent ontologically significant subcategories within the category "book," so the terms "mental property" and "physical property" do not represent ontologically significant subcategories within the category "property". I will return to this point when I discuss the thesis called property dualism.

Now *what* mental properties continue to be true of Sally when the evil genius performs his cosmic conjuring trick? Well, the most important one for our purposes, the one that is, so to speak, operative in the example, is rather hard to express; at least it is hard to express it in a form that does not have misleading implications. We might call it "seeing turquoise", but this phrase makes the word 'turquoise' look like a direct object, a name for something Sally sees. Chisholm suggested that we might remove this implication by inventing an adverb, 'turquoisely'; the property Sally continues to have would, according to this suggestion, be called 'seeing turquoisely' or 'being appeared to turquoisely'. These are bizarre phrases, but I think it's pretty clear that there is such a property as the one Chisholm said they denoted. At least this is clear if we assume that a given piece of turquoise looks the same in respect of color to every human being with normal color vision who observes it in ideal circumstances—and that is an assumption I'm going to make. If you want to have this property then, given that you have normal color vision, examine a piece of turquoise in a good light. If you want to stop having it, close your eyes. I think we all know what this property is, and it's evident that it's a property of *persons*, or at any rate of sentient beings, and of nothing else. It seems to me to be evident that it's possible to have this property even if nothing has the property *being turquoise in color*. I would say that ten thousand years ago, very possibly, nothing had the property *being sky blue*. (Maybe there were sky-blue birds or flowers ten thousand years ago, but let's suppose not.) Although nothing was sky-blue in those remote times, anyone who then looked at the sky on a fine day acquired a certain property, the property Chisholm would call 'being appeared to sky-bluely'. (I'm going to have to insist that it's just false that in such a case the perceiver does see something sky-blue, namely the sky. This is false for the very good reason that there is no such thing as the sky. And I'm going to have to insist, too, on the falsity of the thesis that the mind or consciousness of a person looking at the sky contains a sky-blue quale. I insist on this latter point because no one has ever been able to explain what a quale is. If there are qualia, then, as a simple matter of logic, each quale has, for every property, either that property or its complement, and no one has been able to give a coherent account of what combination of properties a quale has. I am willing to defend this statement not only in this very general form, but in particular application to such alleged examples of qualia as afterimages, sounds, smells, and pains.)

This is the story I promised you. I hope that, as I promised, my way of telling the story displays my rather sparse ontology of the mental. I want to make it clear that, although I believe that lack of attention to ontological questions has led to confusion in the philosophy of mind, I do not deny that there are substantive problems in the philosophy of mind, problems that are by no means artifacts of their first framers' lack of attention to ontological questions. Consider qualia and their role in the statement of problems in the philosophy of mind. Several central problems in the philosophy of mind are usually framed as problems about qualia, but this is not an essential feature of those problems. If, as I do, one denies the existence of qualia, one still faces the question whether there can be what David Chalmers calls zombies, and one still has the inverted spectrum problem. Take zombies. Although the zombie problem is usually stated in terms of qualia, it's easy enough to state without reference to qualia. A zombie is a thing composed entirely of elementary particles, these particles being arranged in more or less the same ways that the particles that compose me or the particles that compose you are arranged, and which, unlike me and you, does not *experience*. Here I use the intransitive verb 'experience' to express the property that comprehends the members of a class of more specific properties, properties such as being in pain and being appeared to redly. Chalmers's problem is this: could there be a zombie? That is, is there in some possible world, a world in which the same physical laws hold as in the actual world, a being made of elementary particles arranged in more or less the same way as the particles that compose us denizens of the actual world, but which, unlike us actual people, does not experience?

Mention of zombies brings us to my final topic, property dualism, for philosophers who say it's possible for there to be zombies are just those philosophers who describe themselves as "property dualists" (as opposed to *substance* dualists, like Plato and Descartes). Property dualists distinguish between the physical properties of human beings and their mental properties, which, they say, are non-physical properties. We know what mental properties are: mental properties are properties that entail thought and sensation. We know what physical properties are: physical properties are properties that entail the property *being physical* or *being composed entirely of elementary particles*. But what are *non*-physical properties? Not, obviously, properties that entail the property *being non-physical*, or physical things could not have non-physical properties, and property dualists say physical things have non-physical properties. I believe the idea of a non-physical property should be spelled out this way: a non-physical property is a property whose distribution or extension in a world does not depend on, is not determined by, does not supervene upon, the way elementary particles are arranged in that world. Thus, if there could be two worlds which were perfect physical duplicates of each other (that is, duplicates as regards the arrangement of elementary particles), and in one world a certain object had F and its counterpart in the other lacked F, F would be a non-physical property. No doubt there are problems with this definition. Definitions involving such notions as supervenience and "perfect physical duplicate" usually have unwanted consequences.[1] But I won't try to answer the question whether there are technical problems with my "supervenience" definition of 'non-physical property', since nothing I want to say is going to hang on esoteric wrangles about supervenience. It will do for my purposes if we have a rough, intuitive grasp of the concepts employed by the property dualist.

Property dualists contend that human persons are physical things, things composed entirely of elementary particles, that they have physical properties (that much follows from their being physical things), that they also have non-physical properties, and that among these non-physical properties, perhaps coextensive with them, are such mental properties as they may have, and, finally, that they have—in the actual world, at any rate—just the mental properties we normally suppose them to have.

I must say that I find property dualism incredible. It seems to me to be evident that, tricky examples involving cleverly contrived properties aside, *all* the intrinsic properties a thing composed of quarks and electrons has at a given time *must* supervene on the properties of, and the mutual arrangement of, and the causal relations that hold among, those quarks and electrons. But I admit I have no argument for this thesis (as David Lewis has said, an incredulous stare is not an argument). I want to make just one point in closing. Whether or not property dualism is an incredible thesis, it seems to me that 'property dualism' is a very odd name to give it. Why is this thesis about supervenience a form of *dualism?* If the thesis is true, there are, or at least there may be, only physical or material substances and abstract objects. Some of these abstract objects, properties like *being appeared to sky-bluely*, properties that are classified as mental not by their nature but by their content, have the following curious feature: they can belong—that is, it is metaphysically possible for them to belong—to a given thing composed entirely of elementary particles and fail to belong to another thing (maybe it would have to be a thing in another possible world) that consists

---

[1] Here's an *odd* consequence of the definition: for all anyone knows, there may be properties that are both physical and non-physical; at any rate, it doesn't seem to be demonstrable that there are no such properties. The following three assumptions jointly entail that some properties are both physical and non-physical, and it doesn't seem to be demonstrable that any of them is false or that their disjunction is false: (i) it is impossible for there to be non-physical substances; (ii) some physical substances have mental properties; (iii) zombies are possible. If (i) is true, then "that it experiences" is a physical property. If (ii) and (iii) are true, then "that it experiences" is a non-physical property. (If these three propositions are individually possible, they certainly seem to be mutually consistent.) This is an odd result, but not a contradiction, since neither 'physical property' nor 'non-physical property' was defined as the contradictory of the other. It, the odd result, could be avoided if one defined 'physical property' as the complement (on substances) of 'non-physical property'. We'd still have the following as a consequence of our three assumptions: Every non-physical property entails the property *being physical*, but I suppose that's no odder than the assumptions of which it's a consequence.

of particles having the same properties, arranged in the same way, and among which the same causal relations hold. An interesting thesis. A *false* thesis, *I* think, but interesting, and well worth extended philosophical discussion. But why call it a form of dualism?

Well, here is a guess. I think it's a plausible guess. If there are non-physical substances, then physical and non-physical substances (a cat and an angel, for example) are clean different kinds of thing. Although they are both substances right enough, the division of the category "substance" into the sub-categories "physical" and "non-physical" is an ontologically significant division. We call Descartes and Plato dualists because they think there are substances in both sub-categories. I would *suppose* that "property dualists" call themselves dualists because they think that the division of properties into physical and non-physical properties is an ontologically significant division of the category "property", a division as significant as the physical/non-physical division of the category "substance". If this is so, I think that the self-chosen description "property dualist" indicates a metaphysical confusion in the way property dualists conceive of properties. For, if I am right, the properties *that it is a cat* and *that it is an angel* are things of exactly the same sort: they are both things that can be said about things. They are both as abstract and bloodless as the Riemann curvature tensor. They differ not in their natures but in their content. If *that it is a cat* is one of the things that can be said truly about Professor Moriarty (who lives in my house) and *that it is an angel* is one of the things that can be said truly about St Michael, then Moriarty and Michael are things of different ontological kinds. But the properties themselves, *that it is a cat* and *that it is an angel*, are of the same ontological kind. And the same goes for *that it weighs 60 kilos* and *that it is thinking of Vienna*; the same goes for these two properties *whether or not* the extensions of properties of the same sort as the latter, mental properties, supervene on the distribution of elementary particles.

9

I Am Not an Animal!

Hud Hudson

1. A PROTEST

I am not an animal!

Well, not literally, at least. Despite my testimony, however, the thesis that a human person is identical to a human animal is a surprisingly popular one—and among the educated elite, the orthodoxy even. Arguments for this thesis come in a variety of flavors from which I would like to single out three for special attention.

The Sophisticated Worldview Defense

Physics, astronomy, chemistry, biology, and geology all point to a picture of the origin of life and to the emergence of consciousness (and personhood) that is utterly grounded in the material. Differences of abilities between space fillers that are persons and space fillers that are nonpersons need not be explained by any mysterious reference to an immaterial mind or soul—any more than the differences in the capacities of my refrigerator and my chalk require those objects to sport immaterial parts to help them perform their characteristic functions. The reasons my fridge keeps my beer cold and not chalky, the reasons my chalk whitens the board rather than damaging it, and the reasons that I cognize are all (in the end) to be cashed out in terms of microphysical parts, their types and arrangements, their environments, and laws of nature. We, like the rest of the furniture of the world, are material objects through and through.

Thanks to Andy Egan, Katherine Hawley, E. J. Lowe, Ned Markosian, Kris McDaniel, Daniel Nolan, Josh Parsons, Joshua Spencer, Christina van Dyke, Peter van Inwagen, Achille Varzi, Dean Zimmerman, and to audiences at Calvin College, the Pew Workshop on the Metaphysics of Human Persons, and the University of St Andrews for comments and criticisms on an earlier draft of this paper.

The Fanciful Thought Experiment Defense

Strategy: tell a moderately frightening, sci-fi-ish story in just the right way and watch the intuitions that back the so-called 'bodily criterion of personal identity' get pumped to the surface. Then drink deeply from the intuition well to steel yourself against conversion when your opponent (as she certainly will) tells her own moderately frightening, sci-fi-ish story designed to pump the intuitions backing the so-called 'psychological criterion of personal identity'. Strategic hints: (i) no real need to invent your own story; save time by getting an advance copy of your opponent's story and be a bit creative in the redescription, (ii) emphasize where you can the things we deeply care about in survival and mix those up with suggestive claims about identity, and (iii) do your best to speak first.

The Big-Picture, Best-Candidate, General Metaphysics Defense

After settling on materialism for human persons (as opposed to idealism or dualism) and on some analysis of 'material object', inquire into the general metaphysics of persistence across time for material things. Consult your best theories of composition and decomposition, of vagueness and the occupation of regions, of temporal predication and transworld identity. Convince yourself that there is usually (at most) one person in your chair. And then—after your general metaphysics has pronounced on just which objects are in the vicinity—go on a hunt for the best candidate to be you.

Some initial observations are in order. Even if it were correct in all points, *the sophisticated worldview defense* is an argument for the wrong conclusion. The best it could hope for is a verdict of materiality not of animality (or at least not without some controversial, auxiliary, metaphysical premises). *The fanciful thought experiment defense* has had a distinguished history, has come under some pretty heavy fire, and has (I think) completely bogged down in a stalemate. The heavy fire is often occasioned by competing explanations of our reactions to the thought experiments, explanations that feature a number of things other than rough and ready insight into or truth-tracking intuitions about the nature of human persons. *The big-picture, best-candidate, general metaphysics defense* is the way to go.

Of course, I don't really expect that casual introduction to convince any fence sitters of the superiority of the third style of defense, but I did want to alert the reader to my take on the current debate and to my own starting assumptions for the discussion that follows. In this paper I would like to avoid entirely the fanciful thought experiment approach that has been so dominant in these debates and to remain absolutely neutral on the bodily criterion/psychological criterion dispute. Instead I intend to explore the prospects for denying that a human person is a human animal by appealing to general metaphysical views about parthood, vagueness, occupation, and *de re* temporal and modal predication.

2. THE ELIMINATION PRINCIPLE

Throughout this essay I will have need of an elimination principle to play a game of 'find the human person among some plausible human person candidates'. Once again, I shall be working with the background assumption that there is usually (at most) one person in your chair, and I will employ the elimination principle to disqualify some of the candidates in the game.[1] Here is an elimination principle that should suffice for the purposes of this paper:

> (EP) If *x* and *y* are both human person candidates and at most one of *x* and *y* is a human person, but *y* has superfluous parts whereas *x* doesn't, then *x* is the better candidate for the office.

Five Clarificatory Notes

1. By 'superfluous parts' I shall mean parts that play no contributory role in supporting a psychological profile constitutive of personhood. Just which sort of psychological profile is constitutive of personhood is, of course, hotly contested. Standard accounts make reference to a certain collection of cognitive abilities and disagree about whether actual or mere potential possession is sufficient and about which other psychological abilities should round out the minimal list. In this paper, I shall assume that a first-person perspective (i.e. the ability to be aware of some of my own acts of awareness and to represent them to myself as mine) is the core condition sufficient for personhood. The ability I have in mind requires more than simply being a subject of thought and experiencing the world from a particular spatio-temporal perspective; it further requires possessing the concept 'being a subject of thought' and the ability to correctly categorize oneself under that concept as a result of reflective representation of one's own acts of awareness. Just to be clear—I am here concerned only with the psychological profile constitutive of being some person or other and not with the relation 'being the same person as' which might well also depend on certain facts about similarity of mental content including facts about memories, beliefs, desires, intentions, and goals, as well as on certain facts about basic mental capacities, dispositions, and character. I should add, however, that the arguments below are consistent with a rather wide range of beliefs about just which characteristics confer personhood.[2]

---

[1] Incredibly, there are some philosophers who think that there are actually continuum-many persons in your chair every time there is at least one! See David Lewis's "Many, but Almost One", in his *Papers in Metaphysics and Epistemology* (New York: Cambridge University Press, 1999), 164–82. I have said what seems right to me against this resolution of what is known as the Problem of the Many in chs. 1 and 2 of my *A Materialist Metaphysics of the Human Person* (Ithaca, NY: Cornell University Press, 2001). In the present paper, I will simply assume that the many-persons solution is false.

[2] For an intriguing discussion of the notion of a first-person perspective and the ability to conceive of oneself as oneself, see Lynne Rudder Baker, *Persons and Bodies* (Cambridge: Cambridge

2. When I speak of a part playing a contributory role in supporting a psychological profile constitutive of personhood, I mean that the part in question manifests certain properties and stands in certain relations upon which a particular collection of psychological properties supervene. It is, for example, the sort of feature almost certainly had by parts of one's cerebrum and almost certainly lacked by parts of one's forearm. Suppose, then, that there is a solitary person in a chair at T and, thus, that certain psychological properties constitutive of personhood are exemplified at T by that person. Now take some object in the vicinity of the chair at T, namely O. Either O manifests properties and stands in relations at T that are among the properties and relations subsumed under the supervenience laws then in play or it doesn't. If it does, then O is non-superfluous, whereas O is superfluous if it doesn't.[3]

3. The basic insight driving the formulation of the elimination principle is simply this: if you must recognize a single human person from two candidates and you are allowed to assume that they are not both human persons, then put your money on the one just big enough to do the job. If a less inclusive thing will do, any larger choice (i.e. anything with parts that are wholly irrelevant to securing a psychological profile constitutive of personhood) is arbitrary and unmotivated.

4. The notion of not having superfluous parts is related to but distinct from the more familiar notion of being maximal; a human person candidate is maximal when it both lacks superfluous parts and is also not a proper part of another human person candidate who lacks superfluous parts. Working with the weaker of these two notions, however, will suffice for the line of reasoning to follow.

5. Won't there be some vagueness in 'superfluous part' that will spell trouble for applications of (EP)? Not if it is epistemic vagueness (and I think epistemicism is the best theory of vagueness on the market).[4] But for those who favor some competing theory of vagueness, I'll restrict my applications of (EP) to cases where one of the candidates is a determinate case of having superfluous parts and the other candidate is either a determinate or a borderline case of lacking superfluous parts, in which case (EP) should be interpreted merely as disqualifying the candidate who determinately has superfluous parts—thereby avoiding (hopefully without serious cost) the quicksand that is the current vagueness literature.

University Press, 2000). On a historical note, I take the main insight behind this minimal condition for personhood to be present and to be the subject of a sophisticated (albeit controversial) defense in Kant's *Critique of Pure Reason*.

[3] It is worth noting that this is not equivalent to a counterfactual test. An object does not qualify as superfluous merely if it is true that if that object were to have been missing, the person would still have existed. For if this were the test, then it would turn out that not a single particle would qualify as non-superfluous.

[4] For defenses of epistemicism see Timothy Williamson, *Vagueness* (London: Routledge, 1994) and Roy Sorensen, "The Metaphysics of Words", *Philosophical Studies*, 81 (1996), 193–214.

A Preview

My intention in the remainder of the paper is to make the case that (given very reasonable metaphysical assumptions) there are just so *many* candidate objects from which to choose a human person that we can always find a better candidate for that office than a human animal. As a bit of biography, I confess to accepting very liberal mereological principles which lead me to endorse an unusually robust view of how many material objects exist in the vicinity of any human animal. As a consequence of the ontology I favor, I embrace the conclusion that an ordinary human person will be located somewhere "within the lifespan and beneath the skin" of a certain organism—it will be a mere proper part of a human animal.[5] But, although I will have occasion to invoke some of these principles at the outset, I won't *insist* on the controversial mereological claims that led me to that conclusion. Instead, I'll relinquish those principles for the sake of the argument and nevertheless do my best to show just how controversial one has to be to identify the human person with the human animal at the end of the day.

3. NONMATERIALISM (AND WHATEVER IT IS THAT AQUINAS IS)

One might complain that I haven't really given nonmaterialism much serious attention yet, and that the most I've said in defense of materialism amounts to asserting that it is the orthodox position among the educated elite. Fair enough—but my aim doesn't require saying much about nonmaterialism. Here's why. A human person is either a material thing or an immaterial thing or a fusion of a material with an immaterial thing. I accept that disjunction, with Idealism represented in the second option and Dualism (and whatever it is that Aquinas is) represented in either the second or third options—depending on the specific account to be given of the relation between the mind (or soul) and the body. Perhaps it is worth calling attention to the fact that I have omitted the minority view that a human person is an event or process, but I don't mind omitting that view. The Idealists and Dualists already grant my primary thesis—that a human person is not identical to a human animal—whether or not they think that human persons represent themselves as having animal bodies and whether or not they think that human persons earn the adjective 'human' by being in a two-way causal relationship with certain animal bodies.

    Does Aquinas grant my thesis, too? I don't know; but I'll hazard a guess and invite the serious Thomistic scholars (who need little encouragement in such matters!) to correct me. Aquinas famously claims that the soul is the substantial

---

[5] Defending (and qualifying) this claim is largely the task of ch. 4 of my *A Materialist Metaphysics of the Human Person*.

form of the human body and that the human body cannot exist without being enformed by the soul. Yet despite the ontological dependence of the body on the soul, the body and the soul are nevertheless numerically distinct, since the soul can be present at times when the body is not (e.g. between the death of the animal body and the general resurrection). Aquinas explicitly denies that the soul taken by itself is the human being or the human person (or any person at all, for that matter).[6] We need not, however, assume that this leaves us only with the option of identifying the human animal body with the human person. Rather, we still have room to identify the human person with the body/soul compound (and not merely with the human animal body that appears as one of its components). Accordingly, whereas the human animal could no more exist without the human person than a body could exist without the soul that enforms it, the human animal is not identical to the human person.

The nonmaterialists, then, I think are already on board. Accordingly, I focus in the remainder of this essay on materialism not simply because I think it is true (which I do), but rather to give the view I wish to refute a fighting chance.

4. FOUR-DIMENSIONALISM

So, addressing ourselves to materialists:

Either four-dimensionalism is true or it is not. At the most general level, four-dimensionalism is a thesis about objects and their parts. The principal idea is that necessarily, for each way of exhaustively dividing the lifetime of any object, x, into two parts, there is a corresponding way of dividing x itself into two parts, each of which is present throughout, but not outside of, the corresponding part of x's lifetime. Or, if we let 'TS(x)' be the set of times at which x is present, we may say more formally:

> (4D) Necessarily, for any object, x, and for any non-empty, non-overlapping sets of times, t_1 and t_2 whose union is TS(x), there are two objects, x_1 and x_2, such that (i) x is the fusion of x_1 and x_2, and (ii) TS(x_1) = t_1, whereas the TS(x_2) = t_2.[7]

The thesis of four-dimensionalism has been center stage in some of the most rich and exciting contributions to the metaphysics literature over the last couple of decades. Prominent defenses of four-dimensionalism arise from exploiting analogies between space and time, from the theory of special relativity, from

---

[6] *Summa Theologiae* Ia.75.4.co, and *ST* Ia.29.1.*ad*5. Thanks to Christina van Dyke for this reference.

[7] In stating (4D) and in its informal gloss, I directly borrow from Theodore Sider's "Four-Dimensionalism", *Philosophical Review*, 106 (1997), 197–231. Some of the material in this brief section (and in Sections 5 and 9) is adapted from chs. 2, 4, and 7 of my *A Materialist Metaphysics of the Human Person*, where I offer a more thorough and sustained defense of the theses I am here concerned with.

a denial of presentism and an affirmation of eternalism, from the problem of temporary intrinsics, from considerations of Humean supervenience, as an answer to puzzles of material constitution, and most recently from reflections on vagueness and composition.[8] Attacks on four-dimensionalism come on all sides, but perhaps the most influential are those that maintain that four-dimensionalism is unintelligible, those that maintain that four-dimensionalism is unmotivated, and those that present modal arguments designed to show that (to his discredit) the four-dimensionalist must consort with the counterpart theorist.[9]

I am currently willing to pass over the debate on its truth, however. Suppose it is true. Consider some uncontroversial case involving a single human organism sitting on a chair (e.g. one not involving future fission or recent fusion or conjoined twins and so on). In such a case, one candidate for being the human person will be a living human organism. But other candidates can be introduced by way of applying (4D) to the organism in question and thus fixing our attention on some of its temporal parts. Well, so what? Why not go with the whole organism anyway? Historically, four-dimensionalists are somewhat reluctant to go this route, since certain puzzles involving longevity suggest that such a metaphysics might do well to untie the knot between the persistence of a human person and organism-continuity.[10] But barring the popularity of this application of four-dimensionalism to such puzzles, another independent reason not to go with the whole organism is simply that, given the wealth of material objects available on this metaphysics, the organism appears to be a wholly arbitrary and unmotivated choice. Everyone grants that the organism has stages when it doesn't appear to have any of the features relevant to personhood at all (e.g. stages of prenatal development or irreversible coma or profound senility). The best we can claim for the organism is that it will later become or once was an item that manifests all the features relevant to personhood. But the best isn't good enough, for it seems to have that latter feature only because it appears to have a human person as a temporal part, and that distinction simply doesn't count for much. It is a feature also had by the fusion of you with the first wheel. A much better choice (if it exists) would be an object each of whose parts plays a contributory role in supporting a psychological profile constitutive of personhood. Significantly, applying (4D) to the organism does seem to yield

---

[8] Richard Taylor, *Metaphysics* (Englewood Cliffs, NJ: Prentice-Hall, 1992), Yuri Balashov, "Enduring and Perduring Objects in Minkowski Space–Time", *Philosophical Studies*, 99 (2000), 129–66, and "Relativistic Objects", *Noûs*, 33 (1999), 644–62; W.V.O. Quine, *Word and Object* (Cambridge, Mass.: Technology Press of MIT, 1960), Trenton Merricks, "On the Incompatibility of Enduring and Perduring Entities", *Mind*, 104 (1995): 523–531; David Lewis, *On The Plurality of Worlds* (Oxford: Basil Blackwell, 1986); David Lewis, "Survival and Identity" and "Postscripts", in *Philosophical Papers*, i (Oxford: Oxford University Press, 1983), 55–77; Mark Heller, *The Ontology of Physical Objects* (Cambridge: Cambridge University Press, 1990); Theodore Sider, *Four-Dimensionalism* (Oxford: Clarendon Press, 2001).

[9] Peter van Inwagen, "Four-Dimensional Objects", *Noûs*, 24 (1990), 245–55; Michael Rea, "Temporal Parts Unmotivated", *Philosophical Review*, 107 (1998), 225–60.

[10] Lewis, "Survival and Identity".

a candidate—a new and genuine material object and not merely another way of referring to the organism at a time it exemplifies a phase sortal—who sports just these qualifications. An application of (EP), then, selects the temporal part in question as a better candidate for the office of human person than the animal.

Objection: Maybe you have the right idea, but you've only learned half the lesson. Suppose you're correct that an early temporal part of a human organism which corresponds to the phrase 'his stage of prenatal development' is among the superfluous parts that disqualify that candidate, and suppose that you then suggest that (EP) favors one of that disqualified candidate's proper, temporal parts. But (EP)—it turns out—is quite unable to give a ruling in this case, for since its antecedent is not satisfied, (EP) has no application at all. Just as the original human organism was temporally too large, so too each of its temporal parts will be spatially too large; that is to say, even the most qualified temporal part will have spatial parts that are superfluous.

In short, then, only if the four-dimensionalist materialists can find a proper spatial part of a proper temporal part to pair with the "host-organism" will I have given them good reason to back my main thesis. Interestingly, this puts them in roughly the same boat (at least on this matter) as their three-dimensionalist opponents. Real and significant differences remain between the four- and three-dimensionalists, but they no longer play a role in the present controversy. Thus, I will now fix my attention on the three-dimensionalists (trusting that the reader will see how the following discussion would play out move by move with the four-dimensionalist).

5. UNIVERSALISM

So, addressing ourselves to three-dimensionalist materialists:

At the most general level, three-dimensionalism is also a thesis about objects and their parts. But for the three-dimensionalist (or at least for the three-dimensionalist who is not also a presentist), parthood is standardly taken to be a three-place relation that has a slot for times; that is to say, there is no atemporal parthood relation of the sort countenanced by the four-dimensionalist, and persistence across time does not turn out to be a matter of having different temporal parts at different times. Since the slightly better candidate for human personhood in the preceding section turned out to be an alleged, proper temporal part of a human organism, the three-dimensionalist should not yet feel compelled to endorse my main thesis.

Either the doctrine of unrestricted composition is true or it is not. Universalism, as I call this doctrine, is the view that any plurality of objects has a mereological fusion or sum (no matter what spatiotemporal and causal relations they may happen to satisfy). In a formulation friendly to three-dimensionalists, the doctrine can be presented as follows:

Universalism: Necessarily, for any objects, *the xs*, and any time, *t*, if *the xs* are present at *t*, then there exists an object, *y*, such that *the xs* compose *y* at *t*.

Universalism and debates about composition in general have also been among the highlights of recent analytic metaphysics.[11] But again, I am willing to pass over the debate on its truth. Suppose it is true.

Then we are free to make use of the same strategy employed in the preceding section. Just as the four-dimensionalist should claim that the human person will be located somewhere "within the lifespan" of a living human organism, so too, the three-dimensionalist universalist should be inclined to locate it "under the skin", as it were. That is to say, there is exactly the same kind of reason for the three-dimensionalist universalist to resist identifying the human person with the whole living human organism (bones, flesh, skin, and all) as there was for the four-dimensionalist to resist identifying the human person with the whole temporally extended, living human organism (prenatal stages, irreversibly comatose stages, and all). Given the wealth of material objects available on the three-dimensionalist universalist's metaphysics, once again the whole living human organism appears to be a rather arbitrary and unmotivated choice. Everyone should grant that living human organisms have parts which are not in any way relevant to any object's being a person (e.g. certain cells on the surface of a hand or even a full head of hair). The best we can claim for such an object is that it has some further object as a proper part, each of whose parts plays some sort of role in furnishing it with the full range of features relevant to personhood. But, once again, the best isn't good enough, for it seems to have that latter feature only because it appears to have a human person as a spatial part, and that distinction simply doesn't count for much. Rather, once again, the only non-arbitrary choice would be an object each of whose parts plays a contributory role in supporting a psychological profile constitutive of personhood. Since (as our best physics teaches us) human organisms are themselves fusions of scattered particles, an application of universalism to a certain subset of such a plurality of particles will yield a candidate—a new and genuine material object—who sports just these qualifications. An application of (EP), then, will select the spatial part in question as a better candidate for the office of human person than the animal.

I happily grant that I have nothing like a comprehensive account of just which parts of a living organism play such a role and which do not. Presumably some parts of the brain are relevant, some parts of the hand are not, and some parts

---

[11] For defenses of Universalism, see David Lewis's argument from vagueness—*On the Plurality of Worlds*, 211–13; Michael Rea's argument from functionality—"In Defense of Mereological Universalism", *Philosophy and Phenomenological Research*, 58 (1998), 347–60; and ch. 3 of my own *A Materialist Metaphysics of the Human Person*. For a widely discussed attack on Universalism, see Peter van Inwagen's *Material Beings* (Ithaca, NY: Cornell University Press, 1990), 72–80. By '*the xs* compose *y* at *t*' I simply mean 'each of *the xs* is a part of *y* at *t* and every part of *y* at *t* overlaps at *t* at least one of *the xs*'.

of the nervous system are borderline cases. But all I need for my present point is that some parts of a living human organism obviously fail to contribute at all (including for example, hair, fingernails, and bone-marrow), and thus mark the animal for elimination when paired with some of its spatial parts and subjected to (EP).

In short, then, three-dimensionalist universalists have good reason to back my main thesis. But what of their opponents?

6. THE DOCTRINE OF ARBITRARY UNDETACHED PARTS

So, addressing ourselves to three-dimensionalist materialists who deny universalism:

The argument of the last section depended upon arbitrary fusions and the empirical claim that the human persons of our world are composed of swarms of particles. Sadly (say I) not everyone is willing to countenance the spectacular array of composite objects that universalism generates—so unwilling, in fact, that it seems better to restrict composition than to accept the existence of a thing that has as its most salient parts the gargoyle on my desk, Nebraska, and all the sunken ships at sea. Such a cautious theorist should not yet feel compelled to endorse my main thesis.

Either the doctrine of arbitrary undetached parts—(DAUP)—is true or it is not. Whereas universalism assures us that many will yield one, DAUP assures us that (an extended) one will yield many; that is to say, whereas universalism provides a liberal theory of composition, DAUP provides a liberal theory of decomposition. These are, it should be emphasized, independent theses, and the three-dimensionalist who denies universalism may nevertheless be attracted to this principle that helps identify the parts of those objects he already acknowledges. In a formulation friendly to such a theorist, DAUP can be presented as follows:

> DAUP: Necessarily, for any material object, x, regions, s and $s*$, and time, t, if x exactly occupies s at t, and if $s*$ is an exactly occupiable subregion of s at t, then there exists a material object, y, such that (i) y exactly occupies $s*$ at t, and (ii) y is a part of x at t.

Debates about DAUP and principles of decomposition have not enjoyed the prominence of recent debates about universalism and principles of composition, but the tide is turning.[12] But again, I am willing to pass over the debate on its truth. Suppose it is true.

[12] For early discussion of this and similar principles, see Peter van Inwagen, "The Doctrine of Arbitrary Undetached Parts", *Pacific Philosophical Quarterly*, 62 (1981), 123–37 and Dean Zimmerman, "Could Extended Objects Be Made Out of Simple Parts? An Argument For 'Atomless Gunk'", *Philosophy and Phenomenological Research*, 56 (1996), 1–29. For recent work on puzzles related to decomposition see the interesting collection of papers on simples and atomless gunk

Then we quickly find ourselves with the same two candidates that helped us close the argument of the last section, but with a somewhat different way of securing our right to assume the existence of the second candidate in question. The first candidate, we may recall, was just the human organism itself. Nothing is dialectically inappropriate about assuming the presence of that candidate, since any adversary inclined to think that this is the human person is, of course, at least committed to its existence. But then, rather than invoking subsets of the particles composing the organism and arbitrary fusions, let us apply DAUP to yield a candidate occupying a subregion of the region exactly occupied by the animal—a new and genuine material object—each of whose parts plays a contributory role in supporting a psychological profile constitutive of personhood. Then, once again, an application of (EP), will select the spatial part in question as a better candidate for the office of human person than the animal.

In short, then, four-dimensionalists and three-dimensionalists who accept either universalism or DAUP have good reason to back my main thesis. It is, however, an easy matter to get common folk to roll their eyes at the allegedly outrageous ontology of temporal parts, arbitrary fusions, and peculiar minima which are championed by four-dimensionalism, universalism, and DAUP. And I suspect that a common reaction thus far might be—"*Sure*—if you accepted some bizarre metaphysics, then you'd deny that you're an animal, and I suppose that if you believed elves spin electrons, you'd change your physics, too. But why should anyone be impressed by those conditional claims?"

7. RESTRICTED COMPOSITION, RESTRICTED DECOMPOSITION, AND BRAINS

So, addressing ourselves to three-dimensionalist materialists who deny both universalism and DAUP:

To be fair—the group just identified makes up the majority of my intended audience. The majority of this majority, however, share a view that can be paired with (EP) to provide a serious challenge to the human-persons-are-human-animals thesis. It is a simple thing to stand with common sense and deny alleged gargoyle-shipwreck fusions or point-sized material objects. It is somewhat harder (but still commonly respectable) to withhold the title 'composite object' from chess sets or solar systems or atoms or even apparently connected objects such as the torso of Michelangelo's *David*. But it is very difficult indeed to deny (with sincerity) the existence of putative objects for which we have familiar (singular) sortal terms, in which we have deep and lasting interests, and for which we recognize a variety of clearly defined functions and purposes—objects such as

in *The Monist*, 87 (2004) and my "The Liberal View of Receptacles", *Australasian Journal of Philosophy*, 80 (2002), 432–9.

a human eye, a human hand, a human heart, or a human brain. Such sincere denials are possible, of course, but don't underestimate their cost. Peter van Inwagen, for example, has given us a wonderful lesson on the possible price such sincere denials may exact and on just what it takes to square the resulting verdicts with both general metaphysics and what we ordinarily say outside the philosophical seminar room.[13] I don't mind the sincere denials; van Inwagen, for example, has a very clear, and (although I think it is mistaken) respectable position on the matter. I mind having it both ways.

Either there are human brains or there are not. Why would anyone be inclined to think there aren't any? Surprisingly enough, there are some pressing reasons: suppose that Victim (a victim) has been kidnapped by the scientists who intend to carve away his body, pare him down to a brain, and let him pass the rest of his days in a vat of nutrients enjoying simulated experiences generated by the scientists' computers. Now suppose that before the surgery Victim has a brain (here named 'Brain') as a proper part. Victim and Brain are not identical, for at pre-surgery times Victim exactly occupies a larger region of space than does Brain, and nothing ever exactly occupies a larger region of space than itself. At post-surgery times, though, Victim and Brain would both seem to have survived the ordeal. Victim is still there, for if a surgery is careful enough, a human animal can be whittled down to a brain and survive as a radically mutilated but nevertheless self-governing organism. Moreover, Brain is still there, for nothing at all happened to Brain except for the annihilation of some of the objects in regions neighboring the region it occupies. But now we have a problem—at least if we are inclined to the highly intuitive view that the co-location of material objects is impossible—for at post-surgery times Victim and Brain would appear to occupy exactly the same region. What to do?[14]

Well, we could simply deny that Victim exists—but no one is inclined to take that very seriously. Or we could deny that Victim could be cut down to a brain and survive as a human animal—but current technological obstacles aside, there seems to be no objection in principle to such a transformation.[15] Or we could maintain that whereas Brain was there to begin with it wouldn't survive the ordeal—but this seems exceedingly implausible, for recall that Brain is the only thing in the story that doesn't get altered by the scientists (save for the alterations generated by certain relational changes to the objects in its environment). Or we could say that our protagonists really do co-locate after all—but this seems to do violence to a popular metaphysics of material objects, one essential feature of which is that material objects of the same fundamental kind resist

---

[13] Van Inwagen, *Material Beings*.

[14] The literature overflows with discussions of this puzzle. See Heller, *The Ontology of Physical Objects* and Sider, *Four-Dimensionalism,* for very nice overviews.

[15] For a philosophically sophisticated introduction to some of the evidence for this claim and for an excellent, book-length defense of the thesis that I am targeting in this paper see Eric Olson's *The Human Animal* (Oxford: Oxford University Press, 1997).

interpenetration and co-location. Or we could revive four-dimensionalism (and a temporal analogue of conjoined twins) arguing that rather than co-locating, our protagonists simply share later temporal parts. Finally, though, we might just maintain that Brain never existed in the first place.

What if Brain (and in general, human brains) do exist, though? Well, then we will have at least two candidates to bring to judgment under (EP). Returning to the case of Victim, the pre-surgery human animal present in the story is a determinate case of having superfluous parts, whereas that animal's brain is either a determinate or a borderline case of lacking superfluous parts.[16] If we work with the double-hypothesis that both exist and that at most one is a human person, then (EP) disqualifies the candidate who determinately has superfluous parts—that is to say, the brain emerges as a better candidate for the office of human person than the animal.

But that just shows that the three-dimensionalist who restricts composition and decomposition might need to impose restrictions severe enough to avoid commitment to human brains, and despite the extreme counter-intuitiveness of it all, we have seen some motivation in the preceding paragraphs for doing just that. So what can be said to secure the support of this remaining group of theorists?

8. CONSTITUTION THEORY

So, addressing ourselves to three-dimensionalist materialists who deny universalism, DAUP, and any theory of composition or decomposition that yields brains:

Either constitution theory is correct or it is not. Constitution theory (of one variety or another) arises largely out of the need to respond to a number of dazzling mereological puzzles. In addition to the relation of identity, such a theorist claims to find a constitution relation that (in the material case) holds at a time between two spatially co-located objects. This is a relation allegedly holding between ever smaller pieces of cloth and the flag they take turns constituting, between distinct hunks of marble and the statue they successively constitute, or (given our present interests) between the human animal and the person it constitutes at some but not all of the moments it is present. The idea is that although the flag may be battleworn at sunset and sport much less cloth than it did at sunrise, one and the same flag is now constituted by a piece of cloth which once was a mere proper part of the cloth originally serving that purpose. Or although the person before us is constituted by a human organism (which itself is constituted by different

---

[16] Depending on one's views about just which parts are superfluous in our preferred sense, one may wish to make the present point with reference to a mere proper part of a brain—perhaps a cerebrum. Curiously, though, whereas an animal may survive being pared down to a brain, it is not at all clear that it may survive being pared down to a cerebrum. Again, see Olson, *The Human Animal*.

aggregates of particles at different times) that very organism had prenatal stages during which it did not constitute any person at all.[17]

Although they are co-located (and are even sometimes taken to share all of their proper parts at a time), the constitutor and constitutee are nevertheless said to be numerically distinct on the grounds that they differ in their persistence conditions (and usually differ in their temporal properties, as well). Yet, despite this distinctness, objects in the constitution relation are so closely tied as to inherit properties from one another—such that if x is F (straightforwardly) and x constitutes or is constituted by y, then y is F (derivatively). The resulting view proves to be a very powerful tool in constructing solutions to outstanding puzzles involving simples, composites, persistence, and change.[18] Whether the solutions are the best to be had is under dispute (I, for one, reject them), but the current point is not to challenge the truth of the constitution theory on which they depend. Suppose this rather popular theory is true.

Then my primary thesis follows straightaway. The human animal is one thing the human person another. Although the person comes onto the scene considerably later than (and sometimes departs considerably earlier than) the animal, throughout its career the person derivatively sports the property of being human by inheriting it from the human animal that constitutes it. Moreover, there is no objection in principle to the person outliving the animal should some distinct material (or perhaps even immaterial) thing come to constitute the same person at later times, in which case it would cease to count as a human animal or else would qualify as human only in virtue of its historical properties.

So far so good. But there is another version of the constitution theory worth mentioning in this context. As it was above, the constitution relation is ordinarily taken to be a relation between two objects. Many of the advantages of orthodox constitution theory could be retained and some of the disadvantages sidestepped, however, if it were instead taken to be a relation between an object and some stuff. Such a move requires a fundamental rethinking of the ontology of space fillers, but a proponent of this view can certainly make the familiar case that the gains in resolving outstanding puzzles involving simples, composites, persistence, and change are well worth the metaphysical costs.[19]

With only one *object* among the relata, it may appear that we would again face some pressure to identify the human person with the human animal. Fortunately, though, the pressure is relieved by even stronger pressure arising from an interplay

---

[17] For a book-length treatment of constitution theory, see Baker, *Persons and Bodies* (together with Theodore Sider's review from the *Journal of Philosophy*, 99 (2002), 45–8). For a slightly different approach, see Kevin Corcoran, "Persons, Bodies and the Constitution Relation", *Southern Journal of Philosophy*, 37 (1999), 1–20, and "Persons and Bodies", *Faith and Philosophy*, 15 (1998), 324–40.

[18] For an excellent introduction to the puzzles in question and the variety of solutions on offer, see Sider, *Four-Dimensionalism*.

[19] See Ned Markosian, "Simples, Stuff, and Simple People", *The Monist*, 87 (2004).

of principles presupposed by such a metaphysics to identify the human person with some stuff that (may or may not) constitute a material object. Without divulging the details, suffice it to say that a dualistic stuff/thing ontology of space fillers, supplemented by a constitution relation uniting some stuff with a material object, ultimately takes a human person to be something rather unexpected while firmly counseling against identification with a human animal.[20]

9. THE DOCTRINE OF THE GENERAL RESURRECTION OF THE BODY

So, addressing ourselves to three-dimensionalist materialists who deny universalism, DAUP, any theory of composition or decomposition that yields brains, and either version of constitution theory:

Either the Christian doctrine of the general resurrection of the body is true or it is not. (Note to the potentially alarmed reader: I understand that the doctrine of the resurrection presents a rather different kind of decision point than do general metaphysical principles about persistence, composition, decomposition, and constitution, and I am not trying to suggest otherwise in this section. However, since a respectable number of theorists still in the target audience are advocates of this particular Christian doctrine, it is fair game.)

The materialist who accepts the doctrine of the general resurrection has some tough choices to make. Such a theorist can accept the replica view according to which individuals (numerically distinct but more or less physically and psychologically indistinguishable from the departed) will rise on the appointed day and will carry on as our successors in the world to come.[21] But this is a non-starter; forfeiting genuine identity is thoroughly at odds with the relevant texts, the staggering tradition of commentary, and the common conviction that the same individual (and indeed, the same body) is resurrected.[22]

Or the materialist can accept the simulacra view according to which God snatches away a body immediately upon its death substituting a simulacrum to be buried and decompose in the place of what we thought were the remains of our beloved. [23] Curiously, however, on this view God perpetrates a systematic and large-scale deception on creaturely persons.

---

[20] Ibid. and see Markosian's forthcoming book-length discussion of these matters.

[21] See John Hick, *Philosophy of Religion* (Englewood Cliffs, NJ: Prentice-Hall, 1983), for a presentation of the replica view.

[22] See Caroline Walker Bynum, *The Resurrection of the Body in Western Christianity, 200–1336* (New York: Columbia University Press, 1995), for a discussion of the same-individual/same-body tradition.

[23] Peter van Inwagen, "The Possibility of Resurrection", *International Journal of Philosophy of Religion*, 9 (1978), 114–21. Note that whereas the view originated with van Inwagen, it was put forth as an answer to a "so-just-how-can-it-be-done challenge" and not as a thesis fully endorsed by its author.

Or the materialist can accept a version of the constitution view just discussed according to which the same person will rise again on the appointed day and will be constituted anew by a new and imperishable body in the world to come.[24] Determining whether the new body is or is not the original animal is no longer crucial to determining the identity of the person, though, since the person is merely constituted by the animal and since constitution is not identity. Whereas there is some room for suspicion that this is just the replica view in disguise (and that at best new persons with mental contents and capacities qualitatively identical to those of the departed will be created in the world to come), any return to the constitution view is a return to the argument of Section 8 above and its conclusion that the human person is distinct from the human animal.

Or the materialist can accept anti-criterialism according to which there simply are no criteria of personal identity.[25] The anti-criterialist can claim to know *that* the dead will be resurrected (on the basis of revelation) while conceding that there is no hope for (and no need of) an explanation regarding *how* this miracle will occur. Some of the most prominent proponents of the identification of human persons with human animals, however, take their view to speak heavily in favor of a bodily criterion of personal identity, and thus would have a difficult time reconciling their identification hypothesis and their reasonably well-worked out views on the persistence conditions of human organisms with anti-criterialism.[26]

Or the materialist can accept the so-called 'jumping animals' view according to which immediately before death one's body undergoes a fission, one branch of which dies and decomposes, and one branch of which jumps a temporal gap into the afterlife. Accordingly, one enters paradise with a body-stage that bears immanent-causal relations to one's body-stages at some moments immediately prior to death.[27] First, whereas it does better than some historical accounts by at least requiring a death—it is perhaps worthy of note that the individual who dies is not the individual resurrected. Be that as it may, however, the much more worrisome feature (compellingly exposed by Zimmerman, who introduced the view into the literature) is that this proposal commits its proponents to a "closest-continuer" theory of personal identity. In short, the jumping animals view yields the unpalatable consequence that whether or not an individual who arrives in the afterworld as a result of a fission is the very same individual

---

[24] See Baker, *Persons and Bodies* 2000 and her "Material Persons and the Doctrine of Resurrection", *Faith and Philosophy*, 18 (2001), 151–67.

[25] See Trenton Merricks, "Physicalism and Immortality: How to Live Forever without Saving Your Soul", in Kevin Corcoran (ed.), *Soul, Body and Survival: Essays on the Metaphysics of Human Persons* (Ithaca, NY: Cornell University Press, 2001).

[26] See particular, the lengthy treatment of this subject in Olson, *The Human Animal*. For a critique of anti-criterialism in general, see Dean Zimmerman, "Criteria of Identity and the 'Identity Mystics'", *Erkenntnis*, 48 (1998), 281–301. Merricks is one animalist who is not open to the complaint registered in the text, however.

[27] See Dean Zimmerman, "The Compatibility of Materialism and Survival: The 'Falling Elevator' Model", *Faith and Philosophy*, 16 (1999), 194–212.

who was born among men (rather than a new creation) can depend entirely on what happens in the other branch of the fission. But to the extent that one thinks that closest-continuer theories posit unacceptable noncausal counterfactual correlations between distinct existants one must regard the jumping animals view with suspicion.[28]

Finally, the materialist can accept the four-dimensionalist universalist's approach to reconciling materialism with the general doctrine of the resurrection. Elsewhere I have put forth a defense of the reconciliation of materialism with the doctrine of the general resurrection which (I believe) bests its rivals by invoking the resources of four-dimensionalism and universalism,[29] but the significance of this resolution for our present concern is just that any return to four-dimensionalism and universalism is a return to the arguments of Sections 4 and 5 above and their common conclusion that the human person is distinct from the human animal.

Given the options just canvassed, then, I suggest the materialist proponent of the doctrine of the general resurrection can best avoid significant objections to his combination of views by relinquishing the human-persons-are-human-animals thesis.

10. ELIMINATION PRINCIPLES AGAIN

There is, of course, lots of room for disagreement here! I acknowledge that my dismissal of *the fanciful thought experiment defense* may have been uncharitable and over-hasty, that the many-persons solution to the Problem of the Many may be more reasonable than I suggested (in n.1), or that my critical evaluation in one of the foregoing sections may have been mistaken. I should think, however, that the most vulnerable feature of the foregoing discussion is the elimination principle. One reasonable response at this juncture is to agree about the maximality of human persons, concede the need for an elimination principle, but then formulate and defend a strikingly different one. Permit me to offer my opponent some ammunition.

Assume once again that we have a solitary person on a chair at T. Assume once again the notion of a non-superfluous object (i.e. an object in the vicinity of the chair at T which manifests properties and relations at T that are among the properties and relations that are subsumed under the supervenience laws then in play). Here are six elimination principles that can each claim (to some degree) the distinction of being non-arbitrary:

[28] For an insightful discussion about just what is (and isn't but is often thought to be) wrong with closest-continuer theories, see Katherine Hawley, "Fission, Fusion, and Internal Facts: Why Only X and Y?" (unpublished).

[29] In ch. 7 of my *A Materialist Metaphysics of the Human Person*, from which the brief descriptions of the preceding five views were adapted and in which one may find a more sustained discussion of the advantages and shortcomings of the competing materialistic positions on the matter.

From all of the relevant candidates (with at most one human person between them) each of which has all of the non-superfluous objects among its parts, the best candidate for the person in question is to be identified with:

(EP1) the mereologically largest object;
(EP2) the mereologically smallest object;
(EP3) the mereologically largest object falling under a natural kind;
(EP4) the mereologically smallest object falling under a natural kind;
(EP5) the mereologically largest living object;
(EP6) the mereologically smallest living object.

Of course, (EP1) should be immediately rejected by anyone who thinks a composite object can have a person as a proper part, and (EP2) is just a version of the elimination principle I have already advocated.

A quick aside: *Question*—but aren't you relying on the unsupported assumption that there will be a unique mereologically smallest object satisfying the relevant conditions? *Reply*—no such assumption is in force: should there be two equally small candidates, then the elimination principle doesn't give the wrong verdict, rather it gives no verdict at all, for the condition in its antecedent which requires that at most one of the candidates is a human person fails to be satisfied.[30]

But (EP3)–(EP6) are somewhat plausible proposals. Perhaps, (EP3) and (EP4) will select the same individual, as will (EP5) and (EP6), but I suppose that's debatable. Nevertheless, what is significant (given our present purposes) is that each of (EP3)–(EP6) can plausibly be thought to select the human animal as the winning candidate.

I am not here at liberty to venture off into a discussion that explains why I find the notion of a natural kind too obscure and the notion of being alive insufficiently relevant to ground a principle whose job it is to select a person from a list of candidates. Accordingly, anyone who finds these avenues of escape attractive has not yet encountered any obstacle from me in pursuing them. Still, I did not want to pass them over in silence, since it seems to me that the best objection to my thesis lies here, and since I am interested in the outcome of others' efforts to upend it.

11. SUMMING UP

Notwithstanding the plausible rivals to (EP) discussed in the preceding section, my own favored version of the elimination principle and the arguments I have

---

[30] I say this because if neither candidate is uniquely smallest, then it would appear that we have a case of mere overlap (as opposed to proper parthood) and that we face the Problem of the Many (as opposed to merely needing to invoke the maximality of 'human person'). But then the two resolutions to the Problem of the Many that I find most congenial agree (albeit for *very* different reasons) that it is not the case that at most one of the two candidates is a human person. See n. 1 above.

produced which invoke it certainly seem right to me. Accordingly, I conclude that holding the human-persons-are-human-animals thesis comes at a fairly high price.

What kind of theorist is left to pay the price? One who (i) is a materialist about human persons, (ii) is a three-dimensionalist, (iii) holds a restricted theory of composition and a restricted theory of decomposition (according to which there is no such thing as a human brain), (iv) takes constitution to be identity, and (v) denies the doctrine of the general resurrection. Once again, to indulge in a bit of biography, I accept (i) and (iv) on this list while firmly rejecting (ii), (iii), and (v). And thus I regard this price as much too high.

Who does not think the price is much too high? This is tricky. Peter van Inwagen and Trenton Merricks hold (i)–(iv), but disagree about the content of Section 9 above which was supposed to show that their adherence to the doctrine of the general resurrection should bring them on the side of my main thesis—with van Inwagen opting for the simulacra view (or else some other three-dimensionalist resolution) and Merricks opting for anti-criterialism. Eric Olson holds (i)–(v), but occasionally writes explicitly as if he rejects (iii) making it difficult for the reader who has access only to his book on this topic (and not to conversations with him or to his other works) to see how he would wish to counter the content of Section 7 above.[31]

Still, these philosophers hold consistent and respectable views that allow them to endorse the human-persons-are-human-animals thesis. What is often overlooked, however, is that adherence to that thesis is *much* more widespread than is adherence to the carefully crafted collection of metaphysical views that it seems to require as support. Accordingly, I suggest that those materialists who are absolutely wedded to the thesis should sign up for a van Inwagean or Merricksish or Olsonian metaphysics of composition and decomposition. On the other hand, if denying the existence of the human brain turns out to be really too high a price to pay, they should relinquish that thesis on the grounds that it is defensible only on an impoverished view of what material things there are.

---

[31] See van Inwagen, *Material Beings*; Trenton Merricks, *Objects and Persons* (Oxford: Clarendon Press, 2001); and Olson, *The Human Animal*, for three excellent book-length discussions of combinations of views that leave the target thesis intact.

PART IV

EMBODIMENT AND THE VALUE OF PERSONS

10

On the Intrinsic Value of Human Persons

Philip L. Quinn

In this paper I offer an answer, which is no doubt incomplete, to the question of what makes human persons intrinsically valuable. Two ways in which my inquiry is limited are worth mentioning at the outset. First, its scope is limited to human persons. For all I know, humans are not the only kind of persons; perhaps there are angels or demons who are also persons. If there are, they may differ essentially from human persons; maybe they are essentially disembodied, while human persons are essentially embodied. It might turn out that something to do with their having or being bodies contributes to the intrinsic value of human persons. If that were the case, it would be natural to expect that what makes human persons intrinsically valuable overlaps but does not coincide completely with what makes angelic or demonic persons intrinsically valuable. I am not concerned in this paper with what might make nonhuman persons of various sorts intrinsically valuable. Nor am I interested in what would make persons as such, including persons of both human and nonhuman kinds, intrinsically valuable. Second, my inquiry focuses on the intrinsic rather than instrumental value of human persons. To take an extreme example, human slaves are instrumentally valuable to their masters. In familiar systems of slavery, slaves constitute a form of wealth owned by their masters. They can be traded or sold in order to secure other things that the masters desire. They can also be forced to produce assets, such as sugar or cotton crops, that their masters can then trade or sell. In such ways, a slave is a mere instrument of the master's will. But human slaves also have value that is intrinsic to them as persons and distinct from their instrumental value to their masters.

It is also worth emphasizing that this is not a paper about the metaphysics of human persons. I do not discuss in it the fascinating topic of personal identity through time; I take no stand on the issue of whether human persons are enduring things or perduring things. What is more, I avoid questions about the nature or

I presented my preliminary thoughts on some of the issues discussed in this paper at a Pew Workshop held in Princeton, New Jersey, on 5 and 6 February 2004. I am grateful to the other participants in the Workshop for critical and constructive suggestions that helped me to clarify and refine the rather inchoate ideas about violations of human personhood with which I began work on this topic.

constitution of human persons when I can. I try to remain as close to neutral as is possible on the question of whether human persons are unextended thinking substances related to bodies as pilots are to ships they steer, or are bodies that are biological organisms, or are tiny physical particles lodged somewhere in gross macroscopic bodies, to mention just a few of the possibilities. However, some of the claims about the intrinsic value of human persons that I shall endorse are in tension, if not outright conflict, with certain metaphysical views of the nature of human persons. I shall in one instance make the tension explicit, but when I do, I shall not attempt to resolve it. I shall therefore not try to evaluate arguments from premises concerning the intrinsic value of human persons to conclusions concerning the falsity or improbability of views about the nature of human persons.

My approach to the question of what makes human persons intrinsically valuable will be indirect. Its starting point is the issue of what bad things that are done or happen to human persons count as violations of their personhood. As it happens, this negative method of addressing the question is employed in several other recent discussions of the value of persons on which I shall draw in the course of my inquiry. Thus a pragmatic rationale for my approach is that it will facilitate making connections with these helpful discussions. I believe there is also a more substantive justification for the approach I have adopted. As we shall see, there are many ways in which the personhood of human beings can be violated. An adequate understanding of what makes human persons intrinsically valuable ought to be broad enough to enable us to comprehend why it is that violations of human personhood of all kinds are in some sense transgressions against what makes human persons intrinsically valuable. Judged by this standard, rationality, which I take to be the leading candidate for what makes human persons intrinsically valuable in the history of Western philosophy, is too narrow to enable us to understand the full range of violations that transgress against the intrinsic value of human persons. There are violations that transgress against the intrinsic value of human persons that do not violate their rationality.

The paper is divided into four sections. In the first, I set the stage for my inquiry by providing a sketch of some of its historical and religious background. The second clears the ground for what is to follow by arguing that rationality does not comprise the whole of what makes human persons intrinsically valuable. The third section, which is the heart of the paper, discusses other characteristics of human persons whose violation transgresses against the intrinsic value of persons of this kind. It focuses on violations of human bodies, particularly sexual violations. In the fourth and final section, I draw some conclusions from the discussion in the second and third parts. My main conclusion is that the intrinsic value of human persons is grounded in a plurality of factors, many of which involve essentially aspects of the human body. The paper thus supports a rejection of the devaluation of the human body that has been an element in some religious traditions.

1. STAGE SETTING

According to Nicholas Wolterstorff, if we wish to identify the theme in Christian thought that provides a reason for favoring the political arrangements typical of modern liberal democracies, we must turn our attention to the great evil of violating human persons. He thinks premodern Christians failed to give sufficient weight to this evil. Appealing to what he describes as historical speculation, Wolterstorff suggests that there is a connection between the increasing weight given to violations of persons by the people of early modern Europe, most of whom were Christians, and the rise of liberal political institutions. Simply put, the suggestion is that

the origins of the liberal polity lie in the people of western Europe, in the sixteenth and seventeenth centuries, slowly giving ever greater weight to the evil of violating a human being's personhood, slowly coming to a more expansive view as to when this evil occurs, and slowly coming to acknowledge that the religious pluralization of their societies meant that forcibly cultivating in others their own understanding of human well-being would require more and more pervasive violation of persons.[1]

He apparently regards this slow process as a transformation of sensibility that goes beyond a mere alteration of opinion. What happened to the people of western Europe, he says, was that "they were increasingly horrified by the violation of the person which occurs in, for example, burning people at the stake for their religious convictions".[2] Such violations more and more came to evoke horror in addition to being judged to be evil.

Wolterstorff's attempt to defend the liberal polity in terms of its potential for preventing, or at least mitigating, the evil of violations of human persons seems to me to place him within the tradition of modern liberal thought that Judith Shklar has called "the liberalism of fear".[3] As she characterizes this tradition, it puts first among the ordinary vices cruelty, which is defined as "the willful inflicting of physical pain on a weaker being in order to cause anguish and fear".[4] Montaigne stands at the origin of this tradition. The sight of cruelty filled him with revulsion; it horrified him because of the anguish and fear it produced; he hated it with the utmost intensity. But, as Shklar sees it, putting cruelty unconditionally first

---

[1] Nicholas Wolterstorff, "Do Christians Have Good Reasons for Supporting Liberal Democracy?", *Modern Schoolman*, 78/2 & 3 (2001), 248.

[2] Ibid.

[3] I spell out the affinities between Wolterstorff's position and the liberalism of fear in more detail in Philip L. Quinn, "Can Good Christians Be Good Liberals?", in Andrew Chignell and Andrew Dole (eds.), *God and the Ethics of Belief* (Cambridge: Cambridge University Press, 2005).

[4] Judith Shklar, *Ordinary Vices* (Cambridge, Mass., and London: Harvard University Press, 1984), 8.

consists of more than just responding to it with horror and hating it intensely. It also involves finding it without justification or excuse. Before the sixteenth century, there were no doubt sensitive inquisitors who were horrified to see their victims burning at the stake or in agony on the rack. Since they were convinced that their behavior was divinely sanctioned, however, they considered themselves justified in tormenting unrepentant heretics. There is neither justification nor excuse for inflicting such cruelty on unrepentant heretics for those who put cruelty first. Shklar concludes that putting cruelty first conflicts with practicing a revealed religion. She says: "To hate cruelty with utmost intensity is perfectly compatible with Biblical religiosity, but to put it *first* does place one irrevocably outside the sphere of revealed religion."[5]

This conclusion is surely too strong. Putting cruelty first will constrain what one can regard as revealed truth. One will have to deny, for example, that putative divine commands to engage in cruel conduct are genuine deliverances of revelation. Taking up a critical attitude toward claims that have historically been advertised as revealed truth may in turn lead to a broader skepticism about claims that are purported to be deliverances of revelation. In the case of Montaigne, it is understandable that skepticism became quite extensive. He was acutely aware of the cruelty practiced by Europeans on one another in the name of Christianity in the course of the Wars of Religion as well as of the cruelty practiced by Spaniards, again in the name of Christianity, in the course of their conquests in the Americas. But none of these factors will necessarily drive anyone completely outside the sphere of revealed religion. After all, not all of the purported content of Christian revelation consists of injunctions to practice cruelty or of doctrines that might plausibly serve to justify or excuse cruel behavior.

When we expand our vision from the ordinary vice of cruelty to the entire spectrum of evils that count as violations of human persons, we may not wish to accept all of the sharp and dramatic contrasts built into Shklar's picture of the liberalism of fear. That picture is, I think, best viewed as a Weberian ideal type rather than a realistic portrait. Thus we need not suppose that violations of human personhood are unconditionally first among evils. It is enough to assume that preventing violations of human persons has come to have a very high priority in modern liberal thought and that it moved up in the ranking of evils to be avoided during the transition to modernity. Similarly, we need not suppose that there are absolutely no justifications or excuses, religious or secular, for violations of human persons. It is enough to assume that the transition to modernity brought with it a significant decrease in the number and kinds of justifications or excuses for such violations whose legitimacy can be taken for granted. And we need not imagine that modern feelings of horror at violations of human persons, particularly bodily violations, are qualitatively different from the affective responses to such violations

---

[5] Judith Shklar, *Ordinary Vices* (Cambridge, Mass., and London: Harvard University Press, 1984), 9.

found in premodern cultures. It is enough to grant that such reactive attitudes have in the modern era become more openly acknowledged, more widely discussed and cultivated, and more routinely accepted as a basis for political conduct.[6] We should not think that all our premodern ancestors were insensitive brutes.

How are we to delimit the range of things that count as violations of human persons? The outline of an answer to this question set forth by Wolterstorff begins with a short list of the targets of violation. First on the list is the person's body. According to Wolterstorff, my body is my own both because it belongs to me in a way that possessions such as a house or car do not and because it is determinative of the narrative that specifies who I am. Next on the list is the person's inner life. My inner life, composed of my thoughts and feelings, hopes and fears, dreams and fantasies, is my own because it too belongs to me in a particularly intimate manner and is constitutive of my narrative identity. The final two items on the list involve moving out from the core of the person's body and inner life to the person's deepest convictions, religious and moral, and fundamental ways of being invested in or attached to the surrounding world. As Wolterstorff sees it, my deepest convictions and fundamental ties to the world are my own in the same double sense as my body and my inner life are. He therefore specifies the targets of violation in the following manner: "violation of a person—or to put the same thing in other words, of a human being's personhood—occurs when someone does something to that person's body, that person's inner life, that person's deep moral and religious convictions, that person's deep investment in the world."[7] Of course, as Wolterstorff knows perfectly well, not everything that is done to a human being's body, inner life, fundamental convictions, or deep investments is violative of personhood. So his next task is to explain how things that are one's own are being treated when one's personhood is violated.

At this point, Wolterstorff's discussion makes contact with a claim about violation made by Robert Adams, whose views will be considered in more detail later in this paper. Adams thinks he can identify two necessary conditions for violating personhood. He spells out the first of them as follows: "An act that violates a person must *attack* the person. Its foreseeable effects must be so damaging to the person, or so contrary to her (actual or presumed) will, that fully intending them, in the absence of reason to believe them necessary for the prevention of greater harm to her, would constitute hostility toward the person."[8] He formulates the second in this way: "A violation is an act that attacks the person *seriously* and *directly*. Most (but not all) violations of a person will assault her body."[9] For Adams,

---

[6] Transformations in modern European attitudes toward the human body are discussed in detail in Roy Porter, *Flesh in the Age of Reason* (New York and London: Norton, 2003).

[7] Wolterstorff, "Do Christians Have Good Reasons", 245.

[8] Robert Merrihew Adams, *Finite and Infinite Goods: A Framework for Ethics* (New York and Oxford: Oxford University Press, 1999), 108.

[9] Ibid.

then, an act is a violation of a person only if it is a serious and direct attack on the person.

Wolterstorff denies that this condition of direct and serious attack on a person is necessary for being a violation of a person. He grants that violations often do take the form of such attacks, but he insists that they do not always do so. He draws attention to two sorts of cases that he takes to be counterexamples. Wolterstorff thinks he would violate the personhood of one of his children if he came across and secretly read the child's diary. He also believes that one would violate their personhood if one secretly watched a couple having intercourse by looking through a one-way mirror. Yet neither the secret reading nor the secret watching would be serious and direct attacks on persons; they would instead be, as Wolterstorff puts it, unwanted intrusions in the personhood of their victims. In the same vein, he claims that eavesdropping violates the person who is its victim, even if it remains undiscovered by the victim and the information it yields is never acted on by the perpetrator. Wolterstorff sums up the way in which he parts company with Adams in this way: "Violation, so I suggest, may take the form of unwanted intrusion as well as the form of direct and serious attack."[10] His conception of which actions constitute violations of human personhood is therefore broader than the conception proposed by Adams.

In this dispute, I am inclined to side with Adams in favoring a narrower conception of which actions to count as violations of personhood, though I admit that my reasons for doing so are not strong enough to be conclusive. I follow Adams in thinking that we may sometimes rely on our sense of what is morally horrible as an indicator of violations of personhood, though I grant that its guidance is fallible. Wolterstorff's examples of secret reading and secret watching do not evoke moral horror in me; I take their failure to do so to give me reason to think that they are not cases of the violation of personhood. Moreover, I do not respond to eavesdropping with feelings of moral horror. To be sure, neither does Wolterstorff. He remarks that "eavesdropping, though a violation of the person, strikes me as more despicable than horrible."[11] But he views the failure of eavesdropping to evoke moral horror as showing only that the moral emotion of horror is a somewhat less reliable clue to when a person has been violated than Adams takes it to be. I am certainly not able to refute his position on this matter. Indeed, I doubt that philosophy will ever contain the resources to provide a decisive resolution of disagreements of this sort.

I have been dwelling on this disagreement because of its methodological significance. It seems to me to indicate that our ordinary conception of violations of human personhood has vague boundaries in some respects. Hence we may expect there to be both paradigm cases and borderline cases of such violations. When I reflect on examples Wolterstorff mentions, I find myself thinking that killing people on account of their religious convictions is a paradigm case of

---

[10] Wolterstorff, "Do Christians Have Good Reasons", 245.   [11] Ibid. 244.

violating human personhood while secretly watching a couple copulating through a one-way mirror is at best only a borderline case. So I doubt that our ordinary conception will support a very precise delimitation of the range of things that count as violations of human persons. We might, of course, impose precision by defining a technical notion of violating a human person, and there could be good theoretical reasons for regimenting the discussion in this way. If this move has not been made, however, we should appeal to examples of putative violations of personhood with some caution. We should not rest much weight on an example unless we can be confident that it falls among or is very similar to the paradigm cases of violating a human person. Since I will not be introducing a technical notion of violating personhood into the subsequent discussion in this paper, I will keep the cautionary note I have just sounded in mind as I proceed.

I draw two lessons from the discussion so far. First, violations of human persons have, as the result of historical developments in the modern period, ascended in the ranking of great evils that urgently claim our attention. It would be a mistake to associate these developments exclusively with the rise of a secular moral culture in the West. Though change has occurred at different rates in different locations, moral worldviews, both religious and nonreligious, all over the globe have been or are being transformed by these developments. Second, central cases of violating a human person involve attacks on something related to the person in some particularly intimate way such as the person's body or the person's inner life. In order to flesh out this abstract description of violations, more must be said about what is attacked when violations occur. It seems initially plausible to suppose that what is assaulted when persons are violated is whatever it is that makes persons intrinsically valuable. What might that be?

2. RATIONALITY

It is tempting to think that what makes human persons intrinsically valuable must be something that all and only human beings possess. For it seems that most of us attribute to human persons a value that is higher than, and perhaps even different in kind from, the value we ascribe to anything else on earth. If forced, for example, to choose between saving the life of a human child and saving the life of an adult sheep, most of us would not hesitate to save the child and would, in so doing, regard ourselves as having shown proper respect for the values at stake in the choice. What grounds this difference in value between human beings and sheep? According to Robert Adams, "*rationality* is the answer most often given, historically and today."[12] The appeal of this answer should not be surprising. A famous definition has it that human beings are rational animals. If we accept this

---

[12] Adams, *Finite and Infinite Goods*, 115.

definition, we will secure an attractive economy in our thought if we suppose that rationality, which is the specific difference between human beings and all other animals, is also the ground of the difference in value between human beings and all other animals. It is then only a small step to the conclusion that rationality is what makes human persons intrinsically valuable, since rationality makes human persons uniquely valuable, as far as we can tell, among terrestrial beings.

If the proposal that rationality is what makes human persons intrinsically valuable is to be illuminating, more needs to be said about what rationality is. Perhaps it is uncontroversial that rationality is a system of complex capacities, but philosophers have disagreed sharply about which capacities are components of the system. Hume reduced practical reason to the capacity to reason about means to ends independently fixed by desire. According to Kant's more capacious understanding of practical reason, it also includes the capacity to set ends, the capacity for self-legislation, and the capacity to transcend natural causation. If rationality is to be what makes human persons intrinsically valuable, an acceptable account of rationality must satisfy some constraints. It should attribute rationality to all human persons, because we are committed to holding that all human persons have this value. And it should attribute equal rationality to them all, since we are also committed to the view that all human persons are equally valuable. Perhaps it should deny rationality to anything on earth other than human persons; many of us think that nothing on earth other than human persons has value of this special kind.

Judged in terms of these constraints, neither Hume's nor Kant's account of practical rationality fares well. Because it is doubtful that any human person has the capacity to transcend natural causation, it is far from clear that Kant's account satisfies the first constraint. What is more, both the capacity to set ends and the capacity to reason instrumentally are possessed by different human persons to different degrees, and so both Hume's and Kant's accounts clearly fail to satisfy the second constraint. A natural response to this difficulty would be to construct a special notion of rationality that does not admit of degrees. In a discussion of the grounds of respect for human persons, Avishai Margalit proposes a threshold concept. He says: "We can determine that the threshold that justifies respecting humans as opposed to animals is their ability to act for a reason. This threshold guarantees respect for every person capable of acting on the basis of reasons."[13] In short, all those whose capacity falls above the threshold deserve equal respect. Concerned with grounds for equal regard for persons as persons, Adams suggests to the rationality theorist a similar idea. His proposal is this: "Rational agency may be a plausible candidate; we could say that one has enough rationality to be a rational agent, and to be as much a rational agent as anyone else (though not

---

[13] Avishai Margalit, *The Decent Society*, tr. Naomi Goldblum (Cambridge, Mass., and London: Harvard University Press, 1996), 65.

as rational in *every* sense), if one is able *at all* to do something *for a reason*."[14] In other words, all those who are rational agents deserve equal regard.

Rational agency as understood by Adams will be equal in all who possess it, and so it will ground an attribution of equal intrinsic value to them all. However, this proposal confronts two other familiar difficulties. The first is that not all human beings are rational agents in this sense; the examples often cited to make this point are irreversibly comatose humans and severely defective human neonates. One might respond to this difficulty by denying that such human beings are persons, and one could then continue to maintain that all human persons are rational agents and so equal in intrinsic value on that account. However, denying personhood to the irreversibly comatose and severely defective neonates will not seem an attractive option to anyone who fears that such a denial will make it more likely that they will suffer from abuses to which they are more vulnerable than normal human persons. The second difficulty is that some nonhuman primates will probably turn out to be rational agents in the sense specified by Adams. Consider, for example, a well-documented instance of chimpanzee behavior. The chimp wants to eat a banana that is suspended out of reach above him in the cage. So the chimp first moves a box under the banana and climbs up on it, and then he reaches up with a stick and knocks the banana down. It seems fairly clear that the chimp does something for a reason in the course of this behavioral sequence and thus exercises rational agency in the sense presently under consideration. One might respond to this difficulty by ratcheting up the threshold for rational agency to a level at which none of the behavior of any nonhuman animal, no matter how intelligent it may appear to be, will count as an exercise of rational agency. If one takes this tack, however, it seems quite likely that, in order to be consistent, one will be forced to conclude that a large number of human beings lack rational agency because their capacities fall short of the elevated threshold. In sum, if we specify rationality in terms of rational agency, explicated along the lines suggested by Adams, we may be forced to conclude either that not all human beings are rational agents or that some nonhuman animals are rational agents. In either case, rationality thus understood will be at best a problematic candidate for the role of grounding the intrinsic value of human persons as such because all and only human persons have it.

Perhaps these difficulties reveal nothing more than a technical problem with the sort of proposals advanced by Margalit and Adams that could be solved with sufficient ingenuity. However, there seems to me to be a much deeper problem with the attempt to understand what makes human persons intrinsically valuable in terms of rationality alone. It betrays an intellectualist bias. Of course, it is not surprising to find a bias of this kind in texts about the value of human persons, because almost all of these texts have been produced by intellectuals. Yet a few

---

[14] Adams, *Finite and Infinite Goods*, 115.

simple reminders should suffice to convince most intellectuals that any account of what makes human persons intrinsically valuable framed exclusively in terms of rationality or closely allied notions will be too narrow. Such an account will be, as Adams puts it, "much too simple and one-sided".[15] Not all violations of human personhood involve violation of the person's rationality, as is indicated by cases of sexual violation such as rape. If rationality alone is what makes human persons intrinsically valuable, Adams asks, "why should we feel so violated by things that are done to our sexual organs?"[16] The victims of rape do feel violated; rape evokes moral horror in us; and most of us are firmly convinced that these responses are appropriate.

Cases of rape do, of course, vary in the effects they have on their victims. But, in some cases at least, rape does little or nothing to damage or impair the victim's rationality. In such cases, we consider the rape to be a violation of the victim's personhood, even though we acknowledge that it is not a violation of the victim's rationality. Thus we are committed to the view that it is not rationality alone which makes human persons intrinsically valuable. This view strikes me as quite correct; indeed, its correctness seems to me almost blindingly obvious. There are, to be sure, other cases in which rape does long-term damage to the victim's rationality. Even in cases of this sort, however, we do not think that the violation of the victim's personhood consists of nothing but the impairment of rationality produced by the rape. Consider a rape that brings about in its victim a phobia which impairs the victim's capacity to act for reasons. Suppose we agree that bringing about the phobia violates the victim's personhood. The phobia would result from a violation of the victim's personhood if it were drug-induced. Nevertheless, when the phobia is a product of rape, the violation of personhood is worse than it would be if the phobia were produced by slipping a drug into the victim's coffee. The rape itself is, at the very least, an aggravating factor in the total violation of the victim's personhood. Depending on how we decide to count violations, we might go so far as to say the victim has been violated twice over, once by the rape itself, considered apart from its consequences, and once by the production of the phobia that is among its consequences. And, again, this way of thinking about rapes that impair the victim's rationality strikes me as entirely sensible and proper.

The upshot is that violation of rationality is not the only kind of violation of human personhood. What makes human persons intrinsically valuable is not exhausted by their rationality. Even though rationality is among the things that make human persons intrinsically valuable, it is not the only thing that performs this function. Once this lesson has been learned, we will be in a position to attend to the variety of ways in which human personhood can be violated. This attention will lead to a fuller understanding of the plurality of grounds for the intrinsic value of human persons and thus to a richer appreciation of their value.

---

[15] Adams, *Finite and Infinite Goods*, 116.   [16] Ibid.

I turn next to an exploration of this variety in which I focus selectively on violations of human persons that involve attacking their bodies.

3. HUMAN BODIES

It might be thought that many of the claims I shall make in what follows about violations of human persons that consist in doing things to their bodies conflict with some metaphysical accounts of the nature of human persons, especially accounts that appeal to substance dualism. Imagine that what I am is an unextended thinking substance, a Cartesian mind. We may suppose that this mental substance is causally related to a portion of unthinking extended substance in such a way that this portion is its body but that the causal linkage in question is as loose as the connection between pilots and the ships they steer. According to this view, the person I am is a mental substance. So it would seem that whatever it is that makes this person intrinsically valuable must be an intrinsic attribute of a mental substance and so can only be something that is itself mental. Rationality, for example, would fit the bill if it were conceived of as a system of wholly mental capacities. It would also seem that whatever violates this person must directly attack something mental, if we equate violations of human personhood with direct and serious attacks on human persons. A violation of the body of this person is not, in and of itself, a violation of this person; such a bodily violation can at most bring about a violation of personhood in this person by causing something bad to happen to the mental substance who is this person. Hence it seems that, on this view, nothing that is done to the body I happen to have is, or even could be, itself a violation of my personhood. And, of course, what holds for me in this regard also holds, *mutatis mutandis*, for every other human person.

I grant that this argument shows that some forms of substance dualism appear to conflict with the view that direct attacks on a person's body can be violations of human personhood. But I deny that all forms of substance dualism, or even all forms of Cartesian dualism, conflict with this view. Subject to correction by Descartes scholars, I conjecture that Descartes himself suggests in some places a dualist position which, when it is suitably developed, avoids even the appearance of conflict with the view in question. Descartes sometimes speaks of the human mind and the human body as being united by a substantial tie. This way of speaking suggests that the person I am is neither the mental substance which is my mind nor the physical substance which is my body; it is instead a third thing, perhaps also a substance, composed of my mind and my body united in a special way. On this view, both my mind and my body are parts or components of the person I am. Hence both violations of my mind and violations of my body, as well as violations of both at once, can qualify as violations of my personhood, because they are sufficiently direct attacks on this person. Some views according to which a human person is composed of a mental substance and a physical substance do not therefore conflict with the claim that direct attacks on a person's body can violate human personhood.

A similar point can, I think, be made about Thomistic accounts of the metaphysical nature of human persons which assert that human persons are composites of soul and body, rather than souls that happen to inhabit bodies. Such accounts do not conflict with the view that human personhood is often violated by bad things done to the bodies of persons. More generally, what seems to matter in determining whether an act counts as a violation of human personhood is whether the target of the violation is related to the person in an especially intimate fashion, not whether the target is metaphysically identical to the person. That is why Wolterstorff's attempt to articulate what the items on his list of targets share in terms of such concepts as intimate belonging and narrative (as opposed to metaphysical) identity appears to be on the right track, even though such concepts are vague and the vagueness is probably ineliminable from them.

Killing and maiming are paradigm cases of violations of human personhood that involve the human body. Adams says: "Killing and maiming, or (to put it more broadly) destruction and lasting damage, are violative independently of questions of voluntary consent. Such acts directly and seriously attack the person whether or not they oppose her will."[17] Killing violates human personhood because it destroys the biological life of the person's body, even if it does not destroy the person on account of the survival of bodily death by a soul which is reunited with a body at the resurrection in order to reconstitute the same human person. Maiming violates human personhood because it does lasting damage to the biological functioning of the person's body, even if normal functioning is fully restored in the person's body after the resurrection. As Adams points out, killing and maiming are sometimes morally justified. Killing in self-defense is perhaps the least controversial example of the morally justified taking of a human life. Amputating a person's leg when doing so is necessary to prevent the person's death from gangrene is a fairly clear case of justified maiming.

Are killing and maiming violative even when they are morally justified? It is hard to say. Support for a positive answer to this question may be forthcoming if we follow Adams in thinking that the response of moral horror tracks violations of human personhood in a fairly reliable manner. For he holds that even justified killings are morally horrible, though they are not morally wrong. He asserts:

Even those who believe, as most people do, that there are at least a few circumstances in which it is right to kill another human being are apt to feel a metaphysical shudder, so to speak, at any prospect of doing it, and rightly so. Not only the death is a bad thing, but being an agent of it is morally horrible, even if morally justified or required.[18]

And I would certainly feel such a metaphysical shudder if faced with the prospect of amputating the gangrenous leg of a fellow spelunker who was trapped with

---

[17] Adams, *Finite and Infinite Goods*, 111.   [18] Ibid. 105.

me in a cave and would otherwise die. It is far from clear, however, that everyone who confronts the prospect of justifiably killing another human being does or should feel an anticipatory shudder. Soldiers preparing to fight in a just war of resistance to aggression by evildoers as monstrous as Hitler are, perhaps, rightly trained not to respond in this way to the prospect of killing enemy combatants. Yet often soldiers who believe they are justified in killing enemy combatants, and do not shudder in advance, are severely traumatized when they kill other human beings in combat. So Adams could take trauma of this sort to be a retrospective indicator that even the justified killing of another human person is morally horrible and hence a violation of personhood.

Adams acknowledges that killing and maiming are things we can do to ourselves. "In these ways," he says, "one can do violence to oneself."[19] I am inclined to doubt that this sort of violence to oneself is always violative of one's personhood. Consider, for example, someone who decides in a cool hour to commit suicide rather than to suffer through a few more weeks while dying of a terminal cancer that is ravaging her body. I think suicide is morally permissible in such circumstances. But is it nevertheless a violation of her personhood? Adams allows that there are cases in which it is very doubtful that being killed was a misfortune for the victim, and maybe he and I could agree that the present example is a case of that sort. He goes on, however, to claim that "even in those cases the killing evokes horror."[20] This killing does not evoke horror in me, and I do not think my response to it is completely idiosyncratic. What differences in the way people respond to the example show, it seems to me, is that the feeling of horror is not likely to be a reliable guide to whether a violation of personhood occurs in the example. So I regard the example as a borderline case. Since I do not wish to put much weight on it, I do not take it to be a decisive counterexample to the claim that killing oneself is always violative of one's personhood. However, I do take it to give me an adequate reason for doubting that claim. What is more, if we alter the example to include the stipulation that the suicide is carried out with the assistance of a physician or a friend, I am not horrified by the actions of anyone who provides such assistance. Thus my doubts about whether killing violates the personhood of the victim also extend to some cases of assisted suicide.

I believe it is significant that in my suicide example, as well as in its amplification to a case of assisted suicide, the killing is in accord with, instead of being outside of or opposed to, the will of the victim. I am therefore also inclined to doubt Adams's claim that killing and maiming are violative of personhood independently of questions of voluntary consent. In the case of maiming, examples of sexual mutilation are worth reflecting on in this connection. Consider the young boys who consented to castration in order to escape the loss of their soprano voices, and consider the men who voluntarily became eunuchs in order to gain the opportunity to rise to positions of great power in the Ottoman Empire. When I

[19] Ibid. 111.   [20] Ibid. 107.

contemplate these cases, I am horrified by the mutilation of male sexual organs in them. And I recognize that it might be objected that the young castrati did not give genuine consent to being mutilated, either because they were too young or too ignorant to give informed consent or because their decisions were engineered by powerful adults. Nevertheless, doubts remain in my mind about whether all the castrati and Ottoman eunuchs suffered violations of their personhood when they were castrated. I would expect Adams to have at least some sympathy for these doubts. When he speaks of sexual relations between consenting adults, he claims that "because of the consent, such relations do not attack, and therefore do not violate, the persons involved."[21] He also notes the existence of cases in which there is authentic consent to sexual behavior that some people do regard with horror. He then says that "in such cases I think we should not accept their sense of horror as establishing that a person has been violated, or that something morally horrifying has been done."[22] And he adds that "this argument is the more compelling to the extent that feelings of revulsion toward voluntary sexual practices are principally a reaction of outsiders, not generally shared by the participants."[23] Of course, male genital mutilation does lasting damage to the bodies of men who undergo it, even when it is consented to, while sexual relations ordinarily do not produce such damage. Yet it seems to me that some legitimate doubt is cast on the claim that voluntary castration is an attack on those who submit to it by the consent. And my own reaction of horror to what was done to the youthful castrati and the Ottoman eunuchs is certainly that of an outsider, apparently not generally shared by the castrati and eunuchs or by others in their social environments. Hence I think there is reason to doubt that the sense of horror I and others like me feel at what was done to them suffices to establish that all of them suffered violations of personhood or that something morally horrifying was done to all of them.

The practices that are often described as female genital mutilation are similar cases that are currently hotly debated. Like many other Western liberals, I am horrified by what is done to the genitals of young women in societies in which such practices are common. But I am hesitant to take my horror to be a reliable indicator that the personhood of the young women is violated, because I know that some of them who understand the moral objections to the practices nevertheless find them acceptable on balance. Such practices are, of course, not above moral criticism, even if it can be reasonably doubted that they are violations of human persons. Judging by what I have read about them, I am fairly confident that they are morally wrong because they are unjust to the young women who are their victims. It is clear, however, that wrongness is not a sufficient condition for violation of human personhood and hence for the propriety of feeling horrified. When he makes this point explicit by citing the example of tax evasion, Adams remarks that "even gross injustices can seem

---

[21] Adams, *Finite and Infinite Goods*, 111.   [22] Ibid.   [23] Ibid.

more appropriate objects of outrage than of horror."[24] From the point of view of refining our moral sensibilities, therefore, we might do well to try to learn how to react to female genital mutilation with outrage rather than horror.

When Adams discusses torture, he is mainly concerned with the infliction of very intense physical pain. Unlike killing and maiming, torture does not always destroy or cause lasting damage to its victims, though it typically does produce such damage. Even when its effects are only temporary, however, it is for Adams a paradigmatic object of moral horror and hence a violation of the personhood of the victim. He also holds that, like killing and maiming, torture is violative of the personhood of the victim whether or not the victim voluntarily consents to it. As he puts it, "if the intensity of pain is so great that we might speak of torture, then I think the consent of the sufferer (if it were ever given) would not remove the moral horror."[25] He tentatively suggests that consent would not cancel the horror because "the most intense pain, even if voluntarily accepted, dominates a person's life in a way that at least threatens, if it does not destroy, all the value of that life to the sufferer."[26] And he goes on to say that "the grip of intense pain on a person's life probably ensures that so much of the person will be unshakably opposed to the pain, no matter what consent may be given to it, that infliction of the pain is bound to have the aspect of a serious and direct attack on the person."[27] This last statement is intriguing because it hints at a picture of the person according to which human persons have the capacity sometimes to be divided against themselves in their response to intense physical pain, with much of the person opposing the pain while some of the person accepts it.

I have doubts about Adams's claim that torture is violative of human person-hood even when the victim consents. In order to articulate them, I shall appeal to an example that is admittedly an extreme case and may also be fictional. According to stories I have read, some Native American tribal societies once had the custom of torturing enemy warriors, who had been captured in battle, to death. The custom was not merely an outlet for sadistic impulses, though it may also have served that function. It was understood by those who lived in these societies, both perpetrators and victims, to be a way of allowing the captives to demonstrate their bravery. They would die with honor if they succeeded in enduring the torture with resolute indifference to their pain. A quick and easy death would be dishonorable, for it would indicate that their captors did not respect them for their bravery. If offered a choice between a quick and easy death and the ordeal of torture to death, a captive would regard the choice of a quick and easy death as cowardly. Better to consent to this last test of one's bravery, since one is going to die anyway! We may imagine a particularly brave captive dying full of contempt for his torturers because they have failed to break his resistance. And we may also imagine that the torturers acknowledge that their victim has proven himself to be a great warrior.

---

[24] Ibid. 105.   [25] Ibid. 110.   [26] Ibid.   [27] Ibid. 110–11.

I do not doubt for even an instant that torturing prisoners of war to death is morally wrong, even if such a trial by ordeal provides a unique opportunity to exhibit bravery. Shaped as they are by modern liberal culture, my sensibilities compel me to judge that the custom I have described displays cruelty in one of its most extreme forms. Even if it is only fictional, the example certainly evokes horror in me when I imagine it vividly. But in this case too I wonder what my sense of horror actually reveals. I am willing to grant to Adams that the torture in the example is a direct and serious attack on the person of the captive warrior. In a way, that is its point. However, since for Adams the condition of direct and serious attack is only a necessary condition for violation of personhood, we cannot legitimately infer from this concession alone that the torture succeeds in violating the personhood of the victim. I am also prepared to grant that the intense pain suffered by the victim threatens the deepest values in his life. For if it breaks him and he begs to be killed, his life will end dishonorably. On the other hand, if he successfully resists complete domination by the pain and dies still defying his captors, those values will not have been destroyed. He will have died honorably and may achieve great renown in tribal traditions. So if the captive warrior consents to the ordeal by torture when offered the alternative of a quick and easy death and if he successfully resists domination by the pain and remains defiant to the end, there may be a sense in which the attack on his personhood fails to violate it or falls short of violating it in a fundamental way. How could this be understood? One way of attempting to render it intelligible would be to say that the tortured warrior is able to identify with something in himself that successfully resists domination by his pain. Another way would be to say that he is able to withdraw into an internal citadel where he is invulnerable to domination by the pain. In speaking of withdrawal into an internal citadel, I am, of course, deliberately invoking stoic imagery. When I do so, I do not mean to suggest that all or even most human persons have the power to execute such a withdrawal and thereby escape domination by physical pain, no matter how bad it gets.

I take the example to give me at least some reason to be suspicious of the claim that torture is violative of human personhood even when the victim consents. More precisely, the claim on which I wish to cast doubt, whether or not it is exactly the claim Adams wants to make, is that torture is violative of human personhood independently of the state of the person's will. But the example is complicated and is sure to prove controversial in several ways. Hence I suppose the example gives me a reason only to doubt and not also to deny these claims and others in the same vicinity.

As Adams sees things, apart from killing, maiming, and torture, "one can be violated only against one's will, or without one's will, or at any rate without one's fully competent consent."[28] His account of rape and other sexual violations emphasizes the involvement of both the victim's body and the victim's will. He

---

[28] Adams, *Finite and Infinite Goods*, 111.

claims: "The involvement of both the will and the body is essential to what horrifies us in sexual violation, which can be contrasted on these points with killing or maiming, on the one hand, and with 'crimes against property,' on the other."[29] Unlike killing or maiming, rape does not always result in the destruction of or lasting damage to the victim's body. Yet rape is violative of the victim's personhood and is rightly felt to be horrible even when there is no serious damage to the victim's body or impairment of its functioning. Hence the involvement of the victim's body does not by itself suffice to account for the moral horror of sexual violations such as rape. Crimes against property, of course, usually do not involve a victim's body and generally are not violations of a victim's personhood.

Adams thinks that the factor which must be added to bodily involvement in order to give an adequate account of the horror of sexual violations is likely to be found in the area of the social definition of selfhood. He asserts that "we may seek it in the thought that the meaning of selfhood, if not the substance of the person, is partly defined by social structures, and that certain boundaries between distinct selves are a crucial part of those structures."[30] Restrictions on sexual contact contribute to fixing the boundary that separates the self from the rest of the world. Crossing this boundary without full consent of the person whose self it helps to define can rightly be seen as an assault on the person's self and hence as a direct attack on the person. Thus understood, such a boundary crossing is a violation of personhood and is rightly seen as morally horrible. Adams takes it to be morally significant that in some cultures people do not respond with horror when sexual boundaries are crossed with full consent but do feel horror when those boundaries are crossed without full consent. In such cultures, he suggests, "the sexual boundary is still seen as important to the meaning of selfhood, but (at least for adults) it is one's own control of one's boundary, rather than conformity to a general rule, that contributes most importantly here to the definition of selfhood."[31] Modern liberal cultures are clearly cultures of this sort. So we will find voluntary control of the sexual boundary crucial to the definition of selfhood and will view involvement of the will as essential to what horrifies us in sexual violations if we subscribe, as Adams and I do, to the central moral assumptions of modern liberal cultures. Yet even if we acknowledge the moral significance of voluntary control of the sexual boundary for the social definition of selfhood, it remains important for understanding the horror of sexual violations that they involve the person's body. Both rape and theft intrude into a rightful sphere of voluntary control without full consent, but rape violates the personhood of the victim while theft typically does not. According to Adams, we are to explain the difference by supposing that the boundary of the sphere of one's property is less important for defining selfhood than one's sexual boundary. The boundaries most important for defining selfhood, including the sexual boundary, must, on his view, "be seen as a tighter perimeter, defining more of an inner sanctum, than

---

[29] Ibid. 109–10.   [30] Ibid. 108.   [31] Ibid. 109.

the privileged sphere of control which typically plays a part in contemporary theories of rights".[32] Presumably the sexual boundary helps to circumscribe the tighter perimeter that defines selfhood, on his view, precisely because it is a bodily boundary and so does not include replaceable possessions such as cars and houses that are not definitive of selfhood.

It seems to me that Adams's discussion leaves an important question unanswered. Why is a sexual boundary important for the social definition of selfhood and thus closely tied to human personhood, while other bodily boundaries that can be drawn do not have this importance? Judging by an example he mentions, Adams feels the force of questions of this sort. He remarks: "To an outside view, nutrition seems as closely connected as sex with our personal being. Yet the force-feeding of a conscious adult, while certainly offensive, and perhaps an outrage, does not seem to reach the same level of horror as rape."[33] Perhaps there are exceptions to this generalization about force-feeding. It seems to me at any rate that force-feeding pork to a devout Muslim who is aware of what is being done to him does rise to the same level of horror as at least some cases of rape. And maybe a similar point could be made with the example of forcing a blood transfusion on an adult Jehovah's Witness. But it is not difficult to understand such cases in terms of socially defined selfhood. Socially defined religious identity is intimately bound up with selfhood for the devout Muslim and the adult Jehovah's Witness, and so it is not surprising that transgressions of the bodily boundaries constitutive of their religious identities tend to be seen as attacks on their selfhood and to evoke feelings of horror. What Adams has to say about the issue that his example of force-feeding is meant to illuminate strikes me as disappointing. After noting that our sense of horror marks sexuality as an area intimately linked to our personhood, he expresses skepticism about whether we will be able to come up with a thoroughly satisfying rationale for the special importance we attribute to sexuality.

Another way of approaching the worry I have is this. In a pluralistic liberal society, there is considerable variation in how deeply people are invested in their sexuality. Some people are completely devoted to religious or artistic vocations. They care deeply about their religious or artistic identities; these identities are closely linked to their selfhood. They may care little or nothing about their sexual identity; this identity is not intimately related to their selfhood. We tolerate and often admire such people, even if we seldom wish to imitate them. Other things being equal, however, we regard the rape of a woman deeply invested in her sexuality, because her socially defined selfhood is most closely tied to her identity as a mother, and the rape of a woman not deeply invested in her sexuality, because her socially defined selfhood is most closely tied to her identity as a servant of God, as more or less equally horrific violations of personhood. As I see it, this casts doubt on whether the appeal to socially defined selfhood can provide all the

---

[32] Adams, *Finite and Infinite Goods*, 110.   [33] Ibid. 116.

resources we need to tell the whole story of why we attribute special importance to the contribution sexuality and its boundaries make to human personhood.

I think the appeal to socially defined selfhood must be supplemented with an appeal to human biology if the whole story is to be told.[34] Though Adams does not bring this point up in his treatment of sexual violations, an important feature of the human condition is that our sexual organs are organs of biological reproduction. The human capacity to reproduce biologically of which our sexual organs are instruments is surely among the things that make human persons intrinsically valuable. It is a capacity for a kind of creativity whose complexity we are only gradually coming to appreciate as our scientific knowledge of human biology increases. Direct and serious attacks on this capacity are violative of human personhood and rightly evoke feelings of moral horror. Because this capacity for biological reproduction is embedded in human sexuality, one of the functions of sexual boundaries in human societies is to define a privileged sphere in which the biological realization of this capacity is contained. As I see it, part of the explanation of the special importance we attribute to sexual boundaries will appeal to their role in protecting the capacity for biological reproduction and regulating its exercise. I find it puzzling that Adams does not draw attention to the connection between human personhood and biological reproduction, mediated by sexuality, in the course of his discussion of sexual violations. It seems to me that his treatment of sexual violations is incomplete and a bit unbalanced because of this omission.

To be sure, reproduction is not the only function of the sexuality of human persons. It is a mistake to regard the contribution of sexuality to what makes human persons intrinsically valuable as exhausted by its role in biological reproduction. Unfortunately, this mistaken has often been made in religious ethics; the result has been distorted teachings about sexual morality in some religious traditions. The distortion seems to me rooted in a view of the human person that reduces sexuality to nothing but a biological phenomenon. Adams's emphasis on the social dimension of human sexuality is a useful corrective to this sort of reductionism. That is why my proposal is to supplement rather than replace it with considerations drawn from human biology. Human sexual boundaries clearly serve legitimate purposes in addition to protecting the capacity for biological reproduction. A rape that destroys or impairs the victim's capacity for biological reproduction is especially horrible because it is a successful attack on a fundamental element of the human person. But rapes violate human personhood and so rightly evoke moral horror, even when they do not destroy or even impair the victim's capacity for biological reproduction.

Most of us feel horror at certain things that are sometimes done to the corpses of human persons. The examples of such things on which Adams focuses

---

[34] In clarifying my own views on sexual violations, I have benefited from reflecting on Claudia Card's *The Atrocity Paradigm: A Theory of Evil* (New York: Oxford University Press, 2002), esp. its chapter on rape in war. Unfortunately, I do not have space in this paper to examine her arguments about atrocities.

are eating the flesh of dead human bodies and using the skin of dead human bodies, as the Nazis did, to make lampshades. Necrophilia seems to me another example. We are horrified at cannibalism, even if the person whose flesh is eaten died of natural causes and so nothing horrible such as killing was done to produce the corpse. And cannibalism evokes horror in us, even if we may think, as in the case of the Donner Party, that it is morally justifiable, or at least excusable, because it is necessary for the survival of human persons who would otherwise starve to death. Should we take our sense of horror at cannibalism to indicate that it is a violation of human personhood? A reason for thinking not is that the corpse whose flesh is consumed by the cannibal seems not to be a human person; the corpse seems to be nothing more than what remains after the person to whom it once belonged has ceased to be or departed.

Adams classifies cannibalism and the making of lampshades from human skin as symbolic violations. He offers two reasons for doing so. First, since we think of what is done to our dead bodies as in some way done to us, we take treating a dead human body as meat or lampshade material to be "profoundly insulting to the deceased person".[35] Second, "acting in a way that expresses a view of the body of a living person as (potential) meat or lampshade material is apt to be in some degree violative of the person (the degree depending in part on the seriousness of the threat that the behavior might reasonably be felt to pose)."[36] As I understand it, his view is that eating human flesh and making lampshades from human skin do not literally violate the personhood of the deceased persons whose dead bodies are employed in these ways. However, such activities do, by our lights at any rate, literally insult those deceased persons. And, because such activities express violative attitudes, they pose a threat of violation to other living persons and on that account may be to some degree violative of the personhood of the living persons thus threatened.

According to Adams, his conception of symbolic violation serves the purpose of "giving objective moral validity to the horror we feel here."[37] Symbolic violations are in some way genuinely horrible. As he recognizes, however, the objective moral validity of symbolic violations is subject to cultural relativity. In the case of cannibalism, he thinks there is not much room for relativity, because eating human flesh seems almost inescapably to mean treating a human corpse as meat. But perhaps this symbolic connection is not altogether inevitable. Adams grants that "if there are cultures in which eating a human body is really honored as a way of gaining possession of some of the 'power' of the deceased, they would not be eating the human body as merely 'meat'."[38] He professes not to have enough understanding of what such a culture might be like to say with confidence whether cannibalism in it would nevertheless be a symbolic violation and hence morally horrible.

---

[35] Adams, *Finite and Infinite Goods*, 128.   [36] Ibid.   [37] Ibid.   [38] Ibid.

I have doubts about one aspect of Adams's discussion of cannibalism. He correctly supposes that in our culture eating a human corpse inescapably has the symbolic meaning of treating it as meat. This he takes to be sufficient to secure objective validity, at least in our culture, for the horror we feel in response to cannibalism. I suspect that the horror we feel at cannibalism lacks objective validity unless the presumption that the person whose corpse is eaten did or would have opposed having her dead body treated as meat is true. In our culture, of course, this is almost always a safe presumption. But consider a case in which it is false. Suppose the leader of a small religious cult whose members live together in a compound somewhere in the mountains of Idaho explicitly states in her last legal will that she wants her closest disciples to consume small bits of her flesh when they have a ceremonial meal together to honor her shortly after her death. Wanting to respect the last wishes of their beloved leader, the disciples do eat parts of her dead body during such a meal, though they all find it unpleasant to do so. It seems that this instance of cannibalism would not be a symbolic violation of human personhood for either of the reasons given by Adams. It would not be insulting to the deceased leader, since she took pains to make it known that she wanted it to happen. Nor would it express any attitudes that pose a threat to other living persons, because we may suppose that the main attitude the disciples express in carrying out their deceased leader's wishes is deep respect for her. Indeed, we may even imagine that the disciples pose a smaller threat to others as a result of their cannibalism than they would otherwise, precisely because their experience of cannibalism was very unpleasant for them. And it is hard to see anything else in the circumstances of the case as described that would make this instance of cannibalism symbolically violative.

Imagine that this incident escapes the notice of the authorities at the time it occurs. Later on, however, it becomes a matter of public knowledge and attracts widespread attention from the media, and I learn about it as a result of the publicity it receives. As an outsider to the cult, I am fairly sure I would find this instance of cannibalism quite disgusting. Maybe I would be horrified. Even if I were, I would doubt the objective moral validity of my emotional response of horror. Perhaps I would also find my feeling of horror inescapable. If I did, I would doubt that this shows anything more than that shared cultural symbols have irresistible power in shaping my subjective feelings. What the example suggests to me is another way, not mentioned by Adams, in which whether activities count as violations of human personhood depends on the wills of the persons involved in them.

4. CONCLUSIONS

My main conclusion is negative: what makes human persons intrinsically valuable is not a single human capacity or characteristic that they possess. I have argued that rationality, which is the leading traditional candidate for the job, is not the only factor that grounds the intrinsic value of human persons. I have also tried to show how the human body is involved in grounding the intrinsic value of human persons in several ways. Many characteristics of our bodies contribute to our intrinsic value as persons; they include its life, its integrity, its unimpaired functioning, its sexuality, and its capacity for biological reproduction. The human will is also involved in grounding the intrinsic value of human persons in a variety of ways.

I am sure that I have not given a complete account of the grounds of the intrinsic value of human persons. In his discussion of what distinguishes human persons from other living things such as dogs and daisies, Adams observes that "it includes rationality, but also emotional, social and creative capacities related to rationality but going beyond it in various ways."[39] Some of these capacities are also among the things that contribute to making human persons intrinsically valuable, as is indicated by our responses to actions that severely impair or destroy them. We are horrified by torture that renders its victims affectless for an extended period of time, reducing them to the level of emotional zombies, even if it does not impair normal bodily functioning. We would also be struck by horror if an evil neuroscientist excised from a victim's brain the parts that provide the biological basis for interacting socially by means of empathetic understanding. And a brutal physical assault that smashed the bones in both hands of an outstanding piano virtuoso would drive our feelings of horror to a high pitch. Actions such as these give us clear examples of direct and serious attacks on their victims. They also seem to be paradigm cases of violations of their victims as persons. There is therefore more to be said about violations of human personhood that can be a source of insight into the many factors which serve to ground the intrinsic value of human persons than what my discussion in this paper has covered.

My discussion of the involvement of the human body in what makes human persons intrinsically valuable has taken the form of critical commentary on Adams's work on violations of human persons because it seems to me to be the best available treatment of this topic. His views are noteworthy for their subtlety and richness of detail. His discussion clearly shows that the human body contributes to grounding the intrinsic value of human personhood in complicated ways. My criticism of his views is directed at the fine details of his accounts of bodily violations of several sorts; it aims to raise doubts about whether he has gotten the details exactly right. I tend to think he has not fully articulated, and may not have accurately grasped, the full range of ways in which the human will is involved in various kinds of violation that also affect human bodies. I hope my disagreements with his views will serve to illustrate two more general points. The first is that there are a lot of issues worth exploring at the level of detail where Adams and I are not of one mind. The second is that it is

---

[39] Adams, *Finite and Infinite Goods*, 117.

unclear how the disagreements between us might be resolved. I am inclined to the pessimistic view that at least some of them cannot be resolved because our conceptual resources do not permit us to achieve the degree of precision that would be required for this purpose. If this is correct, reasonable disagreement is the best that can be hoped for on some of these issues. But even if my pessimism is premature, it is not at all clear to me how further progress might be made toward resolution using familiar philosophical techniques such as constructing hypothetical examples, offering phenomenological descriptions of our emotional responses to such examples, or proposing analyses of the concepts used in the presentation of such examples.

One might wonder whether the plurality of factors that contribute to making human persons intrinsically valuable is unified in some way that we would discern if we stepped back from viewing the details and looked at matters from a more general point of view. It would be natural for religious thinkers to consider the possibility that all these factors contribute in various ways to making human persons sacred. In such a religious perspective, their sacredness would be a plausible candidate for the single theological feature of human persons that makes them intrinsically valuable. And, for religious thinkers for whom the Hebrew Bible is authoritative, understanding the sacredness of human persons in terms of their having been made in the image of God (Genesis 1: 27) would also be natural. Since Wolterstorff and Adams are both Christian theists, it is therefore not surprising that they appeal to the notion of images of God in their discussions of the value of human persons. In the context of remarks on the worth and dignity of human persons, Wolterstorff asserts: "We bear God's image; we are icons of the Holy One."[40] And in the theistic Platonism espoused by Adams, according to which God is the Good, what is postulated to account for the value of human persons "is a transcendent Good, and the sacredness of the image of the transcendent Good that is violated in a horrific evil."[41] I am sympathetic to this theological point of view, though I do not have enough space in this paper to consider it with the thoroughness it deserves. However, I shall conclude by explaining why I think the results of the previous discussion in this paper render the project of understanding the intrinsic value of human persons in terms of their being images of God more problematic than it might otherwise be.

According to mainstream theism, God is not a body and does not have a body. When the capacity of rationality is found in embodied human persons its realization has a bodily basis, but it seems that this capacity could be realized without a bodily basis and hence could be found in a being without a body. Hence it initially seems not too difficult to understand how it could be that both human persons and God are rational, and so it appears that we can make sense of the thought that human persons are images of God in virtue of their resemblance

---

[40] Wolterstorff, "Do Christians Have Good Reasons. . .", 243.
[41] Adams, *Finite and Infinite Goods*, 104.

to God with respect to rationality. If rationality alone were what makes human persons intrinsically valuable, then we would seem to be able to get a good grip on the idea that some respect in which human persons resemble God and so are images of God is what grounds the intrinsic value of human persons. There are, of course, complications that undermine to some extent the initial appearances once they are brought on the scene. Most mainstream theists insist that God is transcendent. As they see it, divine rationality and human rationality differ in many ways; they are at best analogous. And since our understanding of God's rationality is very limited, we do not have a clear understanding of how it is that human persons resemble God with respect to rationality.

But the complications introduced by God's transcendence do not disappear if we adopt the view of what makes human persons intrinsically valuable partially worked out in this paper. And an additional problem arises. For, on this view, the bodies of human persons are deeply involved in what makes human persons intrinsically valuable. The intrinsic value of human persons is thus grounded in part in ways in which they and a God who has no body are not even analogous, indeed are vastly dissimilar. After all, God has no sexual organs and does not reproduce biologically. Because of these vast differences, the task of understanding how it can be that what grounds the intrinsic value of human persons is also made up of respects in which human persons resemble and so are images of God is made more difficult than it would otherwise be. Within the context of Adams's theistic Platonism, it seems fair enough to insist that even the grounds of the intrinsic value of human persons that deeply involve their bodies must, somehow, image God, because they are excellences and God is the paradigm and source of all excellences. For all I know, this claim about imaging God is true, if properly understood. I wish to end, however, with an expression of skeptical doubt about whether we do have a proper understanding of it or can reasonably hope to achieve such an understanding.

11

Persons and the Natural Order

Lynne Rudder Baker

We human persons have an abiding interest in understanding what kind of beings we are. However, it is not obvious how to attain such an understanding. Traditional analytic metaphysicians start with a priori accounts of the most general, abstract features of the world—for example, accounts of properties and particulars—features that, they claim, in no way depend upon us or our activity.[1] Such accounts are formulated in abstraction from what is already known about persons and other things, and are used as constraints on metaphysical investigation of everything else. So, if we accept traditional metaphysics, we should be prepared to yield to abstruse pronouncements—either by giving up our most secure beliefs about the world that we encounter or by abandoning our conception of what those beliefs are really about.

In contrast to traditional metaphysics, a more pragmatic metaphysics does not hold the empirical world in abeyance until we have thoroughgoing accounts of properties and the other topics of traditional metaphysics.[2] Rather, a more pragmatic approach to reality—an approach that elsewhere I have called 'Practical Realism'—reverses the priorities of traditional metaphysics.[3] A Practical Realist starts with the world that people successfully interact with. Instead of holding

Support for this paper comes in part from a grant from the Pew Charitable Trusts. The opinions expressed in this paper are those of the author and do not necessarily reflect the views of the Pew Charitable Trusts. I am grateful to Dean Zimmerman, Gareth B. Matthews, Kevin Corcoran, and Katherine Sonderegger for helpful comments.

[1] For example, see the work of David Lewis, David Armstrong, and Peter van Inwagen. For more recent examples, see Timothy O'Connor and Jonathan D. Jacobs, "Emergent Individuals," *Philosophical Quarterly*, 53 (2003), 540–55, and John Heil, *From an Ontological Point of View* (Oxford: Clarendon Press, 2003).

[2] From a pragmatic point of view, traditional metaphysics has no standards of adequacy other than what is, in Peirce's words, "agreeable to reason"—what we find ourselves inclined to believe. The traditional approach not only makes metaphysics subject to fashion (as Peirce pointed out), but also cuts metaphysics off from all other forms of human inquiry. The more pragmatic philosopher sees the traditional topics to be fanciful unless tethered to something that someone might care about outside the seminar room. Charles Sanders Peirce, "The Fixation of Belief", in *Selected Writings*, ed., Philip P. Wiener (New York: Dover Publications, 1958), 91–112 106.

[3] In *Explaining Attitudes: A Practical Approach to the Mind* (Cambridge: Cambridge University Press, 1995), I developed what I call 'Practical Realism'.

the encountered world hostage to accounts of, say, properties and particulars, the Practical Realist judges accounts of properties and particulars in terms of how well they illuminate matters that everyone—nonphilosophers as well as philosophers—cares about. To use metaphysics as a tool for understanding is not to conflate metaphysics and epistemology; nor is it to follow Quine in taking philosophy to be an extension of science. Rather, it is to pluck metaphysics out of intellectual isolation and to bring it to bear on the world that we all encounter. In this way, metaphysics can earn its keep.

Like David Lewis and Roderick Chisholm, I take ordinary beliefs about human beings and their place in the world to count as data for an ontology that includes persons. But unlike Lewis and Chisholm, I take most substantive a priori commitments to be negotiable. I want to consider the world as we encounter it more or less at face value, and to formulate an ontological scheme that systematizes what we all believe. A Practical Realist seeks a unified theory that hews as closely as possible to what is common currency about the world as we encounter it.

Anyone who takes the world as we encounter it to be ontologically significant—as I do—will be attracted to the more pragmatic line. (By contrast, much traditional metaphysics either has nothing to say about ordinary things that matter, or it treats them in ways that are unrecognizable to science and to common sense.) One way that a more pragmatic metaphysician departs from traditional metaphysics is to accept that what something is most fundamentally may be a matter of what it does, rather than what it is made of. Persons, I believe, are such entities.

'Person', as Locke famously noted, is a forensic term. However, it also denotes a certain kind of being. A metaphysical account of human persons should accommodate well-known established facts. First, there are the facts of biology that situate human persons in the animal world. Darwinism offers a great unifying thesis that "there is one grand pattern of similarity linking all life."[4] Human and nonhuman organisms both find their place in this one grand pattern. Second, there are the facts of self-consciousness that distinguish human persons from other parts of the natural world. People often know what they are thinking, feeling, deciding, etc. They can think about the future, wonder how they are going to die, hope for resurrection. They can reflect on their own motivations—from Augustine in the *Confessions* to former U.S. Presidents in their memoirs. Such descriptions all presuppose self-consciousness: they presuppose beings with the ability to be conscious of themselves from a first-personal point of view. And what they describe is unique to human persons.

The view that I shall propose fully honors both these kinds of fact—the biological facts that pertain to human beings as part of the animal kingdom and, for want of a better word, the "personal" facts that pertain to human beings

---

[4] Niles Eldredge, *The Triumph of Evolution* (New York: W. H. Freeman, 2000), 31.

uniquely. On the one hand, human persons are material objects, subject to all the natural laws that apply to other kinds of material objects.[5] Human persons are wholly part of nature, the product of natural processes that started eons before the existence of our solar system, and that account for the existence of everything in the natural world—from atoms and molecules to solar systems and galaxies. On the other hand, human persons have evolved to have the capacity to think of themselves in the first person. A first-person perspective is the defining property of persons and makes possible their characteristic forms of life and experience.

Not only are human persons a unique part of nature, but also—as I shall urge—they are an *ontologically* unique part of nature.[6] By saying that persons are ontologically unique, I imply that an inventory of what exists leaving out persons would be incomplete. The addition of a person to the world is the addition of a new entity. Being a person is not just a property of some essentially nonpersonal kind of thing. (Fs are essentially nonpersonal if and only if being a person makes no difference to whether or not an F exists.) I realize that many philosophers do not take ontological uniqueness of persons to be a *desideratum* for an account of persons. Such philosophers are often motivated by doubt about the compatibility of persons' being ontologically unique and their being natural products of natural selection. Part of my aim here is to dispel that doubt. (If you do not think that ontological uniqueness of persons is a *desideratum* of an account of persons, then omit the term '*desideratum*' and take my argument to show that if persons are wholly natural, they may still be ontologically unique.) I know of no view of human persons other than the Constitution View that satisfies both these *desiderata* (as I shall continue to say): Human persons are wholly natural, yet ontologically distinctive.

Let me interject a word about my use of the terms 'nature' and 'natural'. I use such terms broadly to apply to anything nondivine or nonsupernatural. So, nature, as I construe it, includes culture.[7] Both biological and cultural processes are natural, in the sense that I intend.

I have set out and defended my view of persons—the Constitution View—elsewhere in detail.[8] Here I want to defend the kind of account that I hold, however the details are worked out, by showing how much better it satisfies the

---

[5] The view that human persons are wholly part of the natural order, I believe, rules out the possibility that human persons have free will, as libertarians conceive of it. They do, however, have free will, as compatibilists conceive of it. See my "Moral Responsibility Without Libertarianism" *Noûs*, 42 (2006), 307–30.

[6] For more detailed arguments, see my "The Ontological Status of Persons", *Philosophy and Phenomenological Research*, 65 (2002), 370–88, and "The Difference that Self-Consciousness Makes", in Klaus Petrus (ed.), *On Human Persons*, (Frankfurt: Ontos Verlag, 2003), 23–39.

[7] In theistic terms, the natural world is the created world, *modulo* angels.

[8] See *Persons and Bodies: A Constitution View* (Cambridge: Cambridge University Press, 2000). Also see "On Making Things Up: Constitution and Its Critics", *Philosophical Topics: Identity and Individuation*, 30 (2002), 31–52. "When Does a Person Begin?" *Social Philosophy and Policy*, forthcoming, contains some further developments of the view.

desiderata than its rivals. After comparing and contrasting three approaches with respect to the *desiderata*, I shall discuss the compatibility of the Constitution View with traditional theism. I hope to show that the Constitution View takes human persons to be wholly in the natural world and wholly material, to come into being without special divine intervention, and yet to be ontologically distinctive in the way required by the great monotheistic traditions. That is, I hold the Constitution View of human persons to be compatible with traditional theism without entailing it.

1. THREE ONTOLOGICAL APPROACHES TO HUMAN PERSONS

There are three main ontological approaches to human persons today: Animalism, Substance Dualism, and (my own) Constitution View.

Animalism

Perhaps the most prominent approach to human persons today is the Animalist View. According to any version of Animalism, persons are most fundamentally animals. On Animalist views, the unique features of persons—for example, features such as wondering how one is going to die, or recognizing and evaluating one's own desires, or inquiring into the kind of being that one is—have no ontological significance at all. Indeed, Eric T. Olson, an influential Animalist, takes mentality in general not to matter to our identity: He says, "[P]sychology is completely irrelevant to personal identity."[9] We are essentially animals and only accidentally persons. Olson has said:

Perhaps we cannot properly call that vegetating animal a person since it has none of those psychological features that distinguish people from non-people (rationality, the capacity for self-consciousness, or what have you). If so, that simply shows that you can continue to exist without being a person, just as you could continue to exist without being a philosopher, or a student or a fancier of fast cars.[10]

On this version of Animalism, what distinguishes "people from non-people" is of no more ontological significance than what distinguishes students from non-students, or fanciers of fast cars from non-fanciers of fast cars. According to Olson, the continued existence of you or me depends on "biological continuity: one survives just in case one's purely animal functions—metabolism, the capacity to breathe and circulate one's blood and the like—continue."[11] Ontologically

---

[9] Eric T. Olson, "Was I Ever a Fetus?" *Philosophy and Phenomenological Research*, 57 (1997), 97.
[10] Eric T. Olson, *The Human Animal: Personal Identity without Psychology* (New York: Oxford University Press, 1997), 17.
[11] Ibid. 16.

speaking, there is no difference between human persons and nonhuman animals; indeed, on some versions of Animalism, there is no ontological difference between human persons and any other organisms. Such is Animalism.

Substance Dualism

Substance Dualism is the view that there are two fundamental kinds of substance: material and mental. Richard Swinburne is a leading Substance Dualist, who explains the view like this:

> I understand by substance dualism the view that those persons which are human beings (or men) living on Earth, have two parts linked together, body and soul. A man's body is that to which his physical properties belong. If a man weighs ten stone, then his body weighs ten stone. A man's soul is that to which the (pure) mental properties of a man belong. If a man imagines a cat, then, the dualist will say, his soul imagines a cat.[12]

"On the dualist account," Swinburne continues, "the whole man has the properties he does because his constituent parts have the properties they do . . . . I imagine a cat because my soul does." The seat of mental states is the soul. Like Descartes, Swinburne offers a modal argument for substance dualism, based on the (alleged) separability of mind and body.

William Hasker offers a different approach to Substance Dualism: Emergent Dualism. Deploying a "unity-of-consciousness" argument, Hasker holds that "a person's being aware of a complex fact cannot consist in the actions of parts of the person, each of which does *not* possess this awareness."[13] This leads to the question, "But what *is* this self?"[14]

The self is an emergent entity "endowed with novel causal powers" and "possess[ing] libertarian free will."[15] As I understand it, emergence occurs when micro-elements, governed by standard physical laws, generate higher-level properties, which, in turn, alter the laws according to which lower-level elements interact.[16] The mind is, then, produced by the brain, and is "not a separate element 'added to' the brain from outside".[17] Emergent Dualism holds that "when suitably configured, [matter] generates a field of consciousness that is able to function teleologically, and to exercise libertarian free will, and the field of consciousness in turn modifies and directs the functioning of the physical brain."[18] Hasker considers the emergent mind to be part of nature, generated by natural processes—an "entity actively influencing the brain but distinct from it".[19]

---

[12] Richard Swinburne, *The Evolution of the Soul*, rev. edn (Oxford: Clarendon Press, 1997), 145.

[13] William Hasker, *The Emergent Self* (Ithaca, NY: Cornell University Press, 1999), 129. Hasker holds that animals have souls (p. 193). But if emergent dualism applies to nonhuman animals as well as to persons, do animals also have libertarian free will? If not, why not? (As I mentioned, I do not see how a being with libertarian free will can be generated by natural processes.)

[14] Ibid. 146.   [15] Ibid. 188.   [16] Ibid. 176.   [17] Ibid. 189.
[18] Ibid. 195.   [19] Ibid. 193.

The Constitution View

According to the Constitution View—the view that I endorse—human persons are wholly constituted by human bodies (= human animals), just as marble statues are wholly constituted by pieces of marble. Every concrete entity is essentially of some primary kind or other. Nothing can be of more than one primary kind. *Person* and *human body* are distinct primary kinds, as are *statue* and *piece of marble*. Ultimately, human persons are constituted by (aggregates of) particles, just as, ultimately, marble statues are constituted by (aggregates of) particles. Primary-kind properties may be exemplified derivatively or nonderivatively. A member of kind K exemplifies the property of being a K nonderivatively: it has the property of being a K essentially, regardless of its constitution-relations. Something constitutionally related to a member of kind K exemplifies the property of being a K derivatively: it has the property of being a K in virtue of its constitutional relations to something that is a K nonderivatively. For example, a particular statue is a piece of marble only derivatively, in virtue of being constituted by a piece of marble, and the constituting piece of marble is a statue derivatively, in virtue of constituting a statue. Similarly, a human person is an animal only derivatively, in virtue of being constituted by an animal, and the constituting animal is a person only derivatively, in virtue of constituting a person. Human persons are just as material as marble statues.

What distinguishes a (nonderivative) statue from the piece of marble that constitutes it are the conventions of the arts—including, perhaps, the intentions of the sculptor. What distinguishes a (nonderivative) person from everything else that exists in the natural world is the first-person perspective—the ability to think of oneself as oneself, without any name or description or other third-person referring device. The constituting animal or body could exist without a first-person perspective (as it did in its early stages, and perhaps will in its later stages); the person could not. When an animal comes to constitute a person, the animal acquires the property of *being a person* derivatively; the person constituted by the animal is a person nonderivatively.[20] In mature persons, to have a first-person perspective is to be able to think of oneself without the use of any name, description, or demonstrative; it is the ability to conceive of oneself as oneself, from the inside, as it were. A first-person perspective is the basis of all forms of self-consciousness.[21]

Many animals that lack first-person perspectives (e.g. dogs, horses, bonobos) are sentient beings. They feel pain, have various desires, and so on. They are conscious, but not self-conscious. They feel pain, but—lacking a conception

---

[20] Not all properties can be had derivatively (e.g. being identical with, having F essentially). For a detailed discussion of the notion of having a property derivatively, see *Persons and Bodies*, pp. 46–57.

[21] I have discussed this at length in *Persons and Bodies*, ch. 3.

of themselves from the first person—they don't know that they are in pain. They have desires, but they don't know what they want. They are not conscious of their own thoughts. Human persons, by contrast, have rich interior lives. Beings with inner lives are fundamentally different—ontologically, but not biologically—from beings without them.

The contrast that I have just drawn between persons and nonhuman animals distinguishes between beings that have robust first-person perspectives and beings that lack first-person perspectives altogether. Human infants, which I take to be persons, may be thought to lack first-person perspectives. However, there is evidence that they have what I call a 'rudimentary first-person perspective': they are conscious; they have a capacity to imitate; and their behavior is explainable only by attributions of beliefs, desires, and intentions.[22] Of course, some nonhuman higher primates may have these features as well, but the difference between human infants and, say, chimpanzees is that human infants are of a kind that normally develops robust first-person perspectives and chimpanzees are not.[23]

It is useful to think of human persons as animals as long as we are thinking biologically, not ontologically. But our animal nature that we share with other higher primates does not expose what we are most fundamentally. Ontology is not a branch of biology. An organism that develops a first-person perspective comes to constitute a new kind of being—one that has a first-person perspective essentially.

Biologically, the appearance of a first-person perspective is not particularly momentous. Considered in terms of genetic or morphological properties or of biological functioning, there is no gap or discontinuity between chimpanzees and human animals. In fact, human animals are biologically more closely related to certain species of chimpanzees than the chimpanzees are related to gorillas and orangutans.[24] So, *biologically considered*, there's no significant difference between human persons and higher nonhuman animals. But *all things considered*, there is a huge discontinuity between human persons and nonhuman animals. And this discontinuity arises from the fact that we, and no other part of the animal kingdom that we know of, have first-person perspectives. (If I thought that chimpanzees or computers really did have first-person perspectives, I would put them in the same category that we are in—namely, persons.)

The evidence for an ontological difference between persons and nonhuman animals lies in the significantly different abilities of persons from all other kinds of beings. The unique features of persons depend on first-person perspectives that underlie self-consciousness. First-person perspectives contribute to features that are distinctive of recognizable human life. To take some obvious examples:

---

[22] See my "When Does a Person Begin?" *Social Policy and Philosophy*, 22 (2005), 25–48.

[23] Gordon Gallup's famous experiments do not show that any nonhuman primates have a *robust* first-person perspective. See Gordon Gallup, Jr., "Self-Recognition in Primates: A Comparative Approach to Bidirectional Properties of Consciousness", *American Psychologist*, 32 (1977), 329–38.

[24] Daniel C. Dennett, *Darwin's Dangerous Idea* (New York: Simon and Schuster, 1995), 336. Dennett is discussing Jared Diamond's *The Third Chimpanzee*.

Natural Language. The first-person way of distinguishing between oneself and everything else is required to have the kinds of natural language that we all speak. In particular, ordinary locutions such as 'I hope that I'll get home safely' or 'I believe that I know the answer' presuppose first-person perspectives.

Cultural Achievements. Cultural achievements likewise depend on first-person perspectives. The ability to wonder what sort of beings we are and to consider our place in the universe are specifically first-person abilities that motivate much of science, art, philosophy, and religion.

Rational and Moral Agency. A first-person perspective is required for rational and moral agency. A rational being must be able to ask, "Is this a goal that I should have?" A moral agent must be able to understand, from the first-person point of view, that she herself has done things.

Control over Nature. Our control over nature depends on first-person perspectives. We can modify our own natural behavior. (We can give up things for Lent, or stick to an exercise regimen.) The ability to conceive of futures in the first person, as *our own* futures, is required to motivate attempts to control over our destinies as individuals and as a species.

Self-Understanding. Making sense of one's life is a first-personal task. Diaries, confessions, and various narratives that we construct about the course of our lives would be impossible without a first-person perspective. Likewise, for good or ill, allegiance to various groups—*my* family, *my* tribe, *my* country—presupposes first-person perspectives. Nationalism and patriotism depend on first-person perspectives.

Inwardness. Finally, first-person perspectives make possible the existence of our "inner lives"—we imagine scenes, say prayers, rehearse speeches. There are incontrovertible facts—for example, that Descartes was thinking that he existed—whose existence would be impossible without self-consciousness beings.

In short, with respect to *the range of what persons can do* (from planning our futures to wondering how we got ourselves into such a mess), and with respect to *the moral significance of what persons can do* (from assessing our goals to confessing our sins), self-conscious beings are obviously unique—significantly different from non-self-conscious beings. The difference that self-consciousness makes, I submit, is an ontological difference. What you are most fundamentally makes possible the life that you lead—a life that is far from exhausted by biological facts. Your biography cannot be written by a biologist.

There are some affinities between the Constitution View and Hasker's Emergent Substance Dualism. Both employ the notion of emergence and both recognize that, in the first instance, the bearer of certain mental properties is the whole person, not any proper part like a brain. But there the similarities end. Whereas Hasker holds that a soul—a distinct spiritual substance that has libertarian free will and that "modifies and directs the functioning of the brain"—emerges from a body, I do not. Let me enumerate some differences between my view and Hasker's: (i) I think that it is implausible to suppose that there are immaterial substances in the natural world. (ii) On Hasker's view, the soul is a proper part of the person; on my view, there are no souls, and hence persons do not have souls as proper parts. (iii) On Hasker's view, the soul directs the functioning of the brain; on my view, the brain functions according to natural processes. (iv) On Hasker's view, the soul has libertarian free will; on my view, there is no libertarian free will. (v) On Hasker's view, the relation between the soul and the body is unlike any other relation that we know of; on my view, the relation between a person and her body is an instance of a very general relation common to all macrophysical objects.[25]

Indeed, one of the merits of the Constitution View is that it can avail itself of many of the fruits of Substance Dualism, without endorsing immaterial entities in the natural world. A proponent of the Constitution View, as well as a Substance Dualist, can endorse the following: (i) a person is not identical to a body; (ii) a human person can survive a (gradual) change of body; (iii) a person has causal powers that an animal would not have it it did not constitute a person; (iv) concerns about my survival are concerns about myself in the future, not just concerns about someone psychologically similar to me; (v) my survival does not depend on the nonexistence of someone else who fits a particular description (like 'is psychologically continuous with me now'); there is a fact of the matter (perhaps not ascertainable by us) as to whether or not a particular person in the future is I. Despite such similarities with Substance Dualism, the Constitution View remains stoutly materialistic.

2. SATISFYING THE *DESIDERATA*

As I mentioned, a view of human persons should take account of these facts:

(1) Human persons are wholly part of the natural world, produced and governed by natural processes;
(2) Human persons are ontologically unique.

---

[25] Hasker, *The Emergent Self*, 188–95. (i)–(v) in the paragraph to which this note is appended answer Dean Zimmerman who has asked what distinguishes the Constitution View from Hasker's. See his "The Constitution of Persons by Bodies: A Critique of Lynne Rudder Baker's Theory of Material Constitution", *Philosophical Topics: Identity and Individuation*, 30 (2002), 295–338.

Let me explain further what I mean by these *desiderata*. First, to say that human persons are wholly part of the natural world is to endorse a kind of quasi-naturalism. Quasi-naturalism is naturalistic in taking the established results of scientific inquiry seriously: science is the source of important knowledge of the natural world that is not subject to reinterpretation by philosophers.[26] The natural world is a spatiotemporal order that has its own integrity and autonomy, and that exhibits regularities that can be understood without regard to any immaterial objects or supernatural beings. The sciences are sovereign in their domains (and they are silent about matters outside their domains). Regularities and processes in the natural world have naturalistic explanations—that is, explanations that make no appeal to any supernatural beings.

However, quasi-naturalism falls short of full-blown naturalism in two respects—one epistemological, the other metaphysical. First, quasi-naturalism does not claim that the sciences are the only source of knowledge; rather, it allows there are kinds of knowledge—such as personal experience, humanistic studies of history and the arts—that are invisible to the sciences. A second way that quasi-naturalism falls short of full-blown naturalism is that quasi-naturalism is not a metaphysical thesis at all: it does not claim that the natural world is all there is to reality; quasi-naturalism remains neutral with respect to the existence of anything that transcends the natural world. Another way to put it is that quasi-naturalism is not metaphysical naturalism, according to which science is the final arbiter of all knowable reality. Rather, quasi-naturalism implies only that scientific explanations are genuine explanations, and that most, perhaps all, events have scientific explanations.

As the sciences have developed, all scientific explanations are naturalistic: they do not ever advert to immaterial beings. Perhaps the sciences could have developed differently. Some contemporary naturalists like Quine would countenance immaterial objects if there were an explanatory need for them. "If I saw indirect explanatory benefit in positing sensibilia, possibilia, spirits, a Creator," Quine said, "I would joyfully accord them scientific status too, on a par with such avowedly scientific posits as quarks and black holes."[27] This passage manifests Quine's scientific pragmatism; Quine is willing to accord scientific status to all and only those posits that have "explanatory benefit". His position combines methodological naturalism with metaphysical naturalism in a way that I would reject as begging an important question: it precludes

---

[26] In reporting the results of science, scientists sometimes give interpretations that depend on philosophical assumptions that philosophers rightly criticize. Although I doubt that there's a sharp line here, I want to rule out philosophers' giving interpretations of scientific results that the scientific community largely rejects.

[27] W. V. O. Quine, "Naturalism; or, Living Within One's Means", *Dialectica*, 49 (1995), 2251–62 (252). Quoted in Michael Rea, *World without Design: Ontological Consequences of Naturalism* (Oxford: Clarendon Press, 2002), 42. I am grateful to Rea for bringing this passage to my attention.

there being genuine explanations that do not fall into the domain of any science.

Methodological naturalism, I believe, has come to be a presupposition of science. It is not an ad hoc assumption, or a bias in science: that scientific explanations make no reference to anything supernatural is partly constitutive of science today and partly responsible for its success. The sciences are in the business of discovering natural causes and only natural causes. They do not and cannot appeal to immaterial entities or to supernatural agents.[28]

The issue of the nature of human persons is philosophical; it is not merely empirical. The sciences can tell us about the biology and biochemistry of human persons, but whether the nature of human persons is exhausted by biology and biochemistry is not itself a scientific question. On the one hand, the sciences do not need a foundation of prior philosophy; on the other hand, philosophy is not just "continuous" with science (here I differ from metaphysical naturalism). Paradigmatic philosophical questions—What is the nature of necessity and possibility? How should vagueness be understood? Is reality ultimately mind-independent?—are questions that do not arise in the sciences. Although not an extension of the sciences, philosophy, according to quasi-naturalism, should cohere with the results of the sciences.[29]

Quasi-naturalism is a *desideratum* of an account of persons because the successes of the sciences in the past four hundred years command respect. (The absence of any reason to believe that theists make better scientists than atheists or agnostics is evidence that we can discover the nature of things without assuming the existence of God.) Moreover, quasi-naturalism offers protection against metaphysical fantasy. Quasi-naturalism, which requires coherence with science, does not allow wholesale reinterpretation of the sciences or of common sense to conform to an a priori metaphysics. For example, it is ludicrous to try to trump evolutionary explanations of fossils by saying that God just planted them in order to mislead secular scientists. (Descartes was surely correct to suppose that God is not a systematic deceiver.) Even if there is more to knowable reality than what the sciences can uncover, the success of the sciences—in shaping and re-shaping our social and physical environment and the framework for thinking about it—still gives them authority in their domains. Philosophers are in no position to reinterpret, in any large-scale or systematic manner, what scientists say in ways that the scientists themselves do not recognize.

So, I hold views of human persons to be accountable to quasi-naturalism. Specifically, a view of human persons satisfies the *desideratum* of quasi-naturalism only if it is consistent with the following description, which has been bequeathed

---

[28] For this reason, it is wrongheaded to hope to find support for theism in science. The theory of Intelligent Design, advocated by certain Creationists, is a nonstarter as a modern scientific theory.

[29] See my "Philosophy *in Mediis Rebus*", *Metaphilosophy*, 32 (2001), 378–94.

to us by the sciences: human persons are part of a natural world that has evolved by means of natural causes over eons. As inhabitants of the natural world, human persons are natural entities that live under the same necessity as the rest of nature (whatever that may be).

The second *desideratum* is that human persons are ontologically unique. To say that persons are ontologically unique is to say that the properties in virtue of which things are persons (nonderivatively) are the properties in virtue of which they exist at all.[30] The claim that human persons are ontologically unique is common to the great monotheistic traditions: Judaism, Christianity, and Islam.[31] But I do not rely on this fact to justify ontological uniqueness of human persons as a *desideratum*; rather, a look at the natural world—in ways that I itemized when discussing the Constitution View—gives ample evidence of the uniqueness of human persons.

That human persons are in some respects unique is indisputable; everything is unique in some respects. What is controversial is whether persons are *ontologically* unique—whether, as I hold, the coming-into-being of a new person in the world is the coming-into-being of a new entity, or whether it is merely the acquisition of a property by an already-existing entity. I submit that our being persons is the deepest fact about us: the properties peculiar to persons are sufficiently different from the properties of nonpersons to warrant the conclusion that persons—with their inner lives that spawn memoirs, confessions, autobiographies, etc.—are a unique kind of being. No other kind of being has values that lead to the great cultural achievements of science, technology, government, the arts, religion, morality, and the production of wealth. The variety and sophistication of the products of human endeavor are good evidence for the ontological uniqueness of persons.[32]

Now consider how the three approaches to the nature of human persons each fares with respect to the two *desiderata*—quasi-naturalism and ontological uniqueness:

Animalism

Animalism does not contravene quasi-naturalism, but some of its proponents do. For example, Animalists consider human persons to be animals, and they consider animals to be what biologists tell us they are. Some Animalists believe that, whereas animals literally exist, their organs (hearts, livers, kidneys and so on)

[30] I am speaking of nonderivative Fs here. See *Persons and Bodies*, ch. 2. For a discussion of ontologically significant properties, see my "The Ontological Status of Persons".

[31] The ontological uniqueness of persons may be explained in more than one way. Some explain it in terms of an immaterial soul; I explain it in terms of the first-person perspective.

[32] For more detailed arguments, see my "The Ontological Status of Persons" and "The Difference that Self-Consciousness Makes" (n. 6 above).

do not.[33] Anyone who denies the existence of items that are (putatively) in the domain of biology contravenes quasi-naturalism.

All Animalists deny that human persons are ontologically unique. The basic metaphysical line, as they see it, is between organisms and nonliving things like artifacts. Let me remark in passing that recent work in biotechnology suggests that that line is not metaphysically basic. Advances in technology have blurred the difference between natural objects and artifacts. For example, so-called "digital organisms" are computer programs that (like biological organisms) can mutate, reproduce, and compete with one another.[34] Or consider "robo-rats"—rats with electrodes that direct the rats' movements.[35] Or for another example, consider what one researcher calls 'a bacterial battery':[36] bacterial batteries are biofuel cells that use microbes to convert organic matter into electricity. They are the result of a recent discovery of a micro-organism that feeds on sugar and converts it to a stream of electricity. This leads to a stable source of low power that can be used to run sensors of household devices. Finally, scientists are genetically engineering viruses that selectively infect and kill cancer cells and leave healthy cells alone. *Scientific American* referred to these viruses as "search-and-destroy missiles".[37] Are these objects—the digital organisms, robo-rats, bacterial batteries, genetically engineered viral search-and-destroy missiles—artifacts or natural objects? Does it matter? I suspect that the distinction between artifacts and natural objects will become increasingly fuzzy; and as it does, the organism/nonorganism line will not be thought to mark a fundamental joint in nature. But even a sharp organism/nonorganism demarcation would not secure the ontological uniqueness of persons, as opposed to organisms generally.

According to Animalists, *person* is a phase sortal. Being a person, like being a student, is a contingent property that some animals have some of the time. A person's persistence conditions are not determined by her being a person. On the Animalist view, being a person is not a deep fact about persons. (Recall Olson's analogy between being a person and being a fancier of fast cars.) Ontologically speaking, the world would be no poorer without persons: if an Evil Genius took away all first-person perspectives, but left lower biological functions like metabolism intact, there would be no loss in what exists. If Animalism is correct, then there could be a complete inventory of the objects that exist that neither mentioned persons nor entailed that persons exist. Therefore, according to Animalists, persons are not ontologically unique.

---

[33] See Peter van Inwagen, *Material Beings* (Ithaca, NY: Cornell University Press, 1990), and Trenton Merricks, *Objects and Persons* (Oxford: Clarendon Press, 2001).

[34] *The Chronicle of Higher Education: Daily News*, 8 May 2003.

[35] *New York Times*, 5 May 2002.

[36] Ibid., 18 September 2003. The lead researcher, Derek Lovley, who coined the term 'bacterial battery', is a microbiologist at the University of Massachusetts at Amherst.

[37] Email update from *Scientific American*, 23 September 2003.

Substance Dualism

Substance Dualism, in contrast to Animalism, does allow for the ontological uniqueness of persons; but Substance Dualism takes human animals to have natures in part outside the purview of biology. Some Substance Dualists take human animals to be radically unlike nonhuman animals in ways that biologists cannot detect.[38] (Hasker takes nonhuman animals, as well as human animals, to have souls.[39]) If part of being a human animal is to have an immaterial soul, and biologists have no truck with immaterial souls, then biologists are not authoritative about the nature of human animals. So, if Substance Dualism is correct, biologists are not authoritative about *biology*.[40] Hence, Substance Dualism violates quasi-naturalism.

The Constitution View

It should come as no surprise that the Constitution View, and the Constitution View alone, satisfies both *desiderata*. First, it is quasi-naturalistic: human animals are exactly as biologists tell us they are. Biologists have animals in their domain, not the persons that animals constitute. (Analogously, chemists have paint in their domain, not the paintings that the paint constitutes.) Biologists are authoritative over the animal kingdom, and they agree that the animal kingdom is a seamless whole that includes human animals; there are no significant biological differences between human and higher nonhuman animals. The Constitution View does not have to put a special gloss on biology to accommodate the ontological uniqueness of human persons.

Second, the Constitution View recognizes—nay, insists on—the ontological uniqueness of persons. *Person* is a primary kind, and each primary kind is ontologically unique. The coming-into-being of human persons introduces entities into the natural world that have the capacity to think of themselves in a unique first-personal way, and to report their feelings and thoughts about themselves. Such reports, when not deceptive, are evidence of a first-personal realm of reality. The coming into existence of human persons in the natural world ushers in a wholly new kind of reality. So, the second *desideratum* is automatically satisfied by the Constitution View.

On the Constitution View, not only are human persons ontologically unique, but they are unique in a special way. Every primary kind—from hydrogen atoms to telescopes to human animals—is ontologically unique. That is, a thing of primary kind K cannot lose the property of being a K without thereby going

---

[38] I take Thomism to be a form of Substance Dualism.

[39] According to Hasker, "Animals have souls, just as we do; their souls are less complex and sophisticated than ours, because generated by less complex nervous systems" (p. 193).

[40] Although I agree with Substance Dualists that our person-making properties are not those that biologists care about, on my view, biologists do have the last word on human animals: human animals constitute us without being identical to us.

out of existence. If a hydrogen atom is "split", it goes out of existence; if a sofa is burned up, it goes out of existence; if a star collapses, leaving a black hole, it goes out of existence. If something of the kind *person* loses the property of being a person, she thereby goes out of existence. So, human persons—like things of other primary kinds—are ontologically unique. But, with their first-person perspectives, human persons are unique in a special way: uniquely unique, we may say.

In sum, the Constitution View makes sense of both the biological claim that we are animals, continuous with nonhuman animals, and the philosophical claim that we are ontologically and morally unique. The Constitution View accommodates both these claims by holding that we are animals in the sense that we are wholly constituted by animals, and yet we are ontologically unique in virtue of having first-person perspectives. A being with a first-person perspective constituted by a human body—a human person—is ontologically distinct from any animal, human or nonhuman.

3. COMPATIBILITY WITH THEISM

The Constitution View is compatible with a robust theism, without entailing it. Since traditional theism entails that human persons have a special place in Creation, there is no tension between the Constitution View and theism with respect to the ontological uniqueness of human persons. If there were any incompatibility between the Constitution View and traditional theism, it would arise from quasi-naturalism.

Quasi-naturalism, however, is compatible with various kinds of theism, with varying degrees of God's involvement with his creation. On the Enlightenment conception—Deism—God is an absent clockmaker. Although he set the world in motion, he is not a personal being and does not intervene in the world. On a more traditional conception, God is an immaterial, personal Creator, who as well as being omnipotent, omniscient, and omni-benevolent, is also Sovereign of the universe—one who makes possible everything that happens, and who cares for his creatures and interacts with them. On a more traditional view, God can and does intervene in the workings of the world. Since it is obvious that quasi-naturalism is compatible with Deism, I'll discuss only the traditional view, which takes God to be a personal being who is omniscient, omnipotent, and omni-benevolent.

Since God is omniscient, he knows which laws of nature and initial conditions have which possible outcomes. Since he is omnipotent, he is able to create laws of nature and the initial conditions that—without his further interven-tion—eventuate in a world like ours. He need not guide evolution at all. Indeed, since he is all-good, he may want to create a world intelligible to some of his creatures. It may well be God's will that the natural order operates by means of natural processes that can be understood in naturalistic terms. The operation of natural processes, understandable in wholly naturalistic terms, is compatible with God's creating and occasionally suspending them.

If the God of the Bible exists, then the natural world is not causally closed. Although God (if he exists) can intervene in the natural world in any way at any time, for the most part, in fact, he does not. For the most part, the world spins on its own natural axis, so to speak.[41] So, even if the natural world is not causally closed, miracles (understood as events that contravene laws of nature) are not very frequent. An omnipotent and omniscient God need not resort to disrupting the natural order (at least not very often). Exercising his will by means of natural processes would not be too much of a challenge for an Almighty God. On this conception, God is active in the world, but works (mainly) through natural processes.

It is part of God's general providence that the world has its own integrity, and that the orderly sequence of events does not require divine intervention for its ongoing operation—even if God actively sustains the world and its laws at every moment.[42] Some hold that, in addition to general providence, there is particular providence, in which God sustains and directs particular events. Even if there is particular providence, the fact that the natural causes would (unbeknownst to atheists) ultimately depend on God's will would not make them less natural or less explanatory. Instead, there would be a "compatibilism"—analogous to compatibilism in the free-will controversy—between natural causes and God's will. For example, if a believer sees God as hardening Pharaoh's heart or as offering someone the gift of faith, natural events (perhaps involving fundamental particles) may well be the vehicle of his hardening or offering. It is within God's power to suspend natural processes (via miracle) at any time. If God intervened at the level of fundamental particles, the resulting miracles may well have naturalistic explanations at the higher levels—the only levels to which we have explanatory access.

Moreover, quasi-naturalism allows for the possibility of veridical religious experience. On the one hand, perhaps there are some religious experiences for which we have no naturalistic explanation. An atheist could hold on to the hope that there really is a naturalistic explanation that has not yet been found; and a theist could hold on to the hope that the same experience is miraculous. But having or lacking a naturalistic explanation does not affect the veridicality of a religious experience. Since God can work through secondary causes, whether or not a religious experience has a naturalistic explanation is independent of whether or not it is veridical. Perhaps there are some veridical religious experiences that are

---

[41] There is a Protestant view that God uses miracles to confirm revelation, and that after the canon of the Bible was closed, miracles ceased. In the seventeenth century Protestants used this view polemically against a doctrine of continuing miracles in the Roman Catholic Church.

[42] There is a minority view, Occasionalism, according to which God is the only causally efficacious being.

explainable naturalistically. Scoffers may argue that if phenomena—such as John Wesley's heart's being strangely warmed—can be understood naturalistically, then it is superfluous to suppose that God exists: he would be redundant. But this conclusion does not follow. It is scoffers, not believers, who advert to a "God of the gaps". The God of traditional believers is not a fillip for explanation in the natural world. The motivation to believe in God comes more from one's own experience than from any paucity of scientific explanation.

In sum, if God has a role in creating and sustaining the natural order, and in caring for his creatures, his role is invisible to science, though it is thought to be visible to the eyes of faith. If theists (at least those who endorse quasi-naturalism) are right, God created the natural order so that natural processes can be understood in naturalistic terms. This picture sits easily with the Constitution View.

The Constitution View is not only compatible with traditional theism, but, more particularly, it can shed some light on orthodox Christian doctrines. I shall briefly discuss two examples—the "two-natures" doctrine of Christ and the doctrine of the resurrection of the body. First, the Constitution View offers a less awkward way to describe the two-natures doctrine of Christ than does Substance Dualism. According to the two-natures doctrine, Christ is one Person with both a fully divine nature (as the Second Person of the Trinity) and a fully human nature (as Jesus of Nazareth).[43] If Christianity is true, the Constitution View draws a metaphysical line in exactly the right place—between the human nature and the divine nature of a single Person. The Constitution View allows believers to hold that Christ is wholly immaterial in his divine nature and wholly material in his human nature. Substance Dualism is less tidy. According to Substance Dualism, Christ is wholly immaterial in his divine nature and partly material and partly immaterial in his human nature. Of course, the mystery of how anything can be both fully divine and fully human remains on any view; but the Constitution View has a neater picture.

Second, the Constitution View sits comfortably with the doctrine of the resurrection of the body. On that doctrine, the fleshly bodies of human persons that are subject to decay will be changed into incorruptible bodies. Some forms of Substance Dualism make it obscure why resurrection bodies are needed at all.[44] On the Constitution View, however, ordinary human persons are essentially embodied. Although human persons cannot exist without a body, human persons

---

[43] The Council of Chalcedon, which took place in 451, declares Christ to be "of one substance (*homoousios*) with the Father as regarding his Godhead, and at the same time of one substance with us as regards his manhood." Definition of the Union of the Divine and Human Natures in the Person of Christ, Council of Chalcedon, AD 451, Act V; quoted in The Book of Common Prayer, p. 864. I should note that the definition also says "truly man, consisting also of a reasonable soul and body". It is not obvious that we should take "reasonable soul and body" to imply two substances since the definition also says "of one substance with us as regards his manhood" rather than "of two substances with us as regards his manhood".

[44] Substance Dualists who are Emergentists (e.g. Hasker, Zimmerman) are exceptions.

can exist without the bodies that they actually have. The very same persons who are constituted at some time by earthly bodies can come to be constituted by resurrected bodies.[45] The bodies on earth (corruptible, organic bodies) and in heaven (incorruptible, "spiritual" bodies) cannot be the same bodies, but the persons are the same persons. The same person, Smith, say, exists on earth and in heaven, because—again, by a miracle—God changes Smith's corruptible animal body into an incorruptible resurrection body that exemplifies Smith's first-person perspective.

Although the mysteries of Christian doctrine remain, the Constitution View of human persons has the resources to describe doctrines in a way that illuminates them. So, the Constitution View is compatible with Christian doctrine, as well as with the great monotheistic traditions generally.

4. CONCLUSION

Many philosophers, especially those with a religious bent, locate the uniqueness of human persons in the alleged existence of an immaterial soul or in the alleged possession of a faculty of libertarian free will that allows persons to intervene in the natural order in a God-like way. Although I share with such religious philosophers the belief that human persons are ontologically unique, I do not believe that these traditional philosophical views are tenable. We must look elsewhere to find an *imago dei* in human persons, and I believe that we can find it in the first-person perspective exemplified in the material world. Only the Constitution View shows how human persons are wholly within the natural order, and yet are ontologically unique.

---

[45] An Animalist holds that an animal cannot exist without the body that it has in the here-and-now. So, an Animalist who believes in resurrection will have to hold that the incorruptible resurrection body is identical to the corruptible premortem animal body. Such an Animalist will have to hold (*per impossibile*, I believe) that a body may be corruptible during part of its existence, and the same body may be incorruptible during another part of its existence. See my "Persons and the Metaphysics of Resurrection," *Religious Studies*, forthcoming.

PART V

PERSONHOOD IN CHRISTIAN DOCTRINE

12

The Word Made Flesh: Dualism, Physicalism, and the Incarnation

Trenton Merricks

The Incarnation is beautiful and mysterious, awe-inspiring and humbling. The metaphysics of "embodiment" is, in comparison, drab and petty. And so a paper on the Incarnation that focused on God the Son's relation to his body would be like a paper on the history of music that focused on the kazoo. Nevertheless, I shall ask: "How is the incarnate God the Son related to his body?"

This is not the most important question about the Incarnation. Nor is it a traditional question. For example, it is not (at least not obviously) a question about human nature or a question about divine nature or even a question about the union of the two. It is not a question explicitly addressed in creedal discussions of the Incarnation. And so, if (for example) this paper were an exegesis of the Chalcedonian Definition, I might have no business asking this question, let alone answering it. But, though I intend to stay within the Definition's parameters, such exegesis is not my project.

My project starts by assuming that God the Son, in virtue of being incarnate, is related to his body just as you and I are related to our respective bodies. This assumption opens up a way to explore the Incarnation, a way in addition to examining the creeds. For, given this assumption, one's view on how each of us is related to his or her body should dictate one's view on how the Son is related to his body. Conversely, if an account of embodiment is untenable in the case of the Son and his body, it is untenable in our case as well. And so my starting assumption opens up not just a way to investigate the Incarnation, but also an Incarnation-based way to investigate the relation between person and body in general.

Although controversial, my starting assumption is quite plausible. For the incarnate Son is fully human and so, presumably, human in the same sense that you and I are. Part of being human, at least in this life, is having a body. And

This paper was presented at the Pew Workshop on the Metaphysics of the Human Person (February 2004) and to the Butler Society at the University of Oxford (March 2004). Thanks to both audiences for helpful comments. Thanks also to Mike Bergmann, Jim Cargile, Joseph Jedwab, Brian Leftow, Mark Murphy, Mike Rea, Richard Swinburne, Patrick Toner, and Thomas Williams.

so, presumably, the Son has a body in the same sense that you and I do. More generally, he is related to his body just as each and every other human is related to his or her body.[1]

1. SUBSTANCE DUALISM

The word 'soul' can be used in many ways. Throughout this paper, I shall use 'soul' to mean a thing or object or substance that has mental properties but lacks physical properties. Because a soul has mental properties, a soul can believe that the sun is shining, hope that rain will come soon, and be appeared to red-ly. Because it lacks physical properties, a soul has no mass, fails to be extended in space, and reflects no light.

Substance dualists (hereafter 'dualists') believe in souls. Indeed, dualists say that each human person just is—is identical with—a soul.[2] Obviously, if we are souls, we are not bodies. Nor do we have bodies as parts. Nevertheless, even dualists believe that, in this life at least, we "have bodies".

According to the typical dualistic picture, a soul's having a body is partly a matter of that soul's having direct causal control over that body. For example, when I—suppose I am a soul—intend that my left arm move, the left arm of "my body" moves. Of course, I can indirectly cause things outside of my own body. I could indirectly cause your arm to rise by my lifting your arm with my hand. But this is not a case of direct causal control, since I cannot make your arm rise simply by intending that it does.[3]

---

[1] A venerable theory of the Incarnation—arguably, the historically dominant theory—seems to reject this assumption. This is the theory that God the Son, in the Incarnation, "took up" an "individual human nature". This individual human nature is supposed to be intrinsically just like a complete human person. Indeed, it would have been a human person had it not—perhaps *per impossibile*—been taken up by God the Son. (A theory along these lines is associated with, for example, Aquinas, Scotus, and Ockham (for discussion, see Freddoso 1986).) But I have a hard time seeing how the individual human nature fails to be a human person (as it must, lest this theory be Nestorian). Moreover, it is hard to see how "taking up" an individual human nature makes God the Son human in the same way you and I are human; and if he is not human just as we are, I do not see how he could be fully human.

[2] Some dualists deny that a person is identical with a soul, saying instead that each human person is a composite of soul and body. This is a minority view among dualistic philosophers, and for good reason. For, if there are souls, they have mental properties. Persons have mental properties, too. So the dualist who denies that a person is identical with a soul must say that there are two objects with mental properties (a person and her soul) where normally we think there is one. (For more objections to the claim that a person is a composite of soul and body, see Merricks, 2001a: 47–53, esp. 48 n. 9, and Olson 2001.)

[3] My intending to raise my arm causes events in my brain, starting a chain of causes, which result in my arm's rising. So I may not cause my arm to rise *directly*. But the relevant point is that, according to the dualist, the only physical events that I directly cause are events in my own body, including my own brain. Along similar lines, suppose my hands are tied behind my back—or the nerves in my arms are injured—so that I cannot raise my arm just by intending to do so. This does not render me disembodied, since my soul could still directly cause events in my brain.

Given typical dualism, the union of soul and body is partly constituted by the soul's having direct control over the body. In addition, the union of soul and body involves the body's influencing the soul. For example, when a blue piece of paper is in front of a body—a body with its eyes open, in plenty of light, etc.—that body causes "its soul" to know that a blue piece of paper is located there.

Dualists are explicit about all this. Thus Richard Swinburne:

> A person has a body if there is a chunk of matter through which he makes a difference to the material world, and through which he acquires true beliefs about that world. Those persons who are men have bodies because stimuli landing on their eyes or ears give them true beliefs about the world, which they would not otherwise have; and they make differences to the world by moving arms and legs, lips and fingers. Our bodies are the vehicles of our knowledge and operation. The 'linking' of body and soul consists in there being a body which is related to the soul in this way. (1986: 146)

According to Swinburne, a person's standing in the appropriate causal relations to a body—or a "chunk of matter"—is all there is to a soul's having a body.[4] Given this picture, embodiment is a cluster of relations, all of which involve some sort of epistemic access or direct control. The more of these embodiment-constituting relations that hold between an immaterial person and a body, the "more embodied" that person is (cf. Swinburne 1986: 151). And so, according to this picture, embodiment can come in degrees. (For example, a soul could leave its body gradually, as one and then another embodiment-constituting relation "shuts off".)

I take this to be the most natural dualistic account of embodiment. Below I shall develop objections to this account. So I shall then consider other accounts, including even one that says that *having a body* is primitive and unanalyzable.[5] But my starting point is Swinburne's account, which I believe reflects the most familiar dualistic understanding of having a body.

The Soul's Influence on a Body

The typical dualist says that a person's *having a body* just is her standing in the relevant causal relations to that body. This leads to the most familiar objection to dualism. As Daniel Dennett says:

---

[4] This account of embodiment seems to rule out one's causing a cup, which is not part of one's body, to levitate simply by intending that it does. And it rules out someone's having knowledge of the physical world via the body of another. Perhaps the dualist might revise this account to permit the possibility of a bit of magic here, a little clairvoyance there. Nevertheless, her account of embodiment should rule out one's consistently having direct control over, and knowledge by way of, a body that is not one's own. If one found oneself regularly enjoying the control of, and knowledge via, a body that is not one's own, the dualist should say that one thereby *has* that body.

[5] Hasker (1999) takes a soul's having a body to be that body's generating that soul. This bodes ill for the Incarnation—surely the body of Jesus does not generate God the Son—so I shall set Hasker's account aside.

The standard objection to dualism was all too familiar to Descartes himself in the seventeenth century, and it is fair to say that neither he nor any subsequent dualist has ever overcome it convincingly. If mind and body are distinct things or substances, they nevertheless must interact; the bodily sense organs, via the brain, must *inform* the mind, must send to it or present it with perceptions or ideas or data of some sort, and then the mind, having thought things over must *direct* the body in appropriate action (including speech) . . . but anything that can move a physical thing is itself a physical thing. (1991: 33–5)

There are a number of replies the dualist could make to the "standard objection". I shall focus on one that is particularly fitting in the present context. This paper explores how a commitment to the Incarnation bears on how we understand embodiment. (It also explores, conversely, how theories of embodiment bear on our understanding of the Incarnation.) The Incarnation entails theism. But theism—with its non-physical miracle-working creator God—entails that the non-physical can causally influence the physical. So, given the Incarnation, the standard objection to dualism ought to be judged uncompelling.

The Incarnation helps the dualist out of a familiar problem, providing a decisive reason to reject the premise that the physical and the non-physical cannot causally interact.[6] But in accepting this help, the dualist takes a poisoned pawn. For, as I shall argue throughout much of this paper, the Incarnation threatens to undermine the dualist's notion of embodiment, thereby undermining dualism itself.

Consider, for example, dualism's claim that having a body is partly a matter of having direct control of a body. Thus God the Son's having the body of Jesus is partly constituted by his having direct control of that body. But that implication of dualism, and so dualism itself, seems to be mistaken. For the Son's being embodied cannot be partly constituted by his having such control over the body of Jesus, lest to that same extent he—along with the Father and the Spirit—have every body that ever was. After all, each divine person, being omnipotent, has direct control over each and every body.[7]

The dualist might reply that while God *has* direct control of each human body, God does not *exercise* such control.[8] (Of course, God continually sustains

---

[6] Indeed, everyone—not just the theist—ought to find the standard objection to dualism uncompelling. Compare: If God exists, then something non-physical (God) causes physical events; nothing non-physical can cause physical events; therefore, God does not exist. This argument seems neither better nor worse than the standard objection to dualism. But this argument is question-begging, or so close to question-begging as makes no difference. So the moral is that the standard objection to substance dualism likewise begs the question. (That is, the argument that takes "no causal interaction between the non-physical and physical" as a *premise* seems to beg the question against the substance dualist. Opponents of substance dualism who *argue* for the impossibility of such interaction—such as Kim (2001) and Sosa (1984)—need not beg the question.)

[7] I shall move back and forth between claims like "God has control" and "the Father, the Son, and the Spirit have control." But I think that the sense in which the Trinity has a property like *having control* is not the same as the sense in which each divine person has that property. For more on this, see §VII of Merricks (2006).

[8] Another reply says that God's control of physical objects is totally unlike our control of our bodies. As a result, God does not have direct control of bodies, at least not in the sense that you and

everything in existence, but that is another matter.) For example, while God could raise my arm simply by intending that it rise, God does not do so, at least not typically. On the other hand, God the Son regularly exercises direct control over the body of Jesus. This avoids the above objection, this reply concludes, because a soul's having a body is not (partly) a matter of that soul's merely *having* direct control of that body, but is instead (partly) a matter of that soul's *exercising* such control.

This reply makes embodiment a matter of a soul's exercising control over a body. And so it implies that whenever one is not intending bodily actions, one is not embodied, or at least not embodied to the extent that embodiment is a matter of the soul's influence on the body. But that implication cannot be right. For my failing to intend bodily actions does not render me totally disembodied. Nor does it even render me somewhat less embodied than I would otherwise be. After all, embodiment does not wax and wane with everyday occurrences, such as my now intending to raise my arm, my now failing to intend any bodily action at all.

For these reasons, I conclude that embodiment is not even partly a matter of the *exercise* of direct control. Rather, insofar as the soul's influence on the body is concerned, embodiment is a matter of the soul's *having* direct control. This allows one to be fully embodied even when intending no bodily actions. (And it implies, quite plausibly, that embodiment is the precondition for, rather than the result of, exercising direct control.) Of course, this returns us to the problem already noted. Insofar as embodiment is having direct control, each divine person is thereby embodied in each human body. Indeed, it seems that each divine person is thereby embodied in each physical object.

The Body's Influence on a Soul

A soul's having a body is not merely its having direct control of that body. That is only one "direction" in the embodiment equation. The other "direction" involves the body's influence on the soul. As Swinburne says above, a person's body is that physical object "through which he acquires true beliefs about the world".

God has direct and immediate knowledge of everything in and around every body. And so insofar as having a body is having knowledge of what is in and around that body, each person of the Trinity has each and every body. This is

---

I do. Defending one version of this reply, Brian Leftow (1997: 120) says "In sum, God cannot in fact move matter by basic acts (again, with perhaps the exception of the Incarnation)." Suppose that God's moving matter in the way that we move our bodies is impossible. Then, given the dualist's account of embodiment, God the Son's becoming incarnate is impossible too. So this reply will not help the dualist. Further, this reply denies that God is a non-physical entity who causes physical events in the sense of 'cause' that non-physical souls cause physical events. And so, given this reply, the dualist loses her theism-based rejoinder to Dennett's "standard objection". Thus, insofar as the dualist thinks the theism-based rejoinder is a good one, she should reject this reply.

all by itself bad enough. And it threatens the Incarnation. For, to the extent that the Son has every body, he does not have the body of Jesus in particular.

I think this point is basically correct. But, to be compelling, it needs to be developed further. Moreover, it is open to more objections than the previous point, the point that the Son's omnipotence gives him the sort of direct control over each and every body that is—according to the dualist—the other "half" of embodiment. So let me consider some objections and offer some replies while, at the same time, clarifying the dualist's problem.

Objection 1: Each person of the Trinity is omniscient. So each knows "everything". Nevertheless, each can know some things the others do not. For example, only the Father knows "I am the Father." More to the point, only the Son knew "I am walking on water." The Son's having the body of Jesus is partly constituted by his knowing such things, things which are appropriately correlated with that body.

Reply: The dualist denies that human persons are bodies. She denies that human persons have physical parts, such as feet. As a result, she must say that when the Son truly thinks "I am walking on water," this is a shorthand way of thinking "my body is walking on water." This in turn is shorthand for "the body of Jesus is walking on the water and the body of Jesus is my body." Such beliefs presuppose that the Son has the body of Jesus. (In this regard, they are on a par with the Son's belief "I have the body Jesus".) Thus they cannot even partly constitute his having that body.

Objection 2: It is one thing to know something. It is another for that knowledge to be caused by a body. Although each person of the Trinity knows what is happening in and around each body, it is not because events in that body cause this knowledge in God. And so it is false that insofar as embodiment involves a body's causing knowledge in a person that the Father, the Son, and the Spirit thereby have each and every body.

Reply: Consider the Platonic claim that God is self-sufficient and unchanging, thus not possibly influenced by goings-on in the physical world. If this claim were correct, bodily events could not cause knowledge in God. And so the above objection would stand. But dualistic Incarnation would not. For God the Son could not be causally influenced by what goes on in the body of Jesus. And so, at least insofar as embodiment is a matter of the body's influence on the person, God the Son could not have the body of Jesus. Therefore, in order to give the dualist a fighting chance, I shall reject this Platonic picture of God.[9]

Besides, I really do think this picture is mistaken. I assume that, typically, God knows something is happening because it is happening, and not the other way round. God knows what is happening in my body because it is happening

---

[9] Another Incarnation-based objection to this Platonic view of God is that in taking on humanity, God the Son underwent some sort of change. (Senor (1990) defends this objection; Leftow (2002) responds.)

there. Moreover, God knows that when particular experiences in my body are caused in particular ways, certain things are happening in the world around that body. Thus, God knows about goings-on in the world because of events in my body. (Of course, God also knows about those goings-on directly.) So it seems that events in my body cause knowledge of the world in each person of the Trinity. At any rate, it is hard to see a principled way of ruling out causation in this case without thereby ruling out something to which the Christian dualist is committed—events in the body of Jesus causing knowledge in God the Son.

Objection 3: A body does not deliver only *propositional* knowledge to its soul. A body also provides *sensory experiential* knowledge. Such knowledge—for example, knowledge of what it is like to see a red-tailed hawk—essentially involves sensory experience, which in turn essentially involves having a body (cf. Aquinas, *Summa Theologica*, 1a.77.8). God the Father and God the Spirit, lacking bodies, lack sensory experiential knowledge. God the Son, however, has sensory experiential knowledge. And we can parlay this knowledge into a way in which the Son is uniquely related to the body of Jesus, a way that at least partly constitutes the Son's having that body.

Reply: Dualists typically endorse the possibility of my having no body, yet everything's seeming to me just as it actually does. (Thus begins Descartes's famous argument for dualism in the *Meditations*.) And so dualists typically think that, possibly, a disembodied immaterial being has sensory experiences. As a result, dualists should say that such a being can have experiential knowledge and, therefore, they should not endorse the above objection.

Besides, presumably, the omniscient God's knowledge of creation is not far poorer than ours. And so, presumably, each person of the Trinity knows, for example, what a red-tailed hawk looks like and what *Eine kleine Nachtmusik* sounds like. Indeed, insofar as we dare speculate on such a thing, I would say that God's knowledge is so rich that each divine person knows what it is like to have your body, what it is like to have the body of Jesus, and even what it is like to be a bat.

Objection 4: It was a mistake to focus on sensory experiential *knowledge*. Let's consider, instead, sensory *experiences* (cf. Cross 2003: 301). To see the distinction, consider that you may not now see anything red, though you nevertheless now know what it is like to see red. Seeing red is one thing; knowing what it is like to see red is another. In general, it is one thing to know what an experience is like and quite another to have that experience.

To have a body is to have sensory experiences caused by that body. For example, if a body's eyes are open and a sheet of red paper is held in front of it, then that body may cause "its soul" to see red, and to see it "from the perspective of" that body. God the Son's experiences are caused in this way by exactly the body of Jesus and no other. (God the Father and God the Spirit may not have sensory experiences, and even if they do, their experiences are not caused by a body.)

Reply: This reply makes embodiment a matter of a body's actually causing a person to have experiences. And so it implies that whenever one is not having experiences caused by a body, one is not embodied. But I object that my body's failing to cause experiences in me should not render me disembodied. My soul might leave my body when I die, but not when I dreamlessly sleep! Moreover, lack of experiences caused by a body should not even result in my being somewhat less embodied. To repeat an earlier point, embodiment does not wax and wane with changes of the sort we encounter every day. Thus I conclude that embodiment is not even partly a matter of a body's actually causing experiences in a soul. (Presumably, embodiment is instead a precondition for having experiences caused by a body.)[10]

Kenosis and Embodiment

The most familiar and straightforward dualistic account of embodiment says that to have a body is to have direct control over, and epistemic access to, that body. But this account stumbles over theism and the Incarnation. So let's consider another account.

Suppose that standing in the relevant relations of control and access to a body is not what it is to have that body. Rather, the dualist might say, to have a body is both to stand in those relations to that body and *to fail to stand in those relations to any other body*. Embodiment, thus understood, is not merely a matter of being "positively" related to a body. It is also a matter of being appropriately limited. It is a matter of lacking control over, and epistemic access to, any other body.

The Father and the Spirit, being omnipotent and omniscient, are not appropriately limited. That is, they stand in the relevant relations of control and epistemic access to each and every body. So this "revised account of embodiment" keeps the Father and Spirit from having bodies. But—by the same token—it robs the Son of his body.

---

[10] Let me address a couple of the most obvious strategies for tweaking Objection 4 in light of my reply. One strategy says that having a body is a matter of the *ability* to have experiences caused by that body. I object that this would give the Father, the Spirit, and the Son each and every body, since each divine person, being omnipotent, is able to have experiences caused by any body he chooses.

A second strategy says that a soul's having a body is a matter of that soul's being such that, were that body in such and such a condition, then that soul would have thus and so experience. (Arguably, even when unconscious, the nearest counterfactual situation in which my body is in sense-experience-causing conditions is also one in which I have the corresponding experiences.) But, I object, whether one is embodied ought to be a matter of how things actually are, not a matter of how they would be, had things gone differently. Moreover, consider a disembodied soul, whose former body has died. If that body were in sense-experience-causing conditions—conditions presumably requiring it to be alive—then I suppose the soul would have the appropriate experiences. After all, the nearest counterfactual situation in which, for example, Lincoln's body is now alive is presumably, given dualism, a situation in which Lincoln's soul is embodied. But this should not imply—as it seems to given this second strategy—that Lincoln's disembodied soul now has a body.

More carefully, this revised account robs the Son of his body if he too is omnipotent and omniscient. But suppose the Incarnation involved a "kenosis". According to Gottfried Thomasius—whose *Person and Work of Christ* (1852–61) contains the first explicit defense of a kenosis—Christ abandoned his divine attributes from birth until resurrection (see McGrath 2001: 377–8). Given a kenosis, the revised account of embodiment might allow the Son to have a body. For, given a kenosis, the Son might stand in the relevant relations of control and epistemic access to only the body of Jesus.

Without a kenosis, the revised account makes it impossible for the Son to have a body. So, given that the Son came to have the body of Jesus, one cost of the revised account is a kenosis. I shall not raise any objections to a kenosis.[11] Nevertheless, I have three objections to the revised account of embodiment.

The revised account implies that no omnipotent and omniscient person can have a body.[12] Given a kenosis, the Lord emptied himself of omniscience and omnipotence at birth and regained these attributes at resurrection. Thus the revised account, combined with a kenosis, has the comic and absurd implication that, upon the resurrection of his body, the Son became disembodied. This—along with the revised account's implying that the Son is forevermore disembodied—is the first reason to reject the revised account.

Suppose a soul starts with a single body and then acquires the appropriate control over and knowledge via a second body, which results in the soul's having two bodies. This idea—one soul's having two bodies—seems possible. Yet the revised account of embodiment renders that idea impossible. (According to that account, a soul has a body if and only if that soul stands in the relevant relations to that body and *fails to stand in those relations to any other body.*) This is the second reason that the dualist should reject the revised account.

The revised account allows the Father to be related to the body of Jesus in each and every way that the Son is, while insisting that the Son, but not the Father, has that body. (According to that account, the Father does not have that body because of how he is related to other bodies.) But, I object, the union of a person and a body ought to be wholly a matter of their relations to each other, not instead partly a matter of how they fail to be related to other things. The revised account does not respect this. This is the third reason to reject that account.

---

[11] The most serious objection to a kenosis says that to be divine just is to have the appropriate array of divine attributes; to shed those attributes is to thereby shed divinity; thus a kenotic Christology denies the Lord's divinity. (One possible reply is that divinity requires only attributes such as being-omniscient-unless-freely-and-temporarily-choosing-to-be-otherwise; cf. Morris 1986: 99 ff.)

[12] That is, such a person cannot have a body *if more than one body exists.* If exactly one body exists, then such a person can have a body. Indeed—given the revised account—that body will automatically be the body of every omnipotent and omniscient person. This result is another flaw in the account, since surely a divine person could create a world with one body without thereby becoming embodied.

Relations R and X

The dualist should reject the revised account of embodiment. So let's return to the original account. That account says that to have a body is to have direct control of, and to enjoy epistemic access to, that body. I have argued that the most obvious and plausible ways of spelling out *direct control* and *epistemic access*, when combined with the dualist's account of embodiment, get the "wrong results". (The wrong results include, among others, your and my lacking bodies when intending no actions and the Spirit's having each and every body for his own.) Of course, I have not examined every possible candidate for what control or access might amount to. And so one might fear that I have overlooked a candidate that gets "all the right results".

So, for the sake of argument, let's grant that there is a relation—call it 'Relation R'—that gets all the right results. That is, R holds between God the Son and only the body of Jesus; R fails to hold between any body and any other divine person; R holds between each of us and exactly each of our respective bodies; and, finally, R is intuitively embodiment-constituting because it is a kind of direct control, a kind of epistemic access, or a combination of both.

Suppose that R, which is an embodiment-constituting relation, holds between the Son and the body of Jesus alone. Even so, the moral of the paper so far is that many more embodiment-constituting relations hold between the Son and each and every body. Thus the dualist cannot say both that God the Son is fully and completely embodied in the body of Jesus and also that God the Son has no other body at all, without qualification. At best, even granting relation R, the Son might be "slightly more embodied" in the body of Jesus than he is in your body or in my body or in a teacup. But that's not good enough. (Moreover, even granting R, the Father and the Spirit are only "slightly less embodied" than you or I.)

This objection presupposes that embodiment is a cluster of relations, only one of which is relation R. The dualist might, however, reject this presupposition. She might say, instead, that embodiment *just is* relation R. Since we have stipulated that R gets "all the right results", this account of embodiment gets the right results as well.

We don't yet know what relation R is, other than that it will be some variety of direct control and/or epistemic access. Insofar as we do not know what R is—given the identification of R with embodiment—we do not know what embodiment is. Thus this suggestion renders embodiment somewhat mysterious.

Moreover, until we know more about R, we have no reason to think that R is intrinsically any more suited to be *the* embodiment relation than any other relation of epistemic access or direct control. The claim that R just is embodiment therefore privileges, in an ad hoc manner, exactly one out of many relations, all of which intuitively constitute embodiment. It would be better to take R as a crucial ingredient of embodiment than to take it to be the whole shooting match.

The dualist might deny that embodiment is reduced to, or analyzed in terms of, any apparently embodiment-constituting relations, including R. That is, she might deny that embodiment is analyzed in terms of any relation of direct control or epistemic access. She might say, rather, that embodiment is a primitive, unanalyzable relation that holds between a person and a body. This too would allow the dualist who believes in the Incarnation to get all the "right results", simply by *fiat*.

But this move, even more than the previous, renders embodiment an occult relation. For once we make this move, then we do not know what the dualist means when she says that each of us "has a body". (She does not mean that we have direct control of a body; she does not mean that we have epistemic access to a body; she does not mean that we have a combination of control over and access to a body . . . .) To simply assert that embodiment is some "relation X" makes embodiment completely mysterious and so is utterly implausible.

Moreover, for all we have said so far, it is possible for me to stand in all the seemingly relevant control and epistemic relations to a body without being X-related to it. Conversely, I could be X-related to a body without being related to it by any control or epistemic relations. *Ex hypothesi*, something is my body if and only if I am X-related to it. And so—at least for all we have said so far—my body might be, for example, the one typically believed to belong to Queen Elizabeth II, the body now in Buckingham Palace. But no account of embodiment should make it possible for that to be my body and not that of Her Majesty, given that HM has (and I lack) causal control over, and epistemic access to, that body.

The defender of relation X could embellish her account to rule out such absurdities. She could insist that although X is not reduced to the relevant relations of control and access, each of these relations—including R, so that we get the cases right—is necessary for X's holding and all of them together are sufficient.

Embellishing the X-account in this way has three advantages. First, there is no chance I have the Queen's body. Second, if X supervenes on relations of control and access, it may not be so mysterious after all. Finally, this account allows one to deny that embodiment comes in degrees. And so its defenders can resist some of my earlier objections. To take just one example, even if God the Father is related to my body by every apparently embodiment-constituting relation except for R, it is false—given the embellished X-account—that there is a degree to which he *has* my body.

Let's focus on this third advantage. The embellished X-account tells us that a soul, standing in all the relevant relations to a body except for R, is absolutely disembodied. This raises the troubling thought that—even though I control a body through which I have knowledge of the world—I might actually be disembodied. This troubling thought is a mere symptom of the real problem. The real problem is that this account puts too much weight on R.

This account says that a soul related to a body by every relevant relation of epistemic access and control except for R is totally disembodied. But I reply that, if I am a soul related to a body by all the relevant relations save R, then surely I am embodied to a significant degree, though perhaps not as embodied as other slightly more plugged-in souls. The X-account—even when embellished—is not plausible. And, besides, we have no reason to think that there really is any relation R, any apparently embodiment-constituting relation that really does get "all the right results."[13]

Embodiment and Incarnation

For sake of argument, let's assume that the dualist can handle the objections above. Let's assume, in particular, that she can account for the Son's having exactly the body of Jesus. Even so, I shall argue, the Incarnation casts doubt on dualism.

This second Incarnation-based objection to dualism begins by considering "Apollinarianism". Here is how Peter van Inwagen describes this heresy:

Apollinarianism (after Apollinarius (c.310–c.390)) holds that Christ did not have a human mind or spirit or rational soul—that he lacked something that is essential to human nature—and that God or some 'aspect' of God (such as the divine *logos*) was united to the human body of Jesus of Nazareth in such a way as to 'be a substitute for' or perform the function of the human mind or soul or spirit. (1998: 727)

Regarding the heresy of monophysitism, Swinburne says:

Monophysitism, holding that the Incarnate Christ had only one nature, normally understood that to be the divine nature . . . He had a human body; and the connection with [that body] that leads to the sensory desires—pain, thirst, etc. So this is not Docetism, the view that Christ's body was mere 'appearance' and Christ did not really suffer. But it is what the century before Chalcedon knew as Apollinarianism, the view that the Incarnation consisted in the Word of God acquiring a human body but not a 'rational soul'. (1994: 224)

With all this in mind, let us turn to:

> *The Heretical Theory*: God the Son is fully divine. But he is not fully human. Nevertheless, ever since the virgin conception and birth over two thousand years ago, he has been related to the body of Jesus just as a normal human soul is related to its body. So God the Son controls the body of Jesus.

---

[13] Some dualists believe that an embodied person is a composite of soul and body. Their resources for accounting for when a soul and body are thus united—for when a soul and body are related by *composing a person*—are no different from those of the standard dualist. (Indeed, Swinburne, whose account of the union of soul and body has been our touchstone, holds that a person is composed of soul and body; see Swinburne 1986: 146.) So this sort of dualism provides no way around the arguments above.

Moreover, he knows what happens in and around that body. He even has experiences such as hunger and pain and seeing red caused by that body.

Arguing that this or that metaphysics of the Incarnation is heretical can be tricky business (cf. Plantinga 1999). Nevertheless, it is safe to say that the Heretical Theory is aptly named. For the Heretical Theory explicitly asserts that God the Son is not fully human. This is a failure of doctrine. It is not, however, a failure of logic. That is, there is nothing incoherent in the claim that a non-human divine person is related to a human body in the ways a normal soul is related to its body. God the Son could "play the role" with respect to a body that, according to dualism, is typically played by a human soul, and the Son could do this without thereby becoming human.

So one moral of the Heretical Theory is that having a body, as understood by the dualist, is not sufficient for being human. Nor would it seem to be necessary. For dualists typically allow that you and I can continue to exist—and continue to be human—after our body dies, even before resurrection. Thus, given dualism, having a human body seems to be neither necessary nor sufficient for being human.[14]

The Incarnation is the Son's becoming human. Given dualism, this cannot be a matter of the Son's coming to have a human body. So the dualist must say that the Son, in addition to coming to have a body, also became human. I suppose that, for the dualist, to be human is to be a human soul. So the dualist must claim that the Son, while remaining divine, became a human soul.

It is neither incoherent nor obviously heretical to say that God the Son's becoming human just is his becoming a human soul. But I would prefer an account of the Incarnation according to which the Son's coming to have a human body is at least a necessary condition for his becoming human. Dualism, as we have seen, is not such an account. Dualism makes the Son's becoming human one thing and his becoming embodied something else altogether. This is my second Incarnation-based objection to dualism.

Besides, whether or not embodiment is absolutely necessary for the Incarnation, God the Son does have the body of Jesus. And the fact that the Son has a body—and the Father and the Spirit do not—undermines the standard dualistic account of embodiment, a straightforward account in terms of knowledge and control. Given theism and the Incarnation, the dualist must exchange the straightforward account for something or other *ad hoc* or implausible or darkly mysterious. (Among the unattractive options are that embodiment turns completely on "relation R" and that embodiment wanes when sleeping.) This, of course, was my first, and more important, Incarnation-based objection to dualism.

In light of this objection, one could conclude that Christians should be dualists who defend one or another ad hoc or implausible or darkly mysterious

---

[14] This is not surprising. Dualistic embodiment is a matter of causal relations that one bears to something contingently, to something not identical with oneself. It would be odd if one's very humanity were a matter of such relations.

claim about embodiment. Similarly, in light of my second objection, one could conclude that the Son could have become human without ever having a body. But, rather than jump to these conclusions, I suggest that we consider another approach altogether.

2. PHYSICALISM

It seems pretty obvious that you have physical properties. You have a height and a weight; you take up space; you have a shape. But only physical objects have physical properties. For to be a physical object just is to be a thing that has physical properties.[15] Given all this, it seems pretty obvious that *physicalism*—the claim that each of us is a physical object—is true.

(Not everyone will agree. Dualists do not think it is obvious that we have physical properties. Indeed, dualists think we lack such properties. For each of us, according to the dualist, is a soul. And souls have no physical properties. Souls have neither height nor weight, shape nor size.)

Physicalism says that we are physical objects. Consider the human-shaped object sitting in your chair and wearing your clothes.[16] Let's call that human-shaped and living and breathing object 'your body'. The sort of physicalism I defend says that you are identical with your body (see Merricks 2001*a*). That is, you are that human-shaped thing sitting in your chair and wearing your clothes. You just are that living, breathing organism.

Physicalism has a straightforward account of embodiment. You have a body if and only if you are identical with that body. I assume that, in the Incarnation, God the Son is related to the body of Jesus just as you and I are related to our respective bodies. So, given physicalism, God the Son, in the Incarnation, is identical with the body of Jesus. That is, in becoming human, he became a body.

Some might object that saying that God the Son became a physical object is deeply inappropriate. Some might object that this is akin to saying that that which spoke the universe into existence is a mere doorstop or a lace doily. But, I reply, to say that the Son became a physical object is just to say that he came to have physical properties. Saying that God the Son became a physical object is no more impious than saying that God came to be such that we could literally touch and see him. The only scandal here is that of the Incarnation itself.

Moreover, the claim that God the Son is identical with the body of Jesus does not mean that God the Son is *merely* a physical object, in the sense that his only

---

[15] More carefully, to be a physical object is to have physical properties *and fail to have a non-physical object (like a soul) as a part.* If we were composed of both a body and a soul, we would have physical properties, but would not be physical objects. But, as already noted, there are good reasons to set aside the view according to which we are composites of soul and body. So I set it aside.

[16] I say there is exactly one such object. Below we shall note a version of physicalism according to which more than one such object exists, each wholly co-located with the others.

properties are physical. Indeed, the physicalist need not say that any human person, divine or otherwise, is merely a physical object. For while the physicalist says that a human person has physical properties, she does not insist that a human person has only physical properties. Persons also have mental properties. And physicalism, as I shall understand it, is consistent with a physical person's mental properties' being *sui generis*, being irreducible to physical properties.[17] (Thus my sort of physicalism is consistent with "property dualism" about the mental.) Moreover, for all I know, we might have properties that are neither mental nor physical. And the same goes for the incarnate Son. *Being the Lord of Glory* is not obviously a mental property, but it is a safe bet that it is not a physical property either.

The claim that human persons are physical organisms is consistent with a variety of views about mental properties. It is also consistent with a variety of views about the further details of human nature. Consider, for example, Aquinas's view. He denied that a human person is a soul that interacts with a numerically distinct body (see *Summa Contra Gentiles*, II.57). Indeed, according to Aquinas, the substantial form of the person is identical with the substantial form of the person's living body (*Summa Theologica*, Ia.76). And so, according to (at least one way of reading) Aquinas, a human person in this life is identical with a living body. And that is physicalism.[18]

Alvin Plantinga says:

Consider again the doctrine of the Incarnation, that characteristic and nonnegotiable Christian teaching according to which the second person of the Trinity became Incarnate and dwelt among us. As *I* understand the scripture and the creeds (Nicene, Athanasian, the Chalcedonian formulation), this involves the second person of the Trinity's actually becoming human. The Logos became a human being, acquiring the property necessary and sufficient for being human. Prior to the Incarnation, however, the second person of the Trinity was not a material object, but an immaterial being. If, however, as materialists assert, to be a human being is to be a material object, then the second person of the Trinity must have become a material object. If he has remained a human being, furthermore, he is presently a material object. But then an immaterial being became a material object; and this seems to me to be impossible. It is clearly impossible, I'd say, that the number seven or the proposition that $7 + 5 = 12$, or the property of self-exemplification, all of which are immaterial objects, should become, turn into, material objects. It is less clearly impossible, but still impossible, it seems to me, that the second person of the Trinity—that personal being with will and intellect and affection—should turn into a material object. (1999: 186)

---

[17] Moreover, the physicalism here is physicalism about *human persons*, saying only that we humans are physical; it does not say that everything is physical.

[18] Physicalism suggests that a person does not exist between death and resurrection. But perhaps a physical person—a human organism—could become non-physical (and presumably non-human) at death and continue to exist in such a state until becoming physical again at resurrection. This seems to be Eleonore Stump's (2002) understanding of Aquinas's view. I think Aquinas can also be read as saying that the person does not exist between death and resurrection, but only the person's substantial form (see Objection 5 and his reply in *Summa Theologica* IIaIIae.83.11).

Plantinga focuses on the physicalist's account of *being human*. But I have been concerned with her account of *having a body*. (I shall address physicalism and *being human* below.) Nevertheless, if Plantinga is right that a non-physical person cannot possibly become physical, then the physicalist's account of embodiment rules out the Son's coming to have the body of Jesus.

Brian Leftow considers the version of physicalism, according to which ". . . the body just *is* the person. On this version, the Son owns [body] B only if the Son *becomes* B; only if an immaterial item becomes material." Like Plantinga, Leftow says: "This does not seem possible" (2002: 284). So, like Plantinga, Leftow thinks that physicalism rules out the Son's coming to have a body.[19]

"Kind-essentialism" says that if something is a member of a natural kind, then it is essentially a member of that kind. Presumably, physical objects constitute a natural kind. And so, given kind-essentialism, physical objects are essentially physical objects. Nothing can start out lacking an *essential* property and then later acquire it. Given all this, kind-essentialism implies that something that starts out as a non-physical object cannot possibly become a physical object. In this way, kind-essentialism threatens the physicalist's account of the Incarnation.

Presumably, human souls would constitute a natural kind. Recall that dualists must say that God the Son became a human soul, though he did not start out that way. Thus kind-essentialism also undermines dualistic Incarnation. Indeed, kind-essentialism undermines the Incarnation on any view. For surely if there are natural kinds, human beings constitute one. Kind-essentialism therefore says that *being human* is an essential property of all humans. But God the Son became human, though he did not start out that way.

Believers in the Incarnation must reject kind-essentialism. Once kind-essentialism is rejected, it is hard to see why the non-physical God the Son could not become a physical human organism.[20] Perhaps this is the sort of thing that might not seem possible merely upon reflection, given no relevant revelation. But the same thing goes for God the Son's becoming human. This is the mystery.

---

[19] It is odd that Leftow thinks that the Incarnation is inconsistent with a normal human person's being identical with a body. For Leftow (2002) endorses a picture of the Incarnation according to which the Son is *not* related to the body of Jesus like each of us is to our own bodies. (So Leftow rejects the assumption that opens this paper.) Thus—given Leftow's view of the Incarnation—an ordinary human person's being identical with a body would not imply that the Son becomes identical with a body in the Incarnation. Moreover, Leftow (2001) himself seems to identify a person in this life with her body, supplementing this with a Thomistic theory of the nature of living human bodies.

[20] C. Stephen Evans rightly insists that we cannot say "the identity of Jesus as the Son of God is grounded in bodily continuity, since the incarnation is a change from a bodiless state to an embodied state" (2002: 269). Some might worry, however, that if we say that God the Son became identical with a human body, we are somehow committed to "a bodily theory of personal identity" that rules out his having existed without a body. But this worry is misplaced. Just so long as *being a body* is a contingent property of what has it, it is possible that that very thing—that very body—could have existed even though it was not a body. (Compare: I am identical with a professor; but this very thing—this very professor—could have existed (and did exist) without being a professor.)

Once we've accepted that possibility, we should accept whatever else comes along with it, including—if part of being human is having physical properties—the Son's coming to have physical properties, that is, coming to be a physical object.

The dualist might still resist. She might object that—even given the Incarnation—God the Son's becoming a human organism seems impossible while his becoming a human soul does not. Presumably, this objection presupposes that there is a "bigger difference" between the divine and (alleged) physical humans than there is between the divine and (alleged) non-physical humans. But, in reply, the difference between God the Son and each of us is staggering. The difference between a non-physical human person and a physical human person is comparatively trivial. If we believe that God the Son became a human being, we have swallowed the camel. To insist that God the Son could not possibly become a *physical* human is to strain out a gnat.

Once we accept the possibility of God the Son's becoming a human being, there remains no good objection to the possibility of his becoming a physical human being. So the Incarnation does not support dualism over physicalism. Quite the contrary. When it comes to the Incarnation, physicalism has two advantages over dualism.

To see the first advantage, recall that dualism—given its account of embodiment—has trouble making sense of God the Son's having exactly the body of Jesus. (It also had trouble affirming that the Father and the Spirit lack bodies.) But physicalism has no such trouble. Physicalism's account of embodiment is that a person has a body if and only if she is identical with that body. Given this account, we can easily state what it is for the Son to have exactly the body of Jesus: God the Son is identical with the body of Jesus and with no other. (And since neither the Father nor the Spirit is identical with a body, the physicalist's account of embodiment tells us that neither has a body.)

To see physicalism's second advantage over dualism, recall that the dualist says that *to be human* is *to be a human soul*. And so dualism makes Christ's becoming human (that is, the Incarnation) one thing, but his becoming embodied something else. But it would be nice to have an account of the Incarnation that required Christ to become incarnate. And we can have such an account, given physicalism. The most straightforward account says that *to be human* just is *to be a human organism*. Christ's becoming human and his coming to have a body—his becoming incarnate—would then be one and the same thing.

There may, however, be a problem with this most straightforward account. To begin to see this potential problem, consider Gregory of Nazianzus's famous anti-Apollinarian remark:

If anyone has put their trust in [Christ] as a human being lacking a human mind, they are themselves mindless and not worthy of salvation. For what has not been assumed has not been healed; it is what is united to his divinity that is saved. . . . Let them not grudge us our total salvation, or endue the Saviour only with the bones and nerves and mere appearance of humanity. (Quoted in McGrath 2001: 362)

The chief objection to Apollinarianism is soteriological. To fully redeem human-ity, Christ must be fully human. He must not be merely physically human—as the Apollinarians said—but also mentally human. (I think this is the point of the creedal insistence that Christ has a "rational soul" (see Kelly 1978: 296–7).) The moral of all this, for our purposes, is that being a human organism—even a human organism with mental properties—might not be sufficient for being "mentally human", for having a "human mind". And if it is not, then the claim that *to be human* just is *to be a human organism* is simply false.

Suppose, for the sake of argument, that being a human organism with mental properties is insufficient for having a human mind. (Presumably, being a human soul with mental properties is also insufficient.) Then the physicalist should say that having a human mind requires thinking in certain ways, having various experiences, and so on (cf. Swinburne 1994: 208). She should say, that is, that to have a human mind is *to be a human organism with a certain sort of mental life*.

The physicalist might say that to be human is simply to be a human organism (with mental properties). Or, instead, the physicalist might say that to be human is to be a human organism with a certain sort of mental life. Either way, physicalism makes becoming identical with (and so having) a body necessary for becoming human. Either way, according to physicalism, the Incarnation—that is, the Son's becoming human—requires his becoming embodied. I say that the Incarnation should be dependent on God the Son's becoming embodied. So, I say, we have another point in favor of physicalism over dualism, since dualism implies the possibility of the Incarnation without embodiment.

I have been treating physicalism as the claim that each human person is identical with a human organism. But a better (and more inclusive) definition of 'physicalism' might be that each human person is a physical object, though not necessarily a human organism. Thus construed, physicalism of course rules out dualism. But it is consistent with a wide range of views. It is consistent with—but does not entail—our being organisms. It is consistent with our being brains. It is consistent with each of us being co-located (but not identical) with a living human body (cf. Baker 2000). And so on.

Each of these versions of physicalism has its own account of embodiment. According to one, a person has a body if and only if she is a (brain that is) part of a human body. According to another, a person has a body if and only if she is co-located with a body. And so on. These accounts of embodiment have none of dualism's problems with Christ's having exactly one body or with the other divine persons having none. For nothing in the omniscience or omnipotence of God suggests, for example, that the persons of the Trinity are proper parts of, or are co-located with, each and every body. Moreover, defenders of each of these accounts can insist that, to become human, Christ had to become a physical object of some sort and so had to become incarnate.

3. CONCLUSION

I assume that we are not events or properties, but rather objects or things or substances. Given that we are objects of some sort, there is no question that we are objects with *mental* properties; obviously we are. The only real question is whether we are objects with *physical* properties. If we are, we are physical objects. If we are not, we are non-physical objects. Given that we are objects of some sort, the only options are physicalism and dualism.[21]

Our options are physicalism and dualism. Which are we to endorse? The Incarnation points us toward physicalism. For the physicalist, unlike the dualist, can insist that becoming embodied is necessary for becoming human; she can insist that the Incarnation requires the Son to become incarnate. Moreover, and more importantly, the physicalist—but not the dualist—can easily and straightforwardly account for God the Son's having the body of Jesus and no other.

Of course, physicalism does not solve every puzzle or answer every question regarding the Incarnation. To take just one example, physicalism is silent on how to reconcile Christ's divinity with his apparently not knowing the hour of his return (Matthew 24: 36). So physicalism is not a cure-all with respect to the Incarnation. Nevertheless, it does cure something, doing away with the embodiment ills brought on by dualism. This gives Christians a good reason to be physicalists.[22]

REFERENCES

Baker, Lynne Rudder (2000). *Persons and Bodies* (Cambridge: Cambridge University Press).

Cross, Richard (2003). "Incarnation, Omnipresence, and Action at a Distance", *Neue Zeitschrift für Systematische Theologie und Religionsphilosophie*, 45: 293–312.

Dennett, Daniel (1991). *Consciousness Explained* (Boston: Little, Brown).

[21] A couple of points will clarify my hasty argument for "only physicalism or dualism". (1) My argument ignores the option of our being composites of soul and body. But since that option just is a form of dualism, that option is consistent with the argument's conclusion, and with the points to follow in this section of the paper. (2) Somewhat misleadingly, I would (in the context of this paper) classify idealism as a form of dualism. For given idealism, we are mental entities that have no physical properties. Given idealism, having a body will presumably be a matter of being associated in the right ways with the relevant ideas. I suspect that, however the "right ways" are cashed out, this will mimic what the standard substance dualist says about embodiment. And so I suspect that idealism is vulnerable to this paper's objections to dualism.

[22] The hope for eternal life, which in scripture is often expressed in terms of hope for the resurrection of the body, gives Christians another good reason to be physicalists (see Merricks 1999; see also Merricks, 2001*b*).

Evans, C. Stephen (2002). "The Self-Emptying of Love: Some Thoughts on Kenotic Christology", in Davis, Kendall, and O'Collins (eds.) *The Incarnation* (Oxford: Oxford University Press).

Freddoso, Alfred J. (1986). "Human Nature, Potency and the Incarnation", *Faith and Philosophy*, 3: 27–53.

Hasker, William (1999). *The Emergent Self* (Ithaca, NY: Cornell University Press).

Kelly, J. N. D. (1978). *Early Christian Doctrines*, revised edn (New York: HarperCollins).

Kim, Jaegwon (2001). "Lonely Souls: Causality and Substance Dualism", in Kevin Corcoran (ed.), *Soul, Body, and Survival: Essays on the Metaphysics of Human Persons* (Ithaca, NY: Cornell University Press).

Leftow, Brian (1997). "Divine Action and Embodiment", *Proceedings of the American Catholic Philosophical Association*, 71: 113–24.

—— (2001). "Souls Dipped in Dust", in Kevin Corcoran (ed.), *Soul, Body, and Survival: Essays on the Metaphysics of Human Persons* (Ithaca, NY: Cornell University Press).

—— (2002). "A Timeless God Incarnate", in Davis, Kendall, and O'Collins (eds.), *The Incarnation* (Oxford: Oxford University Press).

McGrath, Alister E. (2001). *Christian Theology: An Introduction*, 3rd edn (Oxford: Blackwell Publishers).

Merricks, Trenton (1999). "The Resurrection of the Body and the Life Everlasting", in Michael Murray (ed.), *Reason for the Hope Within* (Grand Rapids, Mich.: Eerdmans).

—— (2001*a*) *Objects and Persons* (Oxford: Clarendon Press).

—— (2001*b*) "How to Live Forever Without Saving your Soul: Physicalism and Immortality", in Kevin Corcoran (ed.), *Soul, Body, and Survival: Essays on the Metaphysics of Human Persons* (Ithaca, NY: Cornell University Press).

—— (2006). "Split Brains and the Godhead", in Thomas Crisp, Matthew Davidson, and David Vander Laan (eds.), *Knowledge and Reality: Essays in Honor of Alvin Plantinga on his Seventieth Birthday* (Dordrecht: Kluwer Academic Publishers).

Morris, Thomas V. (1986). *The Logic of God Incarnate* (Ithaca, NY: Cornell University Press).

Olson, Eric (2001). "A Compound of Two Substances", in Kevin Corcoran (ed.), *Soul, Body, and Survival: Essays on the Metaphysics of Human Persons* (Ithaca, NY: Cornell University Press).

Plantinga, Alvin (1999). "On Heresy, Mind, and Truth", *Faith and Philosophy*, 16: 182–93.

Senor, Thomas (1990). "Incarnation and Timelessness", *Faith and Philosophy*, 7: 149–64.

Sosa, Ernest (1984). "Mind–Body Interaction and Supervenient Causation", *Midwest Studies in Philosophy*, 9: 271–81.

Stump, Eleonore (2002). "Aquinas' Metaphysics of the Incarnation", in Davis, Kendall, and O'Collins (eds.), *The Incarnation* (Oxford: Oxford University Press).

Swinburne, Richard (1986). *The Evolution of the Soul* (Oxford: Clarendon Press).

—— (1994). *The Christian God* (Oxford: Clarendon Press).

Van Inwagen, Peter (1998). "Incarnation and Christology", in Edward Craig (ed.), *Routledge Encyclopedia of Philosophy* (London: Routledge).

13

The Tree of Life: Agency and Immortality in a Metaphysics Inspired by Quantum Theory

Peter Forrest

Recently several philosophers including Huw Price, Peter Lewis, and David Lewis have argued that on one interpretation of quantum theory (genus *Indeterminacy*, species *No Collapse*) death is an illusion.[1] Taking Schroedinger's unhappy cat as the standard example, this interpretation tells us that it is as if the whole universe splits into two copies in one of which the cat survives and in the other there is a corpse. Fission into a living organism on the one hand and a corpse on the other is, most of us agree, a way of surviving.[2] So we arrive at the first premise, namely that organisms survive situations like that of Schrödinger's cat. Moreover—and this is the second premise—the causes of death are, it is said, always relevantly similar to those in the Schrödinger's cat thought experiment. From these two premises it is inferred that death is an illusion.

That interpretation also implies *over-survival*, that is, the repeated fission of organisms so that each one of us survives more than once, in fact more times than

Many thanks to the Pew Charitable Trusts, which funded a conference on *Persons: Human and Divine* held at the Nassau Inn, Princeton, on 8 & 9 February 2004, where I read a version of this paper. Many thanks also to all who participated in that conference, and to Dean Zimmerman for his helpful editorial comments. Finally I would like to thank Fiona Utley for drawing the diagrams.

[1] Huw Price, *Time's Arrow & Archimedes Point: New Directions for the Physics of Time* (Oxford: Oxford University Press, 1996), ch. 9; David Lewis in his 2002 Jack Smart lecture, "How Many Lives has Schrödinger's Cat?" subsequently published in the *Australasian Journal of Philosophy*, 82 (2004), 3–22. David Lewis refers to Peter J. Lewis's paper, "What is it like to be Schrödinger's cat?", *Analysis*, 60 (2000), 22–9, as making the same sort of point. Peter Lewis, however, is relying on the Many Minds Interpretation of John Lockwood, in which many minds are posited. See John Lockwood, *Mind, Brain and Quantum* (Oxford: Blackwell, 1989).

[2] There are two assumptions being made here. The first is that the vagueness of the time of death is not an issue, so we may ignore the point that the "corpse" might be not quite dead for a short while. The second is that "corpsism" is incorrect, where corpsism is the thesis that an animal is an enduring thing that survives death as a corpse, until the corpse disintegrates. Corpsism has been discussed but only as part of a *tu quoque* response to an argument for animalism. See Eric T. Olson, "Animalism and the Corpse Problem", *Australasian Journal of Philosophy*, 82 (2004), 265–74.

we naively thought there were human beings on Earth. Moreover, we are ourselves survivors of past fission. Such repeated over-survival is counter-intuitive, and might well be taken as a *reductio ad absurdum* of the interpretation that leads to it.

This paper is not intended as a contribution to a debate over whether quantum theory implies that death is an illusion, although it is inspired by and, as I argue in the Appendix, coherent with contemporary physics. Apart from the Appendix it is an independent investigation of the metaphysical hypothesis that the Universe undergoes fission in such a way that we survive death. I hope it will not cause confusion, however, if the Twin Slit thought experiment is used to illustrate indeterminacy. This is not intended as an appeal to quantum theory; rather, it is just a familiar example.

After a note on coherence with Science, I shall first state the unmodified Tree of Life hypothesis for survival, showing that it has motivation quite independent of the belief in survival after death. Then I explain why it needs modifying, resulting in a rather more complicated Dividing Bundle hypothesis, based upon a *fibrous universe*.

1. COHERENCE WITH SCIENCE

I seek a metaphysics that *coheres* with the sciences. By that I do not mean mere consistency. What I mean by coherence is that the result of adjoining the metaphysics to contemporary scientific theories is an aggregate theory that has the standard theoretical virtue of overall simplicity. If we measure complexity in such a way that the complexity of a consistent conjunction never exceeds, but sometimes equals, the sum of the complexities of the conjuncts, two theories may be said to cohere well if the complexity of the conjunction is significantly less than the sum of the complexities.

My reason for seeking such coherence is a basic commitment to the principle that simpler theories are *significantly* more probable than more complicated ones. That simpler theories are *somewhat* more probable can be argued for on the assumption that we have countably many pair-wise inconsistent theories compatible with the data. They can be arranged in order of increasing complexity with only finitely many simpler than any given theory. The sum of their probabilities cannot exceed 100 percent. So, unless they all have 0 percent (or infinitesimal) probability as Karl Popper taught, their probability must on the whole decrease with complexity. The details of this argument are hardly worth developing, for it does not show that there is *significant* decrease with increasing complexity. I assume, however, that there is a significant decrease and that this applies to philosophy and theology as much as to the sciences.

When it comes to metaphysical hypotheses concerning survival after death, coherence with the sciences is not that easy to achieve. An example of a speculation about survival that is not even intended to cohere with the sciences in this way is Peter van Inwagen's suggestion that God removes the dying, replacing them by corpses.[3] If we postulate an extra spatial dimension, then such removal would merely be a matter of moving sideways. This idea has the advantage of making sense of the accounts of the risen Jesus, who seemed to appear and disappear and yet was solid. I mention this as setting a standard to which other accounts of survival should aspire. In particular, van Inwagen avoids any temporal gaps in persons, avoids fission of one person into many persons, and avoids any appeal to ghostly bodies made of subtle matter. These might all be considered implausible, although subtle matter does have popularity on its side.

2. THE UNMODIFIED TREE OF LIFE HYPOTHESIS

There is a straightforward metaphysical hypothesis that permits survival. It is inspired by Storrs McCall's branching universe.[4] For convenience, I shall throughout this paper take Time to be represented as an extra spatial dimension. Hence the branching universe can be thought of as like a tree. The idea of the Tree of Life is that the universe continually branches but that agents have the power to prune the resulting tree, so that most branches survive for only for a very short time—a jiffy, as Paul Davies would call it: too short a time to support consciousness. (See Fig 13.1, but be warned: in all the diagrams a few branches represent many.)

   Either as a result of divine providence or the human will to survive only once, we undergo no fission ourselves.[5] So on this proposal the universe itself undergoes fission into two or more parts that last for more than a jiffy only if the set of all human beings is correspondingly divided into two or more disjoint subsets. That is, each subset has for its members precisely those who survive in the corresponding branch. Peter Geach suggested something like this as a model for the separation of the blessed from the damned on Judgment Day.[6] But we may use it to provide an account of survival after death. In this context "death" amounts to separation from the rest of us, rather than death strictly speaking. The "dead" person, whom I shall call Mort, lives on in a side branch, presumably alone. I say "presumably" because each death is a distinct event and hence is associated with a distinct branching. Perhaps if you die at the same time as one you love you could go off on in tandem, or perhaps you could ensure your otherwise lonely branches fuse together. But it is highly speculative what

---

   [3] See Peter van Inwagen, "The Possibility of Resurrection", in Paul Edwards (ed.), *Immortality* (New York: Macmillan, 1992), 242–6, repr. from the *International Journal for the Philosophy of Religion*, 9 (1978).
   [4] Storrs McCall, *A Model of the Universe* (Oxford: Clarendon Press), 1994.
   [5] For convenience I am assuming that the only animals who are persons are human beings. Animals that are not persons might well have a will to survive but I doubt that they have a will not to undergo fission.
   [6] Peter Geach, *Providence and Evil* (Cambridge: Cambridge University Press, 1977), 141–3.

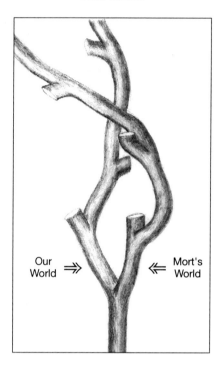

Figure 13.1.

happens in Mort's branch. So my advice to suicidal young lovers is not to count on union immediately after death.

To the obvious objection that the Mort was in a bad way and would die in the side branch, I reply that the branches that begin to form do so in numbers proportionate to the probability of the events occurring in them. Current physical theories allow a very small probability of our surviving just about anything—perhaps even falling into a black hole. So we may suppose that of the very many branches that begin to form a small proportion are ones in which Mort survives if that branch continues for more than a jiffy; and divine providence or a will to survive ensures that Mort continues to exist in one of those branches.

This account, along with the Dividing Bundle hypothesis provided below, has motivation independent of any belief in survival. This motivation is based upon the idea that agency is not the sort of thing for which there is an adequate scientific account. That generates the problem of giving an overall theory that includes agency on the one hand and, without undue alteration, the scientific account of the natural order on the other. The Tree of Life is such a theory. For we replace the usual scientific account of the natural order by a variant, to the effect that so long as a branch exists then the laws of nature hold in it without exception.

We then adjoin to it first an account of universe-fission and then an agency account of pruning. I appeal to readers to judge that this coheres with the sciences somewhat better than van Inwagen's suggestion, and much better than, say, the outrageous suggestion that on apparent death we shrink and come to dwell on the surface of a subatomic particle which looks surprisingly like planet Earth.

The acts of different agents are coordinated in the following way. If X brings it about that a situation of type T occurs, then X prunes all the branches in which X exists but a T does not occur. There are very many branches not thus pruned. If this is the only act occurring at the time then which of these T-occurring branches survives is random. But if there is another agent Y bringing it about that a situation of type U occurs, then Y prunes all the branches in which Y exists but no U occurs. So their combined action results in many branches in which both X and Y exist and situations of types T and U occur. Again if there are no other agents acting apart from X and Y it is random which of these T&U-occurring branches survives.

In what state will Mort be after separation from the rest of us? Divine providence might ensure any possible state for Mort; but if survival is due solely to a will to survive without fission, then the resulting state depends quite critically on whether the pruning occurs before or after further branching. Suppose it occurs after several "generations" of branching, and after enough time has lapsed for very badly damaged organisms to die, but still before it could constitute fission of a person. Then there would be a selection effect, in which the fitter organisms undergo more fission. Hence by the time the pruning occurs it is likely that the random survivor will be fairly fit. If, as I suspect, there is no time for such a selection effect then we may predict that poor Mort only just survives, with whatever degree of consciousness is required for survival. It would be like a brain in as vat, except there is no vat, and only part of a brain. In that case we should expect Mort to "rest in peace", asleep until . . . Until what? The Tree of Life hypothesis does not have much to say about the Resurrection of the Dead, but its successor, the Dividing Bundle hypothesis will.

3. HOW LOVELY IS THE TREE OF LIFE?

The Tree of Life hypothesis is open to the objection that a permanent sleep does not correspond to the hoped for—or feared—survival. To the extent that such hopes are adequately grounded our metaphysics should accommodate them. How could this be done? One suggestion is that there is a further project of providing an eschatology coherent with science, and that Muslims and Jews could think of the dead resting, in peace or otherwise, until Judgment Day. But I fail to see how Christians could fit the Resurrection of Jesus into this scheme. So I for one would not rely on this further project of an eschatology coherent with the sciences.

An alternative is to appeal to the precedent of time reversibility in physics, and allow fusion as well as fission. Hence the side branches that split off containing the dead might fuse together into a heavenly realm. The Resurrection of the Dead would then consist of a final fusion of all existing branches of the universe. On this model the Heavenly realm could itself have undergone fission shortly after Jesus' death, with that branch coming to fuse with the Earthly branch. That is beginning, however, to look rather ad hoc, so I judge that while the Tree of Life hypothesis might be satisfactory for Jews and Muslims, Christians should seek something different. So I shall refer to this as the Christians' objection.

A further theological objection would hold to all the hypotheses proposed in this paper. I call it the Sophisticates' Objection. Surely we do not expect to survive death in a body like this one in a world like ours? Surely, the objection goes, there is a radical transformation into something that we cannot envisage. I reply thus. However radical our eventual transformation turns out to be, we should doubt the metaphysical possibility of our surviving too sudden a change. Life in a side branch could be the first step with more radical changes to follow.

There are three other, non-theological, objections to the Tree of Life hypothesis, which I now note. The first is that this hypothesis does not cohere with the sciences as well as we might like. For although the natural order is not interfered with in the branches that continue, the pruning itself seems to be contrary to the natural order, involving the annihilation of what would be like a whole classical universe. In particular there is the problem with the conservation laws, notably that of mass energy. There are two ways of understanding these in the context of a branching universe. One is to take the mass energy within a branch; the other is to take the totality across branches. But neither works—unless, as Edward Tryon has suggested, the mass energy is zero.[7] If we take the totality across all branches then we would expect some extra energy in the side branches containing the dead. If we consider energy in each branch then pruning violates the conservation. So unless we speculate that the total mass energy is zero or that it is zero on the side branches in which the dead live on then an otherwise well-established conservation law is violated.

We may meet this objection if we allow, along with David Chalmers and Richard Swinburne, the possibility of "zombies", molecule for molecule replicas of human persons but with no consciousness. For simplicity let us temporarily adopt Swinburne's Substance Dualism. Then we may take the universe to branch repeatedly without pruning. At each branch the soul can only go with the one body. So we obtain something similar to the Tree of Life but with the conservation laws holding on each branch. (This is illustrated in Fig 13.2, which is just like Fig 13.1 except that branches are bezombied rather than pruned.) In

    [7] Edward P. Tryon, 'Is the Universe a Vacuum Fluctuation?', *Nature*, 246/5433 (1990), 396–7, repr. in John Leslie (ed.), *Physical Cosmology and Philosophy* (New York: Macmillan).

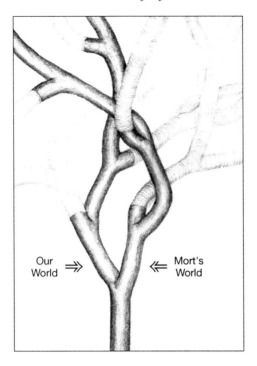

Our World $\Longrightarrow$ ⟸ Mort's World

Figure 13.2.

Section 6, I shall offer a defence of zombies, but this would be premature here since there are other objections to the unmodified Tree of Life.

The next objection is that before mass and energy were equated the conservation of mass was taken to explicate the principle *ex nihilo nihil fit*. And that principle retains its intuitive appeal: stuff, we think, does not just come into existence. And even if the total mass energy is zero we might well consider that stuff would come to exist if the universe underwent fission. Therefore branching would be impossible. To this it might be replied that theists usually accept that God created *ex nihilo*. But if so that was a miraculous act and we should be reluctant to think that this miracle is repeated every fraction of a second as the Universe branches.

The final objection to the Tree of Life hypothesis is that many find the idea of spatially separated branches of the universe implausible. I suspect this is only a genuine problem for presentists for whom a branching universe consists of many unconnected universes. The rest of us may console ourselves with the real connections between the branches in the past.

In addition to these objections there are one or two further reasons for seeking a variant on the Tree of Life. One is that, as I explain in the Appendix, the unmodified Tree of Life is inferior in some respects to the Many Worlds interpretation of quantum theory. The other, for what it is worth, is that the Tree of Life coheres well only with a probabilistic physics and there might be a more fundamental deterministic physics might.

4. THE FIBROUS UNIVERSE

Because of the objections to the unmodified Tree of Life hypothesis, and even to its zombie variant, I now consider the Many Worlds interpretation of quantum theory, proposed by B. S. De Witt as an explication of Hugh Everett's interpretation, and currently championed by David Deutsch.[8] The idea is that a quantum state describes not just what is happening in one world but in many worlds. So, to take an example dear to Deutsch, a quantum computer will have enormous power because it is like a large collection of classical computers in different worlds. For a reason discussed in the Appendix, I hold that even "particles" such as electrons and quarks exist in many worlds simultaneously. And so do we. Therefore I prefer to think of these many "worlds" as themselves all embedded in the one hyperspace. As Dean Zimmerman has pointed out to me, hyperspace does little real work in explaining Mort's survival. It helps the exposition, however, first by overcoming any tendency to think of the separate "worlds" as possible worlds, and secondly as reminding us that we do not have many bodies in different "worlds" so much as one body with parts in different "worlds".

Geometers and topologists often talk of *fiber-bundles*. Why mention this esoteric mathematical terminology? It is because when philosophers talk of *many worlds* or even a *multiverse* this suggests many separate universes, perhaps branches in a McCall branching universe but nonetheless not spatially connected now. As I have said, I want to resist this suggestion, and instead think of what classically we took to be a universe, with three spatial and one temporal dimension, as just one "fiber" in a bundle. So I am thinking of the universe as itself a bundle of universe-fibers, each of which has the usual number of spatial dimensions. Space is to be thought of as having enough dimensions to contain all the universe-fibers at a given time; so it is Hyperspace.

To illustrate the concept of a fiber-bundle consider a familiar three-dimensional space. Now pick a plane K. Then the three-dimensional space can be considered a fiber-bundle with the "fibers" being K and all the planes parallel to K. This does not mean that the planes are somehow separate like cards in a deck, or one dimensional like cotton fibers. All it means is that the three-dimensional space has some extra structure, namely an equivalence relation whose equivalence classes are the fibers.

[8] B. S. De Witt, "Quantum Mechanics and Reality", *Physics Today*, 23 (1970), 30–5; Hugh Everett, ' "Relative State" Formulation of Quantum Mechanics', *Review of Modern Physics*, 29 (1957), 452–64; David Deutsch, *The Fabric of Reality: The Science of Parallel Universes and its Implications* (New York: Penguin USA, 1997).

As I have already mentioned, this way of thinking of the Many Worlds interpretation helps overcome resistance to individuals existing in many "worlds", that is, universe-fibers. When I suggest that the universe is a fiber-bundle, I am suggesting that the "multiverse" or ensemble of "universes" is in fact our universe, perhaps the only one there is, and that it has an equivalence relation on it so that the equivalence classes, which I call universe-fibers, have only three macroscopic spatial dimensions. The whole universe is thus vastly larger than we usually think, and, regrettably, vastly more complicated. It is, however, neither larger nor more complicated than a supposed multiverse made up of distinct universes in the standard version of the Many Worlds Interpretation.

In a classical mechanical theory we would say that each individual fiber evolved deterministically and perhaps hypothesize that nearby fibers had similar initial conditions. In a quantum theory the state of all the fibers taken together might evolve deterministically but not individual fibers.

Now consider an object, as it might be you or I or, again, as it might be an electron. Does it belong to a single fiber or extend across many fibers? If we thought of the fibers as separate universes, it would be natural to assume the former and talk of *counterparts* in neighboring fibers. But if we think of a bundle of fibers we may say that electrons and human beings extend across fibers. In fact I made the distinction between a universe made up of fibers and one that has separate sub-universes chiefly to motivate what might otherwise seem incoherent, the hypothesis that things as we know them extend across many of these universe-fibers. Strictly speaking, however, we do not require spatial relations between the different fibers, such as would exist if they were in a hyperspace. It suffices that there be some physically necessary correlations and that there be simultaneity relations across fibers.

My chief reason for suggesting that things, including we ourselves, extend across universe-fibers is that it is absurd to posit counterparts of ourselves, especially counterparts that are indistinguishable in all mental respects. So our minds extend across fibers. We could hypothesize that the one mind is correlated with a whole collection of brains, each one in a different fiber. Alternatively we could hypothesize that there is just the one brain itself spread out across the many fibers. Perhaps there is merely a verbal distinction between the two hypotheses, but, for reasons indicated in the Appendix, I prefer the hypothesis that objects, including our brains, are spread out across fibers.

Even if this is not merely a verbal dispute the choice of which hypothesis to adopt does not affect the discussion of an afterlife, provided we are convinced there is but a single mind corresponding to the bodies—or the body parts as the case might be—in the different fibers. Nonetheless the question is of intrinsic interest and it is worth noting that given the Whiteheadian account of points as "constructs" (technically *filters)* of smaller and smaller regions this distinction between the two hypotheses would not be merely verbal. For in that case we might for the sake of uniformity take the universe-fibers themselves to be similar "constructs", made up of more and more narrow tubes each representable as, but not constituted by, many universe-fibers side by side.

As Zimmerman has pointed out, this Whiteheadian universe-tube hypothesis is open to the objection that there would then not be any completely determinate states of particles. For their locations and other properties would vary across the tubes, however small. In reply I note that on a Whiteheadian account it is natural to take the fundamental properties to correspond to the integrals of the quantities postulated in a point-based theory. For instance, instead of the mass or charge density at a point we consider the total mass or total charge of a region. This approach may easily be extended to tubes. For example, suppose there are two extra dimensions in the hyperspace, and to avoid confusion let us use the *schmeter* as the unit of length across the extra two dimensions. Then the fundamental unit of mass will not be the *gram* but the *schmam,* where a gram is a schmam per square schmeter. A certain region in a tube could have a total mass of, say, 12 schmams. If the tube was of cross-section 2 square schmeters, then on fiber-based theory we might say that its intersection with a given fiber had density of, say, 6 schmams per square schmeter, that is, 6 grams. And if the volume of the region were itself 3 cubic meters, then the density would be 2 schmams per square schmeter per cubic meter, that is, 2 grams per cubic meter. On a Whiteheadian tube-based account the fundamental mass properties are expressed in schmams, and the ones that appear in a point-based fiber-based account are derivatives. There is no indeterminacy, and there only seemed to be because it was assumed, incorrectly, that the fundamental mass property would be measured in grams not schmams.

Noting, then, that the fibrous universe may be adapted to a tube-based Whiteheadian account I shall, for the sake of exposition, consider fibers rather than tubes and suppose that familiar objects, including our bodies, extend across these fibers. If the neighboring universe-fibers differ just a little, then there is some indeterminacy in what happens to an object. Consider the famous Two Slit thought experiment, in which an electron is fired at a screen with two slits in it without the quantum state being able to specify which slit it went through. If we say that in one fiber one electron-part goes through one slit and in another fiber another electron-part through the other slit, then it is *as if* it is indeterminate which slit the whole electron (extended across the fibers) goes through. This is a harmless quasi-indeterminacy due to the failure to distinguish fibers. Rather than say there is no fact of the matter we should say that there is a more complicated fact of the matter than we first supposed.

The fibrous universe hypothesis provides us with a modification of the Tree of Life. Call this the Pruned Dividing Bundle hypothesis. For a bundle of fibers can undergo fission into sub-bundles without any one fiber undergoing fission. (See Fig 13.3.) If we observers extend across a bundle of universe-fibers and we observe whether or not something has occurred, then the bundle will divide into those fibers in which it has occurred and those in which it has not. Hence our

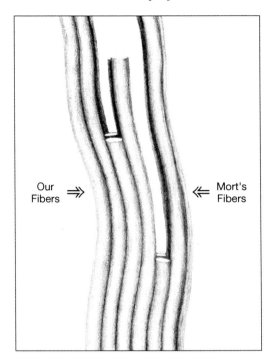

Figure 13.3.

minds would divide also, because in one bundle we observed one thing but in another the other. Given enough different results of observations, we would be forced to say that we do not just have a divided mind but have undergone fission. But that is contrary to the assumption being made in this paper that we survive without fission. Therefore we need something like pruning.

5. THREE FIBROUS UNIVERSE THEORIES

I am now going to a suppose that some version of the Many Worlds hypothesis holds, so that there is a fibrous Universe, and consider three versions of the Dividing Bundle hypothesis. In all three the Universe is made up of fibers that do not undergo fission. Nonetheless, being a bundle of fibers, it can undergo fission by means of the separation of the fibers into two or more sub-bundles. Without something like pruning we would have repeated fission of all of us each minute, and not merely the survival of death but over-survival. On the Pruned Dividing Bundle version whole sub-bundles are pruned, as in Fig. 13.3, where, however, the immense number of fibers cannot be depicted. That is tantamount to terminating many of the fibers.

When an agent X acts to bring about a situation of type T, then, on this Pruned Dividing Bundle hypothesis, X terminates universe-fibers so that of those that remain and contain X, all or most of them are ones in which a T occurs. I say "or most of them" because we would not notice a little bit of (quasi-) indeterminacy. Likewise when Y observes that a U occurs then either all or most of the fibers that remain and which contain Y are ones in which a U occurs.

Which of the objections to the simple Tree of Life hold for this Pruned Dividing Bundle hypothesis? The Christians' Objection will be dealt with in the Section 7. Here I consider the others. There is no insuperable problem due to spatially separate branches; for even if that was a genuine problem we could solve it by saying that the universe-fibers are packed into a higher dimensional Hyperspace rather than occupying separate spaces. Nor is there any violation of *ex nihilo nihil fit.*

The problem of mass-energy conservation still holds, however. Suppose we do not hold the total energy of the universe to be zero. Then terminating universe-fibers violate energy conservation. In any case there is an enormous intuitive difference between short-lived branches of a branching universe and the termination of universe-fibers which have existed from the beginning of the Universe and which are much like most people have thought of the whole Universe. No doubt God has the power to annihilate them, but I have glibly suggested that human beings annihilate them too. Thus if I scratch an itchy toe I have just annihilated half the Universe. Talk of delusions of grandeur! Surely this is crazy. The problem of what happens to the energy is, then, just one, rather minor, aspect of a more general problem, the counter-intuitive character of universe-fiber annihilation.

For fellow friends of zombies, I now present the Zombie Dividing Bundle hypothesis in which the universe-fibers that are to be "pruned" are not annihilated so much as bezombied (Fig. 13.4). If there is no consciousness in these fibers, then they are as good as annihilated. This avoids any problems with conservation of energy, and agency is now just a matter of consciousness retreating away from the unwanted fibers, not massive annihilation.

Many will not only find the termination of fibers counter-intuitive but also dismiss zombification. For them I suggest a variant on which fibers are neither annihilated nor bezombied, so it is not as if the bundle divides. This is the Squeeze hypothesis. On it we must take the supposition of hyperspace as of more than heuristic significance. The universe-fibers are, I am now supposing, packed into Hyperspace. Perhaps they are packed *densely*, in the sense that every (hyper) ball in Hyperspace, however small, intersects some universe-fiber. This is a consequence of a Whiteheadian account in which the fibers are "constructs" out of smaller and smaller tubes, and so is fairly plausible anyway if we adopt a Whiteheadian account of points and instants as "constructs" out of extended regions and intervals. In that case we may no longer equate the probability of an event of type T with the pro-portion of fibers in which a T occurs, for there will be infinitely many in which T occurs and infinitely many in which T does not occur. Rather, we should compare

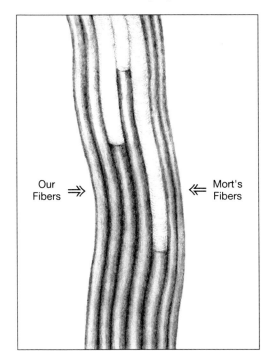

Our Fibers $\Rightarrow$ $\Leftarrow$ Mort's Fibers

Figure 13.4.

the volume occupied by the fibers in which T occurs with the volume occupied in which T does not occur. The fibers do not, therefore, have to terminate in order to provide scope for action. All that is required for the agent to bring about a situation of type T is for the agent to "squeeze" the bundle of fibers in which a T does not occur and allow the corresponding expansion of the bundle in which a T does occur. That is, the action increases the volume of fibers in which a T occurs and decreases the volume in which T does not occur, keeping the total volume constant. Note that in this case the result will never be 100 percent determinate that T occurs, while if fibers are terminated or bezombied total determinacy can occur.

On the Squeeze hypothesis agency does not terminate fibers that have existed from the beginning. Agency, and observation, merely contract or expand the region of Hyperspace these fibers take up. If we picture Hyperspace as a Euclidean plane (so the volume is represented by area,) with time as a third dimension, then we could picture the universe-fibers as curves in the resulting three-dimensional space and it is easy to think of some curves coming closer together so as to occupy less volume while others grow further apart to occupy more.

This Squeeze hypothesis requires that the volume be a suitable measure of indeterminacy and hence be related systematically to the frequencies of types of observation, in such a way that relative frequencies tend to approximate the ratios of the volumes. Thus, if a beam of electrons passes through the twin slits, the relative frequency of detections in a given region R of the screen should approximate the ratio of: (*a*) the volume of the mereological sum of the universe tubes in which the electron hits R; to (*b*) the volume of the mereological sum of the universe tubes in which the electron hits the screen somewhere. Because of the need to posit this systematic connection between the expected frequencies and the volume, we might, on reflection, prefer the first two versions of the Dividing Bundle hypothesis to the Squeeze hypothesis.

6. ZOMBIES TO THE RESCUE!

Any hypothesis that implies that for all we know most or all of those around us now are zombies should, I say, be rejected, as contrary to the presuppositions of morality. This is the *reductio ad zombidum*. Nonetheless we should not dismiss them too swiftly. For if the past but not the future is real then there is a strong case for saying the past is inhabited by zombies, so we need to posit them anyway. The case is that otherwise we cannot reply to the somewhat similar objections made by David Lewis (in conversation with John Bigelow) by Craig Bourne, by David Braddon-Mitchell, and by Trenton Merricks.[9] If the past is real, Lewis asks us to spare a thought for poor old Bonaparte suffering from the delusion that it was still early in the nineteenth century, and then asked how we are justified in our belief that we are not similarly deluded because the present might have already advanced to the year 2500 leaving us stranded in the past! His solution was to adopt the token-reflexive account of the present. Presentists solve the problem by denying Bonaparte any reality. But we Growing Block theorists take the present as an ontologically significant boundary between the actual past and the many merely possible futures. We should, therefore, take the past as zombie-land in order to avoid the Deluded Bonaparte objection.[10]

Likewise those who are realists about possible worlds but reject Lewis's token-reflexive account of actuality should take counterpart human beings in other possible worlds to be zombies. On the Zombie Dividing Bundle hypothesis we may take the bezombied fibers as mere might-have-beens, which have achieved a status like the past without ever having been actually present.

[9] Craig Bourne, "When am I? A Tense Time for some Tense Theorists?" *Australasian Journal of Philosophy*, 80/3 (2002), 359–71; David Braddon-Mitchell, "How do We Know it is Now Now?" *Analysis*, 64/3 (2004), 199–202; Trenton Merricks, "Goodbye Growing Block", in D. W. Zimmerman (ed.), *Oxford Studies in Metaphysics*, ii (Oxford: Oxford University Press, 2006).
[10] For some further details see my "The Real but Dead Past: A Reply to Braddon-Mitchell", *Analysis*, 64/4 (2004). Quentin Smith reaches a somewhat similar conclusion in *Language and Time* (New York: Oxford University Press, 1993), ch. 5.

7. MORT'S FATE

On the proposed Fibrous Universe variants on the Tree of Life there are three different ways of surviving death. First, as in Fig. 13.3 or Fig. 13.4, there could be a complete separation into a universe-bundle in which Mort lives on and a universe-bundle in which the rest of us live on. Or, secondly, the bundle in which Mort lives on might in fact be a very small part of a larger bundle. Or, thirdly, there could be overlap without Mort's sub-bundle being part of ours. Perhaps in these last two cases Mort would become a ghost, but in any case Mort could have little impact on our world as a whole, being reduced to near epiphenomenal status.

In the last two cases there could be an overlap between all the universe-bundles in which the dead live on their solitary lives and the mainstream Earthly bundle. Hence it might subsequently happen that the universe-fibers in the overlap were the only ones not to be terminated. In that case Mort and everyone else who died would, from the perspective of Earth, come back to life. This provides a model for the Resurrection of Jesus, as well as a general Resurrection of the Dead. After the Crucifixion, the fibers in which Jesus did not die but survived in the tomb were only a minute proportion of the actual ones, but at the Resurrection all the other fibers were terminated. As far as I can see this meets the Christians' objection to the unmodified Tree of Life hypothesis.

8. IS THE FIBROUS UNIVERSE TOO COMPLICATED?

The fibrous universe seems rather complicated—neither the sort of thing God would create nor the sort of thing we should posit uncreated. It is, to be sure, no more complicated than other Many Worlds interpretations of quantum theory, but we might reject them as well on the grounds of undue complexity.

The fibrous universe might be too complicated to posit uncreated, but it coheres rather better with creation. To argue for this, I first submit that in addition to any non-sensory ways of knowing, God perceives the world, that is, God knows the world in a sensory fashion. For if God knows everything and if what it is like to see red is itself something to know, then God must know what it is like to see red.[11] It would be a strange imperfection if God knew what it was like to see red but lacked the capacity to see something red, and similarly for other perceptions. I infer that God can choose to perceive the world. Granted that we believe that God can choose to perceive the world, it is better not to multiply mysteries by positing Middle Knowledge as God's way of knowing creatures' choices. Instead we should suppose that God knows these choices by perceiving creatures.

---

[11] Frank Jackson's Mary Argument depends on the premise that what it is like to see red is itself something that can be known. See Frank Jackson, "Epiphenomenal Qualia", *Philosophical Quarterly*, 32 (1982), 127–36.

I cannot understand how God could perceive the Universe unless Berkeleian idealism is correct and the Universe is made up of perceptions, some human perhaps but most divine. Conversely if, for some reason, the theist is already a Berkeleian idealist then this entails that God perceives.

Regardless of whether it is linked with Idealism in this way, the hypothesis of divine perception has considerable appeal. It is, however, threatened by the Perspectives Dilemma, namely: is divine perception perspectival or not? Perspectival perception such as vision contains as part of its content a spatial relation to the apparent object. For example, in out-of-body experiences things appear as if from a point of view which is in fact outside the body. Now for the dilemma: if the divine perception is not perspectival, then it conveys no knowledge of spatial relations and so is inadequate; but if the divine perception is perspectival, then it must be from a single perspective, otherwise it is non-veridical. For the awareness of A from point of view X and of B from point of view Y will in many cases misrepresent the spatial relation between A and B. Suppose, for instance, that X, A, B, and Y are in a straight line, with XA $= 1$ cm, AB $= 3$ cm, and BY $= 1$ cm. Then A and B seem to be 1 cm away from the perceiver, but both A and B being 1 cm away is incompatible with their being 3 cm apart. And presumably God would not create in such a way as to be subject to non-veridical perception.

The second horn of the Perspectives Dilemma is less sharp than the first. For divine perception could always be veridical provided God is confined to a single point of view. In that case we might even think of God as occupying a point. There are, however, two objections to the hypothesis of a single divine point of view. The first is that it is arbitrary where the divine point of view is. (And maybe in Special Relativity the frame of reference is also arbitrary.) The second is that, it could be said, one point of view is not enough for God to have the perfection of knowing every thing in every way. The only reply to these objections that I can think of is to suppose that God creates a fibrous universe, with every point being the divine point of view in some of the fibers. Given Special Relativity, we may also suppose that the divine point of view is in every frame of reference in some fiber. In passing I note that this reconciles Special Relativity with the idea of absolute time and an absolute present, by taking what is absolute to be that which God is aware of.

The resulting system is one in which God perceives everything in every universe-fiber and occupies every point of view in some fiber, without any arbitrary picking out of just one point of view. It therefore provides a satisfactory blunting of the second horn of the Perspectives Dilemma and hence a defense of the hypothesis that God knows things by perceiving them.

9. CONCLUSION

The aim of this paper has been to make progress towards the goal of a metaphysical hypothesis that provided scope for agency, survival of death, and the Resurrection, while cohering well with contemporary science. My best attempt at such a hypothesis is based upon the idea that the "worlds" of the Many Worlds interpretation of quantum theory should be thought of as universe-fibers.

APPENDIX: THE FIBROUS UNIVERSE AND QUANTUM THEORY

I have neither the space nor the expertise to expound the various interpretations of quantum theory, with their strengths and weaknesses. All I can do here is to note the sort of interpretation the simple Tree of Life model provides, the sort of interpretation the more complicated Fibrous Universe hypothesis provides, note the advantage of the latter, and leave it at that.

Interpretations of quantum theory answer the following questions:

- *The Structure Question*: What sort of structure do quantum systems and their states have?
- *The Dynamics Question*: What happens when a system evolves without interference?
- *The Measurement Question*: What if anything novel occurs if there is outside interference, in particular during observation?

The Tree of Life model has nothing to say about the Structure Question. Concerning the Dynamics Question it tells us that between branchings the Schrödinger equation or its relativistic analog holds, governing the deterministic evolution of the state of the system. Its answer to the Measurement Question is that observation is one of those occasions in which the system does not evolve deterministically, and, excepting cases of lasting universe-fission, it evolves probabilistically because just one branch survives more than a jiffy. If there are only finitely many branches then it is not surprising that the observed frequencies of an occurrence of type T would approximate the proportion of branches in which a T occurs. It could be queried whether this proportion of branches counts as a genuine probability of a T occurring, but that is no problem for we would not need to hypothesize any probability in addition to these proportions to explain the frequencies. In particular we need not posit irreducible propensities.

As far as it goes that sort of interpretation is entirely satisfactory. But it does not go far enough. The advantage of the Fibrous Universe is that it inherits the Many Worlds Interpretation's capacity to give more detailed answers to the Structure Question and the Dynamics Question. On the Many Worlds Interpretation we *try* to interpret the state as a probability distribution over various classical states, involving position and momentum of various particles. A well-known difficulty, pointed out by Eugene Wigner, is that the attempt to do so commits us to probabilities less than zero.[12] My preferred response to this is to reinterpret the state not as a probability distribution but in terms of the expected number of particles with given position and momentum.[13] I assume that the "quantum

---

[12] Eugene Wigner, "On the Quantum Correction for Thermodynamic Equilibrium", *Physical Review*, 40 (1932), 749–59, repr. in Y. S. Kim and M. E. Noz, *Phase Space Picture of Quantum Mechanics: Group Theoretical Approach* (Singapore: World Scientific, 1991), 219–31.

[13] See my "Common Sense and a 'Wigner–Dirac' Approach to Quantum Mechanics", *The Monist*, 89 (1997), 131–59; and my "In Defence of the Phase Space Picture", *Synthese*, 119 (1999), 299–311.

vacuum" is a flux of many short-lived particles so that the quantum state specifies the expected number above par where *par* is what occurs in the "vacuum". Then it is quite consistent to allow some expected values below par, holes in the "vacuum", as it were.

Given this interpretation, what we call a particle does not exist in just the one "world" but involves the distribution of position and momenta of particles in the various "worlds". Hence my preference for saying that we have one brain spread across many fibers rather than one mind corresponding to many brains.

On this interpretation an electron stands to the genuine, often short-lived particles much as an organism stands to its constituents, being a self-perpetuating pattern in the flux. Provided we grant that the "particles" that make us up are themselves constituted by what happens in many "worlds" and provided we grant that there is a probability measure over the "worlds" the further identification of the "worlds" as universe-fibers and the probability measure as a (hyper) volume is not strictly necessary, although it has heuristic value.

A little-known implication of this hypothesis about "particles" is that as Wigner also showed there is an informative answer to the dynamics question. The state evolves just as we would expect if the particles within the "worlds" bounce off each other conserving energy and momentum.[14]

Finally, as regards the Measurement Question, recent work on decoherence by Wojciech Zurek, Roland Omnès, and others suggests, although not conclusively proving,[15] that, when an observation is made of whether or not a T occurs, the state evolves into a good approximation to a mixture of states in one of which a T occurs in 100 percent of the "worlds" and in the other a T occurs in no "worlds". Hence the totality of all the "worlds" undergoes an almost complete fission into a T branch and a not-T branch. Moreover the probability of observing a T is equal to the probability measure of the set of "worlds" in which a T occurs. Without some device for pruning the tree, we would say that the observers underwent fission when an observation was made. The proposed Fibrous Universe hypotheses restore common sense while keeping the solution to the Measurement Question provided by the Many Worlds Interpretation.

The result is that the Fibrous Universe has the benefits of the Many Worlds Interpretation without the absurdity of the fission of observers. It is superior to the unmodified Tree of Life as an interpretation because it is more informative. It should be noted, however, that someone who considered some quite different interpretation of quantum theory to be correct would not be impressed. My response to the unimpressed would be that we should not make up our minds on the interpretation of quantum theory independently of the rest of metaphysics but seek a unified account of everything, including agency. If that inclines us one way rather than another when it comes to interpreting quantum theory, so be it.

---

[14] Kim and Noz, *Phase Space Picture of Quantum Mechanics*, 224.

[15] Wojciech Zurek, "Decoherence and the Transition from Quantum to Classical", *Physics Today*, 44 (1991), 36–44; and Roland Omnès, *Understanding Quantum Mechanics* (Princeton: Princeton University Press, 1999).

14

The Metaphysics of Original Sin

Michael C. Rea

Various different doctrines in the history of Christian thought have gone under the label 'the doctrine of original sin'. All of them affirm something like the following claim:

> (S0) All human beings (except, at most, four) suffer from a kind of corruption that makes it very likely that they will fall into sin.

Many (perhaps most) go on to affirm the following two claims as well:

> (S1) All human beings (except, at most, four) suffer from a kind of corruption that makes it inevitable that they will fall into sin, and this corruption is a consequence of the first sin of the first man.

> (S2) All human beings (except, at most, four) are guilty from birth in the eyes of God, and this guilt is a consequence of the first sin of the first man.

The "exceptions" referred to in (S0)–(S2) are the first human beings (Adam and Eve), Jesus of Nazareth, and (according to those who endorse the doctrine of the Immaculate Conception) Mary, the mother of Jesus.

(S2) is known as the *doctrine of original guilt*. It is now common for (S2) to be treated as a doctrine separate from the doctrine of original sin, which many philosophers and theologians simply identify with (S0) or (S1). But it was not always so; and it will be convenient for present purposes just to stipulate that (S2) is part of the doctrine of original sin. I will also stipulate that (S1) is part of that doctrine. Thus, for purposes here, nothing counts as a theory of original

Work on this paper was supported in part by an NEH Summer Stipend (2004). A version of this paper was discussed at the Metaphysics of Human Persons Workshop (February 2004), sponsored by a grant from the Pew Charitable Trust, and also by the weekly reading group hosted by the University of Notre Dame's Center for Philosophy of Religion. I am grateful to the participants in these groups for valuable advice and criticism—especially (from the Pew Workshop) Godehard Bruntrup, Peter Forrest, Hud Hudson, Trenton Merricks, Richard Swinburne, Peter van Inwagen, and Dean Zimmerman; and (from the Center for Philosophy of Religion group) E. J. Coffman, Jeff Green, Tom Flint, Carl Gillett, Todd Long, Michael Murray, James Rissler, and Kevin Timpe. I would also like to thank Michael Bergmann, Jeff Brower and Tom Crisp for their very helpful comments on earlier drafts.

sin or as an expression of the doctrine of original sin (hereafter, 'DOS') unless it includes commitment to both (S1) and (S2). For ease of exposition, I will talk as if the story of the Fall as recorded in Genesis 3 is literally true. I do not think that this story must be literally true in all of its details in order for (S1) and (S2) to be true. But I will not discuss here questions about which details are required by suitably developed versions of DOS, nor will I discuss questions about which details would have to be modified if, as many now believe, the Genesis account of creation were literally false.

DOS has played an important role in the history of Christian thought. Among other things, it provides an explanation for the universality of sin, and it also provides critical underpinning for the view that all human beings—even the youngest of infants—are in need of a savior.[1] It was accepted by most of the medieval philosopher-theologians from Augustine through Duns Scotus, and it is affirmed by many of the most important post-Athanasian creeds of the Orthodox, Roman Catholic, and evangelical protestant churches.[2] Prima facie, however, it conflicts with the following intuitively plausible "principle of possible prevention":

(MR) A person P is morally responsible for the obtaining of a state of affairs S only if S obtains (or obtained) and P could have prevented S from obtaining.

The reason is simple. According to DOS, human beings are born guilty. But one cannot be guilty *simpliciter*. If one is guilty, then there must be something—presumably, the obtaining of some state of affairs—*for which* one is guilty. But, one might think, whatever states of affairs obtained at or before the time we were born were not states of affairs whose obtaining we had the power to prevent. So if (MR) is true, it would seem to follow that we can be guilty only for things that happen *after* we are born. But then we cannot be guilty from birth as DOS requires.[3]

---

[1] Hence, Augustine writes in one of his anti-Pelagian treatises: "Now, seeing that [the Pelagians] admit the necessity of baptizing infants—finding themselves unable to contravene that authority of the universal Church, which has been unquestionably handed down by the Lord and His apostles—they cannot avoid the further concession, that infants require the same benefits of the Mediator, in order that . . . they may be reconciled to God. . . . But from what, if not from death, and the vices, and guilt, and thraldom, and darkness of sin? And, inasmuch as they do not commit any sin in the tender age of infancy by their actual transgression, original sin only is left" (*On the Merits and Forgiveness of Sins*, bk. 1, ch. 39; in Augustine 1999: 30)

[2] See e.g. *The Canons and Decrees of the Council of Trent*, Fifth Session (in Schaff 1998*a*: 83–9); *The Orthodox Confession of Faith*, part I, question 24 (in Mohila 1975); *The Acts and Decrees of the Synod of Jerusalem*, chapter VI, decree XVI (Orthodox Eastern Church 1899: 139–43); *The Augsburg Confession*, part I, articles II–III (in Schaff 1998*b*: 8–9); *The Heidelberg Catechism*, questions 4–11 (in Schaff 1998*b*: 308–11); *The Thirty-Nine Articles of the Church of England*, article IX (in Schaff 1998*b*: 492–3); and *The Westminster Confession*, chapter VI (in Schaff 1998*b*: 615–17).

[3] It has been suggested to me that perhaps the alleged conflict with MR could be dismissed out of hand on the grounds that MR talks about "individual guilt" whereas original sin concerns "collective

Whatever scriptural or systematic theological objections one might have against DOS, the apparent conflict with (MR) is almost certainly the primary source of purely philosophical resistance to it. On the other hand, some theologians, particularly in the Reformed tradition, treat the apparent conflict between DOS and (MR) as reason to reject (MR).[4] In the hands of these theologians, DOS plays an important role in paving the way for the view that moral responsibility is compatible with determinism—a conclusion which, in turn, constitutes an important premise in defense of the view that freedom is compatible with determinism. Thus, Christians who are interested in preserving their commitment to DOS while at the same time resisting compatibilism about freedom and moral responsibility would do well to examine carefully the question whether there is straightforward conflict between DOS and (MR).

In what follows, I will show that there is no straightforward conflict. My discussion will be divided into three sections. In Section 1, I will provide a brief survey of theories of original sin. With the exception of Edwards's theory, which will be deferred to Section 2, all of the theories that I will discuss there are in tension with (MR). We will see, however, that none of these theories explicitly contradicts (MR). Rather, the tension arises because none of the theories offers the resources for denying the following very plausible assumption which, in conjunction with DOS, does contradict (MR):

(A1) No human being who was born after Adam's first sin could have done anything to prevent Adam's first sin; and no human being who is born corrupt could have done anything to prevent her own corruption.

The conflict to be resolved, then, is not, strictly speaking, between DOS and (MR); rather, it is between DOS, (MR), and (A1). Of course, it is a hollow victory to show that DOS can be reconciled with (MR) if the price for reconciliation is denying what any sane person would be inclined to accept. A more substantive victory would be achieved if one could actually develop a theory of original

---

responsibility", the idea being that we humans are somehow collectively, though not individually, guilty or responsible for the behavior of Adam. Peter Forrest (1994) develops a view of original sin roughly along these lines, a view according to which a society itself might be viewed as a moral person and the individuals who comprise it might, accordingly, be held collectively responsible for its acts. My own inclination, however, is to think that groups of persons are not themselves moral persons, and that whatever collective guilt or responsibility might be, it will, in any case, depend on facts about individual guilt or responsibility. For example, the mob is collectively guilty for the damage to the city; but what that means is just that various individuals who were parts of the mob are individually guilty for their contributions to the damage. The notion of collective *debt* is, to my mind, more promising. (As is the notion of collective *liability*. See, on this, Wainwright 1988: 45 ff.) A group might owe $1,000 to someone even if there is no specific amount of money that any particular member of the group owes to that person. But as Richard Swinburne (1989) emphasizes, claiming that we collectively inherit only a *debt* from Adam is precisely to reject the doctrine of original guilt, which I am here taking as central to DOS.

⁴ Jonathan Edwards most notably (*Freedom of the Will*, pt. 3, Sect. 4; in Edwards 1992: 47–51); but see also, e.g. Hodge 2001: ch. 8, and Schreiner 1995.

sin that rests on metaphysical assumptions that are both deserving of serious consideration and inconsistent with (A1). Thus, in Sections 2 and 3 I will describe two such theories. One is a development of a view defended by Jonathan Edwards.[5] The other rests on assumptions that naturally accompany a Molinist account of divine providence. Section 2 describes the Edwardsian view; Section 3 describes the Molinist view.[6]

Both of the views described in Sections 2 and 3 come with substantial and controversial metaphysical commitments. But in each case the commitments in question are ones that have been ably defended and taken very seriously in the contemporary literature. I do not, in the end, claim that any of these commitments ought to be accepted; nor do I claim that they must be accepted by anyone who wishes to endorse both DOS and (MR). For all I am willing to commit myself to here, it might be that there are other ways of reconciling DOS and (MR), and it might also be that none of the ways of reconciling those two doctrines is worth the intuitive price. My aim, again, is simply to show in some detail that there *are* ways of reconciling those doctrines, and that those represent "live options" that cannot simply be dismissed out of hand.

1. THEORIES OF ORIGINAL SIN

I will begin by providing a brief sketch of the various lines along which the central claims of DOS (i.e. S1 and S2) have been fleshed out.[7] The purpose of doing so is to help make it clear where on the landscape of possible views the views developed in Sections 2 and 3 will fall. Doing so will also make it clear just how hard it is to generate a plausible theory of original sin that avoids conflict with (MR). I will organize my discussion around three questions that might be raised about (S1) and (S2): (i) What is the nature of the corruption mentioned in S1? (ii) What is it that we are guilty of from birth? and (iii) Is what we are guilty of something that *we* have done, or not? It is perhaps tempting to think that, once the answer to (ii) is settled, the answer to (iii) will be settled as well. But, as we shall see, that is not the case.

---

[5] Interestingly, the fact that Edwards's theory of original sin can be reconciled with (MR) is bad news for Edwards, since Edwards wants to appeal to the alleged *conflict* between DOS and (MR) to support the claim that moral responsibility is compatible with determinism. Thus, an additional and important lesson to be drawn from the discussion in Section 2 is that, given Edwards's own metaphysical commitments, it turns out that a crucial premise in his defense of compatibilism is undermined

[6] In calling these theories 'Edwardsian' and 'Molinist' respectively, I do not at all mean to suggest that Edwards, Molina, or any of their contemporary followers would necessarily endorse these theories as I am developing them. Edwards, Molina, and their followers might be blamed for saying things that inspired and encouraged the development of these views, but that is all.

[7] In addition to the sources cited throughout this section, the following works have influenced the discussion of different theories of original sin in this section: Adams 1999; Kelly 1978; Quinn 1984 and 1997; Urban 1995; and Wiley 2002.

1.1. The Nature of Our Corruption

S1 says that all human beings (except three or four) are corrupt. But there are at least two different ways of understanding the nature of this corruption. On one view, Adam's first sin brought about a fundamental change in human nature. Whereas human beings prior to the Fall lacked the inclination to disobey God, all human beings after the Fall possess such an inclination. Thus, for example, Augustine writes:

Man's nature, indeed, was created at first faultless and without any sin; but that nature of man in which every one is born from Adam, now wants the Physician, because it is not sound. All good qualities, no doubt, which it still possesses in its make, life, senses, intellect, it has of the most High God, its Creator and Maker. But the flaw, which darkens and weakens all those natural goods, so that it has need of illumination and healing, it has not contracted from its blameless Creator—but from that original sin, which it committed by free will. (*On Nature and Grace,* ch. 3; in Augustine 1999: 122)

And Calvin:

Original sin, then, may be defined as the hereditary corruption and depravity of our nature. This reaches every part of the soul, makes us abhorrent to God's wrath and produces in us what Scripture calls works of the flesh. . . . Our nature is not only completely empty of goodness, but so full of every kind of wrong that it is always active. Those who call it lust use an apt word, provided it is also stated . . . that everything which is in man, from the intellect to the will, from the soul to the body, is defiled and imbued with this lust. To put it briefly, the whole man is in himself nothing but lust. (*Institutes of the Christian Religion,* bk. 2, ch. 1, sect. 8; in Calvin 1986: 90–1)

This sort of view was also endorsed by Luther, and it has been the typical view of theologians in the Reformed tradition.[8]

Another view, however, maintains that the change brought about by the Fall was not so much the positive addition of a new kind of wickedness to a once pristine human nature, but rather the withdrawal of a certain kind of grace that made perfect obedience to God possible. On Anselm's view, for example, original sin is the loss of original justice, where original justice is the *God-given* rightness of will that Adam and Eve possessed but lost for themselves and their posterity when they sinned.[9] Aquinas likewise identifies original sin with the loss of original

---

[8] See e.g. Luther 1976: 95; Edwards, *The Great Christian Doctrine of Original Sin Defended* (in Edwards 1992: 146 ff.); Turretin 1992: 639–40; Shedd 2003: 577 ff. Cf. also *The Formula of Concord,* Article I (in Schaff 1998*b*: 97–106); *The Heidelberg Catechism,* questions 4–11 (in Schaff 1998*b*: 308–11); and *The Westminster Confession,* chapter VI (in Schaff 1998*b*: 615–17).

[9] See his *The Virgin Conception and Original Sin.* As Jeff Brower (2004: 157–78) explains, "Rightness of will, as Anselm conceives of it, is not something that rational creatures, at least in the first instance, are responsible for acquiring; rather it is something they are responsible for preserving once it has been given. In this respect, rightness of will, on Anselm's view, is more like a theological virtue than it is like one of the cardinal virtues—that is to say, it is something supernaturally

justice, but he characterizes original justice not as a sort of God-given *rectitude of will* possessed by our first ancestors, but rather as a supernatural gift that made it possible for Adam and Eve to appropriately order the various inclinations that (in us) give rise to sin. Insofar as they were, in Eden, capable of ordering their inclinations appropriately, Adam and Eve were able to refrain from sinning. The corruption brought about by the Fall was the disordering of our inclinations as a result of the withdrawal of the supernatural gift.[10] This sort of view, according to which original sin consists in the *loss of a supernatural gift* rather than the *acquisition of a new kind of corruption in our nature* is sometimes characterized, by way of contrast with the Augustinian view, as one according to which human nature is *wounded* rather than *totally corrupted*.[11] The major confessions of the Roman Catholic and Eastern Orthodox Churches strongly suggest this sort of view, and it was also tentatively endorsed by James Arminius.[12] So far as I can tell, the Edwardsian development of DOS described in Section 2 is neutral between the Augustinian and Anselmian views. As we shall see in Section 3, the Molinist development of DOS can be made to accommodate both views as well.

1.2. For What Are We Guilty?

According to (S2), we are guilty from birth. But for what are we guilty? As far as I know, all of the existing theories of original sin give one of two answers: (i) we are guilty both for the corruption that makes it inevitable that we will fall into sin, as well as for the particular sin of Adam that caused that corruption, or (ii) we are guilty only for our corruption. The difference between these two answers is commonly characterized as a difference with respect to the question whether the imputation of Adam's sin to his posterity is *immediate* (answer (i)) or *mediate* (answer (ii)).[13] On both views, our own corruption is a consequence

---

infused as opposed to acquired by repeated action. Indeed, according to Anselm, God created rational nature—both angels and the first human beings—with rightness of will precisely because they could not be happy without it. . . . According to traditional Christian doctrine, the first human beings and certain of the angels fell from grace by sinning. Anselm explains their sin in terms of their abandoning, or failing to preserve, rightness for its own sake. . . . [I]n the case of the bad angels (i.e. Satan and his cohorts), Anselm thinks their loss is permanent or irretrievable. In case of the first human beings, however, and their descendants to whom the original loss was transmitted, Anselm thinks that, at least prior to death, their rightness of will can be recovered—though here again the recovery is primarily a matter of grace (co-operating with free will) rather than the result of any effort on the part of individual human beings."

[10] See esp. Aquinas, *Summa Theologica*, part 1 of part 2, Q. 82, Art. 2; in Aquinas 1945: 674–5.
[11] Cf. *The Catechism of the Catholic Church*, 2nd edn, ss. 400 and 405 (Catholic Church 1994: 112, 114–15).
[12] See *The Canons and Dogmatic Decrees of the Council of Trent*, Fifth Session (in Schaff 1998a: 83–9); *The Catechism of the Catholic Church*, 2nd edn, ss. 400 and 405 (Catholic Church 1994: 112, 114–15); *The Orthodox Confession of the Eastern Church*, Questions 23 & 24 (in Mohila 1975); *The Acts and Decrees of the Synod of Jerusalem*, chapter VI, decrees VI, XIV, and XVI (Orthodox Eastern Church 1899: 118–19, 132–5, 139–43); and Arminius 1999: 150–7, 374–6, and 717.
[13] Cf. Crisp 2003 and Quinn 1997 for useful discussion.

of Adam's sin and something for which we are guilty. Thus, either way we bear guilt as a result of something Adam has done. The difference is that answer (i), but not answer (ii), maintains that we are *directly accountable* for Adam's first sin.

Augustine, Aquinas, Luther, and Calvin all explicitly endorsed the doctrine of immediate imputation, and endorsement of that view is typical of theologians in the Reformed tradition. It is harder to find theologians who explicitly endorse the doctrine of mediate imputation. Anselm does.[14] So too does the seventeenth-century Reformed theologian Joshua La Place, though his view was formally condemned at the National Synod of France in 1645, and condemned again shortly thereafter by other churches and theologians throughout Europe in the seventeenth century.[15] The view is also sometimes, though I think mistakenly, taken to be the official position of the Roman Catholic Church.[16] The Molinist view that I will develop in Section 3 is also committed to it.

The main question that arises in connection with the doctrine of immediate imputation is the question of *how* we can be guilty of Adam's sin given the apparent fact that none of us is identical to Adam and none of us existed when Adam sinned. Here there are only two possibilities. One is to deny the appearance, maintaining that we are guilty of Adam's sin because there is some meaningful sense in which *we ourselves* committed or participated in the committing of that sin. The other is to claim that it is somehow just for God to impute to us guilt for a sin in whose commission we did not participate. Adapting some terminology from G. C. Berkouwer (1971: ch. 12), we may refer to views that embrace the first possibility as *Personal Guilt* (PG) theories and to views that embrace the second as *Alien Guilt* (AG) theories. In the next subsection, I will discuss these views in reverse order.

The doctrine of mediate imputation, by contrast, faces only the general problem of explaining how we could justly be held responsible for a state of affairs that we could not have prevented. In other words, it faces only the general problem of apparent conflict with (MR). Notably, Anselm seems content to reject (MR).[17]

---

[14] See *The Virgin Conception and Original Sin*, ch. 22 (in Anselm 1969: 197–8).

[15] See Hodge, *Systematic Theology*, vol. ii. 205 ff. for useful discussion.

[16] See Murray 1955: 153–5. There, Murray claims (again, I think mistakenly) to find the position expressed in the Decree on Original Sin produced by the Council of Trent.

[17] In defending the view that even infants deserve condemnation by God, he writes: "If you think it over . . . this sentence of condemnation of infants is not very different from the verdict of human beings. Suppose, for example, some man and his wife were exalted to some great dignity and estate, by no merit of their own but by favor alone, then both together inexcusably commit a grave crime, and on account of it are justly dispossessed and reduced to slavery. Who will say that the children whom they generate after their condemnation should not be subjected to the same slavery, but rather should be gratuitously put in possession of the goods which their parents deservedly lost? Our first ancestors and their offspring are in such a condition: having been justly condemned to be cast from happiness to misery for their fault, they bring forth their offspring in the same banishment" (*The Virgin Conception and Original Sin*, ch. 28; in Anselm 1969: 209–10). See also ch. 22 of the same work.

1.3. AG-Theories

AG-theories of original sin maintain that we are guilty both for the corruption of our nature and for the sin of Adam, and that we are so guilty despite the fact that we in no way participated in the committing of Adam's sin. The main challenge for such a theory is to explain how it could possibly be just for God to hold a person guilty for a sin she did not commit. The standard response to this challenge is to claim that we are guilty for Adam's sin because Adam is the *federal head, or representative* of the human race. The basic idea is that Adam represented us before God in much the same way that a head of state might represent one nation before another. If a head of state commits a crime against another nation, the nation she represents may well be implicated in that crime and be held accountable for it. War might ensue, and it might turn out that peace can be restored only if the nation whose representative started the war manages to find another representative who can behave in such a way as to rectify the trouble. Thus, for example, Francis Turretin explains:

[T]he bond between Adam and his posterity is twofold: (1) natural, as he is the father, and we are his children; (2) political and forensic, as he was the prince and representative head of the whole human race. Therefore the foundation of imputation is not only the natural connection which exists between us and Adam (since, in that case, all his sins might be imputed to us), but mainly the moral and federal (in virtue of which God entered into covenant with him as our head). Hence Adam stood in that sin not as a private person, but as a public and representative person—representing all his posterity in that action and whose demerit equally pertains to all.

For Adam to be a public and representative person, it was not necessary that that office should be committed to him by us, so that he might act as much in our name as in his own. It is sufficient that there intervened the most just ordination of God according to which he willed Adam to be the root and head of the whole human race, who therefore not only for himself only but also for his (posterity) should receive or lose the goods. (Turretin 1992: 616)

This view is known as the *federalist* theory of original guilt. It is endorsed by many theologians in the Reformed tradition (including Turretin) and also tends to be endorsed by theologians in the Arminian tradition (e.g. John Wesley and Richard Watson).[18]

Not surprisingly, federalism is typically coupled with a doctrine of the atonement according to which Jesus counts as *another* representative of the human race—a "second Adam"—whose behavior, unlike Adam's, is sufficient to restore us to fellowship with God if only we embrace him as our representative. On this view of the atonement, just as the guilt of Adam is imputed to all of us from birth, so too the righteousness of Jesus is imputed to those who embrace

---

[18] Wesley, *The Doctrine of Original Sin, According to Scripture, Reason, and Experience*, esp. part 3, sect. 6 (in Wesley 1978: 332–4); Watson 1834: 52 ff.

him. It is perhaps worth noting that the imputed-righteousness theory of the atonement does not go hand-in-hand with the federalist or any other AG-theory of original sin. That is, one can and many do accept the former without accepting the latter. But, obviously enough, it is hard to see why one should find the imputation of alien guilt objectionable if one is not inclined to object to the imputation of "alien righteousness".

But the AG-theory, as it stands, is in obvious tension with (MR). For nothing in the theory even so much as suggests that there was anything that any of us could have done that would have prevented Adam's sin. In other words, nothing in the theory suggests any reason for thinking that (A1) is false. But, again, (A1) together with DOS flatly contradicts (MR).

Is it possible to produce a credible AG-theory that is inconsistent with (A1)? I doubt it. One might be tempted to suggest that we have *counterfactual power* over Adam's sin. To say that we all have counterfactual power over Adam's sin is to say that, for each of us, there is something we could have done such that, had we done it, Adam would never have sinned. If we do have such power, then A1 is surely false. But, leaving aside worries about the very possibility of our having counterfactual power over the past,[19] the problem with this proposal is that there is absolutely no reason—and certainly no reason arising out of the AG-theory—for thinking that it is true. At best, then, it could only be an ad hoc addition to the AG-theory. Alternatively, one might be tempted to resist (A1) by arguing that there is some sense in which we were all present and able to act at the time of Adam's sin. If that were true, then we would at least be moving in the direction of a reason to think that (A1) is false; and, as we will see shortly, there are various stories one might tell that imply that we were present and able to act at the time of Adam's sin. Unfortunately, however, all of the extant stories of this sort are either incredible or have the implication that we all actually *participated* in Adam's sin (as some PG-theories, but no AG-theories, maintain). Thus, it is doubtful that any of these stories could be used to supplement the AG-theory in such a way as to make even remotely plausible the denial of (A1).

It is worth noting that, on the federalist theory, since part of the explanation for our guilt from birth is the fact that Adam represents us, and since it is within our power to do something—namely, embrace Jesus as our representative—that will make it the case that Adam no longer represents us, it is to some extent up to us whether we *remain* guilty for Adam's sin. But, as the quotation from Turretin makes clear, the federalist theory still takes it for granted that the fact that Adam represented us from birth was not something we could have prevented. Thus, it looks as if those who wish to endorse *both* DOS and (MR) must endorse some sort of PG-theory of original guilt.

---

[19] In Section 3 we will consider another view that presupposes that we can have counterfactual power over the past, and there I will briefly explain why many philosophers think that worries about this presupposition *ought* to be left aside.

1.4. PG-Theories

The main challenge faced by someone who wants to say that we bear *personal* guilt for the sin of Adam is to explain how we could possibly have participated in the committing of Adam's sin.

One way of meeting this challenge is to endorse a view according to which all of us existed as distinct individuals at the time of Adam and somehow participated in or concurred with Adam's sin. One way to motivate this sort of view is to endorse a doctrine of pre-existing souls.[20] Another way is to urge a metaphysically loaded reading of the suggestion (in Hebrews 7: 9–10) that Levi was present *as an agent* in the loins of Abraham, and then to extend this idea to all members of the human race, claiming that everyone was present as an agent in the loins of Adam.[21] But these sorts of view are neither plausible nor popular.

More popular are views according to which we do not coexist as distinct individuals with Adam, but we do somehow enjoy a certain kind of metaphysical unity with him. Here we have two main views, one sometimes, though perhaps mistakenly, credited to Augustine; the other associated with, among others, Aquinas and Edwards. The former view goes under the label 'Realism', and its chief and most explicit proponent is W. G. T. Shedd (2003). The latter view, the one associated with Aquinas and Edwards, is what is sometimes called the 'Organic Whole' theory. I will discuss each in turn.

In three of his anti-Pelagian works, Augustine makes remarks that suggest the rather startling view that somehow we *are* Adam, and that not just Adam but *human nature itself* committed the sin that brought about our corruption. For example:

By the evil will of that one man all sinned in him, since *all were that one man*, from whom, therefore, they individually derived original sin. (Augustine, *On Marriage and Concupiscence*, bk. 2, ch. 15; in Augustine 1999: 288; emphasis added)

All good qualities, no doubt, which [human nature] still possesses in its make, life, senses, intellect, it has of the Most High God, its Creator and Maker. But the flaw, which darkens and weakens all those natural goods, so that it has need of illumination and healing, it has not contracted from its blameless Creator—but from that original sin, which *it committed* by free will. (*On Nature and Grace*, ch. 3; in Augustine 1999: 122; emphasis added)

---

[20] Shedd attributes a view of this sort to Ashbel Green (Shedd 2003: 447). Origen also famously endorsed a doctrine of pre-existing souls, according to which human souls sinned "before their birth in the body" and "contracted a certain amount of guilt" which, in turn, is supposed to explain at least some of the distribution of pain and suffering in the world. (See Origen, *De Principiis*, bk. 3, ch. 3, in Origen 1999: 336–7). But it is not clear whether or to what extent Origen's doctrine of pre-existence is supposed to be connected with the doctrine of original sin.

[21] Berkouwer (1971: 440 ff.) and Murray (1956: 26) both briefly discuss views of this sort without citing references. Anselm (1969: 199 ff.) also seems to take this sort of view seriously.

Anselm likewise makes remarks along these lines:

Each and every descendant of Adam is at once a human being by creation and Adam by generation, and a person by the individuality which distinguishes him from others. . . . But there is no doubt from what source each and every individual is bound by that debt which we are discussing. It certainly does not arise from his being human or from his being a person . . . [for] then Adam, before he sinned, would have to have been bound by this debt, because he was a human being and a person. But this is most absurd. The only reason left, then, for the individual's being under obligation is that he is Adam, yet not simply that he is Adam, but that he is Adam *the sinner*. (Anselm, *The Virgin Conception and Original Sin*, ch. 10; in Anselm 1969: 183–4; emphasis added)

According to Shedd, what Augustine and Anselm are both trying to express with these rather cryptic remarks is roughly this: Human beings have two modes of existence. We can exist *as individuals*, or we can exist *en masse* as a "single specific nature not yet individualized by propagation" (Shedd 2003: 446). When Adam sinned, all of Adam's posterity were literally present in Adam in the latter way, as the undifferentiated human nature. Moreover, as Augustine suggests, it was as much that nature as Adam who committed Adam's sin. Human nature did not act consciously (not being the sort of thing that can *be* conscious); but, he thinks, the nature of its union with Adam and Eve is sufficient to make it blameworthy for their crime. And since all of humanity together is nothing other than human nature as "individualized by propagation", we too are blameworthy.[22]

Shedd's view is a heroic attempt to reconcile the claim that each of us is to blame for Adam's sin with the principle that no one can justly be blamed for a sin in whose commission she did not participate. But even if his view could be made plausible (which seems unlikely), it still would not fare well with respect to (MR). It might turn out on his view that human nature "not yet individualized by propagation" could have prevented Adam's sin; but it will not at all follow from this that *any of us* could have prevented Adam's sin. (For example: the unruly mob could have prevented the riot; but it does not follow that Fred, who was part of the mob, could have prevented the riot.) Thus, though Shedd's view might turn out to be of some help in reconciling DOS with *some* of our moral intuitions, it will not help us to save (MR).

The 'Organic Whole' theory faces similar problems. The idea, in short, is that *humanity*, *human nature*, or *the human race* is an organic whole with the

---

[22] As I have already indicated, however, Anselm explicitly (and repeatedly) denies that anyone other than Adam bears personal guilt for Adam's sin. For example, in ch. 22 of *The Virgin Conception and Original Sin*, he says "I do not think the sin of Adam passes down to infants in such a way that they ought to be punished for it as if each one of them had personally committed it, as Adam did" (Anselm 1969: 197). On Anselm's view, as I have already said, what we are guilty of is *simply* the corruption of our nature. The passage quoted above, and cited by Shedd (2003: 445), is from a chapter wherein he attempts to explain how we could be guilty of *that*, not how we could be guilty of Adam's sin. (Of course, the claim that each of us *is Adam* is in superficial tension with the claim, clearly implied by the remark from ch. 22, that none of us *committed the sin of Adam*. But I will not attempt to sort that out here.)

following properties: (*a*) it is a moral agent; (*b*) every individual human being is a part or instance of it; and (*c*) it committed the sin of Adam by virtue of having a part or instance—namely, Adam—that committed that sin. On this view, it is by virtue of being parts, instances, or members of this whole that individual human beings other than Adam participated in Adam's sin and share the guilt for it. But, as is clear even from this rough sketch, the obvious challenge for the view is to explain in what sense, if any, the non-Adamic parts or instances of the whole could have prevented the sin of Adam. Prima facie, they could not have.

The problem is seen most clearly in Aquinas's version of the view. Aquinas develops his version by way of analogy. Roughly, the analogy is as follows: If you move your hand in such a way as to commit a crime, we won't blame your hand as such; but your hand will share in your guilt and will justly suffer the consequences of your sin. Your hand shares in your guilt because it is a part of the whole person who committed the sin, *and* it is a part that was involved in the sin.[23] Likewise, all human beings together comprise an organic whole, and human nature itself was involved in Adam's sin. Indeed, says Aquinas,

[A]ll men born of Adam may be considered as one man inasmuch as they have one common nature, which they receive from their first parents; even as in civil matters, all who are members of one community are reputed as one body, and the whole community as one man. Indeed, Porphyry says that *by sharing the same species, many men are one man*. Accordingly the multitude of men, born of Adam, are as so many members of one body. (*Summa Theologica* part II, sect. 1, q. 81, art. 1; in Aquinas 1945: 666; emphasis in original)

Thus, when Adam sinned, Humanity—the body of which all human beings are parts—sinned.[24] And just as all of your parts share in the guilt of whatever sins proceed from your will and involve your whole body, so too all of the parts or members of Humanity share in the guilt of this one sin that proceeded from Adam's will and involved human nature; for it was by Adam's will that Humanity committed that sin.

Of course, one worry with this analogy is that it looks like it might imply that more than just the guilt for Adam's first sin could be imputed to Humanity and thus, ultimately, to everyone. Why not Adam's second sin, for example? Or, for

---

[23] Cf. *Summa Theologica*, part 2, sect. 1, Q. 81, Art. 1 (in Aquinas 1945: 664–7), and *De Malo* Q. 4, Art. 1 (in Davies 2001: 327–41).

[24] It is not clear to me how seriously Aquinas really wants to take the idea that there is a physical object composed of every human being who ever did or ever will live. Some of his remarks suggest that the idea might *just* be a metaphor—that it is not literally the case that Adam and the rest of humanity comprise a single body, but that things are only "as if" that were true. But if this is so, then it is hard to see how the hand analogy manages to illuminate the doctrine of imputation. For, after all, the main initial question about the claim that we bear guilt for Adam's sin is how it can be just for God to treat us *as if* we had committed that sin when, to all appearances, we did not commit it. And it is hardly helpful to answer this question by saying simply that God is also treating us *as if* we were members with Adam of a single body, even though we are not. But for now I will simply ignore this concern.

that matter, why not my sins or yours? Aquinas is aware of this worry, and his response, in short, is that only the guilt for Adam's first sin can be imputed to Humanity (and thus to everyone) because Adam's first sin was the only sin that involved human nature as such.

Aquinas's view is more satisfying than Shedd's if for no other reason than that it is somewhat easier to see how all human beings could be at least analogically treated as parts of a common whole than it is to see how we all could exist in an "unindividualized" way in a single person. But it still leaves important questions unanswered. For example, it is hard to see why Adam's first sin, *and that sin alone*, would involve all of human nature in the way required by the analogy. Even if we grant that there is a sense in which your hand, but not your foot, is to blame for sins you commit with your hand, still it is hard to see why Adam's first sin was a sin *committed with his whole nature*, as it were, rather than a sin that simply involved him as an individual. Most important for our purposes, however, is the fact that, as indicated above, Aquinas's view lacks the resources to explain how we could have prevented the sin of Adam. Indeed, if we take the analogy seriously, his view straightforwardly implies that we could not have prevented Adam's sin. According to the analogy, individual human beings other than Adam are related to the impetus behind Adam's sin as a hand is related to a particular movement of the will of the person of which it is a part. But then, just as your hand is powerless to prevent any particular exercise of your will, so too we must be powerless to prevent the exercise of Adam's will that resulted in the Fall. Thus, Aquinas's view, like Shedd's, is of no help in preserving (MR).

We come now, at last, to Edwards's theory (though, as I will note in Section 2.4, it is ultimately only on one of several possible interpretations that his view properly counts as a version of the Organic Whole theory).[25] Famously, Edwards appeals to a sort of divine command theory of persistence over time to account for the possibility of our bearing guilt for Adam's sin. I will save the details of his view for the next section; but what will become clear in that section is that, on either of the two main ways of fleshing out Edwards's view, conflict with (MR) can easily be avoided. Edwards, of course, has no interest in reconciling his views with (MR). But the fact that his view of original sin

---

[25] Interestingly, Edwards's view is often, perhaps even typically, characterized as a *federalist* theory; but I think that this characterization is mistaken. (But see Crisp 2003 for a persuasively argued opposing view.) Part of the problem is that Edwards seems to appeal rather freely to various models for understanding Adam's relation to the rest of the human race. (For example, Charles Hodge 2001: 207–8 finds not only an affirmation of federalism in Edwards, but also an outright endorsement of Shedd's *realist* theory.) The theory I will present here, however, is the carefully worked-out view that he offers in direct response to the question of how it could be just for God to impute Adam's sin to his posterity. And I think that *that* view is not properly understood as a federalist view, even though it is consistent with the claim that Adam is the federal head of the human race. The reason is that, whereas federalism takes it that it is Adam's *federal headship* that explains the imputation of guilt to the rest of humanity, Edwards's response to the question of how it could be just for God to impute Adam's sin to his posterity takes it that something else—a kind of *metaphysical unity* with Adam—is the basis for the imputation.

is consistent with (MR) constitutes at least an *ad hominem* argument against his claim (in *Freedom of the Will*) that attention to the doctrine of original sin provides reason to think that (MR) is false.[26]

2. JONATHAN EDWARDS AND THE DOCTRINE OF ORIGINAL GUILT

As I have already indicated, there are at least two different ways in which Edwards's theory of imputation may be fleshed out. On one way of developing it, Edwards's view counts as a version of the Organic Whole Theory, is committed to a theory of persistence that I'll refer to below as 'worm theory', and suffers from some of the same problems that Aquinas's view suffers from. On the other way of developing it, there is no commitment to worm theory, and the main problems associated with the Organic Whole Theory do not arise.

I will begin in Section 2.1 below by presenting, largely in his own words, the main lines of Edwards's view about how it is that we bear guilt for Adam's sin. In Section 2.2, I will digress briefly and describe several different theories of persistence. I will argue in that section that, contrary to what seems widely to be taken for granted, there is no compelling reason to attribute to Edwards belief in a worm theoretic account of persistence. Then, in Sections 2.3 and 2.4, I will describe in more detail the two different ways of fleshing out Edwards's theory of imputation. We will see that both ways provide theories of imputation that are consistent with (MR), but I will argue that the one that carries no commitment to worm theory has distinct advantages over its rival.

2.1. Edwards's Theory of Imputation

Edwards's theory of imputation is presented in its fullest detail in the last part of *The Great Christian Doctrine of Original Sin Defended* (in Edwards 1992; first published in 1758). Whereas Aquinas uses the metaphor of a body in developing his version of the Organic Whole theory, Edwards relies more heavily on the metaphor of a tree. It is worth quoting him at length since, despite the fact that his theory of original sin is well known and widely discussed, it is often mischaracterized.

He begins thus:

I think, it would go far towards directing us to the more clear conception and right statement of this affair, were we steadily to bear this in mind: that God, in every step of his proceeding with Adam, in relation to the covenant or constitution established with him, looked on his posterity as being *one with him*. And though he dealt more immediately

---

[26] Part. 3, sect. 4; in Edwards 1992: 47–51.

with Adam, it yet was as the *head* of the whole body, and the *root* of the whole tree; and in his proceedings with him, he dealt with all the branches, as if they had been then existing in their root.

From which it will follow, that both guilt, or exposedness to punishment, and also depravity of heart, came upon Adam's posterity just as they came upon him, as much as if he and they had all co-existed, like a tree with many branches; allowing only for the difference necessarily resulting from the place Adam stood in, as head or root of the whole. Otherwise, it is as if, in every step of proceeding, every alteration in the root had been attended, at the same instant, with the same alterations throughout the whole tree, in each individual branch. I think, this will naturally follow on the supposition of there being a *constituted oneness* or *identity* of Adam and his posterity in this affair. (Edwards 1992: 220; emphasis in original)

Then, in a note, he goes on to develop the tree metaphor more fully as follows:

My meaning, in the whole of what has been said, may be illustrated thus: Let us suppose that Adam and all his posterity had co-existed, and that his posterity had been, through a law of nature established by the Creator, united to him, something as the branches of a tree are united to the root, or the members of the body to the head, so as to constitute as it were one complex person, or one moral whole: so that by the law of union there should have been a communion and co-existence in acts and affections; all jointly participating, and all concurring, as one whole, in the disposition and action of the head: as we see in the body natural, the whole body is affected as the head is affected; and the whole body concurs when the head acts. Now, in this case, all the branches of mankind, by the constitution of nature and law of union, would have been affected just as Adam, their common root, was affected. When the heart of a root, by a full disposition, committed the first sin, the hearts of all the branches would have concurred; and when the root, in consequence of this, became guilty, so would all the branches; and when the root, as a punishment of the sin committed, was forsaken of God, in like manner would it have fared with all the branches; and when the root, in consequence of this, was confirmed in permanent depravity, the case would have been the same with all the branches; and as new guilt on the soul of Adam would have been consequent on this, so also would it have been with his moral branches. And thus all things, with relation to evil disposition, guilt, pollution, and depravity, would exist, in the same order and dependence, in each branch, as in the root. (Edwards 1992: 221 n.; emphasis in original)

Here we are just invited to *imagine* that "through a law of nature" Adam and his posterity are unified as parts of a single moral agent. But later in the essay Edwards makes it clear (*a*) that he endorses a theory about laws of nature according to which laws are just divine decrees, (*b*) that he endorses a theory about persistence according to which facts about persistence depend solely on divine decrees, and (*c*) that, by divine decree, Adam and his posterity are "one" in the same sense in which a sapling and the tree that it grows into are one. Thus:

Some things are *entirely distinct*, and *very diverse*, which yet are so united by the established law of the Creator, that by virtue of that establishment, they are in a sense *one*. Thus a *tree*, grown great, and a hundred years old, is *one* plant with the little *sprout*, that first came out of the ground from whence it grew, and has been continued in constant succession;

though it is now so exceeding *diverse*, many thousand times bigger, and of a very different form, and perhaps not one atom the very same: yet God, according to an established law of nature, has in a constant succession communicated to it many of the same qualities, and most important properties, as if it were *one*. It has been his pleasure, to constitute an union in these respects, and for these purposes, naturally leading us to look upon all as *one.* . . .

And there is no identity or oneness [between the successive stages of a created substance] but what depends on the *arbitrary* constitution of the Creator; who by his wise sovereign establishment so unites these successive new effects, that he *treats them as one*, by communicating to them like properties, relations, and circumstances; and so, leads *us* to regard and treat them as one. When I call this an *arbitrary constitution*, I mean, that it is a constitution which depends on nothing but the *divine will*; which divine will depends on nothing but the *divine wisdom*. In this sense, the whole *course of nature*, with all that belongs to it, all its laws and methods, constancy and regularity, continuance and proceeding, is an *arbitrary constitution*. In this sense, the continuance of the very being of the world and all its parts, as well as the manner of continued being, depends entirely on an *arbitrary constitution*. (Edwards 1992: 224; emphasis in original)

So, on Edwards's view, the unity that obtains between Adam and his posterity is metaphysically on a par with the unity that obtains between the successive stages of any ordinary persisting thing.

But here we encounter a fork in the road; for there are two different ways of unpacking the claim that the unity that obtains between Adam and his posterity is metaphysically on a par with the unity that obtains between successive stages of ordinary persisting things. I will refer to these two ways of characterizing Adam's unity with his posterity as the *Organic Whole Theory* and the *Fission Theory*. According to the Organic Whole Theory, Adam and his posterity are all together parts of a single, spatiotemporally extended object. On this view, Adam and his posterity comprise successive stages of a persisting individual which is (in some sense) a moral agent and which is such that all of its stages, or temporal parts, are personally accountable at least for the one salient crime committed by its Adamic parts. I said earlier that it is only under one interpretation of his view that Edwards's theory counts as a version of the Organic Whole Theory, and this is it. The Fission Theory, on the other hand, says that Adam and his posterity are distinct individuals who share a common temporal stage or set of temporal stages (namely, whatever stages of Adam were involved in Adam's sin, and perhaps all of the preceding ones as well). On this view, Adam undergoes fission at the time of his first sin, splitting into billions of different people, only one of whom gets kicked out of Eden, fathers Cain and Able, and does the various other deeds traditionally attributed to Adam. As we will see more clearly in Sections 2.3 and 2.4, the Organic Whole Theory presupposes the worm theoretic account of persistence, but the Fission Theory may be developed independently of that assumption. But first I want briefly to distinguish several different theories of persistence and explain why there is no compelling reason to attribute to Edwards belief in the worm theoretic account.

2.2. Theories of Persistence

Notably, though Edwards is commonly cited as a proponent of the view that familiar material objects are four-dimensionally extended "spacetime worms",[27] the whole of his view as presented above is consistent with an alternative account of persistence. Let me explain.

An object persists just in case it exists at multiple times. But what does it take for an object to exist at multiple times? A fairly commonsensical view about persistence says that existing at multiple times is just a matter of being *wholly present* at more than one time. In other words, an object persists just in case *the whole thing* exists at more than one time. Persisting in this way is typically referred to as 'enduring'; and so the corresponding theory of persistence is typically called 'endurantism'. According to endurantism, every moment of an object's career is occupied by the object itself.

The main rival to endurantism is 'perdurantism', which I will simply characterize as the thesis that objects persist without enduring. According to the most familiar version of perdurantism—I'll call it 'worm theory', for reasons that will become clear shortly—objects persist by having distinct temporal parts at every moment at which they exist. On this view, material objects are extended in time just as they are extended in space; and just as objects have distinct *spatial* parts in every subregion of the total region of space that they fill at a time, so too they have numerically distinct *temporal* parts at every time or period of time in their careers. An object exists at a time, then, just in case it has a temporal part at that time; and an object exists at multiple times just in case it has proper temporal parts at multiple times. A temporal part T of an object X, according to the common intuitive definition, is just an object that exists for part of the total duration that constitutes X's career, and that has X's spatial boundaries at all of the times at which T exists.

As it is usually fleshed out, worm theory says that whatever name we use for an ordinary material object will typically refer to the four-dimensionally extended "spacetime worm" that fills the entire spacetime region that we would normally say is filled by the "career" or "lifetime" of that object.[28] Thus, for example, the name 'David Letterman' typically refers to the four-dimensionally extended object that fills the region occupied by the event that we would call *Letterman's lifetime*; the expression 'that table' refers to the spacetime worm that fills the region occupied by the event that we would normally characterize as the career

---

[27] Chisholm (1976: 138–9), Helm (1997: ch. 7), and Sider (2001: 75) are among those who characterize him as holding this view.

[28] I say 'typically' because worm theorists also say that sometimes (perhaps often) familiar referring expressions refer to temporal parts of things rather than to the things themselves. Thus, for example, I might now say not only that I am human, but also that I am hungry. In the first case, 'I' can clearly refer to a space–time worm; but in the second case 'I' plausibly refers only to my present temporal part.

of the table in question; and so on. Attributions of temporary properties to things are to be analyzed in terms of attributions of permanent properties to their temporal parts. So, for example, to say that Letterman was short but is now tall is just to say that Letterman has a temporal part that is (eternally) short and another temporal part that is (eternally) tall, and that the short part is earlier than the tall part.

But there is another version of perdurantism, usually called "stage theory". Assume that there are instants of time.[29] The stage theorist will agree with the worm theorist that every instant of an object's career is occupied by a distinct thing—a *stage* of the object. She will probably (though not necessarily) also agree that the stages of an object compose a larger, temporally extended object, a spacetime worm of which those stages are temporal parts. But the stage theorist will *not* say that ordinary names typically refer to spacetime worms. Rather, according to stage theory, an ordinary name typically refers to a stage—to what a worm theorist would call the thing's current temporal part. Thus, for example, *Letterman* is nothing other than whatever momentary Letterman-stage exists right at this very instant; and *this table* is just the present table-stage that stands before us.

According to stage theory, attributions of presently possessed temporary properties are unproblematic. The claim that Letterman is tall, for example, is not given an analysis in terms of temporal parts as it is on DTP. Rather, it can simply be taken at face value as expressing the proposition that Letterman himself (the *whole* person) has the property of being tall. Past- and future-tense predications, however, are another story. Letterman was short (when he was a child); but if Letterman is identical to whatever Letterman-stage *presently* exists, then, strictly speaking, Letterman never existed before now and will not exist later than now. Stage theorists handle this problem by offering a counterpart-theoretic analysis of temporal predications. In short, the claim is that predications of the form '*x* was *φ*' or '*x* will be *φ*' are equivalent, respectively, to claims like: 'There is a *y* such that *y* is *φ*, *y* exists at an earlier time than *x*, and *y* is a counterpart of *x*', and 'There is a *y* such that *y* is *φ*, *y* exists at a later time than *x*, and *y* is a counterpart of *x*'.[30] The counterpart relation is then analyzed in terms of *relevant similarity*, which, in turn, is normally taken to be a context-sensitive notion. In

---

[29] There is some question about whether stage theory can be developed apart from the assumption that there are instants, but I won't pursue that here. See Stuchlik 2003 for relevant discussion.

[30] This way of telling the stage theorist's story about temporal predications presupposes that merely past and merely future objects are somehow available to have properties, stand in relations, and fall within the scope of the quantifier. Can this presupposition be done away with? I think that it can be. As I see it, stage theory will fare as well (or not) under the supposition that there are no merely past or future objects as a counterpart theoretic account of modal properties will fare under the supposition that there are no merely possible objects; and most counterpart theorists think that the supposition that there are no merely possible objects poses no problem whatsoever for their view. This view is controversial, but resolving the controversy would take us too far afield. For reasons to doubt that counterpart theory is viable if there are no merely possible objects (reasons which carry over as reasons to doubt that stage theory is viable if there are no merely past or future objects), see Merricks 2003.

most contexts, stage theorists argue, the past stages that are relevantly similar to you are precisely those that the worm theorist would take to be your past temporal parts; and these, in turn, are just the stages that an endurantist would identify with you at various times. Thus, the stage theorist is able, by and large, to affirm temporal predications (like "I was once a baby, but I was never a baby alligator") that respect our commonsense intuitions.

Both stage theory and worm theory are typically—and some would say,[31] necessarily—developed under the supposition that *presentism* is false, where presentism is the view that it always has been the case and always will be the case that there are no non-present objects. Moreover, as I have indicated, stage theory is normally developed under the assumption that some things have temporal parts. Given this assumption, stage theory, like worm theory, is committed to the view that composition is not restricted in such a way that only objects existing *at the same time* can compose something. But suppose we drop these assumptions and yet retain stage theory's counterpart theoretic analysis of temporal predication. We will then have a view according to which, strictly speaking, (*a*) *nothing* that now exists did, does, or will exist, at any time other than the present, (*b*) nothing has temporal parts, and yet (*c*) claims like 'Fred was once a child', 'this table will probably be here ten minutes from now', and so on still express truths. Insofar as stage theory counts as a theory of *persistence* (which is debatable, but generally accepted), this view too should qualify as a theory of persistence. It would be a version of perdurantism without any commitment to the existence of temporal parts.

It is important to point out here that stage theory, unlike worm theory, belongs to a family of theories about persistence whose members maintain that familiar objects exist at multiple times in the "loose and popular" sense while at the same time *denying* that they do so in the "strict and philosophical" sense. In other words, stage theory is one among several views according to which it is appropriate and meaningful, but strictly and literally false, to say of familiar objects that they exist at more than one time. David Hume endorsed a view like this, as did Anthony Collins.[32] Hume is often characterized as a believer in temporal parts. But, in fact, the view he describes—which seems basically the same as Collins's view—sounds a lot more like a view that has, in recent times, been defended by Roderick Chisholm (1976), who is not a temporal parts theorist. According to Chisholm, only mereologically constant things (masses of matter, simples, etc.) persist in the strict sense. But other things (most familiar objects—tables, chairs, human bodies, etc.) persist in a "loose and popular" sense by virtue of having "stand-ins" at the various times that constitute what we take to be their careers. Chisholm's view is not quite stage theory. For one

---

[31] See n. 29 above.
[32] Hume 1978; Collins 1709. See also Bishop Butler's characterization of Collins's view, in Butler 1849: 307–8.

thing, Chisholm believes that some things endure, whereas the paradigmatic stage theorist does not. But still, the two views are similar—and more similar to one another, I think, than either is to worm theory.

I mention all of this because it is relevant to the question of how to interpret Edwards. Clearly enough, worm theory provides one way—and perhaps the most natural way—of fleshing out Edwards's claim that Adam and his posterity are "one" in the way that the root and branches of a tree are one. And this is the view that is commonly attributed to Edwards, particularly by contemporary philosophers interested in saying something about the history of the worm theoretic account of persistence. But to move from Edwards's use of the tree metaphor to the conclusion that Edwards was definitely presupposing a metaphysic of temporal parts is to rest a lot of interpretive weight on the details of that metaphor; and it is not clear that this is warranted. For one thing, Edwards's tree metaphor is substantially similar to Aquinas's body metaphor. But no one wants *on that basis* to credit Aquinas with endorsing the existence of temporal parts. More importantly, we have to reckon with the fact that (*a*) in the eighteenth century, no doctrine of temporal parts had yet been clearly articulated (even by Edwards), (*b*) the explicit (and non-metaphorical) metaphysical claims that Edwards commits himself to are clearly consistent both with stage theory and with the views of Collins and Hume, and (*c*) the views of Collins and Hume were already in circulation at the time when Edwards wrote his treatise. I will not go so far as to say that it is a mistake to attribute to Edwards belief in a worm theoretic account of persistence rather than belief in the Collins/Hume view. But I do think that attributing to Edwards something like the latter view is at least as reasonable as attributing to him belief in the worm theoretic account. Indeed, superficially it seems more reasonable to do so, in light of his remarks to the effect that each successive stage is a "new creation" that is "treated as one" with its predecessors by "arbitrary divine constitution".

That said, let us now compare the virtues and vices of our two interpretations of Edwards. I will begin with the Organic Whole Theory which, again, carries commitment to the worm theoretic account of persistence. After that, I will discuss the Fission Theory, which can be developed independently of worm theory.

2.3. The Organic Whole Theory

According to the Organic Whole Theory, every human being is part of Humanity, a four-dimensionally extended object composed of every individual human being, including Adam. If the worm theory were false, there would be no such thing as Humanity (or, at any rate, it would not be the sort of thing that could include both Adam and us as parts). It is for this reason that the Organic Whole Theory is committed to that view. And, on this view, we all bear guilt for Adam's sin because we are all temporal parts of Humanity, which committed the sin of Adam by way of its Adamic temporal part.

But now four questions immediately arise. First, is it really true that we hold the temporal parts of a person guilty for the sins committed by that person? That is, if I, by way of my current temporal part, commit a crime, do we really blame any of my *temporal parts* for that crime? Or do we simply blame *me*, the entire spacetime worm? Second, is this view consistent with (MR)? Third, is it really appropriate to view *Humanity* as a thing that *acts* and is thereby subject to praise and blame? Fourth, why, if this account is correct, do we bear guilt *only* for Adam's first sin and not (say) for his second sin, or for the sins of people other than Adam? I will take each of these questions in order.

Consider what a worm theorist will say about ordinary ascriptions of praise and blame. Initially, one might think that the temporal parts of a person are fitting objects of praise and blame because those temporal parts have all of the right equipment, so to speak, to think and act in the ways that ordinary persons do. Indeed, on worm theory, the only way an ordinary person can think and act is by having a temporal part that tokens particular thoughts and acts. But is tokening a thought or act sufficient for *having* the thought or *doing* the act? In my view, the worm theorist should say 'no'. The reason is that if she says that tokening a thought or act *is* sufficient for having the thought or doing the act, then she will be committed to the view that, for every thought I have, there is at least one other thinker (namely, the temporal part of me in which it is tokened) that shares that thought; and for every act I perform, there is at least one other agent that performs that act.[33] But that is absurd. If I am a spacetime worm, then the thoughts tokened in my temporal parts are *my* thoughts, not theirs; and the acts tokened by my temporal parts are *my* acts, not theirs. But then the responsibility for those acts is *my* responsibility, not theirs. And so I am the appropriate object of praise or blame for my acts, and they are not. To be sure, if I am punished for my acts, my temporal parts will receive the blows. But that no more implies that *they* are punished or blamed for my acts than the fact that my hand is slapped as punishment for a crime implies that my hand is blamed or punished. In the case of the hand-slap, *I* am punished by having damage inflicted upon my hand. Likewise, in the case of ordinary punishment, the *agent* is punished by having something inflicted upon her temporal parts.

So far, then, the Organic Whole Theory seems to be in trouble. Note, however, that the views just expressed depend crucially on the assumption that the temporal parts of thinkers are not themselves thinkers. But what if this assumption were false? What if each of our temporal parts were an agent and a thinker in its own right? Then it would seem that directing condemnation at or inflicting damage upon a later temporal part for the crime of an earlier one

---

[33] Some worm theorists are apparently content with this consequence. See e.g. Lewis (1983: 74 ff.). Donald Smith (2004: ch. 2) presses this point as an objection against worm theory; but, as the present discussion makes clear, I doubt that worm theorists are, as such, committed to the view that temporal parts of thinkers are themselves thinkers.

would be a way of blaming and punishing the later part for what the earlier one had done. Would this be unjust? Not obviously so. But if not, then it must be the case that those later parts are in some sense guilty of the crime of the earlier parts. Of course, it would be misleading to say that the later parts bear guilt for the crime in precisely the same sense in which the earlier temporal parts, or the person as a whole, bear guilt for it. But perhaps we could do justice to our intuitions here by saying that the parts that commit the crime, and the person as a whole, bear guilt in the *primary* sense whereas the later parts bear guilt for it in a *derivative* sense (derivative upon their standing in the relation of genidentity to the criminal parts).

Presumably this is the sort of thing that Edwards (taken as an Organic Whole Theorist) would want to say about Humanity. On this view, Humanity is a moral person that committed the sin of Adam by way of its Adamic temporal part. Both Adam and Humanity are blamed for that sin, and both bear guilt in the primary sense for it. But the post-Adamic parts suffer the consequences of that sin, and they do so justly. Thus, they bear guilt in the derivative sense for that sin.

But doesn't this violate (MR)? Initially, one might think that it does. The later temporal parts of Humanity could not have prevented Adam's sin, and yet they are held guilty. Note, however, that once we have the distinction between primary and derivative responsibility, (MR) is ambiguous. We can resolve the ambiguity by identifying three distinct readings:

(MRa) One is morally responsible in the *primary* sense for the obtaining of a state of affairs only if one could have prevented that state of affairs from obtaining.

(MRb) One is morally responsible in the *derivative* sense for the obtaining of a state of affairs only if one could have prevented that state of affairs from obtaining.

(MRc) One is morally responsible in *any* sense for the obtaining of a state of affairs only if one could have prevented that state of affairs from obtaining.

The Organic Whole Theorist who believes that the temporal parts of persons can themselves be persons can insist that it is (MRa) rather than (MRb) or (MRc) that best expresses the intuitions that initially led us to endorse (MR); and so she can claim that, once it has been suitably clarified, her view is consistent with (MR). It is so consistent because, though later temporal parts of Humanity are held responsible for something they could not have prevented, they are *not* held responsible in the primary sense.[34] Whether this move will be plausible or not

---

[34] Note that this strategy enables the Organic Whole Theorist to preserve (MR) without rejecting (A1). Obviously enough, then, the claim (which I have made in several places throughout this

is, of course, debatable. But the point is just that once the distinction between primary and derivative responsibility is on the table, the conflict between the Organic Whole theory and (MR) is not at all straightforward.

Still, this version of DOS faces some serious problems. For one thing, it seems wholly inappropriate to view something like Humanity as a moral agent.[35] This is for the same reason that it seems inappropriate to view the temporal parts of persons as moral agents. Many, if not all, of my post-natal temporal parts have the right equipment to be moral agents. They have brains (or, at any rate, temporal parts of brains), and their brains (or brain-parts) token thoughts, acts of will, and the like. But, so I would say, none of my temporal parts is the *subject* of its thoughts, and so the thoughts tokened in my temporal parts are not appropriately ascribed to them.[36] For the same reason, none of my temporal parts are appropriately regarded as the agents of the acts of will tokened in them. It is not *their* experiences, beliefs, and desires that give rise to those acts of will; and so there is no reason to regard them as the agents of those acts. And the same is true for Humanity. It has a brain—indeed, multiple brains. And its brains token thoughts, acts of will, and the like. But, like my temporal parts, Humanity is not the subject of the thoughts tokened in those brains, and so there is no reason to regard it as the agent of the acts of will that are tokened in them.

Moreover, like Aquinas's view, the Organic Whole Theory lacks the resources to explain why it is only the guilt for Adam's first sin that gets imputed to all of the temporal parts of Humanity. And whereas Aquinas could at least *try* to insist that only Adam's first sin involved all of human nature, Edwards (on this interpretation) could not do so, for the metaphysical presuppositions that support the attribution of Adam's guilt to all of us transparently imply otherwise.

2.4. The Fission Theory

The Fission Theory, on the other hand, is much more promising. For one thing, it is more exegetically plausible since it, unlike its competitor, is compatible with theories of persistence that were actually in circulation at the time that Edwards wrote his treatise on original sin. Moreover, it provides the resources either to answer or to obviate all four of the troublesome questions that arose in connection with the Organic Whole Theory.

To see this, let us begin by considering a straightforwardly stage theoretic development of the Fission Theory. Recall the following remark:

---

paper). that the conjunction of DOS and (A1) contradicts (MR) presupposes that (MR) is not ambiguous in the way described here.

[35] Wainwright (1988) raises this objection against Edwards, though he does not develop it in the way that I do.

[36] As indicated above (n. 33), there is room for disagreement on this point. But, as we have seen, saying that each of my temporal parts *is* the subject of its thoughts leads to an absurd multiplication of thinkers.

And there is no identity or oneness [between the successive stages of a created substance] but what depends on the *arbitrary* constitution of the Creator; who by his wise sovereign establishment so unites these successive new effects, that he *treats them as one,* by communicating to them like properties, relations, and circumstances; and so, leads *us* to regard and treat them as *one.* (Edwards 1992: 224; emphasis in original)

In the light of a counterpart theoretic account of persistence (together with a counterpart theoretic understanding of modal predications), we may flesh out remarks like this and others along the following lines. What temporal predications are (objectively) true of an individual depends entirely upon what stages God chooses to treat as counterparts of that individual. The counterpart relation may still be analyzed in terms of relevant similarity; but, on this view, relevant similarity is an *objective* relation grounded in God's judgments. For the most part, we may assume that God's judgments coincide with our own intuitive judgments. In other words, for the most part, those stages that are objectively relevantly similar to us, or to other objects, are precisely the stages we would expect to be relevantly similar to us if our commonsense judgments about persistence were true. And so those judgments *are* true. I was once a baby; I was never a baby alligator. And so on. However, we learn from revelation (plus, perhaps, a bit of systematic theologizing) that a rather unexpected set of temporal predications is true of each of us. It turns out that, according to revelation, the stages of Adam that committed Adam's first sin are relevantly similar to us in a way that suffices for their being our counterparts. In other words, for each of us, there is an *x* such that *x* is our counterpart and *x* committed Adam's sin. Thus, given our counterpart theoretic account of persistence, it is true of each of us that *we committed Adam's sin.* Notably, it is also true of each of us that *we were Adam.* But, as we have seen above, that hitherto cryptic remark has been affirmed by luminaries of the Church since the time of Augustine. Only now we have the resources to make sense of it. On the present view, it is literally true that *we sinned in Adam,* and that by Adam's sin, *the many were made sinners.*[37]

Consider now the four troublesome questions that arose in connection with the Organic Whole Theory. Do we really blame later stages for the sins committed by earlier stages? On this view, yes. For, on this view, what it means to say that I (a momentary stage) committed some sin in the past is just that there is some earlier stage that committed the sin and is my counterpart. Is there conflict with (MR)? No. For, though I am blamed for Adam's sin, it is also true that I could have prevented Adam's sin. After all, *I was Adam,* and, by hypothesis, Adam could have prevented Adam's sin. Thus, (A1) is false, and (MR) is preserved.

---

[37] The claim that "we sinned in Adam" is based on an inaccurate translation of Romans 5: 12b, one which greatly influenced Augustine's development of the doctrine of original sin as well as much subsequent thought on the topic. (See Wiley 2002: 51 for discussion.) The claim that "the many were made sinners" is from Romans 5: 19.

Is Humanity a moral agent? On the present view, that question is obviated; for the present view makes no commitment even to the existence of such an object, much less to its moral agency. Is there an answer to the question of why only Adam's first sin and not his later sins or the sins of other ancestors of ours are imputed to us? Yes: the answer is that, so far as revelation teaches us, only the stages of Adam that were involved in committing his first sin stand to each of us in the (objective) counterpart relation.

Of course, one might well note that, at this point, a fifth difficult question arises: on this view, it is entirely up to God whether, for any person P, the parts of Adam that committed Adam's sin are counterparts of P. Thus, except in the case of those very stages of Adam that actually committed Adam's sin, it is entirely up to God whether claims of the form '*p* committed Adam's sin' are true. Likewise, then, it is entirely up to God whether claims of the form '*p* is to *blame* for Adam's sin' are true. Why, then, would God choose for *everyone* to have those sinning stages of Adam as counterparts? Wouldn't we expect a loving, compassionate, and forgiving God to arrange things so that as *few* people as possible (rather than as *many* people as possible) are to blame for the sin of Adam?[38] Perhaps; but it is important to keep in mind here that, just as it is up to God whether to hold *me* guilty for Adam's sin, so too it is up to God whether to hold later stages of *Adam* guilty for Adam's sin. If it were really true that a good God would minimize overall guilt, then it should follow (if the Fission Theory is correct) that a good God would not even hold later stages of Adam guilty for Adam's sin. But that is a counterintuitive consequence. The Fission theorist therefore has reason to reject the claim that a good God would minimize overall guilt; and, if her theory is to have any hope of respecting ordinary moral intuitions, she will have to sign on to a view according to which there is something good, fitting, or wise about God's choosing to ascribe guilt to a great many more stages than those that are actually involved in the commission of the various sins that have been committed throughout human history. Once she has accepted this sort of view, however, the way is open for her to argue that precisely what makes it good, fitting, or wise for God to ascribe guilt (say) to me for the sins of some of my yesterday-stages also makes it good, fitting, or wise for God to ascribe guilt to me for the sins of Adam's stages. Notably, this is precisely the sort of approach that Jonathan Edwards himself takes in response to the question of why a good God might choose to ascribe guilt for Adam's sin in the ways that the Fission Theorist says that he does (Edwards 1992: 225).

I have so far been fleshing out the Fission Theory under stage theoretic assumptions, but it is important to note that the story could as easily be fleshed out under other assumptions. All we need is a theory of persistence that enables us to make coherent and plausible sense of the central claim that Adam underwent fission, splitting into billions of different people. That claim is

---

[38] I thank Michael Murray for raising this objection.

singularly implausible under, say, endurantist assumptions; for there was simply no event in Adam's life that looked even remotely like an enduring substance splitting into billions of different people. But, to my mind, the claim that Adam underwent fission will be equally plausible (or not) on any theory of persistence according to which, at least for the most part, the persistence of ordinary things is only persistence in the "loose and popular" sense and temporal predications are to be analyzed in terms of predications of "stand-ins" or counterparts. For, on any of these theories, it will not be hard to tell a story according to which Adam, or some stage of Adam, counts as a suitable stand-in for all of us, thus grounding the attribution to all of us of the property *having committed Adam's sin*.

But what about worm theory? After all, worm theory does *not* fit into that family of theories whose members say that familiar things, for the most part, do not exist at multiple times. On worm theory, the central claim of the Fission Theory amounts to the claim that all human beings *overlap* Adam, having some relevant temporal part of him as their first temporal part. There is nothing incoherent in this; but there is at least one worry to be raised. The worry is that this claim does not fit naturally with assumptions that typically accompany worm theory. Worm theorists typically want to say that the temporal parts of persons are unified by spatiotemporal and causal relations of a sort that seem not to hold between (say) Adam's temporal parts and mine.[39] Thus, there is a real question of motivation here: Why, apart from the fact that it is required by a particular theory of original sin, should we believe that Adam has undergone fission and split into billions of different people? Here, worm theory has trouble accommodating the Fission Theory for much the same reason that endurantism does: there is no *event* in Adam's life that looks like his splitting into billions of different people. And so it is hard to see what would explain, or ground, the alleged fact that Adam's temporal parts are among *my* temporal parts. After all, my temporal parts bear relations of biological and psychological continuity to one another that they do not bear to any part of Adam; and it is hard to see any other plausibly relevant spatiotemporal or causal relations that my parts bear to Adam's that they do not bear to the parts of many other people. Thus, absent further argument, the claim that Adam and I share temporal parts in common is implausible.

One might reply by saying that the temporal parts of Adam and me (and so of persons generally) are unified by brute, unanalyzable genidentity relations. But saying this sheds no light on why Adam's initial temporal parts and none other are shared by everybody. To claim that it is just a brute fact that this is so is perfectly coherent, but it is, to my mind, unacceptably ad hoc. But there is a more promising move that can be made. One might say that (*a*) sometimes, even if not always, the temporal parts of persons are unified by nothing more than certain kinds of *similarity* relations, and (*b*) only the temporal parts of Adam up through

---

[39] See e.g., the discussion of identity criteria and persistence across temporal gaps in Hudson 2001 (chs. 4 and 7).

the time of his first sin are similar enough to the temporal parts of everyone else to count as temporal parts of everyone else. So far as I can tell, adding this claim to the worm theoretic development of the Fission Theory puts it on a par with the stage theoretic development of that theory. So long as one is prepared to analyze our genidentity with Adam in terms of relevant *similarity*, there seems to be no reason to prefer one to the other apart from whatever reasons there are in general to prefer worm theory over stage theory or vice versa.

2.5. Conclusion

I have argued in this section that Edwards's theory of original sin is consistent with (MR) regardless of whether it is interpreted as affirming a worm theoretic account of persistence. Moreover, I have identified two interpretations of Edwards's theory (the Organic Whole Theory and the Fission Theory), and I have argued that the Fission Theory is both more plausible exegetically (since it, unlike the Organic Whole Theory, is compatible with theories of persistence that were actually in circulation at the time Edwards wrote his work on original sin) and also more philosophically satisfying than the Organic Whole Theory. The fact that either way of fleshing out Edwards's view is consistent with (MR) is actually bad news for Edwards, since Edwards wants to argue that attention to the doctrine of original sin provides reason to reject (MR) and related principles. Appeal to the alleged conflict between original sin and (MR) is an important premise in his argument for compatibilism about determinism and moral responsibility. But for those who wish to retain (MR) without giving up DOS, this fact is good news—at least if they are willing to reject endurantism and to analyze genidentity at least partly in terms of relevant objective similarity. For many of us, however, this will be too high a price. It would be nice, therefore, if an alternative were available. Happily, one is (though, as we shall see, it too comes with controversial metaphysical commitments). I will develop that alternative in the next section.

3. ORIGINAL SIN AND CONDITIONAL TRANSWORLD DEPRAVITY

The version of DOS that I will develop in this section depends on two assumptions, the first of which is central to a Molinist account of divine providence and the second of which is a natural concomitant. Those assumptions are as follows:

(M1) For every human person P, there are counterfactuals of freedom, including some with false antecedents, that are true of P.

(M2) For any counterfactual of freedom C that is true of a human person P, P is or was able to prevent C from being true of P.

For purposes here, a *counterfactual* is any conditional of the form 'if P were the case then Q would have been the case'.[40] Counterfactuals of freedom, then, are conditionals of the form 'if S were in circumstances C, S would freely do A'.

Many philosophers are inclined to reject (M1) on the grounds that, in the case of counterfactuals of freedom with *false* antecedents, it is hard to see what could possibly ground their truth. The idea, roughly, is that if a person S is free and would remain free if (non-actual) circumstances C were to obtain, then there is nothing about S that makes it the case that she *would* do one sort of action rather than another. Perhaps it is true that S *would probably* do one sort of action rather than another; but, according to those who are inclined to lodge the so-called "grounding objection", that is the strongest that can be said.

Many philosophers are also inclined to think that, even if there are true counterfactuals of freedom with false antecedents, the truth values of those counterfactuals are not in any meaningful sense up to us. It is tempting to say that such counterfactuals are grounded in our character and that, if we are free, our character is up to us. The trouble with this, however, is that our character seems to be entirely constituted by facts about our history plus a variety of 'would probably' facts; and it is hard to see how these facts alone could ground claims about what we would (definitely) do in various kinds of non-actual circumstances. Moreover, those who endorse a Molinist account of divine providence typically want to say that God's knowledge of counterfactuals of freedom entered into his decision about what world to actualize. But this claim, together with the claim that it is up to us which counterfactuals are true of us, might seem to generate a kind of explanatory circle. Since God's knowledge of counterfactuals of freedom plays a role in his decisions about what worlds (and so what individuals) to create, it looks as if the truth of any particular counterfactual of freedom C about an agent S must be explanatorily prior to the existence of S. But if the truth of C is supposed to be up to S (or at least preventable by S), then it looks as if S's existence must be explanatorily prior to the truth of C. And, assuming that explanatory priority is a kind of dependence, it would appear that this little circle is vicious: the truth of C depends on the existence of S which, in turn, depends on the truth of C.[41]

For these reasons and others, (M1) and (M2) are highly controversial. And so, unless the objections can be addressed, any theory of original sin that depends on them must be seen as a theory with substantial metaphysical baggage. My own view is that Molinists have gone a long way, though not the whole way, toward

---

[40] The label applies most naturally when the relevant conditional has a false antecedent; and sometimes the label is used in such a way that a conditional counts as a counterfactual *only if* the antecedent is false. Often enough, though, the label is also used in the way that I am proposing to use it—to cover any sort of 'if...would' conditional.

[41] For discussion of these and related objections, see (for starters) Adams 1977 and 1991; Craig 1991 and 2001; Flint 1998; Hasker 1989; and van Inwagen 1997.

answering the objections that have been leveled against (M1) and (M2).[42] But it is beyond the scope of this paper to defend that claim. For the remainder of this section I will simply assume that (M1) and (M2) are true and attempt to build a theory of original sin around them.

Let us begin by defining some terminology:[43]

> x is *significantly free* $=_{df}$ x is free with respect to some action that is morally significant for x.

> *A* is a *morally significant action for* x $=_{df}$ A is such that it would be morally wrong for x to perform it, but right for x to refrain, or *vice versa*.

> x *strongly actualizes* S $=_{df}$ x causes S to be actual.

> The state of affairs S *includes* the state of affairs S* $=_{df}$ necessarily, if S obtains then S* obtains.

> S is the *largest state of affairs strongly actualized in W by* x $=_{df}$ x strongly actualizes S in W and, for every state of affairs S* that x strongly actualizes in W, S includes S*.

> P *suffers from transworld depravity* $=_{df}$ for every world W such that P is significantly free in W and P does only what is right in W, there is a state of affairs T and an action A such that (i) T is the largest state of affairs strongly actualized in W by God, (ii) A is morally significant for P in W, and (iii) if God had strongly actualized T, P would have gone wrong with respect to A.

Given these definitions, being free and suffering from transworld depravity (TWD) guarantees that one will fall into sin. This may be shown as follows. Let T* be the largest state of affairs strongly actualized in some world W by God; and let P be a person who is both free and suffers from TWD in W. Either W is a world in which P freely does something wrong, or not. By definition, if P suffers from TWD in W, then if God were to actualize T*, P would freely do something wrong. Thus, W cannot be a world in which P fails to freely do something wrong. Thus, necessarily, if P suffers from TWD in a world W, P will freely do something wrong. Obviously, however, it does not follow from this that it is necessary *simpliciter* that P fall into sin. The fact that suffering from TWD guarantees that P will fall into sin is perfectly consistent with the claim that it is possible that P not fall into sin (assuming, of course, that there is a possible world in which either P is not free or P does not suffer from TWD).

Given the truth of (M2), each of us has the power to prevent our suffering from TWD. The reason is that a necessary and sufficient condition for a person

[42] See esp. Craig 1991 and 2001, and Flint 1998.
[43] All of the following definitions are either duplicated or adapted from Plantinga 1974: 166, 173, 186.

P's suffering from TWD is that a certain range of counterfactuals of freedom be true of P; and, according to (M2), for any counterfactual of freedom C that is true of P, P has the power to prevent C from being (or having been) true of her. Still, even though it is up to us whether we suffer from TWD, there is good reason to think that TWD is not an acquired property. To see why, suppose there is a person P who, up until time t does not suffer from TWD and then, at t, comes to suffer from it. Let T* be the largest state of affairs that God strongly actualizes. Now, consider the following counterfactual:

(CF) If God were to strongly actualize T*, P would freely do something wrong.

Given the definition of TWD, if P suffers from TWD after t but not before, then CF is true after t but not before. Could CF change its truth value like that? Some counterfactuals, of course, can become true or false. Suppose you undergo a change of heart toward your enemy. In such a case, it may well be that after the change, but not before, if you were given the opportunity to become reconciled with your enemy, you would do so. Thus, a certain counterfactual would have been true of you at one time but not at another. But CF is not like that; for CF is equivalent to a claim whose consequent quantifies over all times, that is:

(CF*) If God were to strongly actualize T*, it would be the case that there is (was, or will be) a time at which P freely does something wrong.

But now consider the following premise:

(P1) If P does A at t, then the proposition that P will do A at t was true at every time prior to t.

(P1) is very plausible. Moreover, though some philosophers (including some theists) reject it, traditional theists have compelling reason to accept it. For, after all, traditional theists believe, among other things, that God foreknows all of the future free acts of all of his creatures; but such foreknowledge is impossible unless, for every free act A, the proposition that A will occur was true prior to A's occurrence. This, to my mind, constitutes good reason even apart from its intrinsic plausibility to endorse (P1). But if (P1) is true (as I shall henceforth assume), then, obviously enough, (CF*) cannot change its truth value. And if (CF*) cannot change its truth value, then TWD cannot be an acquired property. Thus, if it is ever true that P suffers from TWD, it is *always* true that P suffers from TWD. TWD, then, is a condition we have from birth.

Some, no doubt, will find it hard to swallow the claim that each of us now has the power to prevent the obtaining of a state of affairs that obtained when we were born. But the claim might go down a bit more easily if we keep in mind that one of the most popular responses to fatalist arguments is to say that we have counterfactual power over a great many facts about the past.[44] As we saw in Section 1.3 above, an agent S has counterfactual power over the obtaining of a past fact F just in case there is some act A that S has the power to do such that, had S done A, F would not have obtained. There seems to be no in-principle obstacle to our having such power over at least some facts about the past (e.g. facts like *its having been true one million years ago that I would mow my lawn today*, or *God's having believed one million years ago that I would mow my lawn today*); and Alvin Plantinga (1986) has argued persuasively that divine foreknowledge together with the possibility of divine 'fore-cooperation' imply that *most* facts about the past are such that we might have counterfactual power over them.[45] Thus, it is at least prima facie plausible that we might have such power over the fact that, from birth, we have suffered from TWD.

One might object here that, if we are willing to invoke counterfactual power over the past in our theory of original sin, then preserving (MR) becomes too easy: one might simply say that, for each of us, there is something that we could have done such that, had we done it, Adam would never have sinned. There is, then, no need for controversial Molinist assumptions or a stage theoretic apparatus; MR can be saved by the simple expedient of postulating counterfactual power over the past.

But, as I argued in Section 1.3, the trouble with this proposal is that there is absolutely no reason to think that it is true. Moreover, and perhaps more importantly, even if it were true, we would still face difficult questions about how we could be held accountable for Adam's sin. After all, if there *is* something I can do (or could have done) such that, had I done it, Adam would never have sinned, I have no idea what it is. So it is hard to see how I could be held accountable for not having done it. One might be tempted to think that *refraining from sin* is the thing that I could have done that would have prevented Adam's sin, and I can certainly be held accountable for not doing *that*. But keep in mind that, according to traditional Christian belief, Jesus of Nazareth refrained from sinning; and he did not thereby prevent Adam from sinning. Thus, it is hard to see why we should think that our refraining from sinning would have prevented Adam's sin.

On the other hand, by refraining from sinning, Jesus of Nazareth arguably *did* prevent himself from suffering from TWD; and, likewise, if we were to refrain from sin, we would prevent ourselves from having suffered from TWD. And so here is one of the main advantages that the present Molinist proposal enjoys over the proposal that we have counterfactual power over Adam's sin: Suppose that TWD is identified with the corruption of our nature that was produced by

---

[44] This is the 'Ockhamist' response to fatalism. For discussion and development of this response, see the papers reprinted in Fischer 1989, especially Plantinga 1986.

[45] At any rate, there seems to be no obstacle to our having counterfactual power over the past if presentism is false. As Alicia Finch and I have argued elsewhere, however, if presentism is true, the Ockhamist response is untenable. (See Finch and Rea (forthcoming)).

the Fall. Since refraining from sin would keep us from suffering from TWD, and since refraining from sin is clearly something that we can be blamed for not doing, it is easy to see how we might both have counterfactual power over the fact that we have been corrupt from birth *and* be held accountable for failing to act in a way that would have prevented our being corrupt from birth.

One option, then, for those interested in developing a theory of original sin under Molinist assumptions is to identify TWD with the sort of corruption that DOS takes to be a consequence of the Fall. After all, it seems to be the right *sort* of property. We have it from birth, and we have it contingently. Moreover, there is no in-principle obstacle to supposing that our suffering from it is, in some sense, a consequence of Adam's sin. We have already acknowledged that, though the counterfactuals that constitute us as TWD-sufferers have been true from the beginning of time, there are nevertheless things we can do (or could have done) such that, had we done them, we would not have suffered from TWD. But if it is coherent to say this, then surely it is also coherent to suppose that if there had been no Fall, we would not have suffered from TWD. This by itself doesn't *guarantee* that our suffering from TWD is a consequence of the Fall. But my point here is just that there is no obvious reason to deny that our suffering from TWD could be a consequence of the Fall. Finally, since we have the power to prevent our ever having suffered from it, if TWD *were* identified with the corruption that is brought about by the Fall, the resulting theory of original sin would be consistent with (MR).

But there is a complication worth mentioning. Earlier I said that the Molinist theory of original sin that I'd be developing would be consistent with both an Augustinian and an Anselmian view of the nature of the corruption that is original sin. But if we identify TWD with the corruption in question, it looks as if Anselmian views are ruled out. The reason is that, according to Anselmian views, our corruption consists mainly in the loss of a supernatural gift possession of which would enable us to remain free of sin. Of course, any view according to which we are free and according to which one can be blamed only for things that one freely does will be a view according to which we are in some sense able to remain free of sin. But I take it that, on the Anselmian view, it is not the case that the supernatural gift merely makes it *possible* for us to remain free of sin. (That was possible already.) Rather, the supernatural gift is such that, had God given it to us, we *might have* remained free from sin. In other words, on the Anselmian view there is something that God can do for us (namely, restore to us the supernatural gift that Adam and Eve lost for the human race) such that, had he done it, we might have always freely done what is right. But to say that we suffer from TWD is precisely to deny this. To say that we suffer from TWD is, in effect, to say that even if God had done whatever he does in worlds where we always freely do what is right, we still *would have* sinned. Thus, there is nothing God could have done (consistent with our being free) such that, had he done it, we *might* always have done what is right. The Anselmian view, then, is ruled out.[46]

Perhaps it is not such a bad thing to rule out the Anselmian view.[47] But it would be nice to be able to accommodate it if possible. Thus, I offer the following, second option to the Molinist: build a theory of original sin around a notion of *conditional transworld depravity* (CTWD) rather than around TWD. Informally, to say that someone suffers from CTWD is just to say that there is some condition C such that, even if God had done whatever he does in worlds where both condition C obtains and we always freely do what is right, we still would have sinned. More formally, CTWD may be defined as follows:

P *suffers from conditional transworld depravity* $=_{df}$ there is some condition C that does not include any of P's free acts and is such that, for every world W such that P is significantly free in W, P does only what is right in W, and C obtains in W, there is a state of affairs T and an action A such that (i) T is the largest state of affairs strongly actualized in W by God, (ii) A is morally significant for P in W, and (iii) if God had strongly actualized T, P would have gone wrong with respect to A.

Like TWD, CTWD will be a permanent property of the persons who suffer from it; it will be a contingent property; and whether we suffer from it will be preventable by us. But, unlike TWD, suffering from CTWD is consistent with there being something God might have done such that, had he done it, you might (or even *would*) always have freely done what is right.

We may then flesh out our CTWD-based theory of original sin as follows. Consider again Aquinas's theory about the nature of the corruption that is

---

[46] Here I assume (what is standard in the literature on counterfactuals) that 'if p were true, then q would have been true' entails and is entailed by 'it is not the case that, if p were true, then q might not have been true'.

[47] One reason for thinking that it would not be so bad to rule out the Anselmian view is that the Anselmian view might be thought to raise questions about the goodness of God. On the Anselmian view, we are subject to sin and death only partly, and not entirely through our own fault. For God could have chosen to withhold the sort of grace that was present in Eden only from those who sinned in the way that Adam and Eve did (and he could also have chosen to quarantine such people so that they could not interact with those who had not yet sinned). If he had so chosen, then at least some of us might have enjoyed the great benefit of a perfectly sinless life and a robust friendship with God. And so it seems that it would have been better for God to have so chosen. But if that is right, then it looks as if God's choosing to withhold the grace that was present in Eden from all of Adam's posterity is inconsistent with his perfect goodness. To my mind, however, this objection is far from decisive. For the problem here seems just to be an instance of the problem of evil generally; and so it seems that familiar strategies for responding to the latter problem will also apply to the former. Thus, perhaps there are great goods that God could obtain only by withdrawing his supernatural gift from the human race; or perhaps God's withholding his grace from us is the permission of a gratuitous evil, but, contrary to our intuitions, it is not inconsistent with God's perfect goodness to permit gratuitous evils; and so on.

original sin. On his view, the inclinations that lead us into sin were present in human nature from the beginning, but God had given Adam and Eve a supernatural gift, or a certain kind of grace, that enabled them to order their inclinations in such a way as to avoid falling into sin. On Aquinas's view, *absent that grace*, it is inevitable that we fall. Thus, we might say, it has always been true that human beings (at any rate, all of those who will in fact be created) have suffered from a form of CTWD whose relevant condition is just the absence of whatever gift or grace was initially bestowed upon Adam and Eve. This form of CTWD is not itself original sin; but, as Aquinas might put it, it is the 'matter' of original sin whereas the absence of the supernatural gift is the 'form'.[48] Moreover, we might add, the first sin of Adam brought it about that the relevant condition was satisfied. That is, it is partly because of Adam's sin that God chose to withhold the supernatural gift thenceforth from Adam and his progeny. And so the first sin of Adam is among the salient causes of our being such that we will inevitably fall into sin. But, since (by refraining from sinning) we are able to prevent our having ever suffered from CTWD, and since, on this proposal, we have the power to refrain from sinning, (A1) is false: there is something we could have done such that, had we done it, we would not have suffered from the corruption that makes it inevitable that we will fall into sin. And so our being held guilty for the fact that it is inevitable that we will fall into sin is not contrary to (MR).

We have seen, then, two ways in which our central Molinist assumptions (M1) and (M2) might contribute to the development of a theory of original sin—one Augustinian, the other Anselmian. Both views, however, must come to grips with at least one significant cost (besides commitment to (M1) and M2)) and one important objection (besides those that might be leveled against (M1) and M2)). I'll close this section by discussing each of these in turn.

The cost is that neither version of the Molinist view offers any real explanation for the universality of either TWD or CTWD. On the Augustinian version TWD is universal as a consequence of Adam's sin; but it is hard to see *why* Adam's sin should have universal TWD as a consequence. On the Anselmian version, CTWD is apparently universal simply by divine decree (even Adam and Eve suffer from it). The cost is important since, as indicated at the outset of this paper, one of the main historical functions of the doctrine of original sin has been to explain (ostensibly in a deep, rather than merely superficial, way) the universality of sin. The two versions of the Molinist theory now under consideration purport to explain the universality of sin either by appeal to the universality of TWD or by appeal to the universality of CTWD and the absence of a certain kind of divine grace. But the depth of the explanation is threatened by the fact that it is hard to see what further explanation could be offered either for the connection between TWD and Adam's sin or for the universality of CTWD.

---

[48] Cf. Aquinas, *Summa Theologica*, part 1 of part 2, Q. 82, Art. 3; in Aquinas 1945: 676–7.

The cost, I think, is bearable. But reflection on the cost suggests an objection that, if sound, would be harder to bear. So far, I have simply taken it for granted that the universality of either TWD or CTWD would explain, at least in part, the universality of sin. But one might object that in fact this presupposition is false. For (one might argue) what counterfactuals are true of us depends in large part on what we do; thus, it appears that our behavior explains our suffering from either TWD or CTWD rather than the other way around. If this is right, then if the doctrine of original sin were developed along either of the two Molinist lines I have here suggested, it would be unable to fulfill one of its main historical functions.

Perhaps we could live with this; but it would be better if the objection could be shown to be unsound. And I think that it can be. Consider an analogy. The crystal vase is fragile. What this means, in part, is that, under "normal" circumstances, if it were struck (by a suitably hard, suitably fast-moving object) it would break.[49] But its being struck, even in circumstances that count as "normal", does not *entail* its breaking: there are worlds where it is struck and does not break. So what shall we say about such worlds? Are they worlds in which the vase is not fragile, or are they worlds in which it is fragile but (miraculously) fails to break? Plausibly, they are worlds in which the vase is not fragile. For, after all, a vase that does not break when struck under normal circumstances is clearly not such that it *would* break if struck in such circumstances; and so, *ceteris paribus*, it does not satisfy one of the defining conditions of fragility. Whether a vase counts as fragile, then, depends in part upon what it actually does if and when it is struck; but if it is struck and breaks, its breaking will nevertheless be partly explained by its fragility. Likewise, then, in the case of TWD and CTWD. Those two deficiencies are relevantly like (though perhaps not exactly like) dispositions to sin. To be sure, whether one has it depends in part on what one freely does; but (as in the case of other dispositions) that is consistent with the claim that what one freely does is partly explained by the fact that one suffers from it.

4. CONCLUSION

I have shown in this paper that there are at least two ways of reconciling the traditional doctrine of original sin with (MR), the principle that one is morally responsible for the obtaining of a state of affairs only if that state of affairs obtains and there was something one could have done that would have prevented it from obtaining. The most significant metaphysical commitments associated with the

---

[49] The qualifier "under normal circumstances" is, of course, hopelessly vague. But I include it simply to signal the fact that I am here ignoring complications that arise from the possibility of more unusual circumstances—e.g. circumstances in which the vase's disposition to break is masked, or 'Finkish', etc. Taking account of these issues would add greater complexity to the present discussion but, I think, would not substantially affect my basic point.

strategies that I have developed are, on the one hand, a commitment to some sort of non-endurantist, probably similarity-based understanding of persistence over time, or, on the other hand, a commitment to the claim that there are true counterfactuals of freedom (including ones with false antecedents) and that it is up to us what counterfactuals of freedom are true of each of us. Neither of these commitments is wildly popular; but, if the arguments in this paper are sound, embracing one or the other will provide one with metaphysical underpinnings for an (MR)-friendly development of a fully traditional doctrine of original sin.

REFERENCES

Adams, Robert (1977). 'Middle Knowledge and the Problem of Evil', *American Philosophical Quarterly* 14: 109–17; reprinted with additional notes in Adams, *The Virtue of Faith and Other Essays in Philosophical Theology* (New York: Oxford University Press, 1987).

—— (1991). 'An Anti-Molinist Argument', *Philosophical Perspectives*, 5: 343–53.

—— (1999). 'Original Sin: A Study in the Interaction of Philosophy and Theology', 80–110, in F. J. Ambrosio (ed.), *The Question of Christian Philosophy Today* (New York: Fordham University Press).

Anselm (1969). *Why God Became Man and The Virgin Conception and Original Sin*, trans. Joseph Colleran, (Albany, NY: Magi Books).

Aquinas, Thomas (1945). *The Basic Writings of Saint Thomas Aquinas*, vol. ii, ed. Anton Pegis (New York: Random House).

Arminius, James (1999). *The Works of James Arminius*, vol. ii, trans. James Nichols (Grand Rapids, Mich.: Baker Book House).

Augustine (1999). *On the Merits and Remission of Sins, and on the Baptism of Infants*, in Philip Schaff (ed.), Peter Holmes and Robert Wallis (trans.), *Nicene and Post-Nicene Fathers, First Series*, vol. v, *Augustin: Anti-Pelagian Writings* (Peabody, Mass.: Hendrickson Publishers).

Berkouwer, G. C. (1971), *Sin* (Grand Rapids, Mich.: Eerdmanns).

Brower, Jeffrey (2004). 'Anselm's Ethics', in Brian Davies and Brian Leftow (eds.), *The Cambridge Companion to Anselm* (Cambridge: Cambridge University Press), 157–78.

Butler, Joseph (1849). *The Works of Joseph Butler*, vol. i (Oxford: Oxford University Press).

Calvin, John (1986). *The Institutes of the Christian Religion*, ed. Tony Lane and Hilary Osborne (Grand Rapids, Mich.: Baker Book House).

Catholic Church (1994), *The Catechism of the Catholic Church*, 2nd edn (New York: Doubleday).

Chisholm, Roderick (1976). *Person and Object* (La Salle, Ill.: Open Court).

Collins, Anthony (1709). *An Answer to Mr. Clarke's Third Defense of His Letter to Mr. Dodwell*, 2nd edition (London: J. Darby).

Craig, William Lane, (1991). *Divine Foreknowledge and Human Freedom* (Leiden: E. J. Brill).

—— (2001). 'Middle Knowledge, Truth-Makers, and the Grounding Objection', *Faith and Philosophy*, 28: 337–52.

Crisp, Oliver (2003). 'On the Theological Pedigree of Jonathan Edwards's Doctrine of Imputation', *Scottish Journal of Theology*, 56: 308–27.

Davies, Brian (ed.), and Richard Regan (trans.) (2001). *The De Malo of Thomas Aquinas*. (Oxford: Oxford University Press).

Edwards, Jonathan (1992). *The Works of Jonathan Edwards*, vol. i (Edinburgh: Banner of Truth).

Finch, Alicia and Rea, Michael C. (forthcoming), 'Presentism and Ockham's Way Out', *Oxford Studies in Philosophy of Religion* 1.

Fischer, John Martin (ed.) (1989). *God, Freedom, and Foreknowledge* (Stanford, Calif.: Stanford University Press).

Flint, Thomas (1998). *Divine Providence: The Molinist Account* (Ithaca, NY: Cornell University Press).

Forrest, Peter (1994). 'Inherited Responsibility, Karma and Original Sin', *Sophia*, 33: 1–13.

Hasker, William (1989). *God, Time, and Knowledge* (Ithaca, NY: Cornell University Press).

Helm, Paul (1997). *Faith and Understanding* (Grand Rapids, Mich.: Eerdmanns).

Hodge, Charles (2001). *Systematic Theology*, vol. ii. *Anthropology* (Peabody, Mass.: Hendrickson Publishers).

Hudson, Hud (2001). *A Materialist Metaphysics of the Human Person* (Ithaca, NY: Cornell University Press).

Hume, David (1978). *A Treatise on Human Nature*, 2nd edn, ed. P. H. Nidditch (Oxford: Oxford University Press).

Kelly, J. N. D. (1978). *Early Christian Doctrines* (San Francisco: Harper San Francisco).

Lewis, David (1983). 'Postscripts to "Survival and Identity" ', in *Philosophical Papers*: (Oxford: Oxford University Press), 73–7.

Luther, Martin (1976). *Commentary on Romans*, trans. J. Theodore Mueller (Grand Rapids, Mich.: Kregel Publications).

Merricks, Trenton (2003). 'The End of Counterpart Theory', *Journal of Philosophy*, 100: 521–49.

Mohila, Peter (1975). *The Orthodox Confession of Faith*, trans. Peter Popivchak, http://esoptron.umd.edu/ugc/ocfi.html

Murray, John (1955), 'The Imputation of Adam's Sin', *Westminster Theological Journal*, 18: 146–62.

—— (1956). 'The Imputation of Adam's Sin: Second Article', *Westminster Theological Journal*, 19: 25–44.

Origen (1999), *De Principiis*, 239–384, in Philip Schaff (ed.), Peter Holmes and Robert Wallis (trans.), *Ante-Nicene Fathers*, vol. iv. *Tertullian, Part Fourth; Minucius Felix; Commodian; Origin, Parts First and Second* (Peabody, Mass.: Hendrickson Publishers).

Orthodox Eastern Church (1899). *The Acts and Decrees of the Synod of Jerusalem*, trans. J. N. W. B. Robertson (London: Thomas Baker).

Plantinga, Alvin (1974). *The Nature of Necessity* (New York: Clarendon Press).

—— (1986). 'On Ockham's Way Out', *Faith and Philosophy*, 3/3: 235–69.

Quinn, Philip (1984). "Original Sin, Radical Evil, and Moral Identity", *Faith and Philosophy*, 1: 188–202.

—— (1997). 'Sin and Original Sin', in Philip L. Quinn and Charles Taliaferro (eds.), *A Companion to Philosophy of Religion* (Oxford: Blackwell), 541–55.

Schaff, Philip (ed.) (1998*a*). *The Creeds of Christendom*, vol. ii., *The Greek and Latin Creeds*, (Grand Rapids, Mich.: Baker Books).

——— (ed.) (1998*b*). *The Creeds of Christendom*, vol. iii., *The Evangelical Protestant Creeds*, (Grand Rapids, Mich.: Baker Books).

Schreiner, Thomas (1995). 'Does Scripture Teach Prevenient Grace in the Wesleyan Sense?', in Thomas Schreiner and Bruce Ware (eds.), *Grace and the Bondage of the Will* (Grand Rapids, Mich.: Baker Book House), 365–82.

Shedd, W. G. T. (2003). *Dogmatic Theology*, 3rd edn, ed. Alan W. Gomes (Philipsburg, NJ: P&R Publishing).

Sider, Theodore (2001). *Four-Dimensionalism* (Oxford: Oxford University Press).

Smith, Donald (2004). 'Persistence, Persons, and Vagueness', Ph.D. dissertation, University of Notre Dame.

Stuchlik, Joshua (2003). "Not all Worlds are Stages", *Philosophical Studies*, 116: 309–21.

Swinburne, Richard (1989). *Responsibility and Atonement* (Oxford: Clarendon Press).

Turretin, Francis (1992). *Institutes of Elenctic Theology*, vol. i. *First through Tenth Topics*, trans. George Musgrave Giger, ed. James T. Dennison, Jr. (Philipsburg, NJ: P&R Publishing).

Urban, Linwood (1995). *A Short History of Christian Thought* (Oxford: Oxford University Press).

Van Inwagen, Peter (1997), 'Against Middle Knowledge', *Midwest Studies in Philosophy*, 21: 225–36.

Watson, Richard (1834). *Theological Institutes; or A View of the Evidences, Doctrines, Morals and Institutions of Christianity*, vol. ii (New York: B. Waugh and T. Mason).

Wainwright, William (1988). "Original Sin", in Thomas V. Morris (ed.), *Philosophy and the Christian Faith* (Notre Dame, Ind.: University of Notre Dame Press).

Wesley, Jonathan (1978). *The Works of Jonathan Wesley*, 3rd edn, vol. ix. *Letters and Essays* (Grand Rapids, Mich.: Baker Book House).

Wiley, Tatha (2002). *Original Sin: Origins, Developments, Contemporary Meanings* (New York: Paulist Press).

15

Modes without Modalism

Brian Leftow

The Athanasian Creed has it that Christians

worship one God in Trinity . . . the Father is God, the Son is God and the Holy Spirit is God. And yet they are not three Gods, but one God.[1]

Such odd arithmetic demands explaining. Some explanations begin from the oneness of God, and try to explain just how one God can be three divine Persons. As Augustine, Anselm, and Aquinas pursued this project, let us call it Latin Trinitarianism (LT). I now sketch a Latin view of the Trinity.

1. THE LATIN VIEW

On LT, there is just one divine being, God. The three divine Persons are at bottom just God: they contain no constituent distinct from God. The Persons are in some way God three times over. This way of putting it has roots in certain New Testament texts. John writes, "in the beginning was the Word, and the Word was with God, and the Word *was* God" (John 1: 1). The Word was *with* God suggests that the Word is someone other than God. If I answer the phone and say, "I can't talk right now—I'm with someone," my caller will naturally infer, with someone *else*. I am someone, but if only I am there, I am not *with* someone. So if God is with the Word, God is someone, and the Word is someone else. Yet though the Word was with God, the Word *was* God. So God was with God. Taken at face value, then, the text presents God and God who somehow was someone else, God twice at once, God repeated. This God repeated was incarnate in Christ, according to John. Christians call the "God" who stayed behind when the Word became flesh the Father. The New Testament also speaks of the Holy Spirit. The Spirit descends on the Incarnate Word at Jesus' baptism (Matthew 3: 16). Nobody descends on himself. So the Spirit and the Word are two distinct things. Again, Paul writes "who among men knows the thoughts

[1] The Book of Common Prayer (New York: Seabury Press, 1979), 864–5.

of a man except the man's spirit within him? In the same way no one knows the thoughts of God except the Spirit of God" (1 Corinthians 2: 11). The picture here is that the Spirit is something distinct from "God" as a human soul is distinct from a human. Yet Paul also writes that the Lord is the Spirit (2 Corinthians 3: 17). The Spirit "is" the Lord rather as the Word "is" God: the Spirit who descends on the Lord is somehow the Lord repeated, as the Word is God repeated.

The Latin tradition picks up on Scripture's "repetition" of God. Aquinas writes that

> among creatures, the nature the one generated receives is not numerically identical with the nature the one generating has . . . But God begotten receives numerically the same nature God begetting has.[2]

God begotten is the Son, God begetting is the Father, *per* the Nicene Creed. For Thomas, natures are what we now call tropes.[3] A trope is an individualized case of an attribute. Abel and Cain were both human. So they had the same nature, humanity. But if their natures are tropes, there is also a sense in which each also had his own nature, and Cain's humanity was not identical with Abel's: Abel's perished with Abel, but Cain's did not. For though the two had the same nature, they had distinct tropes of that nature. If there are tropes, bearers individuate them: Cain's humanity is distinct from Abel's just because it is Cain's, not Abel's.

With this term in hand, I now restate Thomas's claim: while Father and Son instance the divine nature (deity), they have but one trope of deity between them, which is God's. While Cain's humanity ≠ Abel's humanity, the Father's deity = the Son's deity = God's deity. But bearers individuate tropes. If the Father's deity is God's, this is because the Father in some way *just is* God: which last is what Thomas wants to say. And God's deity, and so God, is repeated in the Son. Why care about tropes of deity? Deity is a kind. Whatever has a deity-trope is an instance of this kind. An instance of the kind *deity* is a God. So: three tropes of deity, three Gods. This would be polytheism. Polytheism is not an option for Christians. The claim Thomas makes via tropes is intended to rule it out: one God thrice repeated is still just one God.

Making sense of the Latin view does not require treating deity as a trope. Suppose that deity is an immanent universal, *modo* Armstrong. Immanent universals are single items literally present as a whole in many bearers: if humanity is an immanent universal, humanity = Moses's humanity = Aaron's humanity. So too, trivially, the Father's deity = the Son's deity. But on the Latin view, it will in addition be the case that the Father's having deity = the Son's having deity. For both are at bottom just *God*'s having deity, and God's having

---

[2] S. Thomae de Aquino *Summa Theologiae* Ia (Ottawa: Studii Generalis, 1941), 39, 5 *ad* 2, 245a. Translation mine.

[3] See my "Aquinas on Attributes", *Medieval Philosophy and Theology*, 11 (2003), 1–41.

deity, a state of affairs (or on some conceptions an event) is thrice repeated in the Trinity. Things work the same way if deity is a transcendent (Platonic) universal. Latin Trinitarianism does not suppose tropes or universals, either. The Latinists mentioned held to a strong doctrine of divine simplicity (DDS), taking God to be identical to His essence, deity.[4] If God = deity, there is one item where we might have thought there were two. This might be "really" God—that is, where the properties we'd think God would have and the ones we'd think deity would have are incompatible, it might have God's in almost all cases. Or it might be "really" deity or "really" some *tertium quid*, with such a mix of what we'd intuitively think of as God's properties and what we'd think of as deity's that either we shouldn't be comfortable calling it either or we should be marginally comfortable referring to it both ways. If it's "really" deity, DDS in effect eliminates God. So this interpretation isn't open to Christians. One reasonable way to look at the "really God" take on DDS is that it eliminates deity, adopting a form of nominalism for deity. If this is the correct story, then what the Persons have in common on LT is a substantial individual, God. This would hardly be surprising if LT's basic gravamen is that all Persons are at bottom just God. Aquinas takes DDS to imply that God is neither abstract nor concrete, neither universal nor particular.[5] On this *tertium quid* account, what the Persons have in common is not a universal or an abstract entity, so this too could be called nominalist. Thus in fact the Latin view can be explicated whether one is nominalist or realist.[6]

On LT, then, there clearly is just one God, but one wonders just how the Persons manage to be three. If the Father has God's trope of deity, it seems that

(1) the Father = God,

which is after all a natural reading of the Creed's "the Father is God." For like reasons, it seems that

(2) the Son = God.

But then since

(3) God = God,

it seems to follow that

(4) the Father = the Son,

and that on LT, there is just one divine Person. If (4) is true, the Father suffered on the Cross, and so LT falls into the heresy of Patripassionism. Again, if on LT there is really but one divine Person, LT probably slips into the heresy of Modalism. I say "probably" because it is no easy thing to say just what Modalism

---

[4] So e.g. Aquinas, *ST* Ia. 3.3.
[5] *In VII Meta.*, l. 5, #1380; *ST* Ia. 13.9 *ad* 2.
[6] Though not all forms of nominalism will serve—but that's a story for another day.

was. Still, the accounts of it one finds in standard theological dictionaries seem ways of filling out the thought that there is just one divine Person. Such works describe Modalism as holding that the Persons' distinctions are impermanent and transitory[7] (which the distinction between two or more persons could not be) or "a mere succession of modes or operations"[8] (of one person, who is "three" in that He operates in the world in three ways).[9] But not every mode-concept one might bring into Trinitarian theology begets Modalism. Locke used the concepts of some sorts of modes in a way Trinitarians might find profitable. I now explain some of Locke's views and draw from them two morals for Trinitarians.

2. LOCKE, EVENTS, AND ATOMS

Locke called events and processes (motion, thinking and acting) modes.[10] Locke's account of what makes coexisting substances of the same sort distinct and what makes it the case that a later item is identical with an item which existed earlier rests on facts about events and processes, and so "modes". Locke begins the account from a view of events' identity across time. Strictly, he holds, they are *not* identical across time, each being an instantaneous happening "perishing the moment it begins."[11] They can, however, occur in continuous sequences—processes. It is continuous series of point-events that we loosely speak of as the same event continuing. This given, Locke takes up substances' identity. First, basic physical substances:

Let us suppose an atom . . . considered in any instant of its existence, it is in that instant the same with itself. . . and so must continue as long as its existence is continued; for so long it will be the same, and no other.[12]

It continues to be the same item as long as *its* existence continues: this can sound circular and vacuous. But it might not be. For "its existence" might refer to something whose identity is not in turn defined in terms of the atom, appearances notwithstanding. Locke has already argued that there cannot be two things of the same kind in the same place at once.[13] If this is true, then if the contents of a space at one particular instant are the right size/shape to be at least one atom

---

[7] F. L. Cross (ed.), *The Oxford Dictionary of the Christian Church* (New York: Oxford University Press, 1997), 1097.

[8] Ibid. 1102, in an account of Patripassionism, which overlapped Modalism.

[9] I give a fuller survey to the same effect in "A Latin Trinity", *Faith and Philosophy*, 21 (July 2004).

[10] John Locke, "Of Identity and Diversity", in John Perry (ed.), *Personal Identity* (Berkeley: University of California Press, 1975)(henceforth "Locke"), 34. Locke calls other sorts of things modes as well. I do not know whether the Modalists actually used the term "mode" to express their view. If they did, I do not know whether Locke's usage matches up with theirs—though "operations" (in the quasi-definition quoted above) are a type of event.

[11] Locke, 34–5.   [12] Ibid. 35.   [13] Ibid. 33–4.

of kind K and the space can't hold more than one K-atom unless they wholly coincide in space, the space must contain just one K-atom. We sometimes use "existence" to refer to our lives, our careers in time ("after the tragedy I saw no point in my continued existence"). Suppose then that in the text just quoted, "its existence" refers to a continuous spacetime path at each point in which the attribute *being an atom of kind K* is exemplified—a candidate career in time, a path an atom in motion or at rest might follow. On this reading, Locke's view is this: pick out one point in such a path. There is at least one K-atom there. As there cannot be two things of the same kind in the same place at once, and there could be two or more K-atoms there then only if they were in the same place at once, there is just one atom there. And for as long as that path continues, there is the same atom at all points along it. The identity across time of one particular atom, on Locke's account, rests on the continuity of a mode, a process—an atom's moving and resting. Locke may take the process as ontologically basic and "construct" the substance whose path it is from that. But perhaps not: he begins by supposing "an atom" and "its" existence continuing. If we take this at face value, the substance remains prior; the process is *its* moving/resting. Locke's view is that once an atom exists, it continues to exist as long as it either moves or rests, ceases to exist only if it is no longer the case that it is either moving or resting, and so remains the same as long as this process is not interrupted. The text leaves it unclear whether the atom also remains the same *because* this process is not interrupted—this is so, I think, only if Locke really takes the process as prior and "constructs" the substance. Some may wonder whether one atom could "immaculately replace" another along a path continuously occupied by some atom or other—that is, whether it could be the case that up to and including time t, there is one atom in the path, but at every time after t, there is another. But if this occurred, the path would not be one continuous motion/rest, even though it would be mathematically continuous: t would end one motion, and what followed t would begin another.

There can seem to be a second factor in Locke's account. Locke writes,

> every particle of matter, to which no addition or subtraction of matter being made, it is the same . . . having had each its determinate time and place of beginning to exist, the relation to that time and place will always determine to each of them its identity, as long as it exists.[14]

The first part of the text seems to give a purely compositional account of atoms' identity over time. It is the account Locke shortly gives for masses of atoms, adjusted to avoid claiming that atoms have atoms as parts.[15] It in effect treats single atoms as minimal masses. But *can* Lockean atoms gain or lose matter? For Locke as for Democritus, an atom is a partless particle. If a particle has no parts, it cannot lose any. If it lost matter, it would lose a part, unless it could so lose

---

[14] Ibid. 34.   [15] Ibid. 35.

matter that what it lost did not count as part of itself. Aristotelian metaphysics allowed for this, but its way of doing so depended on a notion of substantial form to which Locke seems in general unfriendly. So I take it that a Lockean atom can't lose any matter.

A Lockean atom can gain matter if it can grow. But a Lockean atom could not grow. Locke defines an atom as a "simple substance . . . continued . . . under one immutable superficies."[16] If an atom grew, its superficies—surface—would not be unchanged. It would expand. So the process continuing on from that point would no longer count as the existence of the same atom. Would it be an atom's existence at all? If an atom grew, there might be the part of it that was there before it grew, and the part that arrived afterward, consisting of one or more atoms. This would entail that the result of growth had parts, and so was not simple—not an atom. So a Lockean atom which grew would grow into another atom only if it so absorbed the matter it accreted that that matter would not count as a distinct part of it—to maintain which would require either Aristotelianism or something like the "penetration" account I shortly sketch. Moreover, while masses of atoms can come apart, plausibly atoms cannot—presumably even after growth. For if they came apart, plausibly they would have had the parts into which they split.[17] So if Locke meant to allow atom-growth, he would be saying that atoms come together to compose two sorts of thing, larger atoms which cannot split and masses which can, while giving us no account of why the result of any given combination of atoms is the one rather than the other. So I think the more charitable (as well as coherent) view is that Lockean atoms cannot grow.

This would not rule out gaining matter without growing: perhaps an atom could simply become denser, if this could happen without co-location of matter of the same kind. Again, Aristotelianism allows for this, but Locke is no Aristotelian. For him, increased density would have to come from atoms of a smaller kind being packed into an atom of a larger kind. This would entail gaining parts, and so having parts, unless the new atoms, crowding in, were compressed, so that their prior surfaces (being changed) ceased to exist, but the incoming atoms did not acquire new surfaces separating them from surrounding matter (so as to constitute new atomic parts), being instead merged into the single mass which is the atom's interior. Perhaps this is conceivable, but it would entail an atom's being penetrated. If it were, it would not for Locke be a simple body. Lockean simple bodies are impenetrable.[18] In Locke's scheme of things, penetration can only consist in a body's coming to be lodged among the simple parts of a larger body. So for Locke atoms can neither gain nor lose matter. There is no second factor in Locke's account of atoms' cross-time identity. It rests entirely on the

---

[16] Locke, 35.

[17] Though this can be denied without contradiction, as I show in *Aquinas on Metaphysics* (Oxford: Oxford University Press, forthcoming).

[18] John Locke, *An Essay Concerning Human Understanding*, ed. Peter Nidditch (Oxford: Oxford University Press, 1975), 123.

identity—that is, continuity—of a process. Locke's mention of adding and subtracting matter must just be an allusion to something which *per impossibile* would interrupt this process.

3. LOCKE ON LIVE THINGS

After treating masses, which need not detain us, Locke takes up live things, taking a plant as his example:

An oak [is] such an organization of . . . parts as is fit to receive and distribute nourishment, so as to continue and frame the wood, bark and leaves, etc., of an oak, in which consists the vegetable life. That being then one plant which has such an organization of parts in one coherent body, partaking of one common life, it continues to be the same plant as long as it partakes of the same life, though that life be communicated to new particles of matter vitally united to the plant, in a like continued organization . . . this organization being at any one instant in any one collection of matter . . . is that individual life, which existing constantly from that moment both forward and backward, in the same continuity of insensibly succeeding parts united to the living body of the plant . . . makes the same plant.[19]

Locke writes that "this organization being at any one instant in any one collection of matter . . . is that individual life". This seems to identify a life with an organization in a particular collection of matter. But Locke also calls an *oak* "such an organization of parts". So Locke seems to identify an oak with its life. This is not entirely odd: we would understand a bad poet who wrote "a tree, a life so green". Locke also writes, "That being . . . one plant which has such an organization of parts in one coherent body, partaking of one common life". If a life is an organization here, the last phrase is redundant. Locke also speaks of a life as "existing constantly . . . in the same continuity of insensibly succeeding parts". The continuity of succeeding parts is provided by receiving and distributing nourishment, and an oak, it seems, is something fit (disposed) to continue a "vegetable life" by receiving and distributing nourishment. So there are also life-*processes* in Locke's picture, and it's natural to read "partaking of one common life" in terms of these.

Thus "life" is ambiguous here. A Lockean process, we've seen, is a continuous series of point-events, that is, of states of affairs at instants. These point-events, Locke here tells us, are events of an oak's (a life's) existing at a particular place and time. Or—to the same end—"this organization being at any one instant in any one collection of matter" is an *event* "which existing constantly from that moment" constitutes a continued life-process. Life-processes unite continuous series of these point-events into the lives of single trees. Life-processes are those

[19] Ibid. 36.

processes whose continuity brings it about that there continues to be the sort of organization that supports life processes, that is, that there continues to be an oak and the same oak. Thus, for Locke, we have the same plant just as long as and because the same life-processes continue. So Locke here again rests a substance's identity through time on process-continuity. Plant life-processes can be defined (for Locke) in terms of particular patterns of atom motion, atoms coming to cohere with masses of particular shapes, which slowly gain and lose atoms, that is, are replaced by similar masses of slightly different composition. So a plant life is a process of rightly shaped masses succeeding one another in (loosely) one place, brought about by slow matter-exchange with surrounding places. This account mentions atoms, masses, and processes, but not plants or plant lives. So there is no circularity in Locke's theory at this point. Given an account of what it is for a life to be going on, Locke can again deny that there can be two live things of one kind in one placetime, infer that there is one live thing in any placetime along the spacetime length of a life, and define live things' identity across time via the continuity of life-processes. Further, for Locke the continuity of the life also accounts for the live thing's unity at a moment, for example, for the fact that all its parts compose just one plant: "that being then one plant which has such an organization of parts in one coherent body, partaking of one common life . . . that individual life . . . makes . . . all parts of it, parts of the same plant, during all the time they exist united in that continued organization."[20] An atom is part of a plant, for Locke, just if it has the right relation to that plant's life-processes. This generates Locke's account of plants' distinctness at a time. Locke writes,

one plant . . . has such an organization of parts in one coherent body, partaking of one common life . . . this organization being at any one instant in any one collection of matter, is . . . distinguished from all others.[21]

One plant is distinct from another existing at the same time just in case there are two sets of life-processes, each organizing a distinct set of parts into a plant. For Locke, facts about processes account for live things' unity and distinctness at a time and identity across time. All this does not in Locke's mind make plants modes or events. Rather, for Locke, plants are substances whose identity and distinctness rest on facts about the continuity of a process—a "mode". Now it's one thing for Locke to have thought that he can maintain that plants are not events, and quite another for it to be the case that he has in fact not turned plants into a sort of event. But what Locke has said, in fact, is that an oak's life is a succession of point events in which *an oak* exists, and that if these are related the right way, it is the same oak. So substances remain ontologically basic here. Plant lives exist because plants exist, not vice versa. But plants continue to exist over time because plant lives continue- which is rather commonsensical.

---

[20] John Locke, *An Essay Concerning Human Understanding*, 36.   [21] Ibid. 36.

4. LOCKE ON PERSONS

Turning to persons, Locke again seeks a process:

In . . . consciousness . . . alone consists personal identity . . . and as far as this consciousness can be extended backwards to any past action or thoughts, so far reaches the
identity of that person . . . different substances by the same consciousness [are] united
into one person, as well as different bodies by the same life are united into one animal,
whose identity is preserved in that change of substances by the unity of one continued
life.[22]

It's not obvious what Locke means by "consciousness", but the analogy with a
continued life makes it clear that he's thinking of some sort of mental process.
Locke also extends to persons his process-centered account of unity at a time:
"different substances by the same consciousness [are] united into one person",
and again

in our . . . bodies, all [of their] particles, whilst vitally united to this same thinking
conscious self, so that we feel when they are touched . . . are a part of ourselves, i.e. of our
thinking conscious self . . . Cut off a hand, and thereby separate it from that consciousness
he had of its heat, cold and other affections, and it is then no longer a part of that which
is himself.[23]

whilst comprehended under that consciousness, the little finger is as much a part of
himself as what is most so. Upon separation of this little finger, should this consciousness
go along with the little finger, and leave the rest of the body . . . the little finger would be
the person.[24]

Mental processes account for parts' inclusion in persons, and so, for Locke,
account for the distinctness of two persons existing at the same time.

I want to draw two morals from Locke. One is that it makes some sense to
appeal to events in an account of what makes non-events distinct at one time and
identical across time. Locke's account of live things is incomplete. It does not, for
example, tell us what to say when amoebae split: does the same life-process now
continue in two discrete bodies, and if it does, has the amoeba divided without
multiplying?[25] Yet the broad approach is promising, and has been developed,
for example by van Inwagen. Persons are a sort of live thing. On "animalist"
accounts, they are just a certain sort of organism.[26] So if Locke's account for
live things can be developed, it can provide at least a respectable process-based
account of persons' identity over time. This suggests the more general moral that
process-based accounts of personal identity can be at least respectable. Locke's

[22] Ibid. 39, 40.   [23] Ibid. 41   [24] Ibid. 45
[25] Wiggins and Parfit have of course raised an analogous question about Locke's account of
persons.
[26] See e.g. Eric Olson, *The Human Animal* (Oxford: Oxford University Press, 1997).

own account of personal identity is more problematic.[27] But its main problems cluster around his use of memory to overcome gaps in consciousness (caused by sleep and the like) and counter-examples in which the relevant processes, paths across spacetime, or objects divide.[28] If there were persons who could not fail to be conscious of all of their pasts if conscious, whose consciousness could not be interrupted, and who could not divide or have dividing lives, Locke's account might work for their case even if it does not work for ours.

Because they are omniscient, if they are conscious, the Persons of the Trinity cannot fail to be conscious of their entire pasts, if they have pasts. Because they are always cognitively perfect and being unconscious is a less than perfect cognitive state, the Persons can't suffer gaps in consciousness. Because at bottom they are just God, if a Person split, it would be hard to avoid the conclusion that God had split. As unintuitive as it seems to many now, the doctrine of divine simplicity held sway among Latin Trinitarians *inter alia* because it seemed to follow from the claim that God cannot split, which they took to be obvious.[29] So I think we can simply take it as a datum that LT Persons can't split. But this is also something one can argue. If a Person splits, there are henceforth at least two parts of Him. If there are two parts of Him, some of Him is in one and some in the other. If there is such a thing as some of Him, there is an answer to the question: some *what*? There is *stuff* of which an immaterial deity is made. If there is no stuff to be divided up, there is no difference between an immaterial thing being divided in two and the thing's simply disappearing and being replaced by two other things that are in some ways like it—which is to say that the division claim can't be made out. But what on earth could "immaterial stuff" be?

Persons' lives can't divide. For if a Person's life divided, there would be only a few ways to read this, and none are acceptable. On one, the Person survives without a part: if I lose a finger, my life might be held to split into the life I continue to live and the life my severed finger briefly continues to live. But this would mean that a Person had split. On one, the old Person's life ends, the old Person being replaced by two new Persons. As Persons are eternal, their lives can't end, and so this reading is ruled out. Another is that the Person continues to exist in two parts, as a scattered Person: that Persons divide. Another is that the old Person splits into two Persons, each identical with the pre-split Person. This is impossible: if the results of the split are identical with the pre-split Person, they are identical with one another, and so there is one Person post-split, not two. Another is that the post-split Persons are not identical with the pre-split Person, but that in Parfit's loose sense it "survives" in them.[30] This would mean that, strictly speaking, the pre-split Person no longer exists. This is compatible

---

[27] Some of the important literature on it is collected in Perry, *Personal Identity*.
[28] See Derek Parfit, "Personal Identity", in ibid. 199–223.
[29] So e.g. Anselm, *Proslogion* 17; Aquinas, *SCG* I.18.
[30] Parfit, "Personal Identity".

with its eternally "surviving", but the standard understanding of divine eternality holds that the very same Person always exists, not that there is an eternal series of Persons Parfit-surviving in other Persons.

Finally, one could read "split life" cases in terms of Persons' being wholes of temporal parts. But then, if their lives split, there is again just a limited menu of ways to read this. Perhaps this would just *be* Persons' splitting. Perhaps the split would simply mean that there are two Persons who had earlier shared all their life-segments and later ceased to share them—in which case there really isn't a split of one life into two, but rather there were always two overlapping lives. Perhaps the split would have to be read in another way already mentioned. Perhaps it would entail that there was not always the same number of Persons—which would be unorthodox. Or perhaps it would entail that whenever a Person's life splits and the result is a greater number of Persons than there had been, as many other Persons' lives join as are necessary to keep the number of Persons always at three. In this last case we would again have to ask about the identity of pre- and post-split and -merger Persons. Suppose that at t Person-lives A and B merge and Person-life C splits into lives D and E. If A and B's merger yields a new Person, the Persons living lives A and B have ceased to exist—which is impossible if they are all necessarily eternal. If the merger does not yield a new Person, then either the split also does not yield new Persons or there are four Persons after t. But if the split does not yield new Persons, it is just one Person splitting into parts, and we have ruled this out already. The three Persons, then, seem immune to the sorts of problems that seem to keep Locke's theory from applying to *human* persons.

5. LOCKE-PERSONS

My second moral concerns what I'll call Locke-persons. A Locke-person is a person. It has the full repertoire of personal abilities: it is conscious, acts, loves. What's unique about Locke-persons is just their existence-conditions. Locke held that persons are identical over time just as far as a single "consciousness" extends. This implies that persons come to exist when their "consciousness" begins. A Locke-person, then, is a subject of mental states who exists if a substance or substances generate(s) certain mental states or events. Locke-persons are substances, but event- or state-based substances in the sense that the occurrence of certain events/states constitutes them in existence—and can continue their existence. This last might sound odd, but if live things are essentially live—if, say, dogs don't continue to exist as corpses—then every live thing is in the same way event-based: it comes to exist because life-processes begin and continues to exist as long as and because these processes continue. On Locke's own view, a Locke-person continues to exist only if a stream of the right sort of mental events continues. I suggest only that Locke-persons continue to exist *if* the streams continue. What suffices to generate them at their beginnings suffices to generate them at least as long as the event-stream thus begun goes on. For present purposes, I need say no more about their identity across time.

Even if Locke's full theory of personal identity doesn't apply to us, we may be Locke-persons, as I use this term. Consider: being a person may require having certain psychological abilities. Our having these abilities is our being in certain psychological states, which may be generated and sustained by underlying events and states of our brains, or our brain/soul composites. Our bodies certainly existed before we had these abilities (at least pre-natally). Perhaps we—the persons our "I"-tokens denote—came to exist when our bodies (and/or perhaps souls) acquired these abilities, and continue as long as we continue to have them. Or perhaps we did not exist until their first actual use. We certainly remained in existence as long as this first use continued. So if we by nature begin to exist as persons, we come into existence as Locke-persons do and have as much of their identity-conditions as concerns me. Now even if it takes the right psychological states to become us, we might not depend on continuity of these for our identity across time. Once we reach the threshold of being persons, perhaps our continued existence depends simply on our souls, or the continuity of our biological lives. As far as I can see, there is nothing incoherent in such a complex theory of persons. (It's a hard question whether what begins as a person must be a person so long as it continues to exist.) If there is not, Locke-persons needn't have the identity-conditions Locke placed on persons, and the thought that we may be Locke-persons becomes a bit more appealing. (Note again that I say about them only that they continue to exist *if* certain mental conditions are met.) Even if we are not Locke-persons, cases of split personality might involve the generation of one or more Locke-persons in addition to a body's normal occupant. Locke is quite willing to entertain the thought that more than one Lockean person could be associated in this way with a particular consciousness-generating substance: "if the same Socrates-waking and sleeping do not partake of the same consciousness, Socrates-waking and sleeping is not the same person."[31] My second moral from Locke is simply: there could be Locke-persons. If we are not in fact Locke-persons, we may have no use for such entities in understanding ourselves. But other entities could be Locke-persons: for instance, the Persons could be.

Locke considers a case in which two Locke-persons share a body. Socrates-waking (Socrates$_w$) exists for (say) sixteen-hour periods of uninterrupted consciousness. Then he lies down, a brief period of unconsciousness follows, and a second person, Socrates$_s$, takes over. Socrates$_w$ is a person. So is Socrates$_s$. Each exists at least while the stream of conscious events beginning with his last waking continues. They are distinct persons because for whatever reason, two person-constituting streams of mental events and states are associated with one human body, Body, and their identities depend entirely on the continuing of these streams. (They are Locke-style Locke-persons.) If Body generates only the

---

[31] Parfit, "Personal Identity" 46.

two person-constituting streams, there is never such a person as Socrates. There are only Socrates$_w$ and Socrates$_s$. Strictly speaking, "Socrates", by itself, either names the two jointly or names no person at all. The two Socrates divide Body's person-generating resources temporally.[32] They never coexist, because the mental streams constituting them in existence never go on at once.

Socrates$_w$ and Socrates$_s$ have Body in common: their parts are all and only its parts. (If there is a soul associated with Body, they share use of that, too.) Body generates the two mental streams. Beyond this it's a hard question just how the Socrates are related to Body. It can seem that neither is identical with Body. If either were, we might think, the other would have equal claim to be—and then the two would be identical. That is, it seems that if

(5) Body = Socrates$_w$

then by equal right

(6) Body = Socrates$_s$,

and since

(7) Body = Body,

it follows that

(8) Socrates$_s$ = Socrates$_w$.

Yet this conclusion should puzzle us, and not just because it contradicts our assumption that the two persons never coexist. Suppose that (5) and (6) are true. Then "Socrates$_w$" and "Socrates$_s$" should refer to Body. If they do, it is tempting to treat these terms either as disguised descriptions—such as "Body during the 16-hour periods"—or as names with senses that refer to Body only because it satisfies these. If in fact we should yield to temptation here, this argument isn't fundamentally different from

(5a) Body = Body during the 16-hour periods,
(6a) Body = Body during the other periods,
 (7) Body = Body, and so
(8a) Body during the 16-hour periods = Body during the other periods.

Read one way, (8a) is no trouble, because of course it's the same Body during all periods. The argument ceases to pose a problem once we see that the only referent for any of these terms is Body—but Body in different periods.

The problem, though, is that Socrates$_w$ isn't obviously just Body while waking. Socrates$_w$ seems to be something *other* than Body, constituted in existence by

---

[32] Trenton Merricks divides such resources spatially to much the same end in his "Split Brains and the Godhead", in Thomas Crisp, Matthew Davidson, and David Vander Laan (eds.), *Knowledge and Reality* Dordrecht: Kluwer Academic Publishers, forthcoming). We made these moves independently.

something that goes on *in* Body. Body exists while Socrates$_w$ does not. So how could Body and Socrates$_w$ be simply identical? Any identity between the two would have to be temporary. And the claim that any identity holds only temporarily is counter-intuitive. If Body and Socrates$_w$ are identical, then when Body falls asleep, the same thing both does and does not continue to exist. How could *that* be? And how could a change happening to both of them (as it must if they are identical) remove only one? All the same, I'll now try to say something on behalf of the thought that the relation between Body and a Socrates could be temporary identity. My interest in this claim stems from the fact that I've suggested elsewhere that the doctrine of the Trinity involves something a bit *like* temporary identity.[33] I plump only for a metaphysically unexciting sort of temporary identity. In particular, I do not suggest that we can make any sense of the thought that two things might be identical at some time and co-exist, distinct, at another.

6. TEMPORARY IDENTITY

Identity-statements are true only while both terms flanking "=" refer. When we ask whether a term refers, we must ask whether the term is temporally rigid. Temporally rigid designators refer to their referents at all times if they ever do, as a rigid designator refers in all worlds to what it actually refers to. As a boy, "that boy" referred to me. Taken as temporally rigid, it referred in such a way that I am still that boy: it then referred or was to refer (*inter alia*) to me now. A temporally non-rigid designator with a sense refers to something only at times at which it satisfies the term's sense, as a non-rigid designator with a sense refers to something only at worlds at which it satisfies that term's sense. Taken as temporally non-rigid, "that boy" once picked me out, but ceased to do so when I ceased to be a boy: it referred to me in such a way that I am no longer that boy, because I am no longer a boy. It referred to me only in virtue of my satisfying its sense, and so for only as long as I did so.

While Body is awake, "Socrates$_w$" refers to Socrates$_w$, and to Body if they are identical. If it is temporally non-rigid, it ceases to refer when Body falls asleep. It does not refer to Socrates$_w$, for he does not exist. It does not refer to Body either, for it refers to Body only due to Body's identity with Socrates$_w$, and Body, which exists, cannot then be identical with something which does not exist. (Putting it another way, "Socrates$_w$" has a sense, and it refers to Body only when Body satisfies it.) You might reply that the term then refers back to Socrates$_w$ in the past, as "Lincoln" refers to Lincoln, and so to Body then, and so to everything identical with that Body now, and so to Body. But this is to treat "Socrates$_w$" as temporally rigid, as picking out Body at every time at which it ever exists.

---

[33] "A Latin Trinity".

If it is temporally non-rigid, it goes empty when Body is not awake, as "the inventor of bifocals", taken non-rigidly, goes empty at worlds at which there are no bifocals rather than there referring to the actual inventor, Franklin. So even if "Body = Socrates$_w$" is true, if Socrates$_w$ ceases to exist and "Socrates$_w$" is temporally non-rigid, it ceases to be true. Whether you incline to accept that there are temporally non-rigid designators may depend in part on your view of time. If what is past in no way exists, then it can seem natural to call "Socrates$_w$" temporally non-rigid. There is after all nothing anywhere in reality for it to refer to during the other Socrates' time in the sun, and on this assumption it's hard to make a causal theory of trans-temporal referential relations work. If the past exists, it's hard to see why "Socrates$_w$" wouldn't refer back to Socrates existing in the past. But even so, if I stipulate that "Socrates$_w$" refers in virtue of its sense and has such a sense, who's to tell me that I can't so use the term? There clearly are temporally non-rigid definite descriptions: "the US President" refers to different persons at different times. It's not at all obvious that one of these can't serve as a name's sense.

Falling asleep happens to both Body and Socrates$_w$. Given his existence-conditions, for Body to fall asleep is for Socrates$_w$ to cease to exist. So a change happening to both certainly can remove only one from the scene. This can seem just to push puzzlement back a step. If Socrates$_w$ = Body, two distinct sets of existence conditions apply to one identical thing. How can *that* be? "Socrates$_w$" is just a term for Body when Body has a particular property. When Body ceases to have it, the term ceases to apply. So it's not really correct to describe this situation by saying that the same thing both does and does not continue to exist. The same one thing continues to exist. It ceases to satisfy a description which (speaking *very* loosely) makes it count as another thing. So we can without metaphysical difficulties understand the relation between Body and the Socrates via identity-statements involving temporally non-rigid terms. If we did, we'd say that (5) is true only while Body is awake, (6) only while Body is asleep, and the truth of (5) and 6) does not entail that Socrates$_w$ = Socrates$_s$ because (5) and (6) are never true at once.

But there is a problem for this. If the Socrates never coexist, then while (5) is true, it is true that

(9) Body will exist while (6) is true

but false that

(10) Socrates$_w$ will exist while (6) is true.

But if Body = Socrates$_w$, shouldn't (9) entail (10)?[34] Actually, (9) does not entail (10). (10) entails that Body's temporal location is during the 16-hour

[34] So John Hawthorne, "Identity", in Michael Loux and Dean Zimmerman (eds.), *The Oxford Handbook of Metaphysics* (Oxford: Oxford University Press, 2003), 124–6.

period while (6) is true. (9) does not. But if (9) entails (10), (9) entails everything (10) entails. If you think that (9) entails (10), you believe we can move from (9) to (10) by substituting terms for identicals. But this move can fail where intensionality is in play. And it is in play here. Taken non-rigidly, "Socrates$_w$" contributes to the content of a sentence not merely Body, but a description of Body. (This is why (10) entails that Body is in the 16 hour period.) So Body's failure to meet that description can block substitution for Body under the label "Socrates$_w$" taken non-rigidly. If this is the right explanation of what's going on here, we can allow at least some temporary identities without having to qualify or reformulate Leibniz's Law. I am concerned to allow only temporary identities of this sort. Of course, if Body sometimes exists without being conscious but the Socrates can't exist without Body being conscious, one has to ask how Body can be identical with a Socrates. But this question almost answers itself. You have a Socrates just when you have a conscious Body. Of course it's not possible to have a conscious Body without Body being conscious, and this does not prejudice the fact that Body can fail to be conscious.

Hawthorne suggests that if "Socrates$_w$" behaves as I suggest, then what property predicates attached to it express must depend on context. During the 16-hour period, that

(11) Socrates$_w$ will cease to exist at bedtime

is true and that

(12) Body will cease to exist at bedtime

is false. Since "Body" and "Socrates$_w$" co-refer, Hawthorne suggests, only a difference in the properties the predicates express could explain this.[35] I think not: (11) and (12) are true/false due either to primitive tensed properties attaching (or not) to Body/Socrates$_w$, or (if time is tenseless) to what is the case at a future time. If the latter, at that future time, Body exists but Socrates$_w$ does not. For this reason, (11) is true but (12) is false despite the current co-reference of the terms. The same property attaches to Body and fails to attach to Socrates$_w$ at a future time, and we express this via (11) and (12).[36] If the former, one tensed-time option is to deny that either claim is true or false, as the future is not there to make it so. Once the then-future is actual, of course, it is true that earlier Body was to exist and Socrates$_w$ to not exist at this time, but this is because at this time Body does and Socrates$_w$ does not exist: once again, the predicates express the same property. Another tensed metaphysic would hold that if it is presently determined what the future shall hold, whatever in the present makes this determinate makes it true that such and such will be the case then. But then

---

[35] So John Hawthorne, "Identity", 126–7.

[36] Thus it is not the case, *pace* Hawthorne (ibid. 128), that this sort of view depends on a tenseless metaphysic of time.

whatever in the present makes it true that Body will and Socrates$_w$ won't exist at some future time will make it true that one and the same property, expressed by "___ will exist at (future) t," will and won't be exemplified—by what will and won't exist *then*—despite the current co-reference of "Body" and "Socrates$_w$". That Body will exist at t is true because at t, a temporally non-rigid use of "Body" (or some other name for Body) would refer. That Socrates$_w$ won't exist at t is true because at t, a temporally non-rigid use of "Socrates$_w$" (or some other term with an appropriate sense) would not refer. Nor is this a particularly surprising way to treat uses of "exist". If existence is what the quantifier expresses, then for some A to exist is for it to be such that $(\exists x)(x = a)$: it is for it to be such as to fall within the range of a quantifier. Iff something is such as to fall within a quantifier's range, it could be named, at least by God. One could register ontological commitment by a willingness to use names as easily as by a willingness to quantify.

7. CONTINGENT IDENTITY

Perhaps, then, the claim that some identities hold only temporarily should not be terribly controversial. There is, however, one thing I should take up. If any identity-statement is temporarily true, some identity-statements are contingently true. And this can seem controversial. But this is a controversy I am prepared to accept. It is not at all obvious that all identities must be necessary. It is not true that

(13) $(x) \square (x = x)$.

(13) says that every actual object is identical with itself in every possible world. This is not so. Some actual objects exist contingently. In worlds in which they do not exist, they have no attributes at all, including self-identity. What's true is instead that in every world in which an object exists, it is identical with itself, that is, $(x) \square ((\exists y)(y = x) \supset (x = x))$. Self-identity is an essential property. But to read this as licensing (13) is in effect to introduce an ambiguity into the interpretation of a logical operator, taking it to sometimes mean "in all possible worlds" and sometimes mean only "essentially". This just courts confusion. What I'm defending, of course, is a metaphysically unexciting sort of contingent identity. I'm not claiming that we can make any sense of the thought that two items might be identical at some possible world and coexist, distinct, at another.

8. LOCKE-PERSONS AND THE TRINITY

Locke-persons are particular things made to exist by the occurrence of what Locke called modes. My Lockean "mode"-based suggestion about the Trinity, then, is this. Perhaps the triune Persons are event-based persons founded on a generating substance, God. Perhaps they are to God as the Socrates are to Body. I argue elsewhere that the Trinity arises because God lives His life in three discrete streams of events at once.[37] I now add that these are streams of mental events, and each such stream is the life of a Locke-person. God never exists save *in* the Persons, as Body might never exist save in the Socrates. There is just one God who generates and lives as the three Persons, by generating and living in three distinct mental streams. This is compatible with the traditional claim that God the Father generates the Son and the Spirit: God might generate the other two *by* generating the Father or in having the mind of the Father.

There are two obvious objections to appeal to something *like* temporary identity here. At all times God is all three Persons. Temporary identity at the same time is transitive: if at t A = B and at t B = C, at t A = C. So it seems to follow that the Persons are always identical: that is, (1)–(4) seems to go through. The second concerns Modalism. On Modalism, God is only temporarily Son and Spirit. So talk of God as temporarily identical to the Son and the Spirit seems paradigmatically Modalist.

Both objections are turned if we see the temporal structure of God's life as a bit unusual. I've elsewhere suggested that it has features in common with that of a time-traveler.[38] Suppose that you travel in time, leaving from a time machine at 3:00 and returning at 2:59, just before you entered the machine. Then at 3:00 you are inside the machine, leaving, and also outside the machine, telling someone about your trip. In one sense you are in two places at once. In another you are not. You are at two places at one *public* time: that is, two parts of your life coincide temporally with the 3:00–part of all non-time-travelers' lives. But you are not in two places in the same part of your own life. You are not in two places at one point along your own private timeline. My suggestion is that as (briefly) two parts of the time-traveler's life went on at one public time, God eternally has three parts of His life going on at once, without succession between them. One part is the Father's life, one the Son's, one the Spirit's. To avoid Modalism as described above, Christians must hold the Persons' distinction to be an eternal, necessary, and intrinsic feature of God's life, one which would be there even if there were no creatures. So be it: I now add that these three streams of consciousness and the Persons they generate are eternal, necessary, intrinsic features of the divine inner life. That God lives three lives as three Persons is not a temporary phenomenon. This, however, brings another objection to the fore: how then can I speak of temporary identity here, and how (again) avoid the transitivity problem? Note that at 3:00, the time-traveler is identical both with someone in the machine and with someone outside the machine. Both identities are temporary, because they obtain only in certain parts of the time-traveler's life. This is the sense in which even God's eternal identities with the Persons are temporary: they obtain only in certain parts of His life, which

---

[37] "A Latin Trinity".   [38] Ibid.

are identical with the lives of the three Persons. If time-travel is possible—a matter I discuss elsewhere[39]—then the transitivity argument must fail. It fails, if it does, because the time-traveler's timeline takes precedence over the public timeline. Temporary identity is transitive at the same point along any individual timeline, but if time-travel is possible, it is not transitive at all public times. Thus it does not operate to collapse the Persons into one, since at no point in God's life at which He is one Person is He any other Person. There is a lot more to say here, but I hope to have suggested this much: one can use the concept of a Locke-person to make sense of the Trinity, and if we can make sense of time-travel stories, we can also make sense of a Trinity built on the claim that three Locke-persons have lives which add up to the life of one God.

[39] Ibid.

Index

CPSIA information can be obtained at www.ICGtesting.com
Printed in the USA
BVOW020126160812

297931BV00002B/10/P